STRATIFICATION AND ORGANIZATION

STUDIES IN RATIONALITY AND SOCIAL CHANGE

STUDIES IN RATIONALITY AND SOCIAL CHANGE

Editors: Jon Elster and Gudmund Hernes

Editorial Board:
Fredrik Barth
Amartya Sen
Arthur Stinchcombe
Amos Tversky
Bernard Williams

Arthur L. Stinchcombe
Professor of Sociology, Northwestern University

STRATIFICATION AND ORGANIZATION

Selected Papers

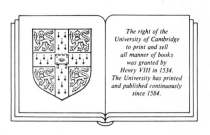

The right of the
University of Cambridge
to print and sell
all manner of books
was granted by
Henry VIII in 1534.
The University has printed
and published continuously
since 1584.

Cambridge University Press
Cambridge – London – New York
New Rochelle – Melbourne – Sydney

Published in collaboration with Maison des Sciences de l'Homme, Paris

Published by the Press Syndicate of the University of Cambridge
The Pitt Building, Trumpington Street, Cambridge CB2 1RP
32 East 57th Street, New York, NY 10022, USA
10 Stamford Road, Oakleigh, Melbourne 3166, Australia

First published 1986

Printed in Great Britain at the University Press, Cambridge

British Library cataloguing in publication data

Stinchcombe, Arthur L.
Stratification and organization: selected papers.
– (Studies in rationality and social change)
1. Social classes
I. Title   II. series
305   HT609

Library of Congress cataloguing in publication data

Stinchcombe, Arthur L.
Stratification and organization.
(Studies in rationality and social change)
'Published in collaboration with Maison des Sciences de l'Homme, Paris.'
Bibliography.
Includes index.
1. Social structure. 2. Social classes. 3. Sociologists.
I. Title.   II. Series.
HM73.S82 1986   305   86-6155

ISBN 0 521 32588 9 (excluding Scandinavia)
ISBN 82 00 07376 9 (Scandinavia only)

CE

Contents

Acknowledgments

The following essays were first printed in the listed publications:

'Agricultural enterprise and rural class relations,' in *The American Journal of Sociology*, vol. 67, no. 2, September 1967.

'Some empirical consequences of the Davis-Moore theory of stratification,' in *American Sociological Review*, vol. 28, no. 5, October 1963.

'Interdependence and inequality: a specification of the Davis-Moore theory,' in *Sociometry*, vol. 32, no. 1, March 1969.

'Marxist theories of power and empirical research,' in *The Uses of Controversy in Sociology*, edited by Lewis A. Coser and Otto N. Larson. Copyright © 1976 by The Free Press, a division of Macmillan, Inc. Reprinted by permission of the publisher.

'Social mobility in industrial labor markets,' in *Acta Sociologica*, vol. 22, no. 3, 1979.

'The sociology of ethnic and national loyalties,' in *Handbook of Political Science, Volume Three*, edited by Nelson W. Polsby and Fred Greenstein, Addison–Wesley, 1975.

'The deeper structure of moral categories,' in *Structural Sociology*, edited by Rossi, Columbia University Press, 1982.

'Bureaucratic and craft administration of production: a comparative study,' in *Administrative Science Quarterly*, vol. 4, September 1959.

'Social structure and the founding of organizations,' in *Handbook of Organizations*, edited by James G. March, Rand McNally 1965. Reprinted by permission of James G. March.

'On getting 'hung up' and other assorted illnesses,' in *Johns Hopkins Magazine*, winter 1966.

'Merton's theory of social structure,' in *Idea of Social Structure:*

Papers in Honor of Robert K. Merton, edited by Lewis A. Coser. Copyright © 1975 by Harcourt Bruce Janovich, Inc.

'A structural analysis of sociology,' in *American Sociologist*, vol. 10, May 1975.

'On journal editing as a probabilistic process,' in *American Sociologist*, vol. 4, no. 2, May 1969.

'Should sociologists forget their fathers and mothers,' in *American Sociologist*, vol. 17, 1982.

T. Robert Harris and Richard Ofshe kindly gave their permission for the essays they co-authored to be reprinted.

1. Rationality and social structure: an introduction

The question of rationality has been reopened gradually in sociology over the past couple of decades. Sociology defended its jurisdictional boundaries 20 years ago by presenting itself as the science of the irrational: of sentiments, of basic value commitments, of the folkways and mores, of informal ties in primary groups. In *The Structure of Social Action* Parsons (1937) had presented us with a birth myth in which sociology was born out of the decay of utilitarianism, as Durkheim, Weber, Pareto, and even Alfred Marshall realized that the framework of rationality was given by deeply irrational value commitments embedded in religion, or in habitual commitments to the values embedded in work activities, or simply, in Pareto, in the unreasonableness of humankind.

Rationality in the sociological writing of those days was the stuff of economics, or of the rational managers who created the formal organizations in which warm irrational workers formed primary groups, or it was what we methodically eliminated to arrive at the core subject of sociology, the irrational residues. Social movements were outbursts of irrational sentiments in the face of social and technical changes that people could not handle by rational means. The rational was none of our business, and we started to claim formal organizations for sociology only when Herbert Simon argued they were not so rational after all.

The boundary defining enterprise of the discipline has broken down in two ways in the last couple of decades. What was inside the boundaries has come to be analyzed as rational, or at least pretty sensible, behavior: people get jobs when they are young and help when they are old through sentimental ties, weak and strong; social movements are attempts to grasp power opportunities for one's own

1

or one's group's ends; informal groups at work defend privileges and form the basis for strong printers' craft unions; basic value commitments against contraception turn out to make very little difference any more in fertility rates, and the best predictor of Catholic fertility turns out to be how many children Catholics want.

But at the same time behavior that is analyzable in rational terms has turned out to have social components: the solutions to games in game theory turn out to depend on the amount and kind of communication, small numbers bargaining and opportunism in markets give rise to rational strategies whose outcomes depend on the numbers of people and the normative arrangements in which they take place, and the outcome strategy is sometimes to build a different, hierarchical, social structure; with highly variable and uncertain markets hiring craft or professional labor is more rational than super-rationalized 'fordism,' because by hiring traditional skills one hires socially maintained human capital and socially induced industrial discipline; Judge Gary's dinner circle turns out to be central in maintaining oligopoly pricing discipline in the steel industry. Of course, if we, and Parsons, had read Weber's *General Economic History* more carefully (1923: e.g. at 356) we would have known the boundaries between the rational and the social had broken down a lot earlier.

This movement to reintroduce rationality into the analysis of social structure and social structure into the analysis of rational action has been closely related to a program of methodological individualism in sociology, or an interest in *mechanisms* by which social structural outcomes come about. In Parsons' version of Durkheim (and to quite an extent in Durkheim himself) the social structure, through value commitments and the like, had direct access to people's feelings and formed the preferences on which rational action was based; Australian aborigines did not make up their minds what social groups to be loyal to, nor did people collect evidence from their social experience on how much their lives were worth which entered into their suicide decisions.

Consequently the mechanisms by which Durkheim conceived social forces to operate were not, by and large, ones of conscious calculation nor other forms of rational maximization. Durkheim had a tendency to raise this opacity to the mechanisms by which social sentiments, norms, or ideas got into the minds of individuals into a methodological principle: one ought not pay attention to individuals at all because individual level explanation was selling our birthright as a discipline for a mess of social-psychological pottage. For a young discipline unsure of its respectability, such voluntary ignorance as a badge of professional identity was appealing, and it did little damage because we did not know how to construct any less opaque mechanism by which social structural forces could operate; the opportunity cost of reputable sociological ignorance was not high.

The search for mechanisms at the individual level has proceeded in several directions, not all of which depend on rationality in any explicit sense. George Homans said he was using mechanisms from behavioral psychology in *Social Behavior: Its Elementary Forms* (1961), and so brought up especially sharply the problem of professional jurisdiction – many sociologists did not so much reject his reasoning as his implication that sociology was a branch of psychology. At any rate rational thought or maximization played no substantial rôle at the individual level in Homans' theoretical work on exchange theory, though the theory clearly had individuals as its basic causal units.

An example that I like illustrates how a social process need not involve rationality to be explicable at the individual level: when two people sleep close to each other all night by 'spooning,' with one's front toward the other's back, then when they turn over the one now in back does the adjusting so that his or her thighs go under the buttocks of the other; then when they turn over again the other adjusts downward. This racheting brings the couple downward to the bottom of the bed during the night. It is clearly social, since when they sleep alone the same people do not end up at the bottom of the bed. Yet it is done at a very minimal level of consciousness; it may reward both, but they are certainly not optimizing.

Besides Homans, R. B. Zajonc's wonderful paper, 'Feeling and thinking: preferences need no inferences,' (1980) supplies psychological mechanisms that are explicitly different from rational analysis of which objects are preferred, in a way much more compatible with Durkheim's original notions about how sentiments get into people's minds than the conceptions common in rational actor theory. But building these mechanisms into sociological explanations will take a lot of work, and will not serve the latent function of defending sociological turf.

The tradition of organizational sociology founded by Herbert

Simon starts with a rational actor model, analyses departures from it ('bounded rationality') more or less in the terms of rational actor models, and then allows social influences into the large areas between the actual 'bounded' calculations and rational optimization. Peter Blau's *Exchange and Power in Social Life* (1964) or various works of James S. Coleman on collective decision theory (e.g. 1973) are conscious attempts to use rational actor theory adopted from economics, and the most vigorous branches of institutional economics, such as 'industrial organization' as represented by Frederic M. Scherer's *Industrial Market Structure and Economic Performance* (1980) or the *Markets and Hierarchies* branch as represented by Oliver Williamson (1975) are not now so much diatribes against the rational actor model after the style of Thorstein Veblen but instead analyses of rational actors set in varying institutional circumstances. That is, rational actors now constitute social structures out of individual acts in much reputable sociological theory.

But these explicit theoretical models of individuals that can produce patterns in social interaction are probably not the main way that methodological individualism and rational or sensible behavior have entered into sociological analysis. Much more often we adduce individual thought about how to behave in various circumstances *ad hoc* in sociological work that attempts to explain particular social structural outcomes. For example, I offer the hypothesis below that in family tenancy systems in which the landlord's only economic rôle is to supply land in return for a rent, the tenants will believe that they could run the farm themselves, while in plantation systems producing agricultural products for export markets on a large scale with extensive onsite capital equipment, the proletarians are not likely to think they could run the farm themselves. This is used to explain why land reform or revolution tends to be an outcome of family tenancy systems.

To make this *ad hoc* psychology believable one need not choose between Oliver Williamson and George Homans, nor explore with Zajonc's psychological mechanisms how much love of the land is induced in the two situations. Similarly when Merton argues that a lot of businesses, especially illegal businesses, will be willing to contribute money and perhaps jobs to a political machine in return for various privileges, privileges which will not in turn hurt the constituencies of the machine (or not hurt in a way that loses votes), he does not need to know whether the businessmen are optimizing or whether their rationality is bounded, or whether they are really just being nice to politicians they have learned to like and trust and not acting rationally at all. Similarly the question of the exact form of individual level calculation involved in food riots need not worry the resource mobilization theorists of social movements, once one can show that participants are not irrationally bursting out because of too rapid social change or because of the disruption of their secure rural folkways by urbanism and capitalism.

In the individual level causation in the mechanisms in the essays in this book I treat the problem of rationality in a thoroughly *ad hoc* fashion. Sometimes the treatment is thoroughly neoclassical microeconomics, as for example in the paper on industrial labor markets as determinants of mobility patterns (though the mathematical treatment is a lot less formal than would be acceptable in economics). Sometimes I assume that people will use whatever categories they are provided by their culture, as in the analysis of the stratification culture of the old regime and the French Revolution, without addressing the question of whether any higher level of rationality might be available to them but certainly not postulating that they are maximizing under the conditions they happen to find themselves in. The fact that both essays appear in the same book in a series on rationality and social change, and the insistence by Cambridge University Press on a higher level of intellectual integration of the book than the essays themselves could provide, provide an opportunity to address the relation between theories of rationality and social structural analysis.

Rationality as a variable

The central trouble with discussions of rationality is that we are taught by economists and decision theorists to treat rationality as an *assumption*. Only if rationality is an assumption can one derive the mathematical results from it by which economists and decision theorists make their livings. But in the real world rationality is a variable to be explained: some people are more rational than others, or we would not need mental tests of mathematical talent (mathematics is certainly one kind of rationality); people are more rational in some rôles than in

others, or we would not need to segregate their work rôles from their
family rôles; people in some concrete social structures are more
rational than in others, or New England manufacturers would not
need to send complex goods through the social structure of the port of
New York where people have more market information rather than
through nearer and cheaper ports; some arrangements of economic
structures facilitate rationality more than others, or neoclassical
economists would not be able advise us about why free competition in
the United States gives such efficiency advantages over the monopolistic Japanese; some decisions induce more rationality than others,
or one could sell more common stocks at higher prices by playing
Muzak, the way one can sell more cosmetics; some cultural subsystems facilitate some kinds of rationality, or we would not teach the
calculus, one small part of our cultural system, as a prerequisite for
engineering or economics or operations research. Much of the discussion of rationality is about the bootless question of the defining
characteristics of the dichotomy, rational versus irrational. But that is
like classifying poker hands into winning or losing – it all depends on
what hands they are up against.

The degree of rationality is at least two types of variable. In the first
place it is a variable describing minds, or bits of minds. People's minds
are more rational in general, for example, if they have a large amount
of causal knowledge about their situations of action; people's minds
are more rational in particular at those kinds of actions they have been
trained in and in which they have a lot of experience, as human capital
theory tells us. In the second place it is a feature of structures of
action, so that people can for example make more rational market
decisions about complex or innovative products in New York than in
New Haven because there is a larger and cheaper supply of worldwide market information in New York. Training and experience that
increase individual level rationality provide the ability to construct
adequate social structures that produce systems of information to
make rational decisions, so that a high toned and experienced
accountant can build a structure of accounting routines that can make
reasonable estimates of the present value of alternative investments
for a chemical company, and an experienced construction engineer
can set up a system of test boring to estimate the load-bearing
capacities of the subsoil before building a dam on top of it. Some of the

variable rationality of social structures is the result of the variability of the individual rationality that designed them.

One of the things that functional structures do is to provide the materials for individual level rationality. The system of market information in a world-class port such as London or Rotterdam or New York is viable because shippers use the port, so that the carriers of that information can make higher profits or wages by working in the port than by working elsewhere. At any given time it is usable to so many shippers because it is there, a deposit of past history of port activity and the wholesaling, banking, stock exchanges, and insurance connected to port activity. But its being usable for increasing the rationality of a great many people ensures that it will still be there to be usable for the people with a use for it a decade hence.

Similarly if a multidivisional decentralized administrative structure results in the capacity to make a stream of more rational decisions for the various parts of a firm selling in various differently organized markets, the various executives of the firm will use that structure instead of fighting it, and it will still be there to adapt to multiple markets next year. If universities that participate extensively in scientific research gain reputations for high quality training that enable them to recruit students who will pay higher tuitions (or to gain higher subsidies per student from sympathetic legislatures), the universities will balance their budgets in more years than less prestigious liberal-arts colleges, and will be here to carry on research again while teaching the next generation. Capitalism came to dominate the world system not by its greater unscrupulousness in conquering colonies than characterized feudal empires, but by its greater capacity to strengthen the metropole by exploiting colonies because of the greater economic rationality of capitalistic production and trade. Structures that facilitate rationality gain viability from that capacity, if they can exact contributions from those that use those capacities.

The causes of the varieties of rationality

The argument above implies that the causes of variations in rationality divide into two great classes: improvements of the minds of individuals and improvements in social structures facilitating rational behavior. It is immediately obvious that the classes are not disjoint, that for example people improve their rationality of investments more by experience in stock markets than by experience with stocks sold by a local prince in Bali in Geertz's *Peddlers and Princes* (1963), where no one thinks of demanding an accounting nor of collecting their profits. One learns more in New York than in Bali because structures that facilitate rationality teach rationality. And conversely rational social structures are quite often set up deliberately by pretty rational people who invent them, as Alfred Chandler's account of the administrative reorganization of du Pont in *Strategy and Structure* (1962) clearly shows.

Nevertheless causes of rationality at the individual level such as relevant personal intelligence, education, experience, a high level of attentiveness to a set of decisions, time to collect and reflect on information and an inclination to do so, are distinct from social structural level causes such as recruitment policies that select for intelligence, education, and experience, or staff administrative structures that provide time and formalized rewards for attentiveness and for collecting and reflecting on information. The rationalization involved in a money economy, much emphasized by Max Weber, is a different level of cause than the facility with arithmetic and a good memory for the details published this morning in the *Wall Street Journal* which makes a person a good stockbroker.

Of course, all social structural facilitators of rationality have to act through individuals who, on the average, come nearer to the right answer (or help others to come nearer), because helped by the structure. But it is quite often not a sensible strategy of sociological investigation to concentrate on this individualistic truism. If one is looking for the origins of the money economy, one would be ill advised to start with the world distribution of numerical talent.

Sociologists have as their distinctive mission in the science of rational decision to analyse the social structural causes of rationality. That does not mean that they must take a professional pledge to remain ignorant of individual causes, such as writer's block as a hindrance to the rational advance of science; it only means they may not be much good at analyzing it (see 'On getting hung-up' below). And it does not mean that sociologists' explanations ought to be of a form in which individual actions cannot be incorporated; it means instead that individual level causes may turn his or her social structural predictions into statistical ones. For example I predict different rates of different kinds of mobility for people differently situated in industrial labor markets, instead of predicting which person will move at which time (see 'Social Mobility in Industrial Labor Markets' below).

The social structural explanations may take various forms, illustrated by various of the papers reprinted here:

(1) General preconditions of rationality. One way to set about the social structural explanation of rationality is to derive the general requirements of rationality from an analysis of action at the individual level. For example, individuals can compare profitabilities of different lines of action better if they can calculate them. Starting with this individual level observation, Weber searches either historically or theoretically for conditions that facilitate the calculation of profitabilities: if all costs and returns can be represented in money terms, if one lives in a business tradition that enters costs and returns in different places in the accounts, if costs and returns do not fluctuate wildly in response to political or military events so that one can control profitability by systematic productive work, if the risks are in small parts of the business at any one time rather than to the whole adventure, and are consequently easy to insure and so to render calculable, then profitablities are more calculable. Weber then sets off to treat each of these determinants as a dependent variable in his historical research and in his theorizing about the causes of rationalization. My review of Weber below treats this as the dominant thrust of Weber's work on the economy.

I have applied this general strategy (without the stage of historical research) in *Creating Efficient Industrial Administrations* (1974), a work too extensive to reproduce here. A somewhat perverse application of the strategy is represented in a paper, also too extensive to reproduce here, on what the requirements are for rationality in the kinds of decisions we make under the influence of love, which I wrote with Carol A. Heimer: 'Love and irrationality: it's got to be rational to love you because it makes me so happy' (1980). There are traces of the same strategy of explanation in the paper, 'On getting hung-up,' below, though choosing research, carrying it through, and presenting it to a scientific public, are a special form of rational behavior and the causes I propose do not have the world-historical sweep of Weber's. This strategy then starts at the level of explaining individual rationality to get its dependent variables, which it then gives social structural explanations for.

(2) Functional explanations of social structures by variations in what is rational in their settings. Much of the sociological work on the determinants of rationality takes the form of what has come to be called 'contingency theory' in the sociology of formal organizations. A representative of this variety of theorizing is the paper on 'Bureaucratic and craft administration of production' below. The argument there explains the existence of craft labor market structures in construction, but not in mass production manufacturing, by the fact that under the conditions of the construction market, it is not rational to construct and pay for a bureaucratic administration that will be running idle all winter. Craft institutions in construction create most of the elements of industrial discipline that are created by bureaucratic administrations in manufacturing. The fact that for most construction jobs one can outcompete a bureaucratically organized construction enterprise with a craft organized one explains why, once the craft structure exists, bureaucratic forms do not drive it out of existence.

But from the point of view of rational actor theory with individuals as actors this is not an adequate explanation, because it does not tell why it was ever rational for people to build such institutions, or how they now meet all their functional prerequisites with actions that seem rational to their members, or why no one reorganizes the market so that the variability that makes bureaucracy irrational disappears (officials in the USSR have reorganized the market, and craft institutions have almost disappeared); in short it does not specify adequate mechanisms at the individual level for the functional explanation to hold water by the high standards Elster has proposed (for example, in his *Explaining Technical Change*, 1983).

But while this strategy of functional explanation by social structural rationality may not be very philosophically satisfying, several of the pieces below urge that it is often empirically fruitful. In one case where it is fruitful below it has a trivial purpose, namely to give a quick memorable summary of causal connections to help a reader remember them ('Agricultural enterprise and rural class relations'). For example, plantation agriculture tends to be found only in the growing of crops for which a great deal of labor is needed throughout the season, if adequate labor can be supplied by supervised gangs working together. Where each plant has to be carefully tended for a long period of time, an adequate incentive system has to be built in which gives the laborer an interest in the total product at the end of the season, so that tenancy rather than plantations are often found, for example, in oriental rice cultivation. Where the ground does not have to be maintained bare of weeds, as with wheat and other grains that grow on praries and shade out their competitors, there is not enough labor required between planting and harvesting so that plantation labor is efficient. Thus it is bare ground crops such as sugar or cotton not requiring much individual care of each plant which can be efficiently grown with plantation labor.

When writing about what sort of stratification systems plantations create and why that system differs from that created by family-sized tenancies, one does not really want a complete functional theory relating the structure of work incentives to the amount of per-plant versus per-acre labor required by different crops. The functional explanation of why plantations are irrational in oriental rice pro-duction but common in sugar and cotton can be left as a hint in 'Agricultural enterprise and rural class relations' below, because that is not the theoretical point at issue.

If there were not such a connection, however, we would not expect to find whole geographical areas in which a plantation stratification system is found, other areas in which a tenancy stratification system predominates, but instead would find in rural areas the helter-skelter mix of stratification systems that one finds, for example, in the factories of New York City. The empirical fruitfulness of the sort of scheme outlined in the paper for such studies as Jeffery Paige's *Agrarian Revolution* (1975) would not obtain unless the stratification results of the organization of enterprises applied to crop areas rather than to individual farms within areas.

The functional connections then are essential to the generalization of the results in the paper, but are not the core of the paper, so their inadequacy at the level of individual rationality is rightly left for anyone to fill in who thinks it worth the while – we can proceed knowing the functional proposition at the social structural level, that forms of agricultural enterprise tend to occur in crops for which they are rational.

The paper on 'Social mobility in industrial labor markets' appears to rest on individual rationality, as employers in certain industries are willing to pay more than employers in others for skill, and employees in those industries are therefore more likely to stay in the industry, to retain occupations in which their skills are valuable, and the like. But there is actually a functional structural analysis back of the analysis of the individually maximizing moves that are the data in the tables. I assume, for example, that when workers change employers but keep the same occupations, this is because their new employer is willing to pay them more in that occupation because their experience in the previous firm is valuable. I further argue that such continuity of value across employers will be most characteristic of industries in the categories we call 'Small skilled' and 'Professional' industries, industries we classified together because they employed a lot of skilled workers or a lot of professional workers, which have labor-market wide institutions for defining and producing competences.

That is, the classification of industries on which the analysis is based is done by supposing the structures facilitating mobility among organizations (by performing professional or skill competence certifications) are functional institutions. It is this functionality that justifies assuming that wherever we find the institutions, we will find that workers and employers will find it rational to preserve occupations during intra-industry moves between employers. And of course these functional institutions are helped to maintain themselves by the fact that both employers and workers find it rational to make use of them to transfer certifications of competence and experience when they make labor market moves between employers.

The functional analysis is essential to the logic of the paper's argument in the following sense. Without the notion that structures predict what is rational for the firms, we would have no reason to expect that people would be any more enthusiastic to preserve the value of their experience during moves in craft or professional industries than in classical capitalist industries such as textiles or apparel or than in bureaucratic industries such as finance and insurance. And we would have no reason to believe that internal labor markets (that is, promotions within firms) would be more important in 'engineering based industries' or 'bureaucratic industries,' and that such markets would lead to increases of earnings with age that are not in general found in the craft and professional industries. The structures are indicators of what is rational only on the presumption that they are functional where they are found.

In the papers on the Davis-Moore theory of stratification, this functional explanation in terms of organizational rationality is even balder. The argument is that if, for example, soloists or movie stars are more important to the quality and success of artistic productions than the best factory workers are to the production of the factory, then there will be more inequality between the best and worst in musical performers or actors than between factory workers, because the Davis-Moore theory says that more inequality will be functional. Similarly if the quality of generals is more important in war than in peace, generals will be rewarded more generously as compared with enlisted people during wartime than in peacetime, because it would be functional if they were. No mechanisms of individual rationality or behavior dependent on reward are offered to explain these correlations indicating the collective rationality of the organizations. Perhaps some such mechanisms could be invented, but the arguments of the papers do not rest on there being sufficient individual level mechanisms to explain the collective level correlation between 'needing' more inequality and getting it.

The 'Norms of exchange' paper applies the same logic to the microsociology of organizations. If we conceive of organizations as being made up of parts, each of which functions like an 'organ' in a body, then the social relationships that are found in the different parts should be different according to the function of that part. Thus the social relationship between the Board of Directors and the stockholder is one in which the stockholder has to trust the Board to manage his investment; it is a 'fiduciary' realtionship. Historically the law of corporations, which is law about the relationship between investments and management, grew out of the law of trusts, the law about the relationship between people who cannot manage their property and the managers appointed to manage it. We should expect that the social structuring of this relationship would be different from that between, say, the management and the production workers, because the function involved in that relationship is to supervise work rather than to ensure trustworthy management of investments. We are not surprised to find that a Board of Directors acts as a committee on the basis of votes, while neither the shop manager nor the worker is involved in a voting group, or that the Board of Directors has its accounts audited while the management of the shop does not get to do its accounting for itself in the first place.

An individual level explanation of why the Board of Directors is created in a legal fashion that grew out of the law of trusts would no doubt be historically grounded in fifteenth- to eighteenth-century English experience, while auditing probably became a separate profession that could be built into the relationship in the nineteenth century. A large variety of historical developments would explain why fiduciary relationships in corporations are the way they are. The reason that the development of modern labor law as it applied to large corporations, say between 1916 and 1937 in the United States, did not touch this ancient deposit of fiduciary law and practice is that it concerned a different part of the corporation, and it touched on relationships that had nothing much of investment and trust about them.

When we look at a cross section of relationships in a modern corporation, we can however use a functionalist shorthand separately on the different kinds of relationships we find. We can explain the existence of committee decision-making and auditing procedures in some relationships and not in others by their function in securing trustworthy management of investments, and the presence of dictatorial structures and accounting outside the relationship in others by their function in supervising production workers. The unit for which we invent a functional theory then is not the organization, but the social relationship within the organization. The functional explanation is still in terms of what sort of structure will give rational results in different circumstances, but the circumstances, the 'niches,' consist of what the relationship is supposed to do in the functioning of the organization, not what the organization is supposed to do in the economy.

'The social biology of survey research centers' below was once rejected because the referees did not see that it was a joke, and as a serious analysis of survey research centers the analogy to hives of bees or wasps or hills of ants or termites is a little strained. The argument in entomology is functionalist in a situation in which hives are the units that survive or perish and that reproduce other hives, and in which survival and reproductive success are functional criteria that determine natural selection of genes. The point which creates the analogy is that a common problem of the survival of hives, such as how to last through the winter and start reproducing in the next season, can have different viable solutions – for example storing food in the hive or in a fat overwintering queen. In a broad ecological niche such as temperate climates with winters in which bee-foraging is unsuccesful, there are alternative sub-niches in which fat queens work better than stored food (for example, for meat-eating wasps), and others in which stored honey works better. The analogy between winter and the policies on social research of the Reagan administration is obvious. In addition, the functional specialization of members of the hive provides easy analogies to the social division of labor within survey research centers.

In this case a variety of reactive problem-solving adaptations to the basic problems of survey research center viability can produce alternative patterns of growth of the internal structure of the center. Which structure is more viable overall will perhaps be determined by selection over historical time – it is certainly not obvious now. And which form will be viable over the short run depends on a good deal on particular characteristics of the micro-environment of particular centers. It is easy to see why audience research on broadcasting might sustain a research center in New York City but not in Ann Arbor. We need not answer the question of which micro-environments will produce which variant of the structure, for our purpose, which is to show that alternative structures can be functional for the major problems of survey organizations.

In an introductory essay about such pieces of functionalism opaque to individuals, one can suggest the direction to go to build a satisfactory theory of social structures selected for their rationality. To do that one suggests how understandable, perhaps even rational, individual actions might be sufficient to create and maintain them. The value of functional theories of rationality of social structures which are not adequate as theories of the mechanisms that create and maintain them is to show that functionalism is very often a useful empirical strategy for explaining the variety of social structures. We show that under some conditions one structure is rational, under others another is, and then show that the appropriate structures indeed occur under the appropriate conditions.

This shows then that there is a functional connection to be

explained. That functional connection can be used then for other scientific purposes, such as predicting the stratification system that will tend to occur with various crops. But its main use is to undermine the general philosophical prejudice against functionalism by showing its empirical strength. If functionalism produces such rich empirical results, then the appropriate way to deal with its philosophical faults is to remedy them, perhaps by investigations which identify adequate mechanisms at the individual level to produce the patterns observed. The 'contingency theory' of organizations, that what organizational form is rational depends on contingencies, on what the conditions are that it has to adapt to, poses a problem for empirical investigation: how are social structures selected so that their structures fit the niches they have to adapt to?

(3) Rational impediments to rational social organization. Clearly the empirical strategy of postulating that structures can be explained by their being rational leads to Dr. Pangloss's view: 'Everything is for the best in this best of all possible worlds.' Equally clearly, serious work in the theory of rational action shows that quite often collective level rationality is in explicit contradiction to individual level rationality, as for example with the 'free rider problem' (Olson, 1965): it is individually rational to take the advantages of a rational social structure without paying one's share of the costs.

The *ad hoc* hedges I put into the section above, that for example the rational structure of the port of New York depends for its viability on people and firms in that structure being able to charge more for their services, turn out to be crucial parts of any actual use of functional explanations. They are statements that the 'free rider problem' has to be solved, though not much of a statement about how it comes to be solved. But this difficulty creates an opportunity for an empirical strategy: systematically looking for the mechanisms at the individual level which undermine rational (or otherwise functional) social structures.

The first strategic fact for developing such theories is that the effect of people's rationality depends on how powerful they are. If plantation owners rationally have different political objectives than, say, bankers, because the suppression of labor is central to a plantation's economic success while freedom of commerce is central to a bank's, then the forces undermining an effective bourgeois democracy should have been more powerful in the old South than in the North, but less effective in Atlanta or Charleston or New Orleans than in the rest of the old South, and so on, because these regional and urbanization variables are indicators of the varying relative power of bankers and plantation owners. Consequently a Marxian functionalism that says that bourgeois democracy will tend to be functional for commercial and financial élites but racist oppression more functional for plantation agriculture makes different predictions for Mississippi back country than for New Orleans, and perhaps different predictions for New York City than for New Orleans.

But now considering American bourgeois democracy as a whole, the functional requisites of labor relations in the rural Old South undermine functionality of the system for bourgeois order in commercial cities. Racial demonstrations depress commercial real-estate values in Mobile and Birmingham, decreasing the probability that the mortgage will be paid. Sufficient police power and control over the political system to disenfranchise blacks is a rational business expense for a plantation, but a charge undermining competitive viability for an urban enterprise or decreasing bankers' returns if they have to pay for it out of mortgage interest. So urban businessmen push instransigent sheriffs to compromise with civil rights demonstrators so as to get the city off the front pages, where it looks like a bad place to invest, while capitalist planters push moderate politicians inclined to compromise to take a hard line with blacks, a soft line with lynch mobs. In the country as a whole, the capitalist planters' strategy undermines the mechanisms of political control most convenient for bourgeois accumulation. At least this is the way I read Marxist theory in 'Marxist theories of power and empirical research' below.

The general argument then is that individual rationality will undermine collective rationality more when those who have individual interests in opposition to collective rationality are more powerful. If bourgeois democracy is generally functional for advanced capitalism, and if those capitalists who grow cotton have individual motives to institute another form of government, then the more powerful cotton planters the less viable the collectively rational form.

In 'Social factors in administrative innovation' (below), the fundamental problem derives from the special moral value of the *status quo*. Administrative innovations in general interfere with the *status quo*, and in particular redistribute privileges which have special moral value simply because the people had them under the old régime. Consequently one of the central determinants of how fast organizations adapt to the conditions of their niches in social life, the rate of administrative reorganization, depends in its turn on the structure of 'vested interests' in the old régime. The micro-sociology of administrative innovation therefore requires us to classify innovations by the kinds of privileges they interfere with.

The same generalization dominates this essay as dominated the grand historical scale of the previous essay, that individual rationality undermines collective rationality more when the people most damaged by collective rationality are more powerful. But here the dependent variables are things like success in taking authority away from the Dean's Administrative Assistant to locate it in the Department, or success in closing down the Edsel Division of Ford Motor Company, or success in taking some officials off the routing scheme for a particular form because they are causing delays in paying requisitions in time to get the discount. Improving the administration may be rational for the organization as a whole, but supporting that innovation may be irrational for powerful people. The privileges that are hard for innovations to dislodge are those generally held by powerful people.

'Social structure and the founding of organizations' originally appeared in a survey of a very heterogeneous literature on the relations between organizations and social structure in the early sixties, with other sections on organizations' effects on revolutions, economic development, the way the upper classes treat the lower classes, and other topics. The description of the secondary labor market and of the internal labor market, extracted from the labor market literature of that time but without the catchy names, has stood up pretty well in the meantime. The rôle such labor market structures play in the essay is not, however, the rôle they play in the current literature: here they do not function as independent variables to explain privilege and oppression, but as existing alternatives to explain patterns of choice in how to build organizations.

The basic argument of this essay is that organizational forms differ at the time of founding of organizations if those forms are being developed in a certain historical period. One can only build organizations with the social materials available. If, in the early modern city, craft forms of organization of the labor market existed, but 'fordism' did not, then the organizational options open to an entrepreneur included craft subcontracting forms but not large scale bureaucratic forms with internal labor markets. Similarly before the development of such kinds of fiduciary social structures as keep most Boards of Directors from making off with the investment, the options for organizing investment were limited to partnerships, and often partnerships limited to a particular sailing of a particular ship (an 'adventure,' in early modern legal terminology). So the possibility space for constructing rational organizations was limited by the stage of social development.

As the paper shows (with more or less casual evidence) there is a great tendency for the organizational forms occupying a certain niche to preserve those forms, so that organizations whose predecessors in a niche originated in a certain historical period now show signs of the preindustrial city, or of the early 19th century, or of the early twentieth century. *Within a given niche of the economy*, people choosing forms for new organizations make use of the social materials available. Individual rationality is limited by the social materials available for constructing an organization to do a given kind of thing.

Sometimes the historically created organizational form for doing a given kind of thing may be continuously the best form for doing that kind of thing, in which case the history of organizational forms bears the same relation to the functional analysis of social forms for different niches that paleontology bears to functional ecology. Paleontology does not provide explanatory information about why the physiology and functional capacities of organisms fit their niches; it instead *perhaps* provides information about what other forms were previously well adapted to a given niche, until the competitive superiority of the presently existing forms dislodged them. If a functional analysis of a social form is a successful explanation, the form's history will not tell much more about it, except to give a date and originating circumstances to its development. In particular, if a given form is *not* functional for a given niche, then its having originated at some period in history will not allow it to occupy that niche now.

But part of the explanatory power of this 'cohort analysis' of organizations derives from two sorts of limitations on individual rationality that are due to the existence of organizations. The first again recurs to the patterning of power in organizations, but now gives an explanation for that patterning. If, for example, craft organizations need craft unions to organize the labor market, to train new workers, to standardize the terms on which labor is available to different short-lived firms, and so on, then such craft organizations not only form a functional structure for craft production, but also form power centers to undermine alternative forms. Craft unions do not always win against alternative forms, as is shown by typesetters' recent failure to prevent their work being done by 'typists', with the introduction of computer typesetting. But such powerful supports for the old régime increase the advantages of whatever social form exists. 'Institutionalization' is a power phenomenon, in which people interested in the institution are given exceptional power to help make the institution go. They can then use that power to keep the institution going even when some of its original competitive advantages have disappeared.

A second advantage of the status quo is that people know quite well, as individuals, how to be rational in it. Organizational learning is basically learning how to do what is usually done in a certain line of business. The learning curve is fundamental to constructing new large-scale machines such as airplanes, and what this means is that a firm which has built a lot of a given kind of airplane has learned how to be rational building it more than a firm that is just starting. But making a new social structure work is subject to the same learning disabilities as making the production line for a new airplane work. It is much easier now, in the historically developed structure of the construction industry, for a great many people to know how to frame, shell, and fit a residence in the organizational form of a craft subcontracting social structure than it would be for them to produce the same product with a bureaucratic fordist assembly line social structure.

Power looms replaced hand looms very slowly because even after one learned to use them they were only about 25% more efficient, while power spinning replaced hand spinning very rapidly because it was several hundred percent more efficient when skillfully run. Similarly a social form to replace craft contract construction will likely die out (except in new environments, such as perhaps the cities of Arizona) unless it is more than 25% better, because people are really good at making contract construction work. The core assertion here is that people may be individually quite irrational in their ability to manage new forms, giving old forms a competitive advantage at any given time. Unless the social structure can take one step back in order to take two forward, the old forms will tend to persist even when competing forms are somewhat more efficient. The rate at which new forms replace the old ones is quite slow if the inherent efficiency of the new forms is only 25% better than the old ones; smaller advantages than 25% may never establish themselves, because of the 'liability of newness.'

'On journal editing as a probabilistic process' (below) treats a rational social form, namely peer judgement of scientific achievements. But it assumes that the individuals who function in that form are simply not very good at producing the judgements that the collective rationality of the system demands of them. Ofshe and I show that under quite reasonable assumptions, the rational structure of peer reviews for journals can nevertheless produce 'the rejection of a great many good papers and the publishing of a large number of mediocre papers.' Measurement error in processes involving individual judgement can produce a good deal of degraded collective performance.

Some of the most famous cases of functional analysis can be conceived as individual rationality at war with collective rationality. The political machine in Merton's essay on manifest and latent functions is 'latent' because there is formal assent throughout the system to a model of city government that should produce technically rational solutions to urban problems, 'without fear nor favor.' The reform charters of city government, whose voting and trustworthy legislative council structures the machine made use of, were manifestly supposed to secure certain collective goods which individuals in cities could not achieve for themselves.

The machine was 'latent' not because the machine politician did not know pretty exactly what he was doing, nor because the businessman who made contributions or paid bribes in return for privileges could have got those privileges cheaper elsewhere, nor yet because the new ethnic voter could have got the 'help, not justice' that he needed from any other institutions in the city. The latent character did not have to do with any of the people acting irrationally, and they certainly would not have been surprised if someone made a speech (a downstate

Republican, perhaps) saying that when they wrote those provisions into the city charters they did not have in mind city judges letting kids in ethnic neighborhoods off with a citation or city cops taking bribes from businessmen who want to have their advertising signs jutting out onto the sidewalk. That is, the machine's functions were not latent because people did not know what was going on, though of course some of the activities of the machine were latent because the officials and the businessmen would go to jail if they were manifest. 'Unconsciousness' has very little to do with something being a 'latent function' here.

What latentness instead has to do with is that the character of the choices presented to people varies with the social structure; this means that the aggregate outcomes of the choices, which in turn form the conditions for future choices, are themselves not chosen, and in fact people may continue to 'choose' consciously to have a reform city government while choosing in their microcontext actions which maintain the machine. Clearly the larger the proportion of recent immigrants in a city's population, the more 'help, not justice' is likely to be what they need, since they do not have the linguistic and other competencies to manage a formal bureaucratic system. Clearly the choice to deliver 'help, not justice' by a public official is more likely if the official serves in a city with a large ethnic population. Clearly the 'Anglo' businessman who is no longer co-member of the country club with the ethnic mayor and ethnic city councilmen is confronted with a different choice about how to get privileges than is a member of an old-time city's old boy network. Paying off a Catholic judge may be a simpler and more effective tactic than letting Catholic politicians into one's country club.

The general point is that the whole structure shapes the choices that rational people make in such a way as not only to undermine the collectively rational reform city charter, but also to maintain the alternative structure, the political machine. It is latent in the sense that the businessmen, for example, if choosing freely what sort of city government to set up, would probably choose a reform administration run by old boys from their country club, while the immigrants would perhaps prefer a village social structure that would make their sons behave rather than a machine that helps keep them out of jail when they misbehave.

Almost all of the arguments in these papers would be called 'latent function' arguments in classical sociological parlance, though they would not satisfy Jon Elster's criterion that people do not know what they are doing when they choose the behavior to be explained (see Elster, 1983: 57). One would not feel uncomfortable talking about the maintenance of peculiar institutions in the South as latently functional for the plantation mode of production while undermining the manifestly functional bourgeois democracy supported (or at least tolerated in their own country, if not perhaps in third world countries) by New York bankers. And locating the powerful interests which prevent rationalization by administrative innovation looks like the work Merton and others included in their *Reader in Bureaucracy* (Merton, et al., eds., 1952), latent function analysis sponsored by the master himself. Merton's own most famous case, the political machine, does not involve anyone being unconscious of what they were choosing, nor any kind of secret rationality unknown to the actor who 'acts rationally' after the fashion of the repressed *id* seeking pleasure.

The key here is that people as rational beings choose in different contexts, even when the world (specifically the social system) connects those choices together causally so that one undermines the other. In the context of city charter writing (or writing up plans for administrative reorganization, or planning a refereeing system for an academic journal, or even evolving the constitution of the United States) one chooses rationally on behalf of the collectivity, with whatever set of individual notions about the utilities of the collectivity and about the causes of those utilities one believes in (whatever one's 'ideology'). When choosing how to get the privilege of putting one's advertising on a public sidewalk (or how to maintain the share of the sharecropper at the level that will just buy him corn meal and molasses, or how to limit the interruptions by students coming into the Department office by sabotaging a new rational space-management plan), one chooses according to individual utilities in the conditions created by the 'ideological' choices one may have contributed to at the collective level.

What makes the pattern resulting from these choices 'latent' is that the different choices making it up are segregated (perhaps by segregation of rôle of legislator from rôle of cotton planter or from the rôle of businessman with a sign a bit too large), not that any of the choices are unconscious. They are not perhaps 'globally rational' choices, in that they do not simultaneously consider all choices together that are casually connected in the world. But there is no secret form of causation at a supra-individual level, a mysterious functional mechanism at the societal level that the people do not know about. There are merely impediments of individual rationality (or at least individual understandable behavior) to collective level rationality.

(4) Cultural forms as things to think with. Thorstein Veblen somewhere talks about the 'trained incapacity' that one learns in an occupation. For example, accountants and financiers learn not to be able to think about the production of substantive goods and services the way an engineer does, because their occupation is to render the monetary accounts of that production (and of the resulting sales) consistent and legally defensible. Conversely an engineer (or perhaps a better example would be a park ranger) may have difficulty seeing why one should destroy something useful because it does not make money. This style of reasoning, that one form of thought (one 'rationality') drives out another, is seen in all sorts of cultural discussions, from the ranting of historical sociologists against the idiocies caused by quantitative methods (and of course vice versa) to the oil-and-water mechanism implicit in third-rate literary history or art history, that for instance romanticism drives out classicism or impressionism drives out academicism from the mind of the artist, so that all important art of a period of transition can be classified as one or the other.

In several of the essays below the basic causal mechanism is congitive limitations produced by a culture. It is very hard here to see exactly what is going on, what the basic form of the theory is. Let me illustrate this more extensively from the process of school formation in sociology; two of the essays below treat this phenomenon at a hortative level ('Should sociologists forget their mothers and fathers?') and at a structural level ('A structural analysis of sociology'). Here I will treat it at the level of the individual, as a problem of culturally induced cognitive limitations, a matter of 'trained incapacity.'

We can think of sociological culture as consisting of various designs for doing sociological work: for understanding phenomena, for building theories, for designing research to test theories, for writing at a length that conveniently fits into journals or that conveniently fills up a whole book (and nothing in between), for having enough references and the right references to show that we know the literature but not saying enough about any of them so as to clutter up the argument, and so on. At any given time the tools available for doing sociological work are more, and more various, than anyone can use in the work they are doing at the time. The variety of tools and models of good workmanship constitutes the capacities of the discipline as a culture to think about things, to establish what is true or false, and to turn what one has understood into science that can be listed on a *vita*. A combination of tools to do the relevant work and models of good workmanship in using them to produce a sociological product constitutes a 'paradigm' of what good work is supposed to look like.

A 'trained incapacity' is produced by a sufficient level of specialization so that some kinds of good work cannot be produced by some of the competent practitioners in the discipline. If it takes so much time to learn statistics up to a modern standard that quantitative researchers do not have time to learn any history, or if the incentive system among quantitative people discourages dillentantism, or if quantitative workers have a positive ideology against becoming learned in 'soft' subjects, or if the social circles that know about hierarchical models do not know about recent good books, then quantitative people will not be able to see things that one can find out about only historically. What one has to look for is not competencies, for there is no general reason that one competence should interfere with another (in fact in general disparate competencies are positively correlated, though generally the correlation is small). Instead one has to look for tendencies for competence in one thing to decrease the ability to develop competence at another thing. Ideologies defending sociological schools are one such force, course requirements for a specialty that take up the first three years in graduate school are another, and so on.

But a second kind of cognitive limitation is produced by tools that do not exist in the discipline at a given time. One then observes a burst of new activity when a cognitive limitation is overcome. When complex intertwining of causes could not be built into our quantitative analyses, our only way of dealing with it was to put different causal connections in different chapters. A table of contents is not a very powerful intellectual integrating device, but since I am now writing an essay on my table of contents I obviously do not believe it is worthless. 'Causal modeling,' in the sense of being able to put several equations together to form a coherent and complete theory, overcame to some degree the cognitive limitations of the sequence that dominated Lazarsfeld's work, from association to partial association to separate examination of the partial relation in different subgroups (what he called 'specification'). What the development of causal modeling showed was the previous limitation of the cultural system of sociology as a whole, of not being able to achieve theoretical coherence quantitatively or mathematically, so requiring coherent theorizing to be done by arguing about the table of contents. The dramatic form of cognitive limitation of thought by cultural systems is produced when the cultural system does not have the tools in it anywhere to think in a certain way.

The essay on 'The deep structure of moral categories, eighteenth-century French stratification, and the Revolution' is an argument about the second sort of cognitive limitation. Its core argument is that the whole cultural system of France in the eighteenth century did not have the conceptual apparatus to think about the semiurbanized, semibureaucratized system, dominated by a helter-skelter system of particularistic privileges and royal ukases for particular cases, that was in fact their stratification system. Consequently the stratification motivations of the Revolution were by and large grievances against a stratification system that no longer existed, and the reforms introduced by the Revolution were often reforms that did not touch the central stratification dynamics of French modernization and commercialization. In particular, the parts of France which most supported the diagnosis of grievances contained in 'bourgeois' anti-feudal ideology, and most supported the reforms, were those which in fact had least of the stratification system that was supposedly being reformed.

The argument then is that the 'deep structure' of French culture in the eighteenth century produced cognitive limitations on the diagnostic and reform analyses of people who thought with that culture, and that this produced some of the most important and indicative features of the stratification ideology and policy of the Revolution.

Ethnic and national identities are similarly lenses through which people the world over perceive the impact of politics and public policy on themselves. The essay on ethnic stratification extracted from a larger piece in the *Handbook of Political Science* (1975) edited by Fred Greenstein and Nelson Polsby asks under what conditions people will come to conceive their identities in national or ethnic terms; when will they feel that they will be better off if the United States succeeds, or if black people's incomes go up relative to white people's incomes, or if Uzbekistan gets an 'autonomous' government whose officials have a larger proportion of Uzbeks (rather than Russians) than under the Russian Empire. There are, as we who specialize in stratification all know, lots of ways to break up the income statistics (or any other measure of 'life chances'). Under what conditions will the people involved tend to use the one of breaking up the world into nations and ethnicities?

The answer the essay gives is largely social structural, that certain types of interdependent organizations of people's lives will tend to produce people who think of themselves first of all as Mexicans, or first of all as members of their village, or first of all as members of the indigenous category, or first of all as members of a particular indigenous tribe, or whatnot. But the dependent variable is a mode of thought, a tendency to see the world as a congeries of ethnicities rather than in the many other ways it can be seen, and so to limit the diagnoses and remedies for injustices produced by stratification systems that they bring to politics.

In the profession of sociology I am more inclined to rant against the cognitive limitations of my colleagues than to analyze the deep cultural sources of those limitations. If one wants to analyze the cultural limitations of a particular person, one has to start by counting up all the various parts of the cultural system that he or she has mastered. In an offhand comment in the essay on Marxist theories of power, I urge that perhaps people should not be allowed to study social change without a course in differential equations. This simply argues that one particularly useful way of thinking about social change is the same way other sciences think about change, by imagining that rates of change are what vary, that the states at any particular time are the cumulation of past rates of change, and that scholars, especially Marxists, would be benefitted by thinking about it in that way as well as in the ways they now think about it. Even if we admit that most people cannot think *simultaneously* in ways treated as distinct in their cultural system, they can then at least think now this way, now that: now as narrative, now as differential equations.

Similarly I argue that while one may want to use Durkheim's *Suicide* to teach about how to link individual pscyhology and social structural forces, or to defend sociological turf, one might also want to use it as a source of possible hypotheses about, say, suicide rates in the Israeli army or in the personal bodyguard of a dictator. Though there is a standard way of treating a classic book when one is teaching theory, and another standard way of treating a book when one is developing hypotheses for a quantitative study, and never shall the twain be linked, they can both occupy different parts of the same mind at different times for different purposes. The essay on when one should forget the mothers and fathers of sociology is an annotated list of the ways a classic book can be a tool for doing sociological work, and a suggestion that we may want to have a full kit of such tools.

'A structural analysis of sociology' is an attempt at the aesthetic form I learned from Thorstein Veblen, the deadpan analysis of the social forms we solve our life problems with as if they were the exotic practices of savages. The central insight of Levi-Strauss is that social groups have to be differentiated if they are to exchange, and that social forms of exchange therefore have to be legitimated by myths of their cultural differentiation (since people are naturally pretty much alike). This insight should apply to the exchanges of people, symbols, and wealth among sociology departments. The hortatory point comes in in the assumption that there is no real intellectual difference, or at most one amounting to six months of further training, between the schools of sociology.

Obviously turning the degree to which different people participate in different cultural subsystems, or the degree to which a society's cultural system is blind to major features of its social life, into a measurable variable, would be a real trick. One may have the intuition that most people who treat social change with differential equations have a trained incapacity to deal with narratives, and vice versa that historians who are good at narratives hardly ever manage differential equations (clearly history of science, especially of physics or chemistry, might be a good place to look for exceptions), but classifying people clearly into competent and incompetent at narrative understanding would be a tricky business, and even understanding differential equations is a subject on which a good many sociologists deceive themselves about their competence. This then is one of those cases of a convincing causal mechanism which one has to treat in a positivistically unsatisfactory way, if one is going to treat it at all. The four pieces treated under this style of analysis of rationality in the introduction are all suitably fluffy, 'essays' rather than 'papers.'

Fitting rationality into sociology

I have chosen to arrange the essays in the book according to their substantive focus, rather than by their strategies in dealing with the problem of the social structuring of rationality. If the strategies outlined above are useful in the way I define 'useful,' they ought to contribute to substantive knowledge about how organizations or stratification systems or politics works. And I hope that people other than those entranced by the problem of rationality will find this book useful. I have therefore divided the essays into those primarily about stratification, those primarily about the sociology of organizations, and those about the discipline of sociology.

PART I

STRATIFICATION

2. Agricultural enterprise and rural class relations[1]

Marx's fundamental innovation in stratification theory was to base a theory of formation of classes and political development on a theory of the bourgeois enterprise (see Parsons 1949). Even though some of his conceptualization of the enterprise is faulty, and though some of his propositions about the development of capitalist enterprise were in error, the idea was sound: one of the main determinants of class relations in different parts of the American economy is, indeed, the economic and administrative character of the enterprise.[2]

But Marx's primary focus was on class relations in cities. In order to extend his mode of analysis to rural settings, we need an analysis of rural enterprises. The purpose of this paper is to provide such an analysis and to suggest the typical patterns of rural class relations produced in societies where a type of rural enterprise predominates.

Property and enterprise in agriculture

Agriculture everywhere is much more organized around the institutions of property than around those of occupation. Unfortunately, our current theory and research on stratification is built to fit an urban environment, being conceptually organized around the idea of occupation. For instance, an important recent monograph on social mobility classifies all farmers together and regards them as an unstratified source of urban workers (see Lipset & Bendix, 1959).[3]

---

[1] James S. Coleman, Jan Hajda, and Amitai Etzioni have done me the great service of being intensely unhappy with a previous version of this paper. I have not let them see this version.

[2] Cf. especially Robert Blauner (1960), in which he compares class relations and the alienation of the working class in continuous-process manufacturing with that in mechanical mass-production industries.

[3] The exceedingly high rate of property mobility which characterized American rural social structures when the national ideology was being formed apparently escapes their attention. Yet Lipset discusses the kind of mobility characteristic of frontiers and

The theory of property systems is very much underdeveloped. Property may be defined as a legally defensible vested right to affect decisions on the use of economically valuable goods. Different decisions (for instance, technical decisions versus decisions on distributions of benefits) typically are affected by different sets of rights held by different sets of people. These legally defensible rights are, of course, important determinants of the actual decision-making structure of any social unit which acts with respect to goods.

But a property system must be conceived as the typical interpenetration of legally vested rights to affect decisions and the factual situation which determines who actually makes what decisions on what grounds. For example, any description of the property system of modern business which ignores the fact that it is economically impossible for a single individual to gain majority stock holdings in a large enterprise, and politically impossible to organize an integrated faction of dispersed stockholders except under unusual conditions, would give a grossly distorted view. A description of a property system, then, has to take into account the internal politics of typical enterprises, the economic forces that typically shape decisions, the political situation in the society at large which is taken into account in economic decisions, the reliability and cost of the judiciary, and so forth. The same property law means different things for economic life if decisions on the distribution of income from agricultural enterprise are strongly affected by urban *rentiers*' interests rather than a smallholding peasantry.

It is obviously impossible to give a complete typology of the legal, economic, and political situations which determine the decision-making structure within agricultural organizations for all societies and for all important decisions. Instead, one must pick certain frequent constellations of economic, technical, legal, and labor recruitment conditions that tend to give rise to a distinct structure of decision-making within agricultural enterprises.

By an 'enterprise' I mean a social unit which has and exercises the power to commit a given parcel of land to one or another productive purpose, to achieve which it decides the allocation of chattels and

small farms systems very well (1950: 33). In 1825 occupational mobility only concerned a small part of the population of the United States. The orientation of most nineteenth-century Americans to worldly success was that of Tennyson's 'Northern farmer, new style': 'But proputty, proputty sticks, an' proputty, proputty graws.'

labor on the land.[4] The rights to affect decisions on who shall get the benefit from that production may not be, and quite often are not, confined within the enterprise, as defined here. The relation between the enterprise and power over the distribution of benefit is one of the central variables in the analysis to follow, for instance, distinguishing tenancy systems from smallholding systems.

Besides the relation between productive decisions and decisions on benefits, some of the special economic, political, and technical characteristics which seem most important in factual decision-making structure will be mentioned, such as the value of land, whether the 'owner' has police power over or kinship relations with labor, the part of production destined for market, the amount of capital required besides the land, or the degree of technical rationalization. These are, of course, some of the considerations Marx dealt with when describing the capitalist enterprise, particularly in its factory form. Plantations, manors, family-size tenancies, ranches, or family farms tend to occur only in certain congenial economic, technical and political environments and to be affected in their internal structure by those environments.

A description and analysis of empirical constellations of decision-making structures cannot, by its untheoretical nature, claim to be complete. Moreover, I have deliberately eliminated from consideration all precommercial agriculture, not producing for markets, because economic forces do not operate in the same ways in precommercial societies and because describing the enterprise would involve providing a typology of extended families and peasant communities, which would lead us far afield. I have also not considered the 'community-as-enterprise' systems of the Soviet sphere and of Israel because these are as much organizational manifestations of a social movement as they are economic institutions.[5]

Systems of commercialized manors, family-sized tenancies, family smallholdings, plantations, and ranches cover most of the property

[4] Occasionally, the decisions to commit land to a given crop and to commit labor and chattels to cultivation are made separately, e.g., in cotton plantations in the post bellum American South. The land is committed to cotton by the landowner, but labor and chattels are committed to cultivation by the sharecropper.

[5] However, the origin of the *kolkhoz* or collective farm does seem to depend partly on the form of prerevolutionary agriculture. Collectivization seems to occur most rapidly when a revolutionary government deals with an agriculture which was previously organized into large-scale capitalist farms.

systems found in commercialized agriculture outside eastern Europe and Israel. And each of these property systems tends to give rise to a distinctive class system, differing in important respects from that which develops with any of the other systems. Presenting argument and evidence for this proposition is the central purpose of this paper.

Variations in rural class relations

Rural class structure in commercialized agriculture varies in two main ways: the criteria which differentiate the upper and lower classes and the quality and quantity of intraclass cultural, political, and organizational life. In turn, the two main criteria which may differentiate classes are legal privileges and style of life. And two main qualities of class culture and organization are the degree of familiarity with technical culture of husbandry and the degree of political activation and organization. This gives four characteristics of rural class structures which vary with the structure of enterprises.

First, rural class systems vary in the extent to which classes are differentiated by legal privileges. Slaves and masters, peons and *hacendados*, serfs and lords, colonial planters and native labor, citizen farmers employing aliens as labor – all are differentiated by legal privileges. In each case the subordinate group is disenfranchised, often bound to the land or to the master, denied the right to organize, denied access to the courts on an equal basis, denied state-supported education, and so on.

Second, rural stratification systems vary in the sharpness of differentiation of style of life among the classes. Chinese gentry used to live in cities, go to school, compete for civil service posts, never work with their hands, and maintain extended families as household units. On each criterion, the peasantry differed radically. In contrast, in the northern United States, rich and poor farmers live in the country, attend public schools, consume the same general kinds of goods, work with their hands, at least during the busy seasons, and live in conjugal family units. There were two radically different ways of life in rural China; in the northern United States the main difference between rich and poor farmers is wealth.

Third, rural class systems vary in the distribution of the technical culture of husbandry. In some systems the upper classes would be completely incapable of making the decisions of the agricultural enterprise: they depend on the technical lore of the peasantry. At the other extreme, the Spanish-speaking labor force of the central valley in California would be bewildered by the marketing, horticultural, engineering, and transportation problems of a large-scale irrigated vegetable farm.

Fourth, rural classes vary in their degree of political activity and organization, in their sensitivity or apathy to political issues, in their degree of intraclass communication and organization, and in their degree of political education and competence.

Our problem, then, is to relate types of agricultural enterprises and property systems to the patterns of class relations in rural social life. We restrict our attention to enterprises producing for markets, and of these we exclude the community-as-enterprise systems of eastern Europe and Israel.

Class relations in types of agricultural enterprise

1. The manorial or hacienda system
The first type of enterprise to be considered here is actually one form of precommercial agriculture, divided into two parts: cultivation of small plots for subsistence by a peasantry, combined with cultivation by customary labor dues of domain land under the lord's supervision. It fairly often happens that the domain land comes to be used for commercial crops while the peasant land continues to be used for subsistence agriculture. There is no rural labor market but, rather, labor dues or labor rents to the lord, based on customary law or force. There is a very poorly developed market in land; there may be, however, an active market in estates, where the estates include as part of their value the labor due to the lord. But land as such, separate from estates and from manors as going concerns, is very little an article of commerce. Estates also tend to pass as units in inheritance, by various devices of entailment, rather than being divided among heirs.[6]

The manorial system is characterized by the exclusive access of the

---

[6] In some cases, as in what was perhaps the world's most highly developed manorial system, in Chile, an estate often remains undivided as an enterprise but is held 'together in the family as an undivided inheritance for some years, and not infrequently for a generation. This multiplies the number of actual owners [but not of haciendas], of rural properties in particular' (McBride 1936: 139).

manor lord (or *hacendado* in Latin America) to legal process in the national courts. A more or less unfree population holding small bits of land in villein or precarious tenure is bound to work on the domain land of the lord, by the conditions of tenure or by personal peonage. Unfree tenures or debts tend to be inheritable, so that in case of need the legal system of the nation will subject villeins or peons to work discipline on the manor.

Some examples of this system are the hacienda system of Mexico up to at least 1920 (Tannenbaum, 1929: 91–133), some areas in the Peruvian highlands at present (Ford, 1955: 93–5), medieval England (Vinogradoff, 1905: 212–35, 291–365), East Germany before the reconstruction of agriculture into large-scale plantation and ranch agriculture (Weber, 1924: 471–4), the Austro-Hungarian Empire, in the main, up to at least 1848 (Blum, 1948: 23, 68–87), and many other European and South American systems at various times.

The manorial system rests on the assumptions that neither the value of land nor the value of labor is great and that calculation of productive efficiency by the managers of agricultural enterprise is not well developed. When landowners start making cost-studies of the efficiency of forced versus wage labor, as they did, for instance, in Austria-Hungary in the first part of the nineteenth century, they find that wage labor is from two to four times as efficient (Blum, 1948: 192–202). When landowners' traditional level of income becomes insufficient to compete for prestige with the bourgeoisie, and they set about trying to raise incomes by increasing productivity, as they did in eastern Germany, the developmental tendency is toward capitalistic plantation or ranch agriculture (Weber, 1924: 474–7). When the waste and common become important for cattle- or sheep-raising and labor becomes relatively less important in production, enclosure movements drive precarious tenants off the land. When land becomes an article of commerce and the price and productivity of land goes up, tenancy by family farmers provides the lord with a comfortable income that can be spent in the capital city, without much worry about the management of crops. The farther the market penetrates agriculture, first creating a market for commodities, then for labor and land, the more economically unstable does the manorial economy become, and the more likely is the manor to go over to one of the other types of agricultural enterprise.

In summary, the manorial system combines in the lord and his agents authority over the enterprise and rulership or *Herrschaft* over dependent tenants. Classes are distinct in legal status. In style of life the manor lord moves on to the national scene, often little concerned with detailed administration of his estate. He often keeps city residence and generally monopolizes education. Fairly often he even speaks a different language, for example, Latin among Magyar nobility, French in the Russian aristocracy, Spanish, instead of Indian dialects, in parts of Latin America.

The pattern of life of the subject population is very little dependent on market prices of goods. Consequently, they have little interest in political issues. Even less does the peasantry have the tools of political organization, such as education, experienced leadership, freedom of association, or voting power. Quite often, as, for example, in the Magyar areas of the Hapsburg monarchy or among the Indian tribes of Latin America, intraclass communication is hindered by language barriers. A politically active and competent upper class confronts a politically apathetic, backward, and disenfranchised peasantry.

2. Family-size tenancy

In family-size tenancy the operative unit of agriculture is the family enterprise, but property rights in the enterprise rest with *rentier* capitalists. The return from the enterprise is divided according to some rental scheme, either in money or in kind. The rent may be fixed, fixed with modification in years of bad harvest, or share.[7] The formal title to the land may not be held by the non-cultivator – it is quite common for the 'rent' on the land to be, in a legal sense, the interest on a loan secured by the land.

This type of arrangement seems to occur most frequently when the following five conditions are met: (*a*) land has very high productivity and high market price; (*b*) the crop is highly labor-intensive, and mechanization of agriculture is little developed; (*c*) labor is cheap; (*d*) there are no appreciable economies of scale in factors other than labor; and (*e*) the period of production of the crop is one year or less.

[7] But share rents in commercialized agriculture are often indicators of the splitting of the enterprise, as discussed above: it most frequently reflects a situation in which land is committed to certain crops by the landlord and the landlord markets the crops, while the scheduling of work is done by the tenant and part of the risks are borne by him.

These conditions are perhaps most fully met with the crops of rice and cotton, especially on irrigated land; yet such a system of tenancy is quite often found where the crops are potatoes or wheat and maize, even though the conditions are not fulfilled. A historical, rather than an economic, explanation is appropriate to these cases.

The correlation of tenancy arrangements with high valuation of land is established by a number of pieces of evidence. In Japan in 1944, most paddy (rice) land was in tenancy, and most upland fields were owner-operated (Klein, 1958: 227). The same was true in Korea in 1937 (Klein, 1948: 246). South China, where land values were higher and irrigated culture more practiced, had considerably higher rates of tenancy than did North China (Han-Seng, 1936: 100–103, 3–4; Klein, 1958: 253). In Thailand tenancy is concentrated in the commercialized farming of the river valleys in central Siam (Jacoby, 1949: 232–5). In Japan, up to World War II, except for the last period (1935–40), every time the price of land went up, the proportion of land held in tenancy went up (Dore, 1959: 21).

The pattern of family-size tenancy was apparently found in the potato culture of Ireland before the revolution, in the wheat culture of pre-World War I Romania (Roberts, 1951: 14–17, Tables ix, x, 363) and also that Bosnia-Herzegovina (now part of Yugoslavia) at the same period (Tomasevich, 1955: 96–101, 355). The sugar-cane regions of central Luzon are also farmed in family-size tenancies, though this is so uneconomical that, without privileged access to the American market, cane culture would disappear (Jacoby, 1949: 181–91, 203–9). It also characterizes the cotton culture of the highly productive Nile Valley in Egypt (Warriner, 1957: 2–26) and the cotton culture of the Peruvian coast (Ford, 1955: 84–5). This pattern of small peasant farms with rents to landlords was also characteristic of prerevolutionary France (Tocqueville, 1955: 23–25, 30–32) and southeast England during the Middle Ages (Homans, 1941: 21). In lowland Burma a large share of the rice land is owned by the Indian banking house of Chettyar, (Jacoby, 1949: 73, 78–88) and much of the rest of it is in tenancy to the other landlords. The land-tenure system of Taiwan before the recent land reform was typical of family-size tenancy (Klein, 1958: 52–4, 235).

Perhaps the most remarkable aspect of this list is the degree to which this system has been ended by reform or revolution, becoming transformed, except in a few Communist states, into a system of smallholding farms. And even in Communist states the first transformation after the revolution is ordinarily to give the land to the tiller: only afterward are the peasants gathered into collective farms, generally in the face of vigorous resistance.

The system of *rentier* capitalists owning land let out in family farms (or *rentier* capitalists owning debts whose service requires a large part of farm income) seems extremely politically unstable. The French Revolution, according to De Tocqueville, was most enthusiastically received in areas in which there were small farms paying feudal dues (commuted to rent in money or in kind) (Tocqueville, 1955: 25). The eastern European systems of Rumania and parts of Yugoslavia were swept away after World War I in land reforms. Land reforms were also carried through in northern Greece, the Baltic states, and many of the succession states of the Hapsburg monarchy (the reform was specious in Hungary). A vigorous and long-lasting civil war raged in Ireland up to the time of independence, and its social base was heavily rural. The high-tenancy areas in central Luzon were the social base of the revolutionary Hukbalahaps during and after World War II. The Communist revolution in China had its first successes in the high-tenancy areas of the south. The number of peasant riots in Japan during the interwar period was closely correlated with the proportion of land held in tenancy. (Dore, 1959: 72; this data disputes with the data on tenancy, p. 21). Peasant rebellions were concentrated in Kent and southeast England during the Middle Ages (Homans, 1941: 119). In short, such systems rarely last through a war or other major political disturbance and constantly produce political tensions.

There are several causes of the political instability of such systems. In the first place, the issue in the conflict is relatively clear: the lower the rent of the *rentier* capitalists, the higher the income of the peasantry. The division of the product at harvest time or at the time of sale is a clear measure of the relative prerogatives of the farmer and the *rentier*.

Second, there is a severe conflict over the distribution of the risks of the enterprise. Agriculture is always the kind of enterprise with which God has a lot to do. With the commercialization of agriculture, the enterprise is further subject to great fluctuation in the gross income from its produce. *Rentiers*, especially if they are capitalists investing in land rather than aristocrats receiving incomes from feudal patrimony, shift as much of the risk of failure as possible to the tenant. Whether the rent is share or cash, the variability of income of the peasantry is almost never less, and is often more, than the variability of *rentiers'* income. This makes the income of the peasantry highly variable, contributing to their political sensitization.[8]

Third, there tends to be little social contact between the *rentier* capitalists living in the cities and the rural population. The *rentiers* and the farmers develop distinct styles of life, out of touch with each other. The *rentier* is not brought into contact with the rural population by having to take care of administrative duties on the farm; nor is he drawn into local government as a leading member of the community or as a generous sharer in the charitable enterprises of the village. The urban *rentier*, with his educated and often foreign speech, his cosmopolitan interests, his arrogant rejection of rustic life is a logical target of the rural community, whose only contact with him is through sending him money or goods.

Fourth, the leaders of the rural community, the rich peasants, are not vulnerable to expulsion by the landowners, as they would be were the landowners also the local government. The rich peasant shares at least some of the hardships and is opposed in his class interests to many of the same people as are the tenants. In fact, in some areas where the population pressure on the land is very great, the rich peasants themselves hold additional land in tenancy, beyond their basic holdings. In this case the leadership of the local community is not only not opposed to the interests of the tenants but has largely identical interests with the poor peasants.

Finally, the landowners do not have the protection of the peasants' ignorance about the enterprise to defend their positions, as do large-scale capitalist farmers. It is perfectly clear to the tenant farmer that he could raise and sell his crops just as well with the landlord gone as with him there. There is no complicated cooperative tillage that seems beyond the view of all but the landlord and his managers, as there may be in manorial, and generally is in large-scale capitalist, agriculture. The farmer knows as well or better than the landlord

---

[8] Though they deal with smallholding systems, the connection between economic instability and political activism is argued by Lipset (1950: 26–36; Heberle, 1951: 240–8; see also Jacoby, 1949: 246; and Lerner, 1958: 227). Aristotle noted the same thing: 'it is a bad thing that many from being rich should become poor; for men of ruined fortunes are sure to stir up revolutions' (*Politics* 1266ᵇ).

where seed and fertilizer is to be bought and where the crop can be sold. He can often see strategic investments unknown to his landlord that would alleviate his work or increase his yield.

At least in its extreme development, then, the landowning class in systems of family-size tenancy appears as alien, superfluous, grasping, and exploitive. Their rights in agricultural enterprise appear as an unjustifiable burden on the rustic classes, both to the peasantry and to urban intellectuals. No marked decrease in agricultural productivity is to be expected when they are dispossesed, because they are not the class that carries the most advanced technical culture of agriculture. Quite often, upon land reform the productivity of agriculture increases (Dore, 1959: 213–19).

So family-size tenancy tends to yield a class system with an enfranchised, formally free lower class which has a monopoly of technical culture. The style of life of the upper class is radically different from that of the lower class. The lower class tends to develop a relatively skilled and relatively invulnerable leadership in the richer peasantry and a relatively high degree of political sensitivity in the poorer peasantry. It is of such stuff that many radical populist and nationalist movements are made.

3. Family smallholding

Family smallholding has the same sort of enterprises as does family tenancy, but rights to the returns from the enterprise are more heavily concentrated in the class of farmers. The 'normal' property holding is about the size requiring the work of two adults or less. Probably the most frequent historical source of such systems is out of family-tenancy systems by way of land reform or revolution. However, they also arise through colonization of farmlands carried out under governments in which large landlords do not have predominant political power, for instance, in the United States and Norway. Finally, it seems that such systems tend to be produced by market forces at an advanced stage of industrialization. There is some evidence that farms either larger or smaller than those requiring about two adult laborers tend to disappear in the industrial states of western Europe (see Dovring, 1956: 115–18).[9]

---

[9] The median size of the farm unit, taking into consideration the type of crops grown on different sized farms, ranges from that requiring one man-year in Norway to two man-years in France, among the nations on the Continent.

Examples of such systems having a relatively long history are the United States ouside the 'Black Belt' in the South, the ranch areas of the West, and the central valleys of California, Serbia after some time in the early nineteenth century, (Tomasevich, 1955: 38–47) France after the great revolution, most of Scandinavia, (Dovring, 1956: 143) much of Canada, Bulgaria since 1878, (Royal Institute of International Affairs, 1939: 106), and southern Greece since sometime in the nineteenth century. Other such systems which have lasted long enough to give some idea of their long-term development are those created in eastern Europe after World War I; good studies of at least Romania (Roberts, 1951) and Yugoslavia (Tomasevich, 1955) exist. Finally the system of family smallholding created in Japan by the American-induced land reform of 1946 has been carefully studied (Dore, 1959).

Perhaps the best way to begin analysis of this type of agricultural enterprise is to note that virtually all the costs of production are fixed. Labor in the family holding is, in some sense, 'free': family members have to be supported whether they work or not, so they might as well work. Likewise, the land does not cost rent, and there is no advantage to the enterprise in leaving it out of cultivation. This predominance of fixed costs means that production does not fall with a decrease in prices, as it does in most urban enterprises where labor is a variable cost (Kahler, 1958: 17). Consequently, the income of smallholders varies directly with the market price of the commodities they produce and with variability in production produced by natural catastrophe. Thus, the political movements of smallholders tend to be directed primarily at maintenance of the price of agricultural commodities rather than at unemployment compensation or other 'social security' measures.

Second, the variability of return from agricultural enterprise tends to make credit expensive and, at any rate, makes debts highly burdensome in bad years. Smallholders' political movements, therefore, tend to be opposed to creditors, to identify finance capital as a class enemy: Jews, the traditional symbol of finance capital, often come in for an ideological beating. Populist movements are often directed against 'the bankers.' Further, since cheap money generally aids debtors, and since small farmers are generally debtors, agrarian movements tend to support various kinds of inflationary schemes. Small farmers do not want to be crucified on a cross of gold.

Third, agrarian movments, except in highly advanced societies, tend to enjoy limited intraclass communication, to be poor in politically talented leaders, relatively unable to put together a coherent, disciplined class movement controlled from below.[10] Contributions to the party treasury tend to be small and irregular, like the incomes of the small farmers. Peasant movements are, therefore, especially prone to penetration by relatively disciplined political interests, sometimes Communist and sometimes industrial capital.[11] Further, such movements tend to be especially liable to corruption,[12] since they are relatively unable to provide satisfactory careers for political leaders out of their own resources.

Moreover, at an early stage of industrial and commercial development in a country without large landowners, the only sources of large amounts of money available to politicians are a few urban industrial and commercial enterprises. Making a policy on the marketing and production of iron and steel is quite often making a policy on the marketing and production of a single firm. Naturally, it pays that firm to try to get legislation and administration tailored to its needs.

Fourth, small-farmer and peasant movements tend to be nationalistic and xenophobic. The explanation of this phenomenon is not clear.

Finally, small-farmer and peasant movements tend to be opposed to middlemen and retailers, who are likely to use their monopolistic or monopsonistic position to milk the farm population. The cooperative movement is, of course, directed at eliminating middlemen as well as at provision of credit without usury.

Under normal conditions (that is, in the absence of totalitarian government, major racial cleavage, and major war) this complex of

---

[10] I.e., as compared with political movements of the urban proletariat or bourgeoisie. They are more coherent and disciplined than are the lower-class movements in other agricultural systems.

[11] An excellent example of the penetration of industrial capital into a peasant party is shown by the development of the party platforms on industry in Romania, 1921–6 (Roberts, 1951: 154–6). The penetration of American populists by the 'silver interests' is another example.

[12] See Roberts (1951: 337–9), and Tomasevich (1955: 246–7). The Jacksonian era in the United States, and the persistent irregularities in political finance of agrarian leaders in the South of the United States, are further examples.

political forces tend to produce a rural community with a proliferation of associations and with the voting power and political interest to institute and defend certain elements of democracy, especially universal suffrage and universal education. This tends to produce a political regime loose enough to allow business and labor interest groups to form freely without allowing them to dominate the government completely. Such a system of landholding is a common precursor and support of modern liberal democratic government.

In smallholding systems, then, the upper classes of the rural community are not distinct in legal status and relatively not in style of life. Social mobility in such a system entails mainly a change in the amount of property held, or in the profitability of the farm, but not a change in legal status or a radical change in style of life.[13]

A politically enfranchised rural community is characterized by a high degree of political affect and organization, generally in opposition to urban interests rather than against rural upper classes. But, compared with the complexity of their political goals and the level of political involvement, their competence tends to be low until the 'urbanization of the countryside' is virtually complete.

4. Plantation agriculture

Labor-intensive crops requiring several years for maturation, such as rubber, tree fruit, or coffee, tend to be grown on large-scale capitalistic farms employing either wage labor, or, occasionally, slave labor. Particularly when capital investment is also required for processing equipment to turn the crop into a form in which it can be shipped, as for example in the culture of sugar cane and, at least in earlier times, sugar-beets, large-scale capitalist agriculture predominates.

The key economic factor that seems to produce large-scale capitalist culture is the requirement of long-term capital investment in the crop or in machinery, combined with relatively low cost of land. When the crop is also labor-intensive, particularly when labor is highly seasonal, a rather typical plantation system tends to emerge. In some cases it also emerges in the culture of cotton (as in the ante bellum American South and some places in Egypt), wheat (as in Hungary, eastern

---

[13] The best description that I know of the meaning of 'property mobility' in such a system is the novel of Knut Hamsun (1921), set in the Norwegian frontier.

Germany, (Weber, 1924: 474–77) and Poland,[14] or rice (as on the Carolina and Georgia coasts in the ante bellum American South) (House, 1954: 18–37).

The enterprise typically combines a small highly skilled and privileged group which administers the capital investment, the labor force, and the marketing of the crops with a large group of unskilled, poorly paid, and legally unprivileged workers. Quite generally, the workers are ethnically distinct from the skilled core of administrators, often being imported from economically more backward areas or recruited from an economically backward native population in colonial and semicolonial areas. This means that ordinarily they are ineligible for the urban labor market of the nation in which they work, if it has an urban labor market.

Examples of plantation systems are most of the sugar areas in the Caribbean and on the coast of Peru, (Ford, 1955: 57–60) the rubber culture of the former Federated Malay States in Malaya (Jacoby, 1949: 106–8, 113) the fruit-growing areas of Central America, the central valleys of California, where the labor force is heavily Latin American, eastern Germany during the early part of this century, where Poles formed an increasing part of the labor force,[15] Hungary up to World War II, the pineapple-growing of the Hawaiian Islands, (Norbeck, 1959) and, of course, the ante bellum American South. The system tends to induce in the agricultural labor force a poverty of associational life, low participation in local government, lack of education for the labor force, and high vulnerability of labor-union and political leadership to oppression by landlords and landlord-dominated governments. The domination of the government by landlords tends to prevent the colonization of new land by smallholders, and even to wipe out the holdings of such small peasantry as do exist.

In short, the system tends to maintain the culture, legal and political position, and life chances of the agricultural labor force distinct both from the urban labor force and from the planter aristocracy. The

[14] See Lesniewski and Ponikowski, (1933: 260–3). Capitalist development was greatest in the western regions of Poznan and Pomerania (cf. p. 264). There seem to have been many remains of a manorial system (cf. p. 277).

[15] Weber shows that, in the eastern parts of Germany during the latter part of the nineteenth century, the proportionate decrease of the German population (being replaced by Poles) was greater in areas of large-scale cultivation (1924: 452–53).

bearers of the technical and commercial knowledge are not the agricultural laborers, and, consequently, redistribution of land tends to introduce inefficiency into agriculture. The plantation system, as Edgar T. Thompson has put it, is a 'race-making situation' (Thompson, 1958: 506–7) which produces a highly privileged aristocracy, technically and culturally educated, and a legally, culturally, and economically underprivileged labor force. If the latter is politically mobilized, as it may be occasionally by revolutionary governments, it tends to be extremist.

5. Capitalist extensive agriculture with wage labor: the ranch
An extensive culture of wool and beef, employing wage labor, grew up in the American West, Australia, England and Scotland during and after the industrial revolution, Patagonia and some other parts of South America, and northern Mexico. In these cases the relative proportion of labor in the cost of production is smaller than it is in plantation agriculture. Such a structure is also characteristic of the wheat culture in northern Syria. In no case was there pressure to recruit and keep down an oppressed labor force. In England a surplus labor force was pushed off the land. A fairly reliable economic indicator of the difference between ranch and plantation systems is that in ranch systems the least valuable land is owned by the largest enterprises. In plantation systems the most valuable land is owned by the largest enterprises, with less valuable land generally used by marginal smallholders. The explanation of this is not clear.

The characteristic social feature of these enterprises is a free-floating, mobile labor force, often with few family ties, living in barracks, and fed in some sort of 'company mess hall.' They tend to make up a socially undisciplined element, hard-drinking and brawling. Sometimes their alienation from society takes on the form of political radicalism, but rarely of an indigenous disciplined radical movement.

The types of agricultural enterprise outlined here are hardly exhaustive, but perhaps they include most of the agricultural systems which help determine the political dynamics of those countries which act on the world scene today. Nor does this typology pretend to outline all the important differences in the dynamics of agricultural systems. Obviously, the system of family-sized farms run by smallholders in Serbia in the 1840s is very different from the institutionally similar Danish and American systems of the 1950s.[16] And capitalistic sheep-raisers supported and made up the House of Lords in England but supported populistic currents in the United States.

However, some of the differences among systems outlined here seem to hold in widely varying historical circumstances. The production and maintenance of ethnic differences by plantations, the political fragility of family-size tenancy, the richer associational life, populist ideology, corrupt politics of smallholders, and the political apathy and technical traditionalism of the manor or the old hacienda – these seem to be fairly reliable. Characteristics of rural enterprises and the class relations they typically produce are summarized in Table 1.

This, if it is true, shows the typology to be useful. The question that remains is: is it capable of being used? Is it possible to find indexes which will reliably differentiate a plantation from a manor or a manor from a large holding farmed by family tenancy?

The answer is that most of these systems have been accurately identified in particular cases. The most elusive is the manor or traditional hacienda; governments based on this sort of agricultural enterprise rarely take accurate censuses, partly because they rarely have an agricultural policy worthy of the name. Often even the boundaries of landholdings are not officially recorded. Further, the internal economy of the manor or hacienda provides few natural statistical indexes – there is little bookkeeping of the use of labor, of land, of payment in kind or in customary rights. The statistical description of manorial economies is a largely unsolved problem.

Except for this, systematic comparative studies of the structure and dynamics of land tenure systems are technically feasible. But it has been all too often the case that descriptions of agricultural systems do not permit them to be classified by the type of enterprise.[17] Perhaps

---

[16] E.g., in the average size of agricultural villages, in the proportion of the crop marketed, in the level of living, in education, in birth rate, in the size of the household unit, in the intensity of ethnic antagonism, in degree of political organization and participation, in exposure to damage by military action – these are only some of the gross differences.

[17] E.g., the most common measure used for comparative study is the concentration of landholdings. A highly unequal distribution of land may indicate family-tenancy, manorial, plantation, or ranch systems. Similarly, data on size of farm units confuse family smallholding with family tendency, and lump together all three kinds of

calling attention to widespread typical patterns of institutionalizing agricultural production will encourage those who write monographs to provide the information necessary for comparative study.

large-scale enterprise. A high ratio of landless peasantry may be invovled in family-tenancy, plantation, or manorial systems. Ambiguous references to 'tenancy' may mean the labor rents of a hacienda system, or the cash or share rents of family-size tenancy, or even tenancy of sons before fathers' death in smallholding systems. 'Capitalistic agriculture' sometimes refers to ranches, sometimes to plantations, and sometimes to smallholdings. 'Feudalism,' though most often applied to manorial systems, is also used to describe family-size tenancy and plantation economies. 'Absentee landlordism' describes both certain manorial and family-size tenancy systems.

Table 1 *Characteristics of rural enterprises and resulting class relations*

Type of enterprise	Characteristics of enterprise	Characteristics of class structure
Manorial	Division of land into domain land and labor subsistence land, with domain land devoted to production for market. Lord has police power over labor. Technically traditional; low cost of land and little market in land.	Classes differ greatly in legal privileges and style of life. Technical culture borne largely by the peasantry. Low political activation and competence of peasantry; high politicization of the upper classes.
Family-size tenancy	Small parcels of highly valuable land worked by families who do not own the land, with a large share of the production for market. Highly labor- and land-intensive culture, of yearly or more frequent crops.	Classes differ little in legal privileges but greatly in style of life. Technical culture generally borne by the lower classes. High political affect and political organization of the lower classes, often producing revolutionary populist movements.
Family smallholding	Same as family tenancy, except benefits remain within the enterprise. Not distinctive of areas with high valuation of land; may become capital-intensive at a late stage of industrialization.	Classes differ neither in legal privileges nor in style of life. Technical culture borne by both rich and poor. Generally unified and highly organized political opposition to urban interests, often corrupt and undisciplined.
Plantation	Large-scale enterprises with either slavery or wage labor, producing labor-intensive crops requiring capital investment on relatively cheap land (though generally the best land within the plantation area). No or little subsistence production.	Classes differ in both style of life and legal privileges. Technical culture monopolized by upper classes. Politically apathetic and incompetent lower classes, mobilized only in time of revolution by urban radicals.
Ranch	Large-scale production of labor-extensive crops, on land of low value (lowest in large units within ranch areas), with wage labor partly paid in kind in company barracks and mess.	Classes may not differ in legal status, as there is no need to recruit and keep down a large labor force. Style of life differentiation unknown. Technical culture generally relatively evenly distributed. Dispersed and unorganized radicalism of lower classes.

3. Some empirical consequences of the Davis-Moore theory of stratification*

Davis and Moore's theory of stratification (1945), though frequently discussed, has stimulated remarkably few studies. Perhaps this is due to the lack of derivations of empirical propositions in the original article. I would like in this note to outline some empirical implications of the theory.

Davis and Moore's basic argument is that unequal rewards tend to accrue to positions of great importance to society, provided that the talents needed for such positions are scarce. 'Society' (i.e. people strongly identified with the collective fate) insures that these functions are properly performed by rewarding the talented people for undertaking these tasks. This implies that the greater the importance of positions, the less likely they are to be filled by ascriptive recruitment.[1]

It is quite difficult to rank tasks or rôles according to their relative importance. But certain tasks are unquestionably more important at one time than at another, or more important in one group than another. For instance, generals are more important in wartime than in peacetime. Changes in importance, or different importance in different groups, have clear consequences according to the theory. If the importance of a role increases, its rewards should become relatively greater and recruitment should be more open.

---

* This note was stimulated by a seminar presentation by Renate Mayntz, who focused attention on the problem of empirical investigation of functional theories.
[1] The theory holds that the most important positions, if they require unusual talents, will recruit people who otherwise would not take them, by offering high rewards to talent. This result would take place if one assumed a perfectly achievement-based stratification system. Some have asserted that Davis and Moore's argument 'assumes' such a perfectly open system, and hence is obviously inadequate to the facts. Since the relevant results will be obtained if a system recruits more talented people to its 'important' positions but ascribes all others, and since this postulate is not obviously false as is the free market assumption, we will assume the weaker postulate here. It seems unlikely that Davis and Moore ever assumed the stronger, obviously false, postulate.

The following empirical consequences of the theory are 'derivations' in a restricted sense. We identify supposed changes in the importance of roles, or identify groups in which certain roles are more important. Then we propose measures of the degree of inequality of reward and openness of recruitment which are consequences of such changes. If changes in importance are correctly identified, and if the measures of inequality of reward are accurate, then the consequences are logical derivations from the theory. If it turns out that generals are not more recruited according to talent in wartime, then it may be because the theory is untrue. But it may also be that generals are not in fact more important in wartime, or that our measures of recruitment do not work.

Consequence 1: In time of war the abilities of generals become more important than in time of peace. According to the theory, this should result in the following types of restructuring of the stratification system during wartime (and the reverse with the onset of peace):

(a) The rewards of the military, especially of the élite whose talents are scarce, should rise relative to the rewards of other élites, especially those which have nothing to do with victory (e.g., the medical and social service élite charged with care of incurables, the aged, etc., see Waller, 1940).

(b) Within the military, the degree of inequality of rewards should become greater, favoring generals, for their talents are particularly scarce.

(c) Even standardizing for the increase in sheer numbers of high military officials (which of itself implies that more formerly obscure men will rise rapidly) there should be pressure to open the military élite to talent, and consequently, there should be a higher proportion of Ulysses S. Grant type careers and fewer time-servers.

(d) Medals, a reward based on performances rather than on the authority hierarchy, should behave the same way. They should be more unequally distributed in wartime within any given rank; new medals, particularly of very high honor, should be created in wartime rather than peacetime, etc.

Consequence 2: The kingship in West European democratic monarchies has consistently declined in political importance as the powers of parliament have increased (this does not apply, for instance, to Japan, where apparently the emperorship was largely a ritual office even in medieval times). Modern kings in rich countries now perhaps have other functions than political leadership. Certainly the rôle requirements have changed – for instance, a modern king's sex life is much more restricted than formerly. Their rewards have also changed, emphasizing more ceremonial deference and expressions of sentiment, less wealth and power. It is not clear whether the ceremonial element has actually increased, or whether the rewards of wealth and power have declined. Investitures in the Presidency in the United States and Mexico seem to have nearly as much pomp as, and more substance than, coronations in Scandinavia and the Low Countries. Changes in the nature of the rôle-requirements and of the rewards indicates a shift of functions. At the least these changes indicate that some ceremonial functions of the kingship have declined much less in importance than the political functions. But to have a non-political function in a political structure is probably to be less important in the eyes of the people. Consequently, historical studies of the kingship in England, Scandinavia, and the Low Countries should show:

(a) The decline of the rewards of kingship relative to other elites.

(b) Progressively more ascriptive recruitment to the kingship. This would be indicated by (i) fewer debates over succession rules, less changing of these rules in order to justify getting appropriate kings, and fewer successions contested by pretenders; (ii) fewer 'palace revolutions' or other devices for deposing incompetent or otherwise inappropriate kings; and (iii) less mythology about good and bad kings, concerning performance of the rôle, and more bland human interest mythology focused on what it is like to occupy an ascribed position.

Consequence 3: In some industries individual talent is clearly a *complementary* factor of production, in the sense that it makes other factors much more productive; in others, it is more nearly *additive*. To take an extreme case of complementarity, when Alec Guiness is 'mixed' with a stupid plot, routine supporting actors, ordinary production costs, plus perhaps a thousand dollars for extra makeup, the result is a commercially very successful movie; perhaps Guiness increases the value of the movie to twice as much by being three times as good as the alternative actor. But if an equally talented housepainter (three times as good as the alternative) is 'mixed' with a crew of 100 average men, the value of the total production goes to approximately

103 per cent. Relatively speaking, then, individual rôle-performance is much more 'important' in the first kind of enterprise. Let us list a few types of enterprises in which talent is a complementary rather than additive factor, as compared with others which are more nearly additive, and make the appropriate predictions for the whole group of comparisons:

Talent Complementary Factor	Talent Nearly Additive
Research	Teaching
Universities	Undergraduate colleges
	High schools
Entertainment	Manufacturing
Management	Manual work
Teams in athletics and other	Groups involved in ordinary competition
'winner take all' structures	in which the rewards are divided among
	the meritorious
Violin concertos	Symphonies

For each of these comparisons we may derive the following predictions:

(a) The distribution of rewards (e.g., income distributions) should be more skewed for organizations and industries on the left, whereas the top salaries or honors should be nearer the mean on the right. In organizations with ranks, there should be either more ranks or greater inequality of rewards within ranks on the left.

(b) Since the main alternative to pure achievement-stratification in modern society is not ascription by social origin, but rather ascription by age and time-in-grade, seniority should determine rewards less in the systems on the left than on the right. There are of course many ways to measure it. For instance, men at the top of the income distribution in groups on the left should have reached the top at an earlier age than those on the right. There should also be a higher proportion of people whose relative income has declined as time passes in the talent-complementary industries and groups.

Other easily accessible empirical consequences of the theory are suggested by the increased importance of the goal of industrialization in many countries since World War II, the rise in the importance of international officials during this century, and the increased importance of treatment goals in mental hospitals. Since these consequences are easy to derive, we may omit their explication here.

Another set of derivations can be made if we add a postulate that a bad fit between functional requirements and the stratification system makes people within the group (and particularly those strongly identified with the group) perceive the system as unfair. For example, this postulate together with the others would imply that where talent is a complementary factor, those organizations with seniority stratification systems should create more sense of injustice than those in which the young shoot to the top. In addition, the alienation should be greatest among those *more* committed to group goals in seniority-dominated talent-complementary groups, whereas it should be greatest among those *less* committed to the group where there is an achievement system. All these consequences ought to be reversed or at least greatly weakened, for groups where talent is an additive factor.

It may be useful to present briefly a research design which would test this consequence of the theory. Suppose we draw a sample of colleges and universities, and classify (or rank) them on the importance of research within them. Perhaps a good index of this would be the number of classroom contact hours divided by the number of people of faculty rank on the payroll, which would be lower, the greater the importance of research relative to teaching.

Within each of the institutions we compute a correlation coefficient between age and income of faculty members. (Since the relation between age and income strikes me in this case as being curvilinear, some transformation of the variables will be appropriate.) The higher the correlation coefficient, the more seniority-dominated the stratification system of the institution.[3] The first hypothesis that we can immediately test is that this correlation coefficient should be generally smaller in research-dominated institutions. This is a direct consequence of the functional theory as originally stated.

Then we could divide institutions into four groups, according to

---

[3] An elimination system, in which young people are either fired or given raises, depending on their performance, will also produce a high correlation between age and income within an institution, and yet may produce (if the institutions with such elimination systems have markedly higher salary scales), in the higher educational system as a whole, a lower correlation. I doubt if the appropriate adjustments for this would substantially affect the analysis except for a very few institutions, but this is of course an empirical question. The adjustments could be made, theoretically, by including the people who have been fired, with their current incomes, in the institutions which fired them.

Table 1. *Hypothetical proportion thinking 'Most faculty promotions go to the people who deserve them most'*

	Institutions with:			
	Substantial research functions and		Mostly teaching functions and	
	Achievement systems	Seniority systems	Achievement systems	Seniority systems
	Proportion thinking the system is fair			
Faculty with:				
Strong commitments	High	Low	Low	High
Weak commitments	Low	High	High	Low

whether they are research or teaching institutions and whether they are seniority-dominated or not. We could ask the faculty within a sample of such institutions a series of questions which would sort out those highly devoted to their work and to staying in the system, and those not highly devoted. At the same time we could ask them to agree or disagree with some such statement as 'Most faculty promotions in this school go to the people who deserve them most.' According to the functional theory with the added postulate on the sense of justice, we could predict results approximately according to the pattern in Table 1.

But adding postulates goes beyond the original theory into the mechanisms by which the functional requirements get met, which is an undeveloped aspect of functional theory generally.

I do not intend to investigate the truth of any of these empirical consequences of the theory here. The only purpose of this note is to point out that functional theories are like other scientific theories: they have empirical consequences which are either true or false. Deciding whether they are true or false is not a theoretical or ideological matter, but an empirical one.

4. Interdependence and inequality: a specification of the Davis-Moore theory (with T. Robert Harris)

The Davis-Moore theory of social stratification (1945) argues that inequality is due to differences in the 'importance' of social rôles, and that recruitment to important social rôles will be more oriented toward getting adequate performance than will recruitment to other roles. Importance of rôles, then, tends to create inequality and to create a force toward recruitment by ability and training. One of the difficulties in working with this theory empirically is to obtain independent measures of the importance of social rôles.

In this paper we will treat the importance of supervision in the productivity of groups. We will show that for groups doing highly interdependent tasks, the marginal productivity of added amounts of supervision (starting from any given level of supervision) will be higher than in groups doing independent tasks. Further we will show that the ability of a supervisor is more important in determining group productivity in the interdependent case.

The derivation of these results will be purely theoretical. If actual stratification systems (in small groups, factories, or societies) actually behave as the Davis-Moore theory implies, then the machinery here will help derive predictions about the relation of task structure to stratification structure. This involves defining the importance of a social rôle by how much difference its performance or non-performance makes to total group performance, and by how much difference it makes to group productivity whether it is well performed or not. We do this by applying the techniques of marginal anaylsis from economics to a mathematical formulation of what it means for tasks to be interdependent.

An intuitive introduction to the argument

Consider the hot processing and cold processing parts of a steel rolling mill. The hot processing part shapes hot steel by passing it through consecutive shaping machines before it gets cold. The cold processing part cuts, grinds, classifies, and otherwise finishes the rolled production.[1] One cannot build up inventories of hot metal between the shaping machines, because maintaining the temperature would require installation of very expensive furnaces and add an input and output worker for each of these furnaces. Cold steel products do not change their state if inventoried temporarily between machines. Under these conditions, the hot shaping machines can only work when the other hot shaping machines on each side of them are functioning. But when a cold processing machine stops, the succeeding machine can work from stock previously produced, and the preceding machine can produce for stock to be processed later by the stopped machine.

Now let us suppose that a single machine breaks down in both sections of the line. A supervisor can, let us suppose, choose where to direct his energies in trying to get the stopped machine running. Let us further suppose that he can get each of the machines running by spending half an hour of time. If he spends a half hour on the hot shaping machine, he will have succeeded in getting the whole hot line running. If he were to spend that half hour on the machine on the cold line, he would get only that machine running, since the others could continue to run anyway. That is, the productivity of his getting a particular machine running on the hot line will be multiplied by all the other machines he gets running. The productivity of getting the machine on the cold line running will be only the productivity of that machine. Hence if he has to choose which to pay attention to first, he will choose to pay attention to the hot line and leave the cold line for later.

Likewise consider the general superintendent's problem in the mill, when deciding where to put his most able supervisor. Suppose, for instance, he has a supervisor whose technical competence is such that

---

[1] The research in a steel plant from which the example comes was done by Stinch-combe, under a grant from the Olivetti Foundation to the Joint Center for Urban Studies of MIT and Harvard.

he only needs three minutes to diagnose and remedy the problem on either machine, rather than 30 minutes. Clearly if he puts the three minute supervisor on the hot line, he will save 27 minutes of the production of the whole line. If he puts the three minute supervisor on the cold line, he will save only 27 minutes of the production of a single machine. The productivity of ability in supervision is apparently much greater in the case of close interdependence than it is in the case of relatively independent production processes.

A formalization of interdependence

For simplicity in presentation, let us consider a productive process in which each machine ('rôle' or any other concrete component of a group process can be substituted for 'machine') is either producing or not producing. When it is producing, it produces at a constant rate. Then production of an individual machine is proportional to the probability that the machine will be running at any given time.[2]

First we consider the total production, T_1, when the production of each of the activities is independent; that is, when variations in the production of one machine have no effect on the output of other machines. This is a rough approximation to the short-run situation on the cold line described above. In this case we merely sum the productions of the individual workers:

$$T_1 = \sum_{i=1}^{n} bp_i = nb\bar{p} \tag{1}$$

where p_1 is a standardized measure of the production of the i'th worker (for example, the probability that he will be working at a given time), b relates this measure of productivity to his or her contribution to total production, $\bar{p}$ is the arithmetic mean of the numbers $p_1, \ldots, p_n$, and n is the number of workers.

In the case of interdependence as described on the hot line above, the probability that the system will be producing at any given time is the probability that everyone will be working, and hence (assuming

---

[2] The following derivation is not restricted to this case, but is valid whenever the production of individuals, however conceived, is related to total production in the same way as we indicate below.

that 'breakdowns,' or failures to produce, are independent for different machines) the average production per unit time is proportional to the product of the probabilities:

$$T_2 = K \prod_{i=1}^{n} p_i \tag{2}$$

where K is the rate of production when the system is producing, and n is the number of machines.[3]

Marginal productivity of supervision in independent and interdependent production

Let us compare the marginal productivity of supervision in these two cases. In general, each worker's productivity will depend on the amount of supervision per worker and the ability of supervisors, which we denote by c and a respectively. The marginal productivity of quantity of supervision is the partial derivative of total production with respect to quantity of supervision. In the dependent case, equation (1) yields:

$$\frac{\partial T_1}{\partial c} = nb\frac{\partial \bar{p}}{\partial c} = \frac{T_1}{\bar{p}}\frac{\partial \bar{p}}{\partial c}. \tag{3}$$

In the interdependent case,

$$\frac{\partial T_2}{\partial c} = K\frac{\partial}{\partial c}\left(\prod_{j=1}^{n} p_j \right) \qquad \text{from equation (2)}$$

$$= K\sum_{i=1}^{n}\left[\left(\prod_{\substack{j=1 \\ j \neq i}}^{n} p_j \right) \frac{\partial p_i}{\partial c} \right]$$

---

[3] We assume the two groups compared have the same number of workers, in order to simplify matters. To avoid confounding the effects of size with those of interdependence on the value of supervision, we hold the former constant. The comparative impact of growth in size on the supervisory problems of independent and interdependent groups could be explored with the theoretical technology developed below, by taking differences for successive values of n, after differentiating with respect to a or c.

$$= K \left(\prod_{j=1}^{n} p_j \right) \sum_{i=1}^{n} \frac{1}{p_i} \frac{\partial p_i}{\partial c}$$

$$= T_2 \sum_{i=1}^{n} \frac{1}{p_i} \frac{\partial p_i}{\partial c} \qquad \qquad \text{from equation (2)}$$

$$\geqslant \frac{T_2}{p_{max}} \sum_{i=1}^{n} \frac{\partial p_i}{\partial c}$$

$$= \frac{nT_2}{p_{max}} \frac{\partial \bar{p}}{\partial c}$$

Thus

$$\frac{\partial T_2}{\partial c} \geqslant \frac{nT_2}{p_{max}} \frac{\partial \bar{p}}{\partial c} \qquad \qquad (4)$$

where p_{max} is the larger of $p_1 \ldots, p_n$.

If $T_2 \geqslant T_1$, and the characteristics of the workers and their jobs are identically distrubuted (drawn from the same population) so that for each level a of ability and c of quantity of supervision, $\bar{p}$ and $\frac{\partial \bar{p}}{\partial c}$ are the same in the two cases,[4] it follows that:

$$\frac{\partial T_2}{\partial c} \geqslant n \frac{\bar{p}}{p_{max}} \frac{\partial T_1}{\partial c} \qquad \qquad (5)$$

where all the symbols are as defined earlier. If we assume also that

---

[4] These are reasonable restrictions. Since our purpose is to study the effects of interdependence or independence, it is appropriate to 'control' other factors. If, for example, the nature of individual jobs were different, resulting in a different effect of supervision on the production of individual workers $\left(\frac{\partial \bar{p}}{\partial c} \right)$, then this fact as well as interdependence would affect the marginal productivity of supervision on the total output of the group. But this is irrelevant to our argument, which is that the same effects on components have a much greater impact on the total output of the system in the case of interdependence.

workers are fairly homogeneous in their productivity,[5] we can conclude from (5) that the marginal productivity of supervision is almost

[5] It is possible to assume instead that $\frac{\partial p_i}{\partial c}$ is uncorrelated with $1/p_i$. This assumption is met, in particular, if $\frac{\partial p_i}{\partial c}$ is the same for all values of p_i. We can also relax an assumption implicit in equation (1) by rewriting that equation:

$$T_1 = \sum_{i=1}^{n} b_i p_i \tag{1a}$$

where b_i, the contribution of worker i to total to total production, may now vary with i. However, we must add the assumptions that p_i and $\frac{\partial p_i}{\partial c}$ are uncorrelated with b_i.

Under these assumptions, we can derive the marginal productivity of supervision in the interdependent case, beginning with the fourth line of the derivation of equation (4).:

$$\frac{\partial T_1}{\partial c} = T_2 \sum_{i=1}^{n} \frac{1}{p_i} \frac{\partial p_i}{\partial c}$$

$$= T_2 \left(\sum_{i=1}^{n} \frac{1}{p_i} \right) \left(\frac{1}{n} \sum_{i=1}^{n} \frac{\partial p_i}{\partial c} \right) \quad \text{because } \frac{\partial p_i}{\partial c} \text{ is}$$
$$\text{uncorrelated with } 1/p_i$$

$$= \frac{T_2 n}{\bar{p}} \frac{\partial \bar{p}}{\partial c}$$

where $\bar{p}$ is the harmonic mean of $p_i, \ldots, p_n$, that is,

$$\frac{1}{\bar{p}} = \frac{1}{n} \sum_{i=1}^{n} \frac{1}{p_i} \ .$$

It is well known that $\bar{p} \leqslant \bar{p}$, and that the equality holds if and only if $p_1 = p_2 = \ldots = p_n$. From equation (1) for independence,

$$T_1 = \sum_{i=1}^{n} b_i p_i = \left(\sum_{i=1}^{n} b_i \right) \bar{p} \quad \text{because } b_i \text{ and } p_i \text{ are assumed}$$
$$\text{uncorrelated.}$$

Thus

$$\frac{\partial T_1}{\partial c} = \left(\sum_{i=1}^{n} b_i \right) \frac{\partial \bar{p}}{\partial c}$$

$$= \frac{T_1}{\bar{p}} \frac{\partial \bar{p}}{\partial c}.$$

Hence if $T_2 \geqslant T_1$, then

$$\frac{\partial T_2}{\partial c} = \frac{T_2 n}{\bar{p}} \frac{\partial \bar{p}}{\partial c} \geqslant \frac{T_1 n}{\bar{p}} \frac{\partial \bar{p}}{\partial c} = n \frac{\partial T_1}{\partial c} \ .$$

This result is slightly stronger than (5). Similar remarks apply to inequality (6) below.

n times as great in the interdependent case as in the independent case (other things being equal).[6]

We can find the marginal productivity of a, the average ability level of supervisors, by differentiating total production with respect to a. The procedure is exactly the same as the above, substituting a for c. The result is:

$$\frac{\partial T_2}{\partial a} \geqslant n \frac{\bar{p}}{p_{max}} \frac{\partial T_1}{\partial a}. \tag{6}$$

Thus (other things being equal) a small increase $\triangle a$ in the level of ability of supervisors will increase production almost n times as much in the interdependent case as would the same increment in the independent case.

Finally, if n is greater than 2 or 3, it is clear that even if our assumptions are only the crudest approximation to reality, the marginal productivity of supervision will still be much greater in the interdependent case than in the independent case.

Empirical implications of the argument

Here we will try to state the logic of several implications of the formal argument above, so that they can be applied to a wide variety of cases and give rise to a rich set of empirical consequences. The implications of such a formal argument depend on adding sociological and economic postulates to the analysis of the productivity of supervision. The examples suggested below elaborate the argument in terms of empirically measurable variables.

1 When the marginal productivity of supervision is higher, more supervision will be used. In particular, the more interdependent the activities of a group:
   (a) the higher the ratio of time spent in supervision to time spent in operative work;

---

[6] This is the result that was suggested in the intuitive introduction to the argument, and it follows for the same reason. The usual mathematical proof of the rule for the derivative of a product of functions, used in deriving the inequality (4), is essentially a generalization of the intuitive idea presented in the introduction.

(b) the more likely is it that full-time supervisory rôles will be established, rather than combinations of supervision with operative duties;

(c) together a and b imply that the higher will be the ratio of full-time supervisors to subordinates (the span of control will be smaller if all 'supervisors' are formal superiors);

(d) hence, in an organization of a given size, the greater will be the number of levels in the hierarchy;

(e) if Simon's postulate of a constant ratio of income between hierarchical levels is true, the more inequality there should be in the overall income distribution.[7]

2 When the marginal productivity of supervisory ability is higher, recruitment should tend to be more on the basis of talent, and talent is more likely to be paid a premium.[8] Hence in interdependent processes we should find:

(a) more recruitment of supervisors on the basis of qualifications and talent, less seniority or nepotism;

(b) more firing, demotion, or transfer of supervisors whose abilities are not adequate to supervisory positions;

(c) more differential wages within the group of supervisors of interdependent processes as compared to the variance within the group of supervisors of independent processes;

(d) more inequality in the amount of overtime by able versus less able supervisors;

(e) more inequality in the informal respect and recognition of ability of supervisors.

3 When rules do not adequalely reflect the contingencies of the productive process, we may postulate that informal adaptations to the reality of the situation will take place more rapidly, the more difference they make to group productivity. Informal adaptations

---

[7] Herbert Simon (1975). Simon is here following the suggestion of Roberts (1956:285n). Strictly speaking, this argument depends on there being a single income rate at each level. As we will show later, interdependence ought also to increase the variance of productivity of operative people at different levels of ability, and it may be that this variance within levels interacts with the variance between levels in such a way as to lower the overall variance.

[8] Compare Stinchcombe's earlier (1963:806–7) somewhat vague suggestions about 'talent complementary' and 'talent additive' industries and activities. The result above may be restated as: "in interdependent activities, supervisory talent is more of a complementary factor of production than in independent activities."

to contingencies are a particular social reflection of supervisory ability. Hence we should expect to find in interdependent processes:

(*a*) more communication outside official channels, backed by more urgent emotional force; in particular, we expect more flow upward of communications about problems from subordinates (Blau, 1957:59–61);

(*b*) more departure of informal, ability-based stratification from formal, especially formal ascriptive, stratification; in particular, the informal status of competent, older, line-foremen, relative to ascriptively higher status but practically less effective new engineers, should tend to be higher in interdependent processes;

(*c*) more departure of actual activities of different supervisors from official manning charts and job descriptions;

(*d*) more esteem, comparatively, of instrumental leaders as opposed to expressive leaders of work groups.

A further line of development

We have concentrated above on the productivity of the supervisor's rôle. There is, of course, no inherent reason for this. Any rôle in the group has a productivity for group performance. If we differentiate the expressions for total production above with respect to the abilities or performances of each worker, something quite similar is derived: the group is more dependent on each worker in the interdependent case.[9]

[9] If we differentiate the total production with respect to the performance of the jth worker, p_j, equation (1) gives:

$$\frac{\partial T_1}{\partial p_j} = b = \frac{T_1}{n\bar{p}}$$

for the case of independence. From equation (2) we obtain for the interdependent case:

$$\frac{\partial T_2}{\partial p_1} = K \sum_{\substack{i=1 \\ i \neq j}}^{n} p_i = \frac{T_2}{p_i} .$$

Thus the marginal productivity of the jth worker's performance is about n times as great in the interdependent case, but varies according to his absolute level of performance. Note that the marginal productivity is greatest for those whose total performance is smallest (p_j then being small). Those with lowest productivity are disproportionately harmful. (Footnote continued on p. 67)

What sorts of things might follow from this? Perhaps the frequency of attempts to control the behavior of others would increase, and hence more total interaction would ensue. This might provide a metric for Homans' 'external system,' (1950:90–4), i.e. the amount of externally induced interaction in a group. Hence we would expect to find more solidarity or mutual liking in interdependent groups, because their activities would produce more interaction.

Conversely any deviant can endanger the payoff to everyone in an interdependent group. Consequently we might expect more instability in such groups, more deaths of groups because of individual variability in performance. We might find more such groups ejecting such deviants. We could thus ask the following empirical questions: do more people get fired from the interdependent parts of production lines? Do more businesses fail in industries with interdependent technologies, controlling for size? Are workers more likely to support firings on the interdependent parts of lines? Is rejection of a deviant more enthusiastic, or quicker, in experimental groups with inter-dependent tasks?

It should be pointed out here that the ratio of rewards of supervisors to the rewards of workers are not predicted by this argument. Both worker ability and supervisory ability are more important in inter-dependent processes. In fact, if we form the ratios between the marginal productivity of supervisory ability and worker ability, we find for the independent case

$$\frac{\dfrac{\partial T_1}{\partial a}}{\dfrac{\partial T_1}{\partial x_j}} = nR \tag{7}$$

Suppose that we conceive of a worker's performance as depending on his own ability as well as on the amount of supervision he receives. Let us call the jth worker's ability x_j. Then, by the chain rule of differentiation, applied to the results in the preceding paragraph,

$$\frac{\partial T_1}{\partial x_j} = \frac{T_1}{n\bar{p}} \frac{\partial p_j}{\partial x_j}, \text{ and}$$

$$\frac{\partial T_2}{\partial x_j} = \frac{T_2}{p_j} \frac{\partial p_j}{\partial x_j} .$$

Thus the organization stands to gain about n times as much in the interdependent case by raising the workers' level of ability.

where R is the ratio between the marginal improvement of performance of the average worker with an improvement of supervisory ability and the marginal improvement of a worker's performance with his own increased ability, i.e. $\dfrac{\partial \bar{p}}{\partial a} \Big/ \dfrac{\partial p_j}{\partial x_j}$. The quantity R might be very important in other applications of the Davis-Moore stratification theory, but we have no ideas about the causes of its variation. For the interdependent case, the ratio of marginal productivities of abilities is

$$\frac{\dfrac{\partial T_2}{\partial a}}{\dfrac{\partial T_2}{\partial x_j}} \geq \frac{p_j}{p_{max}}\, nR. \tag{8}$$

Except for the term p_j/p_{max}, which will be less than or equal to one, the expressions on the right are identical. If workers are fairly homogeneous in their productivity, p_j/p_{max} will be near to one and the inequality, from equation (4), will be close to an equality. Then we would expect the ratios of supervisory to worker rewards for ability to be about the same in the two cases. The greater importance of supervision in the interdependent case does *not* imply greater *relative* importance of supervisors compared to workers.

Summary and conclusions

The purpose of this paper was to give an analysis of the 'importance' of a social rôle and to show how it varied under different conditions. We chose in particular to analyze the importance of supervision under conditions of independent activity and under conditions of interdependent activity. We showed that at a given level of supervision, either an added quantity, or an increase of ability, of supervision had more effect when the supervised activities were interdependent. This argument depends on the accuracy of our formalization of the meaning of interdependence. From this it should follow from the Davis-Moore functional theory of stratification that (1) rôles of supervision are more likely to be differentiated from subordinate rôles, and to be more numerous, in more interdependent activities, (2) recruitment by ability and differential rewards for able supervision will be more common in interdependent systems, and (3) informal adaptation to contingencies will be more common in interdependent systems.

These results should apply to all kinds of groups to which the Davis-Moore theory is supposed to apply. But groups in factories or other natural settings are almost always embedded in larger stratification systems, created by collective contracts, by labor law, by kinship pressures, by pressure toward equilibrium wages in labor markets, and so forth. Further, we have defined 'supervision' abstractly as any activity which improves the performance of a worker. Not all the supervisors in this sense are in formal authority over workers in natural settings. Especially in modern industrial practice, staff people do much of what we have called supervision. Natural groups probably depart radically from our predictions because of the embedding of the task group in larger social structures.

But tasks of groups without previous internal differentiation are easily manipulated in social psychology laboratories. We have argued above that a rich and various body of hypotheses can be derived about stratification patterns in groups with varying tasks. The way seems open for experimental exploration of one of the classical problems of the theory of society.

5. Marxist theories of power and empirical research

I would like to make two assumptions in this chapter that are, I believe, somewhat unusual in the discussion of the Marxist theory of the organization of power. The first is a positivist assumption, that the principal interesting question about the Marxist approach to power is whether or not it is true. The second is the assumption of arrogance, that what the Marxists need is a course in elementary empirical methods.

Given these assumptions, I want to address three principal questions about how to do Marxist research on the ruling class. The first has to do with variations in the mode of production. My argument will be that, just as the Marxist study of the response of workers (say, worker alienation or the strike rate) depends on an analysis of the mode of production (that mode's political and ideological requirements, its authority system, its property system, and its technical organization), so also rulers derive their ideology from their work life, and different modes of production produce different kinds of rulers. This is, of course, a belief that Marx expressed at great length. My proposal is that we find out whether it is true, instead of mixing up all capitalist thought into a gray dough of 'monopoly capitalism.'

The second question appears in two forms in the Marxist literature, that of the role of the vanguard party in Lenin and that of the notion of hegemony of bourgeois ideology. The problem Lenin posed was that in order to win, the working class had to consider its collective interest rather than its individual interests, or its 'trade-union consciousness.' As I understand Gramsci (1973), his point about hegemony of bourgeois ideology is a mirror image of Lenin's analysis of Social Democracy and trade unionism. The notion is that like the vanguard party, the capitalist class collectively so organizes itself to give in easily on the particular, disaggregated interests of individual capitalists, but becomes increasingly hard to deal with as the collective interests of capitalism as a system are threatened. The result is that they easily tolerate professorial vaporings over the dialectic or the crisis of Western sociology, or Social Democratic speeches about the rights of the working man, but are careful that the ideology *actually operating* in work relations, in collective bargaining, in curricular organization of the university, or in foreign policy, is a bourgeois ideology. That is, the hypothesis is that the capitalists, by being the ruling class, have *naturally* the advantages that the proletariat can only achieve by a vanguard party. This inequality means that compromise on the workers' side, that is, Social Democracy, is almost always compromise of basic principles for concrete advantages, while capitalist compromise is almost always an expedient to save the basic features of the system by bargaining away some concrete advantages. My argument will be that there are empirical variations in the preconditions of Lenin's 'trade union consciousness' and Gramsci's 'bourgeois ideological hegemony,' and that these variations allow an empirical test of the relevant theory.

The first of these hypotheses has to do with the bases of differentiation of the ruling class, that it should typically be on the basis of involvement in different modes of production. Gramsci's hegemony and Lenin's vanguard party have to do with the capacity of the ruling class, because it is ruling, to work out an authoritative definition of its collective interests which can overcome its internal diversity, in a way that can only be done by the poor through an agency like a vanguard party. This organization of the ruling class is an empirical variable that ought to have causes and effects that are measurable, and the hypotheses ought to be judged as true or false, rather than as radical or conservative.

The third question has to do with historical processes, specifically with revolution. The core question, as I see it, is: what determines whether socialist governments act differently from capitalist ones? Marxist theory maintains that unless the power of the bourgeoisie is destroyed, socialist governments act like bourgeois governments, but with a different rhetoric. A revolution destroys the power, hence indirectly the property, of the bourgeoisie, since property is basically a political phenomenon. Without a revolution, the power remains behind a socialist façade; hence one way or another property remains. I put it to you that a systematic and empirically responsible comparison of socialism with capitalism, and within each, a comparison of different styles and power constellations, has never been carried out. Instead socialist states are compared with the socialist ideal, and are found to fall short. Capitalist states are also compared to the socialist ideal, and also fall short. The failure of capitalism to achieve socialist ideals is, of course, to be expected. The explanation of the failure of socialist states is usually that people are evil, perhaps because they are bureaucrats, perhaps because they are, like Stalin, insane paranoids, perhaps because of capitalist encirclement.

My argument is terribly naïve empiricism, that things alleged to be due to monopoly capitalism should not be true of the Soviet Union and China. Further, it is that the difference between revolutionary Social Democrats such as Allende or the early Swedish socialist governments and the tame socialism of the British Labour Party or the hollow populism of the average African or South American socialist, must have an explanation. To point out that each is equally distant from revolutionary purity does not advance the analysis. The question is, then, what determines the different degrees of distance of socialist governments from the practice of capitalist governments, and is this distance related to the depth and character of the revolutionary process?

Let me illustrate these major questions with the example of the Marxist theory of race relations, specifically the 'internal colonialism' theory. I rely heavily on Robert Blauner. The first question is whether the economic, enterprise authority and political requirements of different industries lead to different ideologies and practices of race relations, and specifically whether the colonial character of an industry affects capitalist ideology and practice. By the colonial character of a mode of production, we mean three things: (1) does the enterprise produce raw materials shipped to a national or world market from a distinct region, raw materials requiring a large input of relatively unskilled labor, as opposed to producing services for a local market, manufacturing goods out of the raw materials, or providing government services? (2) Do the labor relations in these regional enterprises depend on the political suppression of class conflict, in such a way that they would be undermined by independent local self-government of a bourgeois-democratic kind, allowing workers' representation – or more briefly, does the labor relations system depend on disenfranchised workers? (3) Are the other middle classes and the governmental leadership of the region in question dependent on the colonial enterprises, so as to constitute a dependent comprador class, and so that the conflict of capitalist interests that Marx argued produced bourgeois-democratic pressures does not take place? For example, the plantation mode of production of cotton in the American South or vegetable farming in the irrigated Southwest or Hawaii has had a colonial character to a high degree, by all three criteria, while government services in the industrial North and West are at the opposite extreme. The question is, do upper-class ideologies and institutional practice show a more racist character, the more colonial the mode of production?

The question of hegemony, and its mirror-image problem of Social Democracy and trade-union consciousness, has two components for the colonialism model. First, it urges that as the rôle of blacks or Chicanos in the mode of production changes in the aggregate from colonial to bourgeois, the centers of organizing power in the capitalist class (the banks, the peak associations of business, the conservative parties) manage the change of the class as a whole from a colonial model of race relations to a free labor market, bourgeois-democratic model. This movement by the bourgeoisie toward Social Democracy is predicted to show changes relatively rapidly on the trade-union type of issues, but to be very sticky on all sorts of questions having to do with the rights of property in the market, and specifically to be against paying minority people more than their productive value in the market. That is, capitalist ideology should move in a 'liberal' direction much faster on questions of improving the market value of black or Chicano productivity, for example, by educational reforms, and much slower on questions of redistributing income and wealth. Conversely, without a vanguard party, the Social Democratic part of the thesis would be that the protest ideology and practice of minority groups should tend to move over time, and to move especially in concrete bargaining and legislative arenas as opposed to speechmaking, in a direction compatible with capitalist hegemony. That is, in practice such movements will more and more accept the improvement of minority market position and participation in limited bourgeois democratic politics as evidence of the advance of collective ethnic interests, replacing or playing down the objectives of redistribution of income and wealth, challenge to capitalist authority in the enterprise, and so on.

The third major question is whether, say, the treatment of Chicanos and blacks in the United States differs in a significant way from the treatment of Muslim, Caucasian, and Ukrainian minorities by Russians in the Soviet Union; the treatment of Macedonians or Bosnians by the Serbs or Croats in Yugoslavia; the treatment of Tibetans by the Chinese in China; the treatment of blacks in Cuba. If inequality of races is produced by colonial capitalism, it ought not be regularly produced by revolutionary socialism.

My general impression from a casual acquaintance with the facts is that the Marxist theory of race relations stands up pretty well. But the fact that at this late date I am giving my impressions is an indictment of the empirical quality of Marxist scholarship on how the power networks of capitalist and socialist societies work, and of the lack of theoretical imagination of the positivist opponents of the Marxist view. These are empirical propositions derived from the theory of internal colonialism by straightforward applications of conventional Marxist reasoning. I put it to you again that the interesting question about them is whether or not they are true, not whether some fact-free version of the Marxist 'approach' is better because it is dialectical, or useful for identifying oneself as radical, or in some other nonempirical way a superior philosophy.

Elementary methods applied

The first thing we learn in elementary methods, starting with a quotation from John Stuart Mill if we like, is that causal inference depends on comparisons. We have to so choose our units of analysis that the causal variable of interest varies over these units. The usual practice in power studies in America is to show that people with power are rich. What that shows is, whatever the mode of production of their business, they are good at it, they know how to make it go. It requires a considerable gift to read Marx's long discussions of the stages of evolution of factory enterprises, or variations in bourgeois political behavior in France, Germany, and England, and completely miss the point of the comparisons. As Marx observed repeatedly, it is branches of industry that have distinct technical, enterprise government, and economic requirements. Thus they produce different types of upper class, different kinds of the rich.

There are three main units of analysis that vary in their mode of production: individuals, firms or government organizations, and countries. If the oil business has a monopoly, capital-intensive, skilled-labor mode of production, for example, Standard Oil capitalists are capitalists in such a mode of production; Standard Oil as a firm should show the characteristic labor relations of such a mode of production; and the Arab oil-exporting nations should be distinctive in having their capitalist parts be monopolistic, capital-intensive, and high-skill. All three kinds of units of analysis vary in their mode of production both over time and cross-sectionally. It is true both that Arab countries now have more monopolistic capitalism than the United States, and that their capitalism is more monopolistic now than fifty years ago; a capitalist in food retailing fifty years ago was in a petty bourgeois mode of production; now he is liable to be either in petty bourgeois or oligopolistic corporate competitive modes of production; a firm in cotton culture fifty years ago needed a labor relations system to manage black cotton pickers, which wheat farmers did not need, while now it needs one to manage cotton-picking machines.

That is, history should be disaggregated by industrial modes of production, into separate industry evolutions of the ideology and practice of individual capitalists, separate industry evolutions of the practice of firms, and separate comparative histories of countries with different modes of production. The prediction would be, for example, that the king of Saudi Arabia, as Rockefeller's successor to the oil monopoly, should act pretty much like Rockefeller, except perhaps for being cleverer and more powerful, and should act in quite a different way from a sheik based on nomadic subsistence camel herding, pilgrimage services, and petty trading by camel caravans.

But further, the Saudi king should act differently than Sra. Perón, who is based on a competitive agricultural export sector and a nationalist, protected industrial base. That is, besides the historical continuity of the types of upper classes produced by a given mode of production, and historical change as the mode of production changes, individuals, firms, and countries should have different ideologies and practices at a given time, depending on their industrial base.

The main units of analysis that vary with respect to the hegemony variables are social and political protest movements, and upper-class establishments. Here we have three aspects of variation: I will call one the 'class organizational health' aspect, the second the 'linking' aspect, and the third the 'oppositional arena' aspect. First, social movements or establishments *as a whole* vary in the degree to which they are so set up as to be able to make the class collective interest dominate the individual, sectoral, trade-union, or particular interests. Second, given any degree of collective organizational health, particular segments of the class may be tightly or loosely linked to the organizational center. Thirdly, the process of class negotiation may be so set up that what is hegemonic or central among capitalists is what Social Democrats and trade unions give up first, and conversely that what is peripheral to the capitalists is easily won by the Social Democratic workers. Or it may be the case that capitalists foolishly fight on irrelevancies, and Social Democrats can find no one to compromise with and so lose out to a vanguard party for the constituency of the poor.

So what we have, then, are again three types of units of analysis. The first are collective organizations of the contending classes, which vary over history and between countries, and are to be classified by their degree of capacity to make class interests dominate particular interests. The second are segments of the contending classes, classified by the tightness of their links to the center. The third are oppositional arenas, like industry-specific collective bargaining, or legislatures, or riots, which are to be classified by the degree to which hegemonic content gets into the practical deals made in those arenas.

Since this is pretty abstract, let me specify the interrelations among these types of variation a bit more, using our example of internal colonialism. The argument would be that as a society moves from a mode of production that uses black people and Chicanos in a colonial mode of production, effective bourgeois hegemony would be reflected in a movement, *including* dominant Southern capitalists in places like Atlanta and Dallas, toward a bourgeois democratic incorporation of blacks and Chicanos. Effective ethnic vanguard organizations would be reflected in continuing insistence that black and Chicano incomes have to go up, regardless of whether their market value as laborers in capitalist enterprise goes up.

Now, if we classify parts of the internal colony by its degree of linkage with the hegemonic capitalist organization – say, for instance, by the involvement of national banks in the investment in the colonial section, the degree of incorporation of blacks and Chicanos into less colonial modes of production, and so on – we should find that the closer the linkage, the more dominant the hegemonic (progressively more bourgeois democratic) ideology and practice becomes. The stronger the hegemony the less rapidly, however, this falloff toward the periphery takes place. That is, if New York banking already controls cotton plantations, then plantation counties will be as easy to move toward modern race relations as Atlanta. Further the *content* of the hegemonic ideology can be diagnosed by those aspects of bourgeois opinion and practice that slope most sharply with the strength of the links. So, for example, capitalist support (or at least tolerance) for voting rights, collective bargaining rights, and schooling should slope from black reaction among peripheral capitalists to enlightened conservatism among Atlanta bankers, while opposition to improving black and Chicano situations by taxing the wealth being made off their backs should not slope toward the peak, with Chase Manhattan being just as defensive of property rights as a rural Alabama cotton grower on a family plantation.

On the other side we have two predictions about protest ethnic movements. The first is that, in the absence (or weakness) of a vanguard party, over time there will be increasing demands for programs compatible with bourgeois democratic hegemony, that is, demands for educational equality, individual promotion opportunities for ethnic minorities rather than collective redistribution, voting participation rather than national self-determination, and the like. The second is that among countries, those with stronger collective organization of oppressed ethnic groups should evolve in the direction of trade union consciousness more slowly than they do in the United States.

Finally, arenas of conflict vary in the degree to which they are dominated by the hegemonic organizing center for capitalists, and the older, compromising, Social Democratic movements for the poor. For example, national collective bargaining as an arena has least participation of primitive Southern racists, Congress has somewhat more,

Southern state politics has more yet, and labor relations in plantation agriculture most of all. What we should find is that the more the dominance of hegemonic institutions in an arena of conflict, and the less the dominance of loosely linked peripheral sectors of the Establishment, the more rapid the drift of the protest movement in a bourgeois democratic or trade-union direction.

A second source of variation is in the substantive content of the issues in an arena, with questions of taxation, expropriation, property rights and revolution being central to the system; education, promotion policy in the civil service or the military, collective bargaining over the price of labor, social security paid for by a tax on workers, being more peripheral. The argument implies, for example, that the Ways and Means Committee will underrepresent the interests of the poor, while the Health, Education and Labor Committee will overrepresent them (relatively). Further it argues that bourgeois courts will not decide to bus black people into Wall Street, but will be much more open to busing them to a white school, or to giving them membership in a trade union. It further argues that as time goes on, Social Democratic movements will focus more on the arenas with open competition, and will count their victories in Health, Education, and Labor rather than their defeats in Ways and Means.

So much for hegemony and Social Democracy.

For the third variable, the revolutionary process, the primary unit of analysis is the political system, that is, nowadays, the nation, and within nations, different historical times. The variable we want to classify political systems by is the degree of destruction of the special access of bourgeois interests to those parts of the system that are crucial for bourgeois rule, specifically the property system. The general argument is that the more integrated the working-class movement around an ideologically organized party, and the more that party controls the state apparatus, the less influence bourgeois interests will have in those parts of the system having to do with taxes, expropriation, property rights. Further, the argument implies that the greater the development of Social Democratic or trade-unionist trends in the left movement, the more its coming to power will leave the channels of access open to bourgeois interests in these crucial sectors, and the more they will open channels for workers only in the trade union, education, and welfare aspects of the system.

For example, with respect to internal colonialism and race relations, the argument implies that a revolutionary socialist regime (or a Social Democratic regime less penetrated by hegemonic bourgeois ideology) is more likely to expropriate properties in businesses with a colonial mode of production and rebuild them on a noncolonial basis, to intervene directly in the labor market decisions of firms to achieve fair employment goals, to organize equally strong worker protest organizations in the colonial periphery as in the metropolitan center, to intervene in the process of appointment of general managers of firms when goals of ethnic equality are undermined, and for all these reasons to move the income and wealth of oppressed minorities more rapidly toward equality than do capitalist or tame Social Democratic régimes.

Thus it should be the case both that Uzbeks and Ukrainians have moved faster toward Russian standards of income than blacks or Chicanos have moved toward whites in the United States, and also that they have moved faster since the Revolution of 1917 than under the Russian Empire.

To summarize the application of John Stuart Mill to the comparison problem, the units of analysis that have to be compared for different parts of the Marxist analysis of power are:

1 For the mode of production
   (*a*) capitalists as individuals
   (*b*) firms as organizations
   (*c*) countries
   (each compared cross-sectionally and historically, by industrial types)
2 For hegemony–Social Democracy
   (*a*) class organizations, cross-culturally and historically
   (*b*) sectors with different linkages to hegemonic or vanguard class centers
   (*c*) arenas of conflict, by the participation of hegemonic centers and by substantive centrality to capitalist viability
3 For revolutionary process
   (*a*) countries, comparative and historical, by degree of control by worker interests of the property system

For the internal colonialism model of race relations, the variables we have to evaluate for these units of analysis are:

1 For the mode of production
  (*a*) labor-intensive raw material production for capitalist markets
  (*b*) labor relations systems depending on a disenfranchised labor
  (*c*) dependence of other regional middle classes on the colonial enterprises
  (*d*) as the dependent variable, racist ideology and institutional racism, measured for individuals, firms, and political systems
2 For hegemony–Social Democracy
  (*a*) the variation over time from black reaction to enlightened bourgeois conservatism (as the rôle of blacks and Chicanos changes from colonial labor) in the centers of banking, corporate management, and peak associations
  (*b*) the same variation within the colony as we move from family plantations to corporate plantations to nationally oriented manufacturing to regional banking and investment centers to local representatives of the national bourgeoisie
  (*c*) the content of protest programs as the protest movement ages or becomes more involved with hegemonic centers, varying from redistribution to improving the market value of black or Chicano labor through education
  (*d*) the degree of representation of the interests of the poor as we move from arenas peripheral to capitalism such as Health, Education, and Labor to arenas that are central such as Ways and Means (which considers tax and expenditure bills)
3 For revolutionary process
  (*a*) special access of capitalists in the political system at points where policy touches on the property system, presumably from high access in capitalist and tame Social Democratic régimes to low access in revolutionary socialist regimes
  (*b*) the speed of movement toward racial equality, supposed to be especially marked in the former colonial areas in revolutionary régimes

Sources and types of data

Now we turn from the point that one has to have comparisons, and units of analysis and variables that yield comparisons, in order to make causal inferences, to the point that one has to have observations on those variables for those units in order to test the causal ideas.

The first point to note about the units of analysis above is that they are mostly *collective, cross-cultural or cross-industry*, and *historical*. As long as positivist observation in race relations insists on studying the social psychology of prejudice in the mass public of *individuals*, in one country, ignoring people's location in the productive order except for a loose social-class variable, at one point in time, there is not much chance that they will speak to the issues. As long as Domhoff shows again that the people who run things tend, as individuals, to be rich and to live their lives with other rich people, and forgets that the king of Saudi Arabia is also rich, we are not likely to see any advance. As long as the pluralists insist on counting a black speechmaker on the Health, Education and Labor Committee as equal to a friend of oil depletion allowances on Ways and Means, we have no hope of studying variations in arenas. The individualist illusion, ethnocentric parochialism, and historical shortsightedness of the positivist tradition in sociology tend to make its observations irrelevant to any sophisticated theory of the power system.

The second point is that one has to observe at least two values of the variable in order to get anywhere. If internal colonialist theorists insist on calling New York equally colonialist as Mississippi, which rather strains one's capacity for belief but seems to be respectable nowadays, then they will have to observe what happens in Soviet Central Asia to the Muslims. If 'monopoly capitalism' means anything observable in the world, some modes of production such as the oil industry must be more monopolistic than some others such as retail trade; some countries such as Saudi Arabia must have more monopolistic capitalism than others such as the United States; socialist countries must have less monopoly capitalism than capitalist countries. The careful absence of comparative study among students of internal colonialism suggests an overwhelming desire to be ignorant about whether what they say is true or not.

The third point is that there are a lot of things to count and measure in the variables above. There is no reason that the column inches of capitalist testimony to the Ways and Means Committee cannot be compared to column inches on Health, Education, and Labor. The evolution over time of the demands of social movements ought to be codable by criteria of redistributiveness versus improvement of labor market position, and the rates of change of the ratio of Social Democratic or trade-union consciousness types of demands to challenges to central capitalist institutions compared in the different situations where Marxists predict different rates of change. The rate of approach to income equality by Uzbeks in Uzbekistan as compared to blacks in the South is theoretically observable, although the Soviet government does not go out of its way to facilitate bourgeois sociological analysis. If the racial employment of firms classified by monopoly position can be calculated by Gary Becker (1971) for his neoclassical economic purposes, it is hard to see why Marxists cannot do the same thing. Incidentally, in every respect Becker's results support the Marxist analysis of race relations given above, whenever they are relevant to the issues. Firm policies in race relations are measured both by contract compliance officials and by Parsonian investigators like Leon Mayhew. There is no particular reason for a Marxist to be less competent than a routine civil servant or than a Parsonian. The race relations ideology that pervades different industries can be easily calculated, even for the self-employed and managerial personnel alone, by simply coding the industry questions asked in every respectable academic national survey study. The industry code is now used for the propose of coding occupation, but this bourgeois shortsightedness of survey researchers need not hinder its use to study the impact of the mode of production. Southern states can be statistically described by the dependence of their middle classes on peculiarly colonial modes of production with little difficulty. The distinction in closeness to national capitalist banking centers between Atlanta or Dallas on the one hand, and Birmingham or Tallahassee on the other, can be found in a half dozen statistical sources available for metropolitan areas.

In short, Marxist variables are variables in this world; variables in this world can be observed; things that can be observed can be counted or measured or both, with a little bit of scientific ingenuity. If Marxist studies cripple themselves by not observing comparatively, they double their disability by refusing to use the inherently quantitative and countable nature of their variables for precision of empirical analysis.

Now we turn to the analytical technology necessary to turn the raw facts into facts of parameters relevant to the theory. Marxist theory is about comparative rates of change in different circumstances: for example, rates of change of the mode of production in which blacks and Chicanos are involved are supposed to determine rates of change of hegemonic institutions toward bourgeois democratic types of reforms; or, for example, sectors closely linked to capitalist centers are supposed to respond to this change faster than loosely linked peripheral sectors. The ordinary analytical technology for studying causes of rates of change is differential equations. In my most intransigent moments, I sometimes urge that people without the calculus should not be allowed to study social change, because their comments on the value of quantitative and mathematical theories are necessarily incompetent. But even in reasonable periods, I would urge that Marxists need the calculus more than Parsonians, because they have theories of the causes of different rates of change, while Parsonians usually have theories of the form that eventually change will happen by social differentiation.

It is not much wonder that the positivists have not made much contribution to the study of Marxist theory, because their analytical technology has been peculiarly inappropriate to the questions at hand. Cross tabulations, or a panel at time one and time two, are hardly adequate to the empirical issues. The statistical problems are those of relating time series data to differential equations models of the social process.

The fifth point has to do with interaction, or as Lazarsfeld called it, 'specification' (1955: 122). The prediction of the theory of hegemony, for example, is that as we go closer to capitalist centers, the slope of consent to racial reform of a bourgeois sort (education, voting rights, collective bargaining) is steep, while the slope of consent to redistributive programs (collective contributions to black income out of taxes on wealth, self-determination by blacks governing central economic institutions such as property) is essentially flat. The analytical technology for studying interaction effects or differences in slope is analysis of covariance, or its analogue in the log-linear model for cross tabulations. Elementary multiple regression without interaction, or path analysis, simply are not adequate to the question. The average level of statistical ingenuity required for studying Marxist theory is going to have to be *above* the competence necessary to be an ordinary social-psychological kind of positivist, in order to turn a set of raw facts into a fact about a statistical parameter that speaks to Marxist theory.

How did we get into such a mess?

Let me suppose for the sake of argument (what I don't suppose for a minute in reality) that I have convinced the reader that Marxism is an empirical theory, testable by the methods of quantitative investigation, when these methods are suitably improved over the present dismaying state. How does it come about that investigation in this area is so far below what is required – in fact, so far below the level of empirical investigation of Marx and Trotsky? I want to offer three hypotheses to account for this situation. The first is that we allow people to be theorists in the discipline. The second is that we have turned over the development of methodology to the social psychologists. The third is the ethnocentrism of the American ideological left, the audience to which many Marxists hope to speak.

When I compare the travesty of Marxism I learned in a theory course to the sophistication of Marx's empirical analyses of nineteenth-century English capitalism and of French politics, I am persuaded that the central cause of theoretical disability is to pose as, and aspire to be, a theorist. This empirically empty schematism that generates no investigable results is only possible because we provide sociologists a social rôle as theorist. Furthermore, a Marxist is not a specialist in a subject, so has to be a theorist, and is shaped by the tradition of empirical emptiness by which we sociologists recognize something as theoretical. If there were no specialists in nonempirical investigations of ideas in the discipline, we would not channel Marxists into such nonempirical activities.

The overdevelopment of quantitative methods for social-psychological studies, and their underdevelopment for structural and historical units of analysis, is primarily due to the fact that only survey researchers specialize in methods. This has two effects. The first is that most of what we learn in methods courses is irrelevant to the study of structural problems, especially structural change. The second is that a Marxist has to show that he can hardly count in order to show he is not a social psychologist. Usually the demonstration is convincing, if not very fruitful for testing Marxist ideas.

The third problem comes from the peculiarly untheoretical nature of the American left ideological public. It is very hard to get the *New York Review* interested in race relations outside the United States, or in the oil monopoly when it passes from Rockefeller, Governor of New York, to the king of Saudi Arabia. What use is it to find out who in abstract terms is responsible for racial oppression or oil prices ten times the cost of production, if you cannot, respectively, keep him from becoming chairman of the Judiciary Committee or vice-president? This ethnocentric view is, perhaps, appropriate for a general intelligentsia, for intellectual consultants to American left politicians. It is radically inappropriate for the scientific investigation of Marxist ideas.

The general practice of Marxist investigations results in their not having much to say to the profession. Their orientation to a particularly parochial ideological community, as an alternative audience, confirms them in a kind of research strategy that keeps them from making causal inferences, which keeps them from having much to say to the profession, and so the sterile circle is closed.

6. Social mobility in industrial labor markets[1]

The purpose of this paper is to analyze the partition of the labor market into segments, and to show how this affects the process of social mobility. By labor market segments we mean bounded areas within the labor market such that people within those boundaries do not compete with people outside to more than a limited extent. For example, if physicians are licensed, other people who are not licensed compete with physicians only at a substantial disadvantage, as 'quacks.' If the vice-president for sales of a corporation is recruited only among middle managers in the corporation, then contenders for the job do not need to worry about what the going wage for vice-presidents is, for they will get somewhat more than a middle manager and less than a chief executive. When a labor market is divided up into segments, we can speak of the structure as a whole as 'balkanized'. (Cf. Clark Kerr 1954. Recent work by Ross Stolzenberg (1975) and Aage Sørensen & N. Tuma (1978) bear very directly on the relation between Kerr's arguments and the modern mobility literature.) We will apply the ideas to some data on social mobility in Norway.

There are two dimensions to labor market segmentation which can be illustrated by contrasting farming with university teaching. Among

[1] The analysis in this paper involved some complicated data manipulation designed by Knut Holmqvist and carried out in part by Sten-Erik Clausen. I am convinced they got it right, but this is not a competent judgement since I could not have done it myself. Natalie Rogoff Ramsøy remembers how variables generated several years ago were defined, or remembers how to look them up. I have never worked on a project in which this was true, since I have mainly worked on projects I have administered myself. When I consulted her about these matters, she fortunately insisted on discussing the substantive issues, which I believe led me to function at much above my usual intellectual level. I do however realize that it is not my beliefs that count, and in agreeing to have my belief judged by the profession I want to protect the people above from being blamed for my faults.

farmers in the United States or Norway, most of the labor is recruited from among the families of farm owners of the previous generation. Positions as 'helper' around a farm generally go to sons of the farmer, and the only people who become farm owners (for all practical purposes) are the sons of farmers. But, especially in the United States and other agricultural exporting countries, the commodity market is highly competitive, so that the return to farm labor (mostly received by owners and taking the legal form of 'profits') is kept down below the level of competitive wages in the labor market as a whole. So there is a monopoly over jobs by the sons of farmers (because they need land to farm, which ordinarily they get only from their parents), but there is no monopolistic pricing of that labor (this statement should be read for the Norwegian case to apply only to the period during which the careers we will be studying were formed – the present policy is to create a monopoly in the commodity market by legal means, so as to give farmers incomes competitive with urban workers' wages).

In university teaching, in contrast, recruitment is controlled by the members of the university as a corporation, usually by consultation with people who are already working in the discipline. But the education system generally speaking produces more qualified people than there are jobs as university teachers, and university professors are generally willing to do so. So the general situation is that no young people have a monopoly over the jobs of university teachers, except that they have to be trained for them, but as a practical matter only people hired by the university are allowed to 'sell' university education. So there is a monopoly in the product market, allowing university professors' wages to be raised to a level considerably above what one could get people to do the work for. But there is no monopoly in the labor market at the beginning level (as a practical matter, only younger scholars who are already hired in some university are normally competitors for professorships).

To provide a general classification of labor market structures, then, we need to take into account the degree to which there is a monopoly in the product market which allows wages to remain above the competitive level, as well as whether there are boundaries in the labor market that cut off one segment from another. The three most important types of monopoly in the product market are (1) government monopolies, as for instance in education, postal services, military and police work, (2) licensing of professions and crafts, so that physicians' or plumbers' services can be bought only from firms that use the labor of qualified and licensed professionals or craftsmen, and (3) monopolies created by technical or administrative constraints on the efficiency of competitors, such as for example those created by large economies of scale in the production of iron and steel, or those created by technical monopolies (created by research and development and reinforced by patent laws) in the computer industry.

On the side of the labor market, noncompetitive segments are created 'naturally' by skill differences and by a normal requirement that hierarchies be constructed (generally at least) in such a way that the superior could do the inferior's job. Hierarchy creates 'careers' in which qualification in one job is a prerequisite for entry into another job. Both kinds of 'natural' processes are often reinforced by normative or contractual regulation, so that skills may be made more monopolistic by licensing, careers may be made more rigid by seniority provisions, careers may be created where there is no natural hierarchy (e.g. in universities) by administrative regulations, craft unions may get control over recruitment and training for a given occupation and over bargaining about the wage rates, and so on. Generally speaking we can distinguish here *craft and professional* normative structures, which establish a *general* labor market status which has a monopoly over positions in a given line of work in a large number of organizations, and *bureaucratic* structures, which establish seniority rights and career lines within a given organization. There are mixed cases in which a bureaucratic-type career structure is imposed on a large group of organizations and a given individual may have a status in which he can be hired by many organizations, which status he has however got by following a 'bureaucratic' career path which leads to that status in late middle age. Ship captain in the merchant fleet is an example of such a mixed bureaucratic-professional status.

In addition to these boundaries in the labor market as such, we have already mentioned the binding together of a job and a property ownership status in agriculture. In Norway such 'petty bourgeois' structures in which some kind of labor is combined with property ownership occur also on a large scale in fishing, and to some degree in forestry, and are also very frequent in wholesale and retail trade.

Many of the possible combinations of these divisions of the commodity and labor markets do not really occur. For example, almost all enterprises which provide services under government sponsorship are either bureaucratically organized or organized as professions – then among the bureaucratically organized parts are some which have large categories of skilled manual workers (e.g. the railroads or the post and telephone system), but almost none which have unskilled labor. Consequently the classification of industries we will develop below does not have all the possible combinations of the variables mentioned above.

Our general purpose now is to classify parts of the labor market in accordance with the general character of segmentation that occurs in an industry (we use here industry as a translation of *næring*, and 'manufacturing' as a translation of *industri*). Then we will try to use that classification of industries to analyze the typical structure of careers within those industries.

A classification of industries in Norway by labor market structure

Traditional primary industries

Traditional primary industries (excluding mining, including farming, fishing, hunting and forestry) tend to be organized with family property in small enterprises, with some or all of the labor going into the enterprise coming from the family itself. There is relatively little supply of labor from outside the family, either in the form of skilled labor or proletarian seasonal labor, in Norway. (This is not, of course, true of a good many other agricultural systems. See for example Jefferey Paige (1975)). Recently fishing has become more of a floating factory enterprise, especially fishing on the high seas on distant fishing grounds. But a very large share of Norwegian fishing is in coastal waters, as when there is a run of codfish in the north, or the more continuous catches of herring and brisling along the coast. Such coastal fishing does not give very large advantages to larger ships, and can be combined with part-time farming by people with access to relatively small capital investments in fishing boats. Hunting of whales and seals has been carried out with larger ships, but has occupied only a very small part of the labor force. Consequently, without too much loss of precision, we can classify all the industries with a first digit of 1 in the 1970 Norwegian census as being in the petty bourgeois primary sector.[2]

The characteristics of this group of industries can be summarized as (a) recruitment is almost entirely from families of people in the industry already, especially from families of owners of a petty bourgeois enterprise; at any given time a large share of the workers themselves have property rights in the enterprise they work in, and if they do not they have a good chance of having such a property interest by the time they reach middle age, (b) a general decline in the overall labor force due to the fact that demand does not increase as fast as productivity – this in turn means that if a relatively 'free' market is allowed in the commodity market, the returns to the enterprises will be forced down low enough to drive a good proportion of the labor force out of the industry (very roughly at the rate of one new recruit for every three retiring or dying workers). Thus roughly five out of six sons of farmers and fishermen will not enter these family enterprises, but will instead go to urban employments. Their skills in fishing or farming will not in general be of any value on the urban labor market, and will not be of any value on other farms (not because they are irrelevant, but because the other farm is now no longer profitable enough even to support that farmer's own son, let alone supporting a neighbor's son as well). This is one main source of the 'reserve army of the unemployed' in recent history.

'Classical' capitalist industries

By 'classical' capitalist industries I mean those which formed Marx's (and Ricardo's) picture of how the labor and commodity markets relate to each other. It includes in particular the textile industry from which Marx took many of his examples and much of his evidence. It is characterized by relatively small firms in a competitive commodity market, using unskilled labor in the labor market. That is, there is no appreciable technical or scientific apparatus of staff employees in research and development or in engineering in the managerial struc-

---

[2] Statistisk Sentralbyrå *Standard for Næringsgruppering, Håndbøker* 9, Oslo 1972. All references to numbers for industries correspond to this publication. This is a five digit code. When all of an industry grouping is classified in the same place, I have only specified as many digits as needed. E.g., when I below classify 'Building and other construction' all in the same place and give the number as 50, that means that all five digit codes having 50 as the first two digits are included.

ture, but instead an authoritarian 'people-driving' administrative apparatus. Higher productivity comes from the 'stretch out' rather than from technical improvements. See Robert Blauner (1964). Workers tend to be recruited from whatever the underprivileged group in the labor market is at the time – blacks, guest workers, women, cottagers driven off the land, or generally the 'reserve army of the unemployed'. (See Gary Becker's *The Economics of Discrimination* (1957) for a demonstration of the connection between competitiveness in the commodity market and hiring of underprivileged workers.)

In these industries we expect there to be no positions of privilege, or only very minimal ones, to be defended by trade unions. Seniority systems will probably not be highly developed, because seniority rights are only useful if they defend a good (highly paid and secure) job. But if competitive pressures push wages down to the wage acceptable by the most desperate members of the reserve army of the unemployed (or to the legal minimum wage if that is higher), then the job being defended by seniority rights will not be one of privilege. Because the main component of the value added by classical capitalist manufacture is direct labor by unskilled workers, getting more (but not more skilled) labor out of cheaper laborers is a central determinant of a firm's profitability and competitive viability. Over time we would expect such industries to move out of high wage (and high education) economies. They would move to the south or to Puerto Rico in the United States and would move internationally to Taiwan or Hong Kong or Korea. In short, the general principles of Marx and Ricardo about how the labor market should work are likely to apply with full force to such industries, which means that there will not be much labor market segmentation in them in advanced economies, but that the advanced economies will not have much such industrial work because internationally it follows the reserve army of the unemployed to third world countries where that army is now found.

In the Norwegian system for classification of industries, examination of characteristics of firms and of their labor forces suggests that the following industries should be classified here: Other mining (mainly sand and gravel production and quarrying) (29), food and drink (31), textiles, clothing, and shoes (32), wood products and furniture (33), plastic goods (356), other mineral products (mainly ceramics and glass) (36) and other manufacturing industries (39). The numbers in parentheses refer to the 1970 classification of industries of the Norwegian Central Statistical Bureau. See Note 2.

Competitive or small-scale industries with skilled workers
Some manufacturing industries, building and other construction, and some repair industries are characterized by a small-firm structure, generally competitive commodity or service markets, but they require the manual work force to be experienced and skilled. This means that besides the competitive structure, they also need to have a labor market so structured that people can have careers – in order to motivate them to learn a skill. The manufacturing subsections of this group are the 'job shops' and small producers of specialty lines which tend to grow up in industrial districts. Typically they buy a good many of the parts that go into what they produce, so that for example a lathe manufacturer may buy the motor, the cutting tools, and other parts, and himself produce only those parts which are distinctive of lathes. Some of these he will subcontract, e.g., to a small foundry for the frame. This in turn means that such manufacturers tend to be located near other industrial producers, generally speaking in the heavy industrial districts near primary iron and steel producers, such as the industrial belt in the United States that stretches from New York–Baltimore at one end to Chicago–St Louis at the other, and includes most of the industrial East and Midwest. Other examples are the midlands complex in England, or the Saar–Ruhr districts in West Germany.

Another manufacturing subsection is concentrated in metropolitan areas, graphical and printing industries. It is often classified together with publishing industries (publishing industries are actually professionally organized and do not belong here, but the classification system in some countries does not allow their distinction. We will make the distinction below, but it cannot be carried backward in time in Norway).

Construction entrepreneurs usually hire skilled workers for a given construction project, and then lay them off, but these people often go to work on another construction project. Finally, repair of machinery is usually skilled work, but is organized on a small scale much like other services delivered to the general public.

What we expect to characterize these industries is that *as a group* they may well be in a noncompetitive situation, but they are *in firms* that compete with each other within that market. It is impossible, of course, to build a road in Hong Kong and ship it to Norway, or to send one's refrigerator back to Japan to have a loose wire connected or a new charge of refrigerant put in. Highly specialized production in manufacturing may involve technical monopolies, or depend on ready availability of parts, or need a large market, to remain competitive. Much building of capital equipment such as machine tools can only rationally take place in heavy industrial districts for this reason. Thus a partial monopoly in the commodity markets is combined in these industries with skilled (and hence generally well organized) workers who cannot be replaced from the reserve army of the unemployed. We expect then a 'craft' organization of the labor market.

The industries that should be classified here, together with their code numbers in the Norwegian 1970 system, include: Metal goods (381), machines other than electrical (382), building of small boats (38 412), technical and scientific instrument production (385), graphical and printing work (3421), building and other construction (50), repair services for machinery (951).

Large-scale engineering-based industries with skilled workers and bureaucratic administration
Much manufacturing, utilities, transport, and communications have a common basis in applied physical science, so that a large share of their middle class labor force has been trained in some kind of engineering. They also have in common large-scale enterprises, so that bureaucratic administration is more rational than small firm entrepreneurial administration. Quite often they have a quasi-monopolistic position, perhaps for technical reasons (e.g. telecommunications or sewerage need only one network), for reasons of minimum scale for efficiency (e.g. primary iron and steel production require a large market for each plant of the minimum effficient size), for reasons of technological monopolies due to patents, research and development, or simply experience in difficult production processes (e.g. in production of drugs), or for reasons of government monopolies (e.g. the post office). This means that their wages can be raised above those of the reserve army of the unemployed, that they are often viable in internationally open economies even if those economies compete with

countries with low labor costs, that they can provide reasonably stable careers for skilled workers and for professional engineers or scientists, and that in other ways they are capable of sustaining a 'modern' form of the labor market with extensive normative provisions for seniority rights and skill monopolies.

The labor market structure we expect in these industries depends somewhat on exactly how the education for higher positions is arranged. In particular, in Norway several other organizations are organized the way the military and police forces of the United States are organized, with recruitment (essentially) only at the bottom and promotion from within, with schooling arranged by the organization itself at crucial career stages. (The United States military have such an organization except that they recruit officers and enlisted men separately, perhaps making them more similar to ordinary industrial and governmental bureaucracies.) The post office, telecommunications, the merchant marine, and the railroads have been organized like that in Norway.

With these exceptions, the usual situation is that two separate career lines exist for the middle classes (usually recruited from higher education) and for the working classes. Both of these groups have careers, and many of the manual workers are classified as skilled, and are paid at considerably above the competitive wage rate for unskilled workers. Manual workers do not ordinarily obtain these skilled wages until they have been with the same organization for some time, and generally in the working class part of the labor force rights to good jobs are distributed rather strictly on seniority lines. In the middle class part of the labor force seniority plays a very large rôle, sometimes explicitly (e.g. the rule in the American army that unless otherwise provided, the officer with the highest rank, and if of the same rank with the longest 'time in grade', is commanding – there are some special rules to ensure that this does not result in high ranking physicians commanding an infantry battalion), but always implicitly. People are rarely jumped several grades in the hierarchy, and the amount of time spent in a given grade, while variable, is moderately uniform. In this industry group, however, we would expect that education would be a determinant of the speed of promotion and of the ultimate level to which a person is promoted, because the industries do depend on abstract knowledge, and because education is one of the criteria of merit which is easiest to defend normatively when authority has to be unequally distributed (see Eric Wright and Lucca Perrone, 1977).

The industries included here, with their Norwegian Central Statistical Bureau codes, are: Coal, oil, and metal ore mining (21, 22, and 23), tobacco products (314), pulp and paper production (341), chemical, petroleum and rubber products except plastic goods (351, 352, 353, 354, 355), primary metals production (37), electrical apparatus and machines (383), transportation equipment except for small boats (38 411, 38 413, 38 414, 3842, 3843, 3844, 3845, 3849), power and water supply (4), transportation other than taxis and car rentals (7111, 7112, 712, 713), post and telecommunications (78), sewerage and sanitation (92).

Small competitive trade and services

This fifth group is being reorganized, especially by the vertical integration of retail and wholesale trade in chain stores of supermarkets and department stores. The main reorganization from an economic point of view seems to be that chain stores greatly reduce the costs of wholesaling, but the main effect from the point of view of the labor market is that it substitutes an organization much like the 'classical' capitalist industries above, competitive enterprises with unskilled labor, for the traditional petty bourgeois organization. However, this reorganization has not gone very far in Norway, probably because the regional diversity and the small size of the country makes many of the savings of chain stores harder to obtain there. It is therefore still the case that a large share of the labor force in the trade and personal services sectors are self-employed, or are small employers with an average of about ten employees. So a total of about a fifth are petty bourgeois proprietors, and four-fifths are employees of relatively small firms which are in at least locally competitive situations. Most of these services are not however competitive internationally, so the pressure of the price of labor in Hong Kong has little bearing. Otherwise the situation for the employees is much like that of the 'classical' capitalist industries above.

We expect these industries, then, to recruit their workers from whichever groups *within society* provide the reserve army of the unemployed – women first of all, guest workers, ethnic minorities, youth taking time out from their education to accumulate some money. There will be few careers, and those will not lead to much higher wages than the minimum standard. Since there are no positions of privilege to be defended, we would expect few and weak seniority provisions. The middle class has very little reason to introduce science or sophisticated accounting into their enterprises – 'bookkeeping' is enough – and this combines with the petty bourgeois character of many of these enterprises to make the principal career of the middle classes one of either inheritance or borrowing and paying back. Education probably makes very little difference in career chances.

The industries included here, with their Norwegian Central Statistical Bureau 1970 numbers, are: Wholesale trade (61), retail trade (62), hotels and restaurants (63), taxi and rental cars (7113, 7114), services connected to transportation (travel agencies, freight forwarders, etc.) (719), real estate agents and managers (831), rental of machines (833), distribution and display of movies (9412), sport and other entertainment and recreation (9490), personal services other than repair of machines (9052, 953, 959).

Professional services
The central feature of professional services is that the professionals have a status obtained by education which is valuable in many different organizations, which is often protected by formal monopolies (e.g. lawyers), by the service being provided by the state itself (e.g. in most countries' education), or by both (e.g. in many countries' medicine). However, a number of competitive industries require such a high level of professional skill, and that skill is so publicly observable, that a person has a status in a labor market rather than in a given firm. The other people who work in professional organizations may be aspiring professionals (e.g. young researchers in museums or research enterprises), subordinate professionals (e.g. nurses in hospitals), or service and communications personnel (e.g. secretaries or janitors). Generally speaking they are disproportionately recruited from underprivileged groups (especially women, but also the young, guest workers, ethnic minorities, and the like). They tend to be paid at the going rate for the reserve army of the unemployed, or less because their work is 'volunteer' work for such valuable purposes that they need not be paid – for example, underpayment of alternative service

which replaces military service is common, and provision of services either free or under the going rate in such industries is often part of religious devotion, of conspicuous leisure for upper middle class women, and the like. Apprentices to such professions are often given scholastic credits or certificates of professional competence rather than wages. The point here is that the dynamics of the wage rates of the nonprofessional workers in professional organizations is often determined by considerations internal to the status system of the organization, rather than by any labor market process whatsoever. And such systems are in general designed so as to maximize the status and rewards of the professionals, and to demean and underpay the nonprofessionals as much as possible. This is more true of the public and private charitable sector than of the business sector of professional services, but in both, the manual and service workers are part of the Ricardian labor market.

The industries included here are: Publishing (3422), business services (832), various professional services provided in Norway mainly through the state, including education, health, religious services (93), artistic production other than distribution and display of films (9411, 9413, 9414, 9415, 942).

Bureaucratic services
Some bureaucratic organizations do not administer a production process, do not usually apply engineering knowledge, and are not dominated by professionals who do deliver the services. Their main business is the processing of claims of one kind or another – claims on checking and saving accounts, claims to rights (and duties) toward the government, claims against insurance policies – and the work entailed in making sure that the total sum of claims is not larger than the total that can be paid out. Generally then this involves the government, banks, and insurance organizations, and some part of the work of interest organizations.

The general labor market structure of bureaucratic services is determined by the general tendency toward monopoly, or at least reduced competition, of these organizations. Sometimes the sales parts of the organizations compete in minor ways. The monopoly allows them to develop extensive bureaucratic career structures, with relatively little transferability of the competence from one organization to another (this makes them different from professional organizations), and without the subordinate structure of skilled and operative manual workers found in engineering-based industries. The Norwegian Central Statistical Bureau numbers that correspond are 81, 82, 91, and 935.

In the following analysis, we have used an approximation to this industry classification, because the data were coded in two-digit industries by the 1960 standard of the Central Statistical Bureau. The classification below is quite close to that described above, but we cannot sometimes distinguish details – for instance small boat building cannot be distinguished from shipbuilding, and so we are forced to put it into the engineering-based industries rather than into the category with the other relatively small machines produced in small lots, small competitive skilled industries, where we believe it belongs.

The gross mobility pattern by industry

Table 1 shows the proportions of men for whom we have data showing that they stayed within the same two-digit industry even though they changed employers during the five-year period previous to a given age.[3] The essential points of the table are two. First, there is a great difference between the sorts of labor market experience of people before they are 25 and after they are 25. This shows up in a great many features of the data base, but here in particular Table 1 shows that the job changes of men recently entering the labor market are much less likely than later job changes to be 'career' changes in the sense that they use past experience. That is, after 25 years old, a man can evidently often get a better job if he stays in the same industry as his previous job, indicating that there is often some value in his previous experience even though he is changing employers. This is much less likely to be true of changes of employers before the age of 25 years.

---

[3] The analysis that follows is of the Norwegian occupational life history data, whose collection was directed by Natalie Rogoff Ramsøy (see especially Ramsøy 1977: 43–60 for a brief description of the data and some validation studies). It obtained interviews with random samples, very slightly clustered, of three one-year age cohorts. Complete occupational, migration, family and household status, and educational life histories were collected, with interviewer cross-checks between these areas to use the respondent's memory of each to help his memory of the others. My own opinion is that the data are of an exceptionally high quality, and that there are only trivial errors in what follows due to sampling variations or measurement errors.

Table 1 *Of all men who changed employers during a five-year period, percentage who did not change two-digit industry during that period.*

Age at end of period	Year of birth		
	1921	1931	1941
25 years	14.2 (883)	10.3 (822)	11.7 (822)
30 years	26.8 (745)	28.3 (583)	27.5 (652)
35 years	28.7 (534)	32.6 (429)	
40 years	31.2 (423)	29.2 (404)	
45 years	36.0 (386)		
50 years	29.7 (330)		

Beyond 25 years, the proportion staying in the same industry remains about constant. A weighted estimate of the probability that one will remain in the same industry if one changes employers would be 29.4%. The weights used here are $N_i/p_i (1-p_i)$, where N_i is the number of workers in a given category (e.g. number working during a given five-year period), and p_i is the proportion of these with some characteristic (e.g. proportion changing industries). That is, after age 25, just about three out of ten employer shifts involved no change of industry, for all three cohorts and for all the periods of history covered by the data. The main point here is that this figure of three out of ten is a lot larger than would have been expected by chance, and is also a lot larger than is characteristic of the period before a man's experience is of much value on the labor market, before 25 years old. After 25 there are in fact boundaries (obviously highly permeable boundaries) around the labor market of an industry, such that people already within the industry have evidently some substantial advantages over new entrants, and also have advantages by staying in their own industry as compared to any jobs available to them if they change industries.

This constancy of the ratio of changes of employers which remain within the same industry (after 25 years old) combines with an increasing tendency over time to stay with the same employer to produce the gross pattern of industrial stability shown in Table 2.

The results in Table 2 can be predicted by knowing the constancy of the ratio (after age 25) of moves which entail staying in the same industry and which entail changing industry, and the increasing percentage of people who do not change employers as a cohort ages. That is, the new piece of information for each cohort and each five-year experience period in Table 2 is the percentage at the top of each set of three, the percentage remaining with the same employer throughout the period.

In all three cohorts the number remaining with the same employer throughout the period was very small in the five years before 25 years old, running to about one out of eight. In the period between 25 and 30 years old, however, about two out of five or 40% remain with the same employer throughout the period. By the age 30–35 this proportion is over half, and after 35 years it runs near to two-thirds. That is, from the period 25–30 to the period 35–40, the proportion changing employers drops from very roughly two thirds to very roughly one third, to remain somewhere near that second figure up to 50 years old. When we combine this with the fact that about one third of those changes involve staying within the same industry, we then obtain that about two-ninths will have the experience of staying within the same industry and changing employers between 25 and 30 years old (the actual figure is nearer a sixth, because not quite two thirds change employers), and this should go down to one ninth (or about 11%) and remain there for all periods after 35 years old.

Overall then the proportion of all people spending a given five-year period in the same industry, either by staying with the same employer or by moving to another employer within the same two-digit industry, increases from about one out of four or five in the five-year period before 25 years old, to about three out of four or four out of five in the five-year periods after the age of 35. Thus industrial labor markets are much more bounded for older workers than for younger workers. There are two sources of this increase in boundedness. First, starting at about age 25, some proportion of the people who leave one employer have enough better chances with another employer in the same industry that they find it profitable to stay within the industry. Second, continuing throughout the ages for which we have data, older men are more likely to stay with the same employer throughout the whole five-year period than are younger men.

Table 3 shows that this fact of increasing industrial boundedness of employment with ageing is a principal source of the greater continuity

Table 2 *Percentage who spent a specified five-year period with the same employer, different employer in the same industry, or different employer and different industry.*

	Year of birth		
	1921	1931	1941
20–25 years old			
Same employer	15.1	13.1	8.1
Different empl., same industry	12.0	9.0	10.7
Diff. industry	72.9	77.9	81.2
NUMBER OF CASES	1040	946	894
25–30 years old			
Same employer	38.4	43.6	36.9
Same industry	16.5	16.0	17.3
Diff. industry	45.0	40.5	45.8
NUMBER OF CASES	1210	1033	1033
30–35 years old			
Same employer	57.2	59.1	
Same industry	12.3	13.3	
Diff. industry	30.5	27.5	
NUMBER OF CASES	1248	1050	
35–40 years old			
Same employer	66.5	61.9	
Same industry	10.5	11.1	
Diff. industry	23.1	27.0	
NUMBER OF CASES	1261	1061	
40–45 years old			
Same employer	69.7		
Same industry	10.9		
Diff. industry	19.4		
NUMBER OF CASES	1274		
45–50 years old			
Same employer	74.0		
Same industry	7.7		
Diff. industry	18.3		
NUMBER OF CASES	1268		

of occupational experience with increasing age. The numbers are the percentages who changed their occupations at any time during a five-year period, classified by whether they changed employers, and if so, whether they also changed industries. If we look first at people over 25 years old, we find that the two right hand columns are very nearly constant. A weighted average of column 2 for ages after 25

Table 3 *Percentage who changed occupations during a five-year period, by whether they changed employer, and if so whether they changed industry, of those not working as unpaid family workers at the end of the period**

	Same employer	Changed empl., same industry	Changed empl., changed industry
20–25 years old			
Born 1921	26.4 (157)	76.8 (125)	99.2 (758)
Born 1931	61.3 (124)	78.8 (85)	99.7 (737)
Born 1941	72.2 (72)	84.4 (96)	99.0 (726)
25–30 years old			
Born 1921	24.3 (465)	65.0 (200)	93.9 (545)
Born 1931	24.9 (450)	58.2 (165)	90.7 (418)
Born 1941	22.0 (381)	55.3 (179)	92.0 (473)
30–35 years old			
Born 1921	12.7 (714)	55.6 (153)	93.4 (381)
Born 1931	15.8 (621)	53.6 (140)	86.9 (289)
35–40 years old			
Born 1921	11.6 (838)	55.3 (132)	92.4 (291)
Born 1931	15.2 (657)	55.9 (118)	89.9 (286)
40–45 years old			
Born 1921	9.6 (888)	51.8 (139)	89.9 (247)
45–50 years old			
Born 1921	9.9 (938)	54.1 (98)	92.2 (232)

*A movement out of unpaid family work is not counted as an industry change, even if the father was in a different industry than the first paid employment or other paid employment. However, a person who works, for example, in forestry, goes back home for a while, then works in forestry again, is counted as changing employers even if he goes back to work for the same employer the second time. Changes in which one of the industries or occupations could not be determined were counted as not changing that variable.

yields 56.7% of all men who change employers but stay within the same industry, change occupations during the five-year period. A weighted average of column 4 for all ages after 25 is 91.9%. That is, about one out of eleven men (at all ages above 25) keep their same occupations if they change industries, while about three out of seven keep the same occupation if they change employers but stay within the same industry. It is clear from an examination of these columns that all the figures in both after the first set are quite near the average.

This means that since the ratio of within-industry job changes to cross-industry job changes remains about constant, and the proportion of each of those which also involve changing occupations is also constant, the proportion of all changes in employer that involve a change in occupation is nearly constant. We multiply 0.294 (proportion of all job changes not involving changes in industry) by 0.567 (proportion of within-industry changes which involve changing occupations), and add 0.706 (proportion of all job changes involving change in industry) times 0.919 (proportion of all cross-industry changes which involve changing occupations), and get that after 25 years old about 81.6% of all changes of employer involve changes in occupations. This is approximately constant across cohorts and across this (small) segment of labor market history.

The increase in continuity of occupation with increasing age after age 25 is therefore due to two factors: the decreasing tendency of men to change employers as they get older, and the decreasing tendency of employers to change the occupations of their employees as those employees get older. The first factor we have already noted in Table 2. The second factor appears in the leftmost column of numbers in Table 3. After 25 years of age there is a regular decline in the proportion of men who have not changed employers who have changed occupations. Otherwise put, either the frequency of 'promotions' goes down with age, or the proportion of all promotions which involve changes in occupational titles in the Norwegian occupational classification system decreases. From ages 25 to 30, roughly a quarter of all men who remain with the same employer change occupations. This decreases to about one out of seven changing occupations between the ages of 30 and 35, about the same from 35 to 40, then about one out of 10 from ages 40 to 50.

We can distinguish then four types of labor markets in the data on gross mobility. The first kind characterizes people under 25, and involves a great deal of 'non-career' movement, with very few men remaining with the same employer throughout the period, very few who change employers while remaining within the same industry, and fewer changes of any kind involving keeping the same occupation. Even if these young men stay with the same employer, they are very unlikely to keep the same occupation throughout the period (the exception is the oldest cohort, which has some continuity if they keep the same employer).

The second type is the internal labor market within firms, which both becomes more important as men get older (because fewer change employers) and changes its mobility features (because fewer men change occupations during any given five-year period). Almost all of the increase in the continuity of occupational experience with increasing age is due to the increasing importance of these internal labor markets, and the increasing continuity of job title within these labor markets. That is, the serial correlation of job at the beginning of the five-year period and at the end increases dramatically with age. Most of this increased serial correlation is due to more and more men keeping the same employer *and* the same occupation throughout the period. There is very little other increase in stability of occupation in the labor market for older men.

The third kind of labor market is that manifested by employer changes which do not involve changes in industry. Roughly one third of all employer changes are within two-digit industries. These are characterized by a great deal *more* occupational change than is characteristic of men who do not change employers, but a great deal *less* occupational change than is involved in cross-industry transfers. Roughly three out of seven men who change employers within an industry take up the identical occupation with the new employer that they had with the old one. This must mean that their previous experience in the occupation is valuable to their new employer.

The fourth kind of labor market is manifested in between-industry movement of older men. In general about two thirds of all moves by older men are between industries. In only about one out of eleven cases does the mover take up the same occupation with the new employer – while this is much higher than it is in the labor market for men under 25, it still indicates that the previous experience of the worker is not usually valuable to his new employer when that employer is in a different industry. We will expect such labor markets to work in a way more like that predicted by Ricardian labor market theory.

Industrial variations in types of mobility: internal labor markets

Clearly from the analysis embedded in the classification of industries, the industry types we have defined should be related to the types of mobility which we have just been analyzing. In particular, we would expect industries characterized by 'bureaucracy' to have highly developed 'internal labor markets' – that is, labor markets in which jobs are more available to people already employed by the firm. 'Bureaucracies' have 'promotions'. We expect that if these internal labor markets apply to all employees and all positions, then ordinarily an employee of such an establishment will find it to his advantage to stay with the same employer.

In Table 4 we have therefore provided three replications of 'promotion' measures for each of our seven industry types, one for the overall experience of each cohort. For each cohort we give the average percentage of all employees spending an entire five-year period with the same employer who changed occupations during that period. Since as we saw before this proportion declines with age, and since the earlier born cohorts have had more time at older ages, the averages are generally higher for the young cohort (proportion of all employees staying with the same employer who were promoted between ages 25 and 30) than for the old cohort (in which the high index mentioned for the younger cohort is combined with low indices for later five-year periods). However, what we are interested in here is the relative rank of the industries, and that is very nearly the same for all three cohorts.

The probability of staying with the same employer throughout a five-year period was predicted to be different for low status jobs than for high status jobs in some of the industries. An approximation to this is the distinction between young and older employees. Consequently we have provided two indications of 'tenure' with a given employer, one being an average proportion staying with the same employer for those five-year periods we have observed after age 35 (three periods for the 1921 cohort, one period for the 1931 cohort, and of course none for the 1941 cohort who were only 30 when interviewed), and the other the proportion staying for the full five-year period with the same employer at ages below 35.

The results of Table 4 are simplified in Table 5. The 'purest bureaucracies' in Table 5 should appear in the upper left cell, characterized by high career stability among both young and older employees and a great deal of 'promotion'. The industries where we find employees with such careers are exactly the ones where we expected it, namely the public administration and finance industries that we have labeled 'bureaucratic' and the large-scale engineering-

Table 4 *Indicators of 'internal labor market' for industries classified by labor market types. Men over 25. Percentages.*

Industry type[c]	Average 'promotion' old cohort[a]	Average 'promotion' middle cohort	'Promotion' young cohort	Tenure[b] over 35	Tenure under 35
	(1)	(2)	(3)	(4)	(5)
Bureaucratic[c]	36	39	62	82	61
Engineering	15	21	22	75	50
Petty bourgeois services	16	17	24	70	46
Professional	14	11	13	70	44
Classical capitalist	11	14	16	68	49
Small skilled	11	14	9	58	42
Primary	6	10	12	62	42

[a]. 'Promotion is the percentage of those who stayed for five years with the same employer who changed occupations. The averages are over all the five-year periods available (i.e. all five-year periods after age 25 for the three cohorts), 5 for the old, 3 for the middle, 1 for the young cohort. People who remained in or moved to unpaid family work are excluded, as are people for whom some of the data are missing.
[b]. 'Tenure' is the proportion of those employed in the industry at the beginning of the five-year period who stayed with the same employer for five years. Over 35 includes three periods of the old cohort, one of the middle cohort. Under 35 includes five five-year periods, two for each of the older cohorts and one for the younger cohort.
[c]. See the text above for the industry classification.

Table 5 *The relation between indicators of internal labor markets. Data from Table 4.*

High mature tenure (Col. 4 over 69%)	Steady young employment (Col. 5 over 47%)	'Promotion' always over 15%	'Promotion' always under 15%
Yes	Yes	Bureaucratic Engineering	
Yes	No	Petty bourgeois	Professional services
No	Yes		Classical capitalist*
No	No		Small skilled Primary

* In the youngest cohort 'classical capitalist' industries show 16% 'promotion'.

based manufacturing industries and transportation and utilities services. Likewise in the lower right we should find the least bureaucratic
industries, with unstable employment among both young and old and
little internal promotion. And we find exactly the industries we expect
there, namely the small-scale industries producing small metal wares
and the building industry, and the primary industries, farming, fishing
and forestry.

Between we have some mixed cases, which also correspond to our
analysis. The industries we have labeled 'petty bourgeois service'
industries, including retail and wholesale trade and a large number of
services organized in small firms, tend to have tenure and promotion
for older workers and unstable employment (with, however, considerable occupational change) among younger workers. The 'professional' industries have relatively little promotion (after all, many
people start occupationally 'at the top' of these industries), relatively
good security of employment of the older people, and unstable
employment for the young people. The 'classical capitalist' industries
in textiles, food and drink, and wood products, have a sort of 'almost
bureaucratized' pattern with less promotion and less tenure than the
engineering industries but more of each than the small-scale skilled
worker industries.

Industrial variations in types of mobility: industry-wide labor markets

Table 6 presents two indicators of the degree to which experience
gained in one establishment is valuable to another employer in the
same industry. The first is simply the proportion of all men who
change employers during a five-year period who stay within the same
industry throughout the five-year period, averaged over all the
five-year periods for which we have data. The second is the proportion
of these within-industry job changers who retained the same occupation throughout the five-year period.

This table is simplified in Table 7. In the upper left are those
industries high on both criteria – i.e. those in which employees
apparently get an industry-specific skill which makes the industry into
a bounded labor market. As expected we find the professional
industries like schools, hospitals, business services here, and also the

small skilled manufacturing and building industries. It is characteristic of these industries that they have apprenticeship or professional training which establish a certificate of competence that is valid in *an area of occupational service*, a craft or profession, which is essentially different from a *rank in a bureaucracy* which is not ordinarily transferable across employers.

At the other extreme are the classical capitalist industries that Marx and Ricardo theorized about, the small business services sector which has been the focus of modern studies of the 'secondary labor market', and the traditionally depressed primary industries. (This does not mean, of course, that experience on one farm or one fishing boat is of no use on another – rather the problem is either that the worker does not have capital to invest in the other farm so goes to the city, or that the other fishing boat is not hiring because the quotas on the fishing banks are already allocated.)

The intermediate cases are somewhat understandable. The engineering industries have a good many positions as operatives, 'appendages to the machine' as Marx puts it, whose experience would give them no particular advantage in another firm – instead their status depends on seniority and promotion within a single firm. But some of the employees in these industries do have generalizable skills, such as toolmakers or electricians or engineers, which are transferrable among firms. If they do transfer among firms within an industry, we would expect that it would be more profitable both for them and for the new employer to keep them in the same skilled occupation. The intermediate classification of bureaucratic industries is based on relatively few movements (it is a smaller industry group, and as we saw most of its employees stay with the same employer), and may simply be an error. The data say that employees stay within the same industry but change occupations – perhaps being 'promoted' in the same line of work at the same time they change employers. If it is not an error, we have no explanation of it.

Labor market structure and the age pattern of earnings

In order to connect the traditional sociological concern with career development, and with the impact of moves between jobs or migration between places on social status, with the theory of the structuring

Table 6. *Indicators of industry-wide labor markets beyond the firm. Averages over nine five-year periods in three cohorts. Percentages.*

Industry type[c]	Industry continuity[a]	Occupational continuity within industry[b]
	(1)	(2)
Professional	37	53
Small skilled	35	52
Engineering based	24	45
Bureaucratic	38	34
Classical capitalist	23	40
Petty bourgeois services	26	40
Primary	24	35

[a]. Of those employed at the beginning of the five-year period in a given industry who changed employers during the five year period, percentage who never changed out of the same two-digit industry.
[b]. Of those who changed employers but stayed within the same industry, percentage who never changed occupation during the five-year period.
[c]. See text for classification of industries.

Table 7. *Relation between indicators of industry-wide labor markets.*

	Labor market relatively closed (Col. 1 over 30%)	Labor market relatively open (Col. 1 under 30%)
Occupations continuous (Col. 2 over 42%	Small skilled Professional	Engineering based
Occupations not continuous (Col. 2 under 42%)	Bureaucratic	Classical capitalist Petty bourgeois services Primary

of markets for human capital in different industries developed above, we need to relate industry and mobility to earnings. Table 8 gives the mean income in constant kroner (estimated real values of nominal income, inflated or deflated to 1968; the actual numbers are hundreds of 1968 kroner), by the seven industry groups developed above, for each of the three cohorts for five-year periods. That is, for example, the cohort born in 1921 was 25 years old in 1946. Some 290 of these men were at that time in primary industries, fishing, farming, and forestry, of which 215 provided income data. After inflation of the

Table 8 *Mean annual income in hundreds of 1968 kroner, by industries grouped by labor market type, for three cohorts at five-year intervals.*

Industry type	Cohort	Year of income					
		1946	1951	1956	1961	1966	1970
Primary	Old	111	157	186	194	198	210
	Middle			156	202	209	227
	Young					200	247
Classical	Old	131	190	207	235	251	275
capitalist	Middle			206	265	277	283
	Young					223	274
Small	Old	145	213	232	270	289	306
skilled	Middle			210	263	296	315
	Young					247	292
Engineering	Old	159	215	239	286	305	333
based	Middle			203	266	306	329
	Young					246	291
Petty	Old	160	232	270	330	341	358
bourgeois	Middle			196	268	317	365
services	Young					226	301
Professional	Old	139	223	322	361	381	387
	Middle			199	317	403	429
	Young					256	320
Bureaucratic	Old	147	200	253	300	343	400
	Middle			208	296	348	387
	Young					239	323

nominal 1946 income according to the value of the krone for 1946 to give constant values, the mean income of these farmers and fishermen was 11,000 1968 kroner. The 98 men in classical capitalist industries who provided usable income data for 1946 earned an average of 13,100 1968 kroner.[4]

[4] Estimated errors in Table 8 vary somewhat, depending on the number of people in a particular cohort and at a particular age, how many of these gave usable income data, and on the size of the variance of income within groups – this variance appears not to be homogeneous on casual inspection. The standard errors as estimated for each figure vary between 600 1968 kroner and 2,300 1968 kroner, with the great majority being under 1,500 1968 kroner. An average standard error figure then would be about 1,200 1968 kroner, or 12, as the numbers appear in Table 8. This means that the figures in Table 9 will have a standard error of about 1.414 times this, or 1,700 1968 kroner, and a difference between two such figures in Table 9 (which is what our real inferences are based on) would be about 1.414 times larger still, or about 2,400 1968 kroner. So individual differences in Table 9 which are larger than 48 are likely to be significant at the 5% level, and differences smaller than this should only be bases for inference if they fall into a regular pattern.

The substantive considerations above for this table lead to predictions about the pattern of reward for factors associated with age in the different industries. The theory bears most directly on the relative rewards for older as compared to younger men in an industry at a given time. Indirectly the pattern of reward for seniority and experience in a labor market at a given time, repeated over time, will generate a typical career pattern for people who are employed in an industry, so the secondary predictions have to do with industrial differences in earnings careers. Consequently we can extract from Table 8 two sorts of measures of the premium for age associated with different labor market structures in different industries, the cross sectional relation at a given time, and over time biographical development of the individuals in the industry.

Table 9 presents the 'age premium' in different industries. The first three columns compare mean income at various older ages with mean income at 25, on the general ground that most of the good that experience does for the labor market value of a person happens after he has settled down into a job, and after (as we saw above) the labor market behavior becomes less random.

The first column gives the two-decade age premium of 45-year-olds to 25-year-olds in 1966. That is, it is the difference between the old cohort and the young cohort in 1966. The second and third columns give the one-decade difference between people 25 and 35 years old, in 1956 and 1966, in each industry type.

The next group of three columns contrasts older men to men who are 30 (or 29, because the income year of 1971 was not finished at the time of the interview). The fourth column then compares the incomes of 49-year-olds to 29-year-olds in the labor market of 1970, while the last two contrast 40- (or 39)-year-olds with 30- (or 29)-year-olds.

From a statistical point of view, then, the argument above leads to the prediction that in Table 8 there will be a statistical interaction between industry and age. The differences between incomes at different ages in Table 9, then, ought to show a systematic pattern, with some industries giving large age premiums and other industries giving small ones. In general the premiums should be larger toward the bottom of the table than toward the top, since as we move toward the bottom our general idea is that labor markets depart more from the classical Ricardian labor market with homogeneous labor and no

Table 9 *Age premiums (differences) in hundreds of 1968 kroner for various age intervals in various years, by industry type. Computed from Table 8.*

Industry type	Age intervals starting at 25			Age intervals starting at 30 or 29		
	20-year premium 1966	10-year premium 1956	10-year premium 1966	20-year premium 1970	10-year premium 1961	10-year premium 1970
Primary	−2	30	9	−37	−8	−20
Classical capitalist	28	1	54	1	−30	9
Small skilled	42	22	49	14	7	23
Engineering based	59	36	60	42	20	38
Petty bourgeois services	125	74	91	57	62	64
Professional	125	123	147	67	44	99
Bureaucratic	104	47	109	77	4	64

career development. The main predictions have to do with the urban section of the table, so we will ignore the primary industries here.

We can summarize the results of Table 9 as follows:

1. In every case the age premium of older men as compared to men of 25 is larger than the age premium for the same number of years after 30 years old. This implies that the slope of the income curve between 25 and 30, is, in all the industry types, larger than the slope of the age curve of income after age 30.

2. In every case for the ten-year premiums, where the ages are the same, the premium for a later labor market is larger. That is, measured in constant kroner, the gaps between wages at different ages are becoming larger.

3. In every case but one (small-skilled in 1966 for the ten-year age gap), classical capitalist industries give less age premium than any other type of urban industry.

4. In every case but one (1961 Bureaucratic industries ten-year) the age premium in the industries classified as Small Skilled is less than that of all industry groups below it in the table, i.e. the more bureaucratized and professionalized industries have more age premium than do these craft industries.

5. In every case but one (same exception), the age premium in the engineering-based manufacturing and service industries is lower

than in the more middle class service industries below it in the table.

6. In every case but one (1961 Petty Bourgeois Services ten-year gap), the age premium in the professional industries is the largest or tied for largest in the column.

To put these conclusions more briefly, if we grouped petty bourgeois services and bureaucratic services together, and put them in the 5th rank behind professional industries, the departure of the age grading of income from that modeled in the classical economic theory (classical theory predicts trivially small age premium) would be in the rank listed. Or to put it another way, examining the cross sectional age distribution of incomes in order to indicate the premium on experience in a type of industry, we expect more systematic career development in small skilled industries than in classical capitalist industries, more in engineering-based manufacturing and services than in small skilled industries, more in petty bourgeois services or bureaucratic industries than in engineering industries, and more in professional industries than in any other type.

Table 10 confirms this inference in most of the details. Here we have treated age as a quasi-biographical fact, and traced incomes of the members of a cohort who are employed in an industry type at a given age. That is, in real income the 1921-born men employed in the classical capitalist industries gained 14,400 1968 kroner per year from 25 to 49 years old, while those in professional industries gained 24,800 1968 kroner. These are not all the same men at the two dates.

Part of this increase was, of course, a general increase in real wages – in classical industries 25-year-olds earned 13,100 constant kroner in 1946, 22,300 in 1966. But we will expect this gain to be larger in those same industries in which there is a cross sectional age premium. Except for some tendency for bureaucratic industry employees to show more age grading than professional industry employees, and some uncertainty about exact ranks in the right hand column (the age premium between 25 and 29 years old), the pattern here is also perfectly clear. The industries which we expect to be 'balkan' bounded areas in the labor market on the basis of theoretical analysis show the most fully developed departures from the classical assumption of homogeneous labor, by showing more age grading and more evidence of systematic career development.

Table 10 *Age premiums within cohorts over time, by industry type (calculated from Table 8). Differences in hundreds of 1968 kroner.*

Industry type	Premium 25 to 49 yr. 1921 cohort	Premium 25 to 39 yr. 1931 cohort	Premium 25 to 29 yr. 1941 cohort
Primary	99	71	47
Classical capitalist	144	77	51
Small skilled	161	105	45
Engineering	174	126	45
Petty bourgeois services	198	169	75
Professional	248	230	64
Bureaucratic	253	179	84

Types of mobility and labor market returns

The general conclusion from all of the foregoing is that all young and some older people are in an open labor market in which their previous experience does not do them much good, and which consequently works according to classical competitive processes. We expect in particular that people in such labor markets will generally get lower wages because the reserve army of the unemployed press upon their wage levels. The alternative view is that experience is a generally valuable trait of a worker, and that a worker will seek out whatever place his experience has the most value, so there will be no relation between types of labor market structure and wage rates. We have just explored whether *industries as structures* show a pattern of movement of wages which indicates that they have different labor market structures, and the evidence that they do is overwhelming.

The second question then is whether the differences between industries in the pattern of career development do indeed reflect the effects of different kinds of movements within those structures, or whether there is some other reason that industries have different wage structures. Generally speaking we can distinguish four broad kinds of movement that men can go through in a five-year period. The first is the kind of movement that indicates that they are in an open labor market in which not much of their previous experience would be valuable, labeled 'Mobility indicating open labor market processes' in Table 11. In our data this includes the following movement categories: (1) if a man ends the five-year period in his first job, then he has certainly not obtained that job by virtue of his experience, and is presumably competing openly (though of course with varying amounts of educational and other human capital resources developed elsewhere) with everyone else on the labor market, (2) if a man changed employer, industry, and occupation, it seems unlikely that he brought much experience of value to his new employer, and (3) if a man changed employer and occupation, but not industry, then it is possible that he brings some small experience and general orientation of some value to his new employer, but we would not expect the effect to be large. If people have this kind of open labor market movement, then whatever their ages we expect them to be in open competition with the lowest paid workers available in the market, so we would not expect much age premium, and we would expect that the wages would be generally lower than for men who are in more protected markets.

The second kind is the ambiguous category of men who have kept the same employer and the same occupation throughout the period. They may either be in an internal labor market in a firm, or in an open labor market but at their equilibrium wage.

The third general category of movement we can call 'professional and craft movement', because people keep the same occupation but move among employers. Presumably the most common cause of this phenomenon is that they are more valuable in the occupation in which they have experience than they are on the open labor market. We would expect people with such movement during a five-year period to obtain higher wages than would people who change employers with no indication that their experience will be valuable to a new employer, and we will expect there to be larger age premiums for people in such labor markets because their valuable experience will have had longer to accumulate, to make them valuable to their new employer, if they are older.

While we have shown above that most movements among industries do not preserve occupation, we have no particular reason to expect previous experience in the same occupation to be less valuable for a person who continues in that occupation with a new employer when the job shift involves an industry shift than not. That is, usually the

Table 11 *Unweighted average final yearly income at the end of five-year periods by the type of mobility during those periods, for periods up to and including 25–30, for all three cohorts, and for periods from 30–35 to 45–50 for the two older cohorts. Hundreds of 1968 kroner.*

Type of mobility	Time of mobility		
	Young (up to 30)[a]	Older (over 30)[b]	Difference
Mobility indicating open labor market processes			
Ends period still in first job	110	–	–
Changed employer, industry and occupation	221	269	48
Changed employer and occupation, but not industry	236	285	49
No movement			
Same employer and occupation	254	291	37
Professional and craft movement			
Changed employer and industry, same occupation	269	326	57
Changed employer, same industry and occupation	216	313	97
Movements in internal labor markets in firms			
Same employer, same occupation, but place of work changed	262	339	77
Same employer, different occupation	262	333	71
Mean of all but first job	*246*	*308*	*62*
Standard deviation of income in all but first job	*21*	*27*	

[a]. This means the incomes were received at age 25 and age 30, or 29 for the young cohort in 1970, two incomes for each cohort enter into the analysis if there were enough cases.
[b]. This means the incomes were received at ages 35 and older. There will ordinarily be six annual incomes averaged, two for the 1931 cohort and four for that of 1921.

reason an employer wants to hire a man who had the same occupation with his previous employer is that the new employer is in the same business. But when, for example, a builder of oil refinery installations hires a welder who previously worked in shipbuilding, the welder's previous experience would be expected to be as valuable as if it had been in oil refinery building. Consequently we will not expect there to be much difference in either the level of wages, nor in the wage premium for age, depending on whether the shift was across industry lines, provided the shift does not involve a change in occupation.

Finally, two kinds of movement indicate that the man is involved in an internal labor market in his firm or establishment. If a man keeps the same employer and occupation, but is moved from one place to another, this indicates that the post in the new place has some characteristics which make (some) present employees more valuable for it than are people on the local labor market in the new place. Thus we expect such men to be more highly rewarded, and to have a larger age premium, than are men who are closer to the open labor market. Similarly we expect most movements that involve staying with the same employer but changing occupation indicate promotion, hence involvement in an internal labor market in which within-firm experience makes a person more valuable than a person on the open labor market. So it too should have larger returns and a larger age premium.

The general pattern of Table 11, which gives mean annual income at the end of five-year periods by types of movement experienced in the previous five years, divided by the ages of the movement (and so by the ages of the incomes), supports this analysis. In general the incomes for men who have had the kinds of movements indicating that they have worked in either professional and craft labor markets or internal labor markets, are higher than the wages of those whose movements indicate an open labor market situation (the bottom half of the table shows higher incomes than the first group in the Table), and also higher than the ambiguous case in which probably some people are in internal labor markets, and some in open labor markets (same employer and occupation). Further, the difference between younger and older workers is consistently higher in the bottom half of the table than in the top half, indicating that the age premium is larger when people have the kinds of movements indicating that they are in protected markets.[5]

This implies that the differences among young men by types of movement ought to be smaller than they are for older men, i.e. that

[5] Estimated standard errors in Table 11 vary for the same reasons specified in the note about Tables 8 and 9, and in addition because the number of five-year periods averaged to get each number varies. Since it is the gross pattern that is of interest, and since that is clearly non-random, I have not calculated estimates of these errors. Note that using unweighted averages in this table is slightly inefficient, so the pattern comes through clearly even in the face of some (slight) extra noise.

the *between group variance* in Table 11 ought to be larger for older men than for younger men. At the bottom of each column I have simply computed the standard deviation of the entries in the columns, i.e. the sum of squared differences from the column mean of *the entries* in the columns, omitting the first job, divided by $(n-1)$ or six entries. These figures are not, then, standard deviations of income at different ages, but a reflection of between group variances in the respective columns. As predicted this measure is larger at later ages.

Conclusions

The fundamental premise of this paper is that the status attainment literature has been crucially crippled by not noticing that it is employers who pass out good jobs. Consequently the theory of status attainment must be a theory of what employers find valuable, and only secondarily a theory of which individual workers get the characteristics that employers find valuable. Consequently, the first part of a theory of social mobility should be a theory of what employers want, and what kind of structural constraints there are in the labor market that make it harder or easier for them to get it. In particular, the presence of monopoly or 'protection' in the commodity and labor markets affects the degree to which a firm or an industry can develop a status system in which the wages of some people are substantially above the wage for which the reserve army of the unemployed would be willing to work.

Our first task was to classify industries in Norway by rough categories of the type of labor market structures they had. We distinguished: (1) primary industries with large recruitment through families and declining total employment, (2) classical capitalist industries with low skill requirements which ought to have classical Ricardian or Marxian labor markets, (3) industries with small competitive firms but skilled workers in building, metal wares, and repair, (4) engineering based manufacturing and services which combine a professionalized bureaucratic administration with extensive use of skilled workers, with firms which generally operate in monopolistic or oligopolistic markets, (5) petty bourgeois services of retail and wholesale trade and small-scale services to a general public with a petty bourgeois administration recruited partly by family lines, and a general low-skill service staff on the open labor market at the bottom, (6) professional industries delivering highly skilled services to the general public or the business community, and (7) classical bureaucratic structures in public administration and finance.

Part of the general task of this paper was to show that this classification of industries by their expected labor market structure did in fact differentiate labor markets that operated differently. This had two major parts: to show that the patterns of types of mobility within careers were significantly different in different industries, and to show that this resulted in a different pattern of income distribution by age and type of mobility in different industries.

There are a great many details in a great many tables that bear on this question, but the overall result is clear. There are very large variations in the amounts of different kinds of mobility in different industries, which agree in very large measure with the expectations that guided us in constructing the classification. Further, there are differences in the wage structure of industries and the kinds of career development of incomes by age which correspond very closely to the theory that premiums above the competitive wage develop in the kinds of structures in the labor market which the theory of balkanized labor markets in different industries would predict. Unprotected workers do not get nearly as large age premiums for their experience, and wages above the Ricardian competitive level occur among experienced workers in those kinds of labor markets protected by the kinds of barriers we outlined in our classification of industries.

Finally, this connection of labor market structures to labor market outcomes for income extends to the details of the movements within the labor market, for people who have movements in the labor market of the kind that show they are probably in a given kind of protected structure have both higher wages and more age premiums, than do men having had kinds of movement indicating that they are probably on the open competitive labor market.

We have not related these results to the traditional concerns in the mobility literature, which relate human capital accumulated before entry into the labor market to final career attainment. The part of the career attainment model we have been concentrating on is that part between the end of education and the peak of the career, in which the traditional path models show four main features: (1) men's status increases with age, as do its separate components of prestige, income, and authority within the enterprise, (2) the variance of attainments of men increase with age, again as measured by prestige, income, or formal authority, (3) the correlation between attainments at one age and attainments at an age five or ten years later increases with age, and (4) the correlations with social origin variables of father's prestige and own education (especially the latter) increase with age.

All these four traditional results (the first and third were in the sources for the original Duncan paper on path analysis, 1966 – the other two are documented for these data by Hernes & Knudsen, p. 55, for occupational status, and by Rogoff Ramsøy, pp. 127–9, also for occupational status; the variance of income rises to about 40 years in these data, then levels out) indicate that status and income are coming into equilibrium with total human capital endowment, presumably by movements within the labor market in which people move closer to their equilibrium market value more often than they move away from it. But what that has to indicate is that somebody is evaluating the value of these men in order to offer them an income nearer the equilibrium. Consequently the structuring of that movement and of that evaluation is crucial for the last 40 years of the status attainment model. It is not very relevant to the first 20 to 25 years of that model, in which teachers rather than employers do the evaluation. This paper then is mainly about that last two thirds of the status attainment model.

What the overall pattern of the results shows is that there is not one such process of equilibration, but at least seven markedly different ones in different industries. Further, those different labor market structures manifest themselves in different kinds of career movements within the career of individual men, and those career movements have different effects on the outcome of the final status attainment. Promotions within an internal labor market in a firm *do not* result in the same status attainment effects as movements from one industry to another, changing occupations in the move. That is, the overall equilibrating process works concretely by different subprocesses, and those different subprocesses have different effects in how they move a man toward equilibrium.

So we can take the central premise of this paper as both demonstrated, and demonstrated to be important to status attainment models: men do not determine their own status and labor market value – employers do. Consequently if one wants to understand how status resources on entry into labor markets affect attainments, one must study how employers organize themselves to evaluate workers and relate to labor markets. The reason this is productive of new insights is that different employers in different industries organize themselves differently and relate to labor markets differently, and that makes the careers of the people they are deciding about develop differently.

7. The sociology of ethnic and national loyalties

By national or ethnic loyalty we mean the identification by an individual of his or her interests with the interest of a nation or ethnic group. A person is loyal if he or she is willing to sacrifice some personal interests for the sake of group interests. This often is caused by a persons's belief that the group interests are truly his or her personal interests rather than by any special altruism. Thus nationalism is in part a *belief system* which asserts that one's own interests are promoted by the promotion of the group and are damaged by damage to the group.

But often, perhaps usually, there is really no cognitive separation between individual and group interests, so 'belief system' is too flattering a word. 'Of course we have to resist invasion' – this leaves the 'we' unanalyzed, a part of the natural order of things, a natural subject of the verb 'have to.' The analogies that naturally occur to people defending the national draft against pacifists are family analogies: 'Wouldn't you kill a man to defend your mother from being raped?' The assumption that the 'we' of a nation is like the 'we' of a family is implicit in this argument. What we want to do here is to develop a theory of the social conditions under which such unanalyzed 'we' concepts come to be the natural subject in sentences about political values and policies.

Likewise it seems perfectly natural to a nationalist that my income and your income should be added together to make up the National Income and that you and I should both praise the politican who increases the sum of our incomes. It is not that we *believe* that if you are better off and I am worse off this is a good thing; instead the sum itself has an unanalyzed magic as a measure of a good thing.

Further, many of the psychological phenomena of nationalism have very little cognitive content at all. They consist of direct sentimental ties to the nation or ethnic group and to its symbols, possessions, prestige, and history. A massacre of comembers of the group hurts more than a massacre of other strangers, even though one had no personal ties with those killed. Trampling the flag or writing an unflattering history of a national or ethnic hero makes a loyal person angry. That is, national or ethnic loyalty consists in large measure of an unreflective tendency to take joy in the successes of a group and sorrow in its failures and to devote oneself to the promotion and defense of the group as if one was promoting and defending one's own integrity and honor.

Clearly ethnic groups and nations vary in the degree to which they have such loyalty among their constituencies. And different potential constituents of an ethnic or national group will have different degrees of loyalty. Thus there are two separate problems for explanation: the variation among groups in the average level of national and ethnic loyalty and the variation among individuals or subgroups in their degree of loyalty. Below we will offer a theory of these variations in terms of the degree to which a person's social identity depends on the group.

But so far we have not touched on the use of national and ethnic hatreds in politics. Under what conditions are governmental policies justified (or attacked) in terms of national or ethnic solidarity and loyalty? There surely is a sense in which the Nazi regime was more nationalistic than the socialist regime of the Weimar Republic that preceded it. The American Legion's patriotism is different from the loyalty of the American Civil Liberties Union to the Constitution and in some sense is more nationalistic. Black Power movements that involve distrust of any whites in positions of power over blacks are more nationalistic than Civil Rights movements that aim to make powerful whites behave decently. The people who wanted to win in Vietnam were more nationalistic in some sense than those who wanted to get out, though the question of what was 'in the national interest' was open (in fact, it was what the debate was mainly about).

What all these various nationalistic movements have in common is a wish to suppress internal divisions within the nation and to define people outside the group as untrustworthy as allies and implacably evil as enemies.

The problem of creating a theory of nationalism, then, is that it is composed of diametrically opposed forces, which have opposite explanations. It is on the one hand a generous spirit of identification with the sufferings of a group, a love of compatriots. As such it has the causes of generosity and solidarity as its causes. But it is on the other hand a spirit of distrust of the potential treason of any opposition within the group and a hatred of strangers. As such it has the cause of hatred and suspicion as its causes. Thus an explanation of why a society *can* wage war, can call on its young men to sacrifice their lives and its workers to sacrifice real wages and consumption so that war material can be supplied, is somewhat the opposite of the explanation of why a society *wants* to wage war or why some people call so exquisitely loud for the suppression of trade unions and strikes so that we can unite against the enemy.

We need a theory with two parts: one of them an explanation of the solidarity of groups, the other an explanation of why solidarity goes sour. We need to understand how a person mixes his or her own identity with the fate of a group and why he or she chooses to defend that identity by hating outsiders and suspecting insiders. It is the great tragedy of social life that every extension of solidarity, from family to village, village to nation, presents also the opportunity of organizing hatred on a larger scale. The first half of this paper will be directed to the explanation of variations in solidarity; the second half to variations in hatred.

The normative system and identity

By a person's 'identity' we mean the set of social statuses in which one expects to pursue one's purposes, gratify one's lusts, solve one's problems, find fellowship and support.[1] An identity then is an organization of one's social life in the future, in the light of one's motives and future motives, in relation to one's social opportunities. An identity is solid when one has an expectation that he or she can marry, make a living, keep out of jail, make friends, have and educate children, by doing the sorts of things that he or she now knows how to do. A firm sense of identity then is an accrued confidence in the social

---

[1] The ideas here are derived from some combination of Erikson (1959) and Grodzins (1956).

validity of one's problem-solving capacities. It consists concretely in the expectation that one's competence will allow him or her to get a good job, find a spouse to love and be loved by, throw darts or cook or play poker well enough to be accepted as one of the crowd, and so on.

When one's identity is attacked, as it is by unemployment, retirement and loss of capacity with old age, exile, a crippling injury or brain damage, a person's fate passes psychologically out of his or her hands. The things he or she has learned how to do are no longer worth anything. Such a person can no longer rely on being loved and appreciated for being the kind of person he or she has learned how to be. The usual symptoms of severe identity crises are apathy, free-floating rage, and availability for new identities that would have been uncivilized by a person's old standards.[2]

In order to understand what social conditions might produce a solid identity, we have to analyze under what conditions the culture that a person learns will actually solve his or her life problems. A culture, in the famous definition, is a 'design for living.' But like architectural designs, cultural designs sometimes work and sometimes do not. From the point of view of identity formation, a culture is integrated if the design for solving life problems taught by a culture does in fact solve those problems. Broadly speaking our hypothesis is that if an ethnic group or nation teaches a person techniques for making a living, defending his or her rights, marrying and raising children, *and can make those techniques work for him or her*, then there will be a direct tie between a person's identity and the group. This direct tie is where the energy of ethnic and national loyalty comes from. An attack on such a group is an attack on a person's capacity to solve the problems of his or her life, and so it releases great patriotic energies. The promotion of such a group is, in a sense, an expansion of an individual.

Ecological range and citizenship

We can define a person's *ecological range* as the set of social relations within which most of his or her problems arise and have their solutions. In a subsistence farming village in the jungles of southern

---

[2] The analysis of the apathy of Sioux Indians by Erikson (1950, pp. 114–65) is the classic source. For unemployment see Jahoda *et al.* (1933); for the effects of total institutions with total unpredictability of life and more or less complete identity destruction, see

Mexico, in which the people speak an indigenous language, most problems arise and are settled (if at all) in the village itself. As the inhabitants go out for wage labor, their wages are settled in a national labor market, exploitation is controlled by national political movements and laws, education is provided by a national school authority, and so forth. The ecological range of a typical person in such a modernized village is the nation. The 'brain drain' from poorer countries to the United States indicates that some professional people's ecological range is worldwide. A civil servant or a military officer almost invariably has a national ecological range. One of the main causes of maimed identities in developing countries is that the solutions to life problems learned for an ecological range of village level must be applied to cope with problems whose solution is only possible with national institutions.

A person's 'citizenship' in the normative system of a group may be defined as the proportion of his or her life problems which is solved according to the normative system. The question we ask is: of all the institutional services a person gets, how many are provided within the group?

From the point of view of the group, this is a question of 'institutional completeness.'[3] Groups that provide within themselves the institutions by which people make a living, defend their property, marry, school their children, and retire make members highly dependent on the group. If in addition people within the group have a good deal of influence through representative institutions on how the problem-solving organizations are set up, then their fate in life depends in great measure on their activity within the group. Thus groups that are highly institutionally complete will tend to have people solving the problems of their lives within the group.

The same variable appears for individual attachment as for group

Bettelheim (1943). For various kinds of imperfect or maimed identities see Goffman (1963).

[3] This concept is used by Breton (1964). A very similar conception, in completely different language, is developed by Marshall (1950) in talking about different types of citizenship. If a government provides civil legal institutions and 'equality before the law' it is less institutionally complete than one that also provides political and group representation institutions but more complete than one that provides no access to the king's courts. When governments provide for various life crisis (old age, sickness, child support, and schooling) they are still more institutionally complete. Marshall calls these different institutional services types of citizenship rights.

attachment. If a person's problems typically require that he or she go beyond a group to work them out, then the person is dependent on the larger setting for the normative regulation of his or her central life concerns. If a person's problems typically can be resolved in the village by influence on neighbors, then he or she need take no interest in larger national institutions. If a person is downtrodden and exploited in a group, he or she cannot solve any problems by means of influence on group institutions. That is, one's citizenship in a group is a product of how much one is *subject to* the group, multiplied by how much one is *influential in* the group. If one is highly subject to a group, then the more influential one is, the more one can control his or her fate by group activity. If one is influential in a group *but* has no interest in group arrangements because he or she acts on a larger stage, then one fails to be incorporated in the group.

Clearly the average ecological range of a national society will determine to what extent people are dependent on national institutions. In 'traditional' societies only civil servants, merchants, military men, and a few others have an ecological range as large as the nation, and often many of them have an international range. For instance in colonial societies a large proportion of the production that is shipped out of any given local area is shipped abroad. In that case the merchants depend on international, 'imperial' institutions rather than on national institutions. The higher the rate of interchange of people, goods, and communications among the subparts of a national society, the more an individual's problems will typically be solved only in national institutions (Kunkel, 1961; Deutsch, 1953).

Further an individual's identity will depend more on a group the more his or her individual ecological range corresponds to the range regulated by group institutions. Retail traders will tend to have more local identities than wholesalers, domestic wholesalers more national identities than cosmopolitan importers and exporters, importers and exporters more national identities than shipping lines flying flags of convenience; tankers registered in Liberia or Panama are not noted for Liberian or Panamanian nationalism. That is, a person's social rôle and the normatively regulated social solutions to a person's life problems will tend to be created by a set of institutions whose own range corresponds to his or her own. Hence a person's identity will tend, given reasonably benign social institutions, to correspond to his or her ecological range. An economy like that of the United States, which exports and imports about a fourteenth of its national income each year, will tend to give people more national economic identities than an economy like Scandinavia or the Low Countries which have a much higher ratio of foreign trade to national income, because a person's daily economic life in the Low Countries depends on the world trade situation more than on national regulation of economic life.

In general we would expect that when citizens of imperial and international countries (e.g., Britain or the United States) emigrate, they will probably be incorporated into foreign societies *less* than immigrants whose national loyalties are not reinforced by international institutions. For instance, we would expect the English community in Argentina to have assimilated into Argentine society less than the Italian or Chilean immigrant streams, because an Englishman's economic and political rôle *in Argentina* depended on his relationships to metropolitan economic and political institutions.

If an ethnic group such as the French Canadians is large and geographically segregated, has its own local government institutions (especially schools) and a well-developed religious and social welfare organization, then it is likely to get the loyalty of most of its members. But if an individual French Canadian is isolated in Saskatchewan, is well served by local governmental and social welfare institutions, comfortable in a Catholic Church dominated by immigrants from Eastern Europe, and has children progressing well in an English-language school, then he or she as an individual may have very little French Canadian loyalty. If on the contrary he or she is a professional, French-speaking intellectual, for instance a broadcast announcer or a French-speaking Catholic theologian, then his or her ecological range in Canada will be exactly the French cultural group.

Now our problem is to formulate these complex interdependencies among the ecological structure, the institutional structure, and people's loyalties in a sufficiently clean form so that we can work with them. What we are trying to explain first is the embedding of people's political conflicts and the formulation of their planning problems in a set of general national or ethnic loyalties. That is, the significance of loyalty for the political process is that it brings to bear on particular political conflicts and particular governmental administrative problems those considerations of other values and of the general health of the social system which limit the conflict. Conversely, if a conflict of interest occurs between different national or ethnic groups and those groups have high degrees of internal loyalty, then each of the conflicting parties can call on the loyalties of the nation or ethnic group as a whole to support its particular interests. Roughly speaking, then, loyalty explains why there is social peace within groups and great risks of war among groups. The empirical proposition here is that generalized or diffuse loyalty of a group depends on that group being in fact the locus of normative solutions to life problems, resulting in the group being a central point in the organization of people's personal identities, in their confidence that their competencies and social rights will in fact solve those life problems.

This proposition can be elaborated by defining a set of related concepts: 'ecological range,' 'institutional completeness,' and 'citizenship.' The definitions of these concepts rather go around in circles, because each specifies an aspect of the relation between the problems a person has in his or her life and the problems solved by the institutions of a group. (1) The degree to which a person is subject to a group depends on (a) the degree to which the group has institutions for solving the problems of given kind (the degree of institutional completeness of the group), times (b) the degree to which the person has those problems. (2) A group's institutional completeness for a given set of people (a above) will depend on (c) the aggregate ecological range of the set of people, times (d) the ecological range of the institutions of the group itself, times (e) the number of areas of life for which the group has institutions. (3) The degree to which a person can control his or her own fate through action within the group (a person's citizenship in the group) depends on (a) the degree to which the person is subject to the group (1 above), times (g) the degree of influence or representation he or she has in the group's government. The central hypothesis restated is that a person's loyalty to a group depends on the degree to which the person can control his or her own fate through action in the group, that is, his or her citizenship in the group (3 above).

Propositions on national loyalty

From this general line of argument we can derive the following propositions about the degree to which a person's identity will be invested in an ethnic or national group, the degree to which a person is likely to sacrifice his or her individual interests (e.g., interest in staying alive) for group interests (e.g., national defense), the degree to which a person conceives of his or her own and the group's interest to be identical so that when pursuing the national defense he or she is pursuing the defense of an unanalyzed 'we,' the degree to which a person's particular conflicts within the group will be limited by considerations of the general value of the institutional life of the group as a whole.

1.   For an ethnic or national group, the *average* level of loyalty will rise as the group becomes more institutionally complete. More specifically: (a) the more functions that are performed by group organizations, the more loyal its members; (b) the greater the coverage or content of the rights of citizenship in a group and the more a person has a *right* to the institutional services provided by the group, the more loyal the group's members (this may be roughly estimated by the proportion of a country's gross national product spent by the government on social and educational services); (c) the more representative a group's government, the more loyal its members, because then the institutions of the group are likely in fact to solve the members' problems; (d) the more segregated territorially a group is, the more loyal its members, because many institutions that solve people's problems are, more or less necessarily, geographically organized.

2.   The greater the proportion of members of an ethnic or national group who have an ecological range identical to the boundaries of the group, the greater will be the average level of loyalty of the group, and hence: (a) the greater the internal development of markets for labor and goods and the less the dependence on local subsistence economy, the greater the national loyalty; (b) the less the international market for labor and goods, the greater the national loyalty; (c) the larger the employment by institutions that themselves have a national ecological range (e.g., the civil service or national army), the greater the national loyalty.

3.   The more an *individual's* life problems have their solutions within an ethnic or national group, by use of group institutions, the greater the individual level of loyalty, and hence: (a) the more the defense of an individual's property, job rights, or livelihood depends on a national legal or trade union system, the greater his or her loyalty; (b)

the more that the success or failure of an individual's employing organization is defined in national terms (e.g., this is very high for military men), the greater his or her loyalty; (c) the more the individual's developed needs (e.g., religious preferences) are the same as the needs developed by his or her conationals (and served by national institutions), the greater his or her loyalty; (d) the more the individual's ecological range is extended above the local community and kin relations to dependence on ethnic or national institutions (e.g., the more the individual migrates to find work), the greater his or her national loyalty; (e) the more solid an individual's enfranchisement in the group, that is, the greater the individual's rights and the less exploitation there is of that individual, the greater his or her loyalty.

'Racism' and ethnic loyalty

In many societies some large group of families and their descendants are given a distinct social and legal status because they are thought to belong to a distinct 'people.' Such a 'people' is most often created by forced migration (e.g., Negroes in the United States), by conquest (e.g., Catholic Irishmen in Ireland), or by voluntary migration of a group with a distinctive set of institutions (e.g., Jews or Gipsies in Eastern Europe). Very often the distinctive social position of these families is explained ideologically by a theory of genetic differences among the peoples involved, that is, by a 'racist' ideology. For the sake of convenience and evocativeness, we will call the general phenomenon of differential status that is determined by communal attachment by the name of one of its most common ideological defenses, 'racism,' but the analysis is supposed to apply to all communally organized status systems.

Racist systems may be classified by the proportion of the areas of life of the people of subordinate status which is administered by ethnic criteria. In the extreme of *apartheid* systems, the economy, the civil courts, rights of travel, political citizenship, as well as residence, schooling, marriage, and sociability are all administered with ethnic criteria dominant. In the American North, the civil courts, the voting booths, and large parts of the economy are administered on formally nonracial grounds, while residence, schooling, marriage, religion, and large parts of recreational life are highly racist for blacks. Jews in most

American cities have moved from the present position of blacks (Jews seem to me to have been about at the same state as black people now around 1920) to a position of exclusion only from marriage and religious institutions of the gentiles (and those exclusions are not perfectly tight).

The point of this definition of racism is that in addition to depending on his or her group's internal institutions, a person may be more or less dependent on the jural status of his or her group in a societywide normative system. That is, regardless of the institutional development of the individual's own group, if a dominant group has developed special ethnic institutions and imposed them on him or her, so that the individual's life problems must be solved in relation to institutions informed by ethnic criteria, then the jural status of the ethnic group penetrates his or her identity. A person cannot solve the problems of his or her life without reference to his or her ethnic identity unless other people treat the person (with respect to those problems) without reference to ethnic identity. The greater the degree of racism in a society, the greater the extent to which we will expect the minority groups to have intense ethnic loyalties. For example, to a considerable extent putting Japanese in concentration camps during World War II created the Japanese ethnic group in the United States (Grodzins, 1956).

There should be a greater effect of racism on the ethnic loyalty of minorities than of majorities, and this should apply whether the minority is subordinate, as the Negroes and Jews in the United States, or superordinate, as the whites in colonial Rhodesia or South Africa. The reason is that a minority member will be distinguished by race from the person he or she is dealing in many more relations in daily life than will a majority member. If there are, say, a hundred thousand interracial contacts per day in an area, that hundred thousand will be a much larger proportion of the contacts of a minority of a hundred thousand (one per person per day) than of a majority of a million (one contact per person every ten days).

The cognitive construction of citizenship

The analysis above has been almost entirely an 'objective' analysis, in the sense that it assumes that if people depend on a nation they will see that they do depend on it and direct their attention to the national scene. Or we assume that if the true reason people are poor is racial discrimination, they will see it. I believe that in fact groups of people are, in the long run, statistically right about such questions. But at any given time there will be differences in the degree of correspondence between the objective and the ideological situations.

For the average person, institutional problems take the form of difficulties in his or her interaction with particular other people in particular settings. A worker's problem is not, in the first instance, that the wage rate in his or her occupation is too low – it is that the employer will not pay a fair wage. To manipulate the employer by changing the structure and government of the national labor market is not the most obvious way to get more money. As Lenin taught us to formulate the problem, the masses, by themselves, can reach only the level of trade-union consciousness.

Changes in the ecological range of people's problems tend to be perceived in the first instance by intellectuals and publicists, secondly by the leadership of concrete groups, and lastly by the membership of those groups themselves. Thus we find broadly speaking that early in the course of national development, intellectuals are more nationalistic than the population.[4] Later on in national development, intellectuals tend to be more internationalist than others. The same generalizations apply, though in lesser degree, to group leaders as compared with members.

The social causes of group hatred

By outgroup hatred I mean the infusion in a group on which one's identity depends (as analyzed above) of an ideology that says (a) that the only acceptable relation of the ingroup to the outgroup is unconditional surrender or extinction and (b) that those in the ingroup who have attachments to or tolerance of the outgroup are traitors and should be treated as enemies. This is a caricature (commonly called an 'ideal type') of aggressive nationalism but identifies the core of the concept. Any sort of solidarity can have such outgroup hatred attached to it. It produces the 'liquidation of the *kulaks* as a class' in the Soviet Union in the 1930s as well as 'the final solution of the Jewish question' in German-ruled Europe in the 1940s. Class, ethnic, relig-

---

[4] For two monographs using extremely divergent methods but coming to the same conclusion on this point, cf. Kohn (1951) and Lerner (1958, pp. 221–32).

ious, or familial solidarities as well as more implicit solidarities of 'normal' people against 'deviants' (witches, lunatics, juvenile delinquents) can produce patterns of group hatred, Our problem is to outline the social sources of such hatreds.

The classic case of nationalism as outgroup hatred is Nazism. What we need then is a sociology of Nazism. The combination of the Nazi movement of outgroup aggression and internal suppression of dissent as treason is characteristically authoritarian. But the same pattern can be seen in, for example, some police-oriented movements to stomp out juvenile delinquency; the delinquents are seen as embodiments of the satanic principle rather than as human beings, and judges or criminologists who want to 'mollycoddle' them (treat them as people) are seen as subversive of the normative order. This similarity suggests that a common orientation to the nature of the normative order is involved. The orientation is that (1) the privileges of those now advantaged by the normative order are especially valuable or sacred – the *conservative* principle, (2) the advantages of that normative order should be reserved for those now protected by it – the *exclusiveness* principle, (3) the normative order is under attack by evil forces outside and also within the group – the principle of *satanism*, (4) normative judgements are easy to make and involve simple and fundamental values – the *fundamentalism* principle.

We argue then that any normative order is subject to movements showing conservatism, exclusiveness, satanism, and fundamentalism. When the normative order that primarily organizes the institutional life of groups is embedded in a nation-state, the form that such fundamentalist movements takes is nationalism. That is, part of the explanation of extremist nationalism is the same as the explanation of the extension of citizenship discussed above. It is exactly because the principles of solidarity, justice, and the good life are now embedded in nation-states that fundamentalism now so often takes a Nazi style rather than, as formerly, a witch-burning style.

The embedding of fundamentalism in other ideologies

The conservatism of the psychology of fundamentalist movements of all kinds can be revolutionary. This is of course true of all conservative ideologies; there have probably been more conservative revolutions than radical ones. But it is peculiarly true of fundamentalist movements that all sorts of sophisticated established systems of administration and privilege can come under attack. There were strong fundamentalist elements in the Reformation, which was certainly revolutionary toward established church organization. Fundamentalist patriotism often attacks such sophisticated systems of privilege as universities or supreme courts. There is in fact a certain inherent affinity between fundamentalism and populism. If all the complexities of the normative order are merely veils to hide the simple truth, the 'people,' with the simple truth, are more to be trusted than the élite with their pettifoggery. One of the complexities of the Roman Church, for example, was to treat sin realistically, to forgive heresy on renunciation of heresy, to consider infidels as creatures created in the image of God. That is, a simpleminded statement that Christians were more worthy than agents of the devil, a common theme in fundamentalist parts of the Reformation, is simultaneously a conservative defense of the privileged position of Christians and a radical critique of the 'corrupt' élite of the Church.

But the problem of isolating national and ethnic hatred for a unified explanation is more complex still. For fundamentalist ideals and movements can be identified with the most various conceptions of the nature of the normative order. Consider for example the following varieties of racist ideology. By racist ideology I mean a fundamentalist ideology in which the privileges to be preserved are the privileges of an ethnic group, the principle of exclusion from the normative order has racial content, the satanic principle is applied to mean corruption by another race, and the simpleminded solution to normative questions is to apply hostility to racial groups. This ideology is not to be confused with institutional racism described above, though of course they are generally linked in practice.

Racism in an attack on the lumpenproletariat
All modern societies have a subpopulation that has failed to make a satisfactory connection with the world of work. Some people in the subpopulation have spoiled identities because they have prison records. Some cannot perform the required activities of work rôles because of illness, alcoholism, drug addiction, or mental incapacity. Some cannot form the will to perform work rôles because they lack

faith that the system will reward them, because they do not want those rewards, or because they lack faith in their own capacities. Some have a run of bad luck – getting jobs for which they were not qualified, getting laid off because they were hired last in a declining industry. Some leave spouses with whom they have quarrelled for years. These people form the lumpenproletariat, the ragged casual laborers, petty criminals, drunks, and cast-offs of urban society.

Such people offend the principles of bourgeois society. They are the kind of people that respectable workers fear their sons-in-law will turn out to be. Respectable middle-class people use them as a symbol to explain why the poor must always remain poor – they obviously lack the bourgeois virtues of thrift, hard work, and keeping out of prison. By serving as a counterexample, they reinforce the self-satisfied complacency of respectable people. (Conversely, of course, they are also a symbol of romantic rebellion; serving for a period as a member of the lumpenproletariat is almost a qualification for the career of a radical writer.) The point is not that the lumpenproletariat is not really what respectable people think it is, although many careful studies by novelists and a few careful studies by social scientists show that it is mostly not – that in fact the values of the lumpenproletariat are similar to the values of the respectable middle class.[5] Rather we want to identify the rejection of the lumpenproletariat as a general ideology held by the hard-working proletariat and the bourgeoisie.

This rejection of the lumpenproletariat often takes a racist form in which, without much reflection or evidence, the characteristics of the lumpenproletariat are attributed to a low-status ethnic group, such as Negroes in the United States. All the attributes of fundamentalism can be associated with racism of an antilumpenproletarian variety. For example a typical ideology would hold that (1) the respectability of neighborhoods where whites now live ought to be preserved against black-lumpenproletarian contamination (conservatism); (2) the rights of respectable people should not be extended to respectable black people (exclusivism); (3) various satanic forces (communists, 'block-busters' (speculators who specialise in ethnic transition areas, exploit-

---

[5] I especially like Orwell (1933) and Hamsun (1920). Studies by Lewis are perhaps more prolix than realistic. See for example 1964 and 1965. Whyte (1961) does one of the best portrayals of the variety of people and conditions. A very careful statistical study that shows that the values of the young potential lumpenproletariat are not very different from those of other people is by Gordon *et al.* (1963).

ing fear) and real estate speculators, outside agitators), including both misled whites and blacks, are trying to undermine the integrity of neighborhoods by integration (satanism); and (4) one need not answer the question of where a growing population of blacks *should* live – it is enough to follow the simple principle that they should not invade white neighborhoods (fundamentalism). Such fundamentalist racism, with the basic function of praising respectability in a fundamentalist way, can also have international political repercussions, as when it informs the American immigration laws (Higham, 1965).

Populist racism

Often the group that relates a traditional feudal land tenure system to the institutions of international capitalism is an urban commercial ethnic group. Such a group seems, to residents of the societies, to have the functions both of shoring up the worst features of the old régime by bringing money to landlords, collecting their rents, and so on and introducing the worst features of the new capitalist régime: usury, unsteady prices, the use of the law rather than the local norms of justice in commercial dealings, treatment of customers and laborers as strangers, the principle of *caveat emptor*, and so on. The Jews in Eastern Europe, the Chinese in Southeast Asia, the Indians in Kenya and Uganda are examples of urban commercial groups that function to create these combined conservatizing and subversive effects.

The response to this structural situation by the peasantry subject to it and often by the landlords and bureaucrats (colonial or native) disturbed by capitalistic invasions into the old régime is 'anti-Semitism.' The anti-Semitism of Eastern Europe was often associated with populist ideas. The 'social racism' of the Nazis, in which the evils of credit and money and cosmpolitan contamination of the nation were identified with Jews, had a great appeal in Poland. Similar populist racism is characteristic of the response to the Chinese in Southeast Asia or to the Indians in Kenya and Uganda.[6]

[6] Much of the anti-Semitism of Eastern Europe was thoroughly reactionary, characterized by feudal romanticism, clericalism, and bureaucratic conservatism. The anti-Indian sentiment in Kenya and Uganda was undoubtedly shared by colonial English administrators and commercial agents. Populist movements often call upon the same themes of a golden age corrupted by evil modern forces as do reactionary movements, and hence reject the same bearers of modern commercial impersonality. Commercial impersonality invades personal dignity. Personal dignity means, to a colonial administrator or a feudal lord, the personal subjection of others to him –

Populist racism therefore claims to restore the normative order, reclaim virtues of the old régime, and take from the ethnically alien exploiters their illgotten gains. Its fundamentalist forms lead to pogroms, concentration camps, and the creation of 'displaced persons' deprived by popular national revolutions of their status in the societies in which they were born, with no place else to go. Such displaced persons can sometimes be recognized by their British passports, which once allowed people to come to Britain.

Racism as a justification of exploitation

In situations in which plantation labor is imported, in colonial or semicolonial circumstances, or the native population of a conquered territory is put to work, the workers are usually deprived of all political rights, all access to coercive power. This means on the one hand that they cannot defend themselves against exploitation and on the other that they cannot tax themselves to build communal institutions or to sue runaway fathers for child support. The reason they are denied political rights is that they would use these rights to temper the rate of exploitation. In this circumstance a racial ideology alleging communal incompetence of the proletarian race, lack of integrity and good faith, incapacity for the higher forms of civilization, justifies continued governance by the plantation élite.

That is, a racial ideology may serve the function of giving a lesser value to the grievances and aspirations of one social class as compared with another, when the social classes belong to different 'peoples' with different conditions of immigration and citizenship. This is the 'gentlemanly racism' of the plantation counties of the American South, where, typically, innocent men were not lynched; only rebels were.

The fundamentalist form of exploitative racism is characteristic of South Africa, where fundamentalist racism seems to be mixed with a good dose of religious Boer fundamentalism as well. It (1) preserves the monopoly of political and economic rights to the whites (conserva-

---

servility. Personal dignity means to a peasant a proper respect for the economic value of his work, a defense of his ancient tenure, and help in time of need. The reasons Jews are the image of unpleasant servility in, for example, Elizabethan drama is because their servility was not personal subjection, and hence honest, but rather it was impersonally given to anyone with money, and hence dishonest.

tism); (2) excludes black people, who are set apart by racial norms, and lately also civilized white people who oppose apartheid, from the benefits of citizenship (exclusivism); (3) sees the possibility of subversion of the system of stratification in every white-black contact, even playing tennis (satanism); and (4) upsets delicate and complex institutions (e.g., the exploitive labor market itself) by applying simple norms of apartheid (fundamentalism).

Thus even though there is some inherent tendency for fundamentalist movements to be populist, fundamentalism can be embedded in ideologies having quite different social and historical functions. The same is true of the opposite, of course: the main artistic, scientific, and legal achievements of human civilization have been embedded in ideologies justifying all sorts of exploitation and all sorts of revolution. The reason is, of course, that what people think the normative order is and ought to be is determined by their positions in it. For their positions create the grievances and aspirations and interests that a just order would remedy, satisfy, and serve. The grievances of a Malaysian peasant against a Chinese moneylender give the peasant a notion of what a just order should do that is different from the notion held by a white South African who has grievances against the belated constitutionalism of the British Colonial Office. Responding to the normative order in one's own interest gives rise to an appropriate form of racist fundamentalism. Because each of us internalizes a different part of the normative order, a part in keeping with our own interests and grievances, our fundamentalism takes different substantive forms.

Alternative explanations of aggressive fundamentalism

If fundamentalism can be embedded in different substantive ideologies, then it can be explained neither by the content of those ideologies nor by the causes appropriate for explaining that content. The populist (and reactionary) character of anti-Semitism in Eastern Europe must be explained in terms of the rôle of Jews in Eastern Europe and the grievances of peasants (and landlords or bureaucrats) against that rôle, by the rôle of Jews in Christian popular theology, and the like. This explains why, *when pogroms and concentration camps come*, they are directed against the Jews. But what we want to know is whether, given the content of a loyalty to a normative order, we can locate conditions that will make the level of hostility embedded in that loyalty increase and the cognitive and normative complexity decrease, so as to produce a fundamentalist variant of that loyalty.

1. *Reality*. In social scientific explanations of people's beliefs, the first hypothesis should be that the people are right. If for example the leaders of Arab states proclaim that they want to destroy Israel, shoot artillery at Israel, expel Jews from their countries, refuse to negotiate with or to recognize Israel, it is not terribly surprising if Israelis think Arabs are out to get them. Conversely of course, Israeli bombers flying over Cairo seem hostile, and the fundamentalist solution of shooting them down seems simple in normative theory, if practically somewhat difficult.

War causes fundamentalism. When someone really is out to destroy a person's normative order and to kill that person and his or her conationals, it tends to produce in that person a feeling of simpleminded patriotism.

2. *Fundamentalism as a mental disease*. The thesis of the *Authoritarian Personality* (Adorno *et al.*, 1950) can briefly be summarized in two propositions: (1) conservatism, exclusivism, satanism, and fundamentalism form a unified psychological entity, roughly measured by the famous *F*-scale and (2) certain disturbances in people's biographies which produce other sorts of psychological disorders also produce the *F*-scale complex. The first of these propositions seems to me very well established for Western democracies by repeated demonstrations of correlations among the items of the scale. (Note however that conservatism as defined above does not necessarily imply support for conservative parties, though in the United States at high levels of political activity it generally seems to do so in fact.) The second proposition really has two components, that the *F*-scale complex is *associated in fact* with other symptoms of mental disease and imperfect social functioning and that both *are produced by* disordered biographies. The first seems to have been thoroughly demonstrated by McClosky (1963). The second component has been repeatedly demonstrated for one aspect of biography: education discourages fundamentalism (except of the realistic variety mentioned above: educated Arabs are just as hostile to Israel as Arab peasants

are).[7] No other biographical inferences seem to me to have been solidly established.

3. *Fundamentalism as a movement of desperation.* None of the above explanations could account for the rapid growth of fascist movements in most advanced capitalist countries during the depression of the 1930s. People's social identities had been deeply attacked: capitalists who thought their skills would always make them money were going bankrupt, and profits were cut drastically in the most powerful companies, especially in heavy industry; workers were thrown out of work; students faced careers without prospects, if they could find jobs at all; shopkeepers extended credit to respectable people who then couldn't pay. It did not seem to matter which government was in power, for they were all (save perhaps the Soviet Union) impotent to reconstruct satisfactory lives for people. Since the sophisticated answers, ranging from Hoover's stalwart capitalism in the United States to social democracy in Germany, did not work, their advantage over the simple answers of fascism were not obvious. (In fact, if one is willing to ignore the ultimate consequences of war and extermination camps, one can conclude that the simple fascist answer worked somewhat better than the others.)

When people who do not ordinarily much analyze public questions have deep and persistent grievances because of a historical crisis, fundamentalist answers to those questions have a disproportionate appeal. The fundamentalist elements of much of the Black Power movement in the United States can perhaps be explained in this way. An elaborate theory maintaining essentially this proposition is argued by Smelser (1962).

4. *Fundamentalist cultural traditions.* Fundamentalist Christianity is associated with anti-Semitism in the United States (Glock and Stark, 1970). The traditional 'isolationist' vote in the American Congress, which I think can be called fundamentalist, is disproportionately concentrated in the midwestern rural home of northern religious fundamentalism. Education, which decreases fundamentalism in religion, also decreases commitment to racism and to oversimplified punitive treatment of deviants. The more funda-

---

[7] The argument that lack of education causes fundamentalism in personal ideology is the brunt of Lipset's controversial article (1959).

mentalist religion of the Boers in South Africa coincides with their more fundamentalist racial policies.

From such bits and pieces of evidence one can suggest that socialization into one sort of fundamentalism predisposes people to other forms. One may first learn to explain one's troubles in satanic terms, for example, by learning about a literally fallen angel. But Jewish conspiracies may easily substitute for fallen angels psychologically, once the efficacy of satanic agents is firmly implanted in the mind.

5. *Fundamentalism as an ideology of policies which will not bear examination.* Systematic hysteria and rejection of critical reason may be a tool in the hands of people who know perfectly well that the policies they are following would not be acceptable to the public if the public knew what was going on. Politicians who promise all things to all people, give rich-rolling oratory that we associate with Southern demagogy in the United States, or constantly change the number of communists in the State Department, may allow the government to follow no policy at all but rather respond to particular pressures or to follow a policy that serves secret devious interests. The lack of correspondence between promise and delivery is covered with a rhetoric of national unity of a fundamentalist kind.

It is hard to think of the evidence that would support or refute this view. It is true that much nationalist rhetoric is strangely silent on who get what, but that may be because to a fundamentalist it is obvious that everyone should get what he ought to get. It seems to me that our sociology of conflict and solidarity and the functions of wrong-headed ideologies is too primitive to deal productively with the rôle of conspiracy and deliberate obfuscation in nationalist movements.

Summary

Our problem in this section has been to describe the social sources of system loyalty. That loyalty can take a generous form of willingness to sacrifice one's own interest for perceived group welfare. It can take a selfish form of willingness to sacrifice outsiders or opponents within the system for perceived group welfare. The pervasiveness of loyalty in political affairs is illustrated by the large majority of group decisions, especially decisions about group defense against outsiders, which are not the focus of political divisions. Bipartisan foreign policies or socialist parties' 'betrayals' of their pacifist positions in times of war are examples to be explained. Ethnic groups and nations are much more unified than one would predict from the sociology of partisan clashes.

But not all nations and ethnic groups have the same level of consent, the same confinement of loyalties within the group. We have been trying to suggest why nationalism is more of a political resource of some governments and élites than of others. We have also tried to specify why that resource is sometimes used in primitive and obnoxious ways.

The core idea of our theory of when a nation will be able to call on its citizens and diverse interest groups to sacrifice for the group is the institutional grounding of people's identities. The more a person's life problems have their solution in the institutional order created by the political system, the more that system becomes identified in that person's mind with his or her own life. The capacity of individuals to solve the problems of constructing a satisfactory life in a group's institutional order depends on a complex interrelation between his or her particular social location and the character of the group's institutional order. Thus that interrelation will tend to predict the frequency of 'statesmanship' in that group, if we understand by statesmanship the special priority of conceptions of collective welfare over partisan interests.

The variables we have suggested to use in analyzing this problem are the institutional completeness of the group, the group's ecological range, the ecological range of various types of individuals within the group, and the particular relation of each person's needs in constructing his or her type of life to the needs satisfied by the institutional order. Propositions relating these variables to loyalty are outlined.

Then we turned to ethnic relations, to the fact that institutional solutions to the problems of the lives of some ethnic group with high internal loyalty often imposes a 'racist' institutional order on another group, so that the others are repetitively in all institutional areas treated as outsiders, as rightless. The more pervasive that jural exclusion, the more ethnic loyalty will be imposed from outside. Thus the extreme of ethnic loyalty would come when people are involved in a rich institutional order *within* their own groups and are systematically treated as rightless outsiders in a normative order imposed from outside. Some colonized peoples have approximately confronted those extreme conditions.

In the last sections above, we have tried to outline some alternative explanations for why ethnic and national loyalties are sometimes infused with fundamentalist group hatred. That is, the statesmanship produced by group loyalty mentioned above can consist of sacrificing partisan interest to wage holy wars against outsiders or to establish concentration camps for minorities. The alternative theories of fundamentalist nationalism offered were: that outsiders and minorities really are conspiring to destroy the group; that fundamentalists are mentally diseased; that the identities dependent on group institutions are maimed by extensive malfunction of the problem-solving techniques, as in economic depressions; that fundamentalism in one area of life (e.g., religion) tends to produce fundamentalism in other areas; and that fundamentalist loyalties are a resource of leaders of nations to distract people from the leaders' incapacity or unwillingness to solve the actual problems of people's lives in the group.

Because of the superposition of group loyalty and fundamentalist ideologies, the sociology of nationalism is filled with theoretically intractable ironies. One symptom of a high level of group loyalty, for example, is a large number of issues in a political system which are resolved without partisan conflict. But another symptom of a high level of group loyalty in its fundamentalist variant is partisanship carried to the extreme of genocide, treason trials, and inter-group hatred. The sociology of nationalism depends for its future development on an adequate theoretical composition of the variable to be explained.

8. The deep structure of moral categories, eighteenth-century French stratification, and the Revolution

I shall apply structural analysis to the system of moral categories into which any society's population is classified, to the categories of the stratification of the old régime in eighteenth-century France, and discuss how the deep structures of the stratification culture of the old society shaped the nature of the Revolution which abolished that stratification structure.

The social functions of moral categories

In every society there are some categories into which people can be classified that pervade their whole lives: child–adult; male–female; citizen–alien; black–white; crazy–sane are examples of such categories in the United States. Further, there are other categories that pervade particular situations or social systems: in a house there is the owner or renter (and his or her family) and the guests. These categories dominate the situation of the particular house, in the sense that few of a guest's acts are not affected by his being a guest.

Furthermore, these categories have extension into the larger institutional order. If a guest oversteps his rights, the police and the courts will distinguish the tenant from the guest. If an insane person comes to criminal court he or she will be treated differently from a sane person. Blacks appear in the administrative records of fair employment enforcement with a different significance than do whites. Children are required to go to school – adults not.

These categories used to classify people for social purposes have moral obligations attached to them. A guest has responsibilities, ranging from the most subtle obligation to pick up cues about when to go home to the legal responsibility not to break and enter. Children

145

have privileges and obligations distinct from adults; citizens privileges and obligations distinct from noncitizens (e.g. noncitizens are not expected to be 'loyal'); a white or a black come by accident to a neighborhood bar with the opposite color clientele can feel his lack of moral privilege with the hair on the back of his neck.

On the one hand these categories seem to be features of institutions. For example, the category 'child' is a part of the institution of the school, and its moral significance constituted by the obligations it lays on the child in the teacher–child relation, the principal–child relation, the child-bringing-home-grades-from-the-teacher-to-his-parents relation, and so on. Child is also a category of the institution of the family, as a person subject to adult authority; in the political system as a nonvoter; in the system of civil law as a person who cannot sign contracts. We do find a certain amount of variation between these institutions in exactly who is a child: in schools there is a variable age of final graduation to an adult rôle (from about 16 to about 30); for voting there is a single age of 18; for the family adult rights and duties are granted so gradually and so variably among families and among children that legal majority has little to do with it. In any event, the age of legal majority varies for different areas of life.

But somehow this misses the essence of the social status of being a child. After all, being a child in the civil courts (i.e. not being able to be held liable for contracts) is very closely related to being a child in the family (being subject to the head of the household's decisions about money) and in the labor market (not being employable) and the school (being prepared for the labor market). The status of a child is pervasive among institutional areas, and 'hangs together' in a meaningful sense. That is, it is dominated in each institutional area by the notion that this is a person who needs to be taken care of, who cannot make his or her own decisions. Though the details (e.g., the age of majority) vary among institutions, the child–adult contrast has roughly the same significance in all of them. It is a 'structural' distinction, in the sense that it gives structure to a wide variety of superficially different situations.

Likewise the status of 'owner or tenant' and 'guest' is structural in the same sense. A guest in a restaurant is a client whose rights and obligations differ substantially from those of the man who came to dinner, but beneath the superficial differences we find that both the housewife and the waiter can keep the guest out of the kitchen, and can send him home at closing time. Thus there is a deeper continuity in meaning in the tenant–guest distinction between superficially different situations.

Now consider the problem of quickly constructing a moral order for conversations at a dinner party. Who is in charge? The owner or tenant, the 'host.' Who can be shooed out? Children. How should people be arranged at the table? Alternate men and women, but do not seat women next to their husbands. The moral order is thus quickly blocked in – its main features are known – just by making use of the structural or pervasive distinctions of the culture. Although the montage of a particular dinner party may have aesthetically unique qualities, its basis is constructed from standard materials. These categories are, so to speak, the ideological raw materials from which a moral order may be constructed to suit the occasion. Since, by and large, one can depend on children to be willing to be shooed, husbands to give up their wives for the sake of dinner conversation, hosts to take charge, there is a certain amount of reliability, of known qualities, in the raw materials.

Much more complex and continuing systems can be built with the same sort of raw materials. Schools shoo children on a complex and well worked out schedule, combining the shooability of children with many other moral characteristics of the structural position of a child (such as listening when he or she is told to listen) to build the complex moral order of 'education.'

The problem of structural analysis of a moral order is therefore one of finding the basic or pervasive categories of the normative system, out of which (with suitable modifications) the basic moral order for different situations is constructed.

Universal moral categories?

People categorize other people into morally significant categories primarily in order to carry out action toward, or with, them. Commonalities of human action therefore tend to produce commonalities of moral categorization. For example, in most male social groups in all societies, women are of more sexual interest than are other men, and women in child-bearing ages are of more reproductive interest than are girls or older women. In all societies this sexual and reproductive interest results in men classifying women differently from men. The reproductive interest results, in all societies, in the classification of women according to who their children 'belong to,' by marital status, by who is responsible for supporting the children, for claiming children's labor services, for arranging their social placement, marriage, etc. This classification by marital status often also results in the establishment of moral (if not always practical) sexual monopoly over the woman, so that she becomes (morally) of no sexual interest to men aside from her husband.

That is, in all societies there is a moral category of female, and a moral category of wife.

Likewise for age – all societies distinguish children and adults. All must take some cognizance of those adults who cannot assume adult responsibilities because of mental or physical disabilities. All must recognize that a dead person can no longer fulfill his social obligations in the same way as one who is alive, and consequently (for example) that a *widow* is in a somewhat different situation than a wife, and a farm or herd whose owner has just died has to be run in some different way (by an 'heir').

And finally we come to the most pervasive category of all, the category that distinguishes those people who can be trusted to form reliable parts for the moral constructions we make to run our lives, and those who are outside the pale. Moral reliability usually depends on social enforcement, ultimately economic sanctions or violent punishment. People whose social and economic fate, or their life and liberty, are not subject to the moral order are not reliable parts of it. The boundaries around a 'society' are boundaries that mark off people who are moral entities in the normative system, in the sense that their behavior is subject to that system and can, to that degree, be relied upon.

For example, there is a reasonably close correspondence between 'residing' in the United States and being a 'citizen' of the United States. About 1% of the population in the territorial United States at any one time is likely to consist of aliens. But in hundreds of ways, aliens living in the United States are part of American society – and when they are not, as some diplomats are not, the legal status of diplomat is defined by American law and American treaty obligations.

Aliens (except perhaps diplomats) must drive on the right, pay their bills, sent their children to school, leave when the host starts yawning after a dinner party, and keep their hands off other men's wives in public. Thus the category 'resident alien' is a status in American society. But there is no morally significant sense in which 'Japanese citzen living in Japan' is a category of the moral system of the United States. Such people are merely 'foreigners.'

Every society, indeed every corporate moral system whatever, has a categorical distinction between members and nonmembers, that is, between morally responsible constituent elements for social action governed by the norms of the group, and people who are not governed by those norms. These categories may be shadings of grey rather than black and white distinctions, and there may be 'resident aliens' or 'apprentices' or 'probationary members.' And there are always ways of showing oneself to be sufficiently unreliable and hence to be expelled from the society as criminal, insane, incompetent, or disloyal, so that membership is never completely inheritable.

But having said all this, we must recognize that we have said very little. Although there is a category 'wife' in all societies, the moral accompaniments of the category are not very similar at all. For example, in eighteenth-century France and in Karimoja in Northern Uganda (Dyson-Hudson, 1966) a wife is only represented in the legal system by her husband or father-in-law; in the United States she can make contracts and sue in her own name. In the United States and Karimoja she can get divorced, while in old régime France she could not, but in Karimoja she leaves the children to her husband's family, while in the United States she almost invariably takes them with her on divorce. In Karimoja the wife works in agriculture, the husband does not – in eighteenth-century France the reverse. The amusement of playing with fire by encouraging conversations between a wife and other men, so characteristic of the upper middle classes in the United States, would be foreign to the conversational rôle of a wife in eighteenth-century France or Karimoja. A wife among the Karimojong has no legitimate claim to sexual monopoly over her husband; in eighteenth-century France she had a strong claim unless her husband was politically upper class, in which case she shared him with mistresses. In the United States she has a strong claim to sexual monopoly *especially* if the husband is in the political upper class, and people lose political offices for scandals that would have contributed to political prestige in eighteenth-century Paris.

Thus except for one common feature of these moral situations of wives – that they are all centrally determined by what men want women to do as wives – the category wife is a different one in the three societies. In each case there will be a moderate degree of predictability, so that by and large one can depend on wives' behaving as they are supposed to. In each case one builds the moral order of families *and* conversations *and* casual sexual encounters with the moral raw material that includes the concept wife.

In the same way 'foreigner' means to the modern United States 'the subject or citizen of another state, or a refugee.' Foreigner to a Karimojong means 'enemy' (with some exceptions), a person to be either attacked or avoided. In eighteenth-century France, the category of foreigner was in rapid evolution, as a medieval jumble of crosscutting feudal ties was being reorganized into nation-states; roughly speaking, it had the modern meaning of someone to be dealt with through his political leaders. The Karimojong do not have diplomacy, so foreigners cannot have the moral meaning of 'people dealt with by diplomacy.' There is a similarity again at a deeper level, like the similarity in the meaning of 'wife' as 'someone at the disposal, in certain respects, of her husband.' Foreigners in all three moral systems come under a 'principle of lesser eligibility' for all sorts of privileges and rights created by the moral order. Only if diplomacy gives a foreigner a right to travel in the United States, or to sell his or her goods there, does he have that right – all American adults except prisoners or mental patients have those rights.

We are clearly in a dilemma here if we treat such concepts as 'wife' and 'foreigner' as universal components of normative systems, and to ignore the immense variety. If we do, we shall not take into account that foreigners entering Karimojong territory stand a good chance of getting killed, while foreigners entering the United States only get humiliated by an Immigration Officer. The difference between getting killed and getting humiliated is sufficiently important to take account of, at least if one is a foreigner rather than a social theorist. Nevertheless, there is a good deal in common between an Immigration Officer and his enforcement of lesser eligibility and an indignant Karimojong meeting a foreigner at his waterhole.

The method of structural analysis

The problem we have just outlined is basic to the cultural sciences. It is the question of whether it makes sense at all to use common categories across cultures for cultural or 'mental' phenomena. Clearly it makes sense to talk of sexual intercourse or eating as phenonema that take place everywhere. But is 'wife' a phenomenon everywhere? If so, what about 'mistress'? Is 'feast' a cross-cultural category? If so, what about 'communion'? Unfortunately these empirical questions have become tangled up with epistemological questions, about whether we can ever know what is in someone else's mind, and if we can, whether we can measure it. Though this is a very interesting question, it is only in the case of the solipsist resolution of it that it has any implications for scientific practice. If we resolve the epistemological question by saying that there are better and worse guesses about what people have on their minds, and that we know generally speaking how to make our guesses gradually more accurate, we can address the question of what to do with the guess that 'foreigner' means something similar, yet crucially different, to a Karimojong and to an Immigration and Naturalization Hearing Examiner. That is, we suppose that we have solved the epistemological problem enough to guess that intending to kill someone is different from intending to change the conditions of a visa, and that in both cases the principle of lesser eligibility is applied to foreigners. Now we want to know what to do with this guess. We leave the question of the ultimate philosophical value of that guess to philosophers.

There are two main methods that have been proposed to deal with this question: the 'ideal type' method and the 'structuralist' method. In both cases 'method' is perhaps too strong a word: 'intellectual strategy' or 'orientation' might be better.

The 'ideal type' strategy starts with a common problem of human action, for example, of a decison-maker controlling an administrative apparatus which he wants to have execute his decision, or a religious leader justifying God's ways to Man by explaining how evil and injustice come about. The notion is that there will be a limited number of basic types of cultural patterns that *can* do the job: charismatic, traditional, or bureaucratic authority; transcendental gods, exorable gods, or a purposeless universe. The reason that only a limited number of basic strategies will be found is that the nature of the problems of human action everywhere have basic similarities. Getting willful men to obey, or explaining to a man with boils all over himself why he should love God, are everywhere basically similar. And since the problems are similar, only a few types of cultural frames will provide the materials for constructing a moral order that can solve them. Thus the ideal type approach depends on what might be called 'strong functionalism.' Although the kinds of gods may vary, the nature of the problem of explaining evil and injustice is everywhere sufficiently the same that only a few basic forms of solution will be found.

The 'structuralist' strategy tries to avoid the strong functionalist postulate by analyzing each cultural concept in terms of the particular cultural system as a whole. For example, the concept 'wife' among the Karimojong would be described by the conjunction of all the contrasts between adult women and children, all the contrasts between unmarried and married adult women, all the contrasts between married women and widows. Thus 'wife' among the Karimojong means a person without the right to own cattle but with the right to use a garden and a milk cow, without the right to participate in religion and politics, without the right to take lovers, but with the right to have a baby's father support it, with the right to live with the husband she married rather than one of her husband's heirs (as a widow must), and so on.

The bundle of distinctions, of rights and duties, liberties and immunities, that make up the moral concept 'wife' among the Karimojong may be unique. There is no 'strong functional' hypothesis here that only a few sorts of cultural patterns can fill the rôle of bearing legitimate children. Where then does the universality come in? It comes with the attempt to specify a cross-cultural set of contrasts which *will be a sufficient language* for, say, describing all rôles as wives. The question is now, if we take all the components used in the description of a Karimojong wife's status, can we use that set to describe any other human family system we choose?

What then would this language look like? First we have a set of exclusions: in all known societies some family members are excluded from some ownership rôles but not others, from some religious ritual rôles but not others, from some political decisions but not others.

Thus in every society family rôles can be divided from each other by ownership, by ritual capacities, by citizenship rights.

Now we know that this small set of distinctions is not a complete language for describing the rôle of a wife, for even among the Karimojong it does not yet distinguish a wife from a widow. And yet it makes perfect sense to us to use the same language to say that in the United States wives typically own family property jointly with husbands, but the children and grandparents typically own none of the nuclear family's property; that wives and children participate in religious ceremonies but usually in subordinate rôles, that wives but not children have legal political citizenship.

The reason for calling this approach 'structural' is that it presumes that the concrete concepts of a moral order such as the concept 'wife,' will vary from one 'moral language' to another. But the basic pattern of contrasts out of which these concepts are constructed, say contrasts between excluded and included rôles in property, religion, and politics, will tend to be universal.

An example of the contrasting strategies would be in the analysis of rules of succession. Radcliffe-Brown's famous essay argues that the predominance of *either* matrilineal *or* patrilineal succession in most societies of the world was caused by the fact that only a few cultural solutions existed to the problem of continuity of corporate action, when the corporation consisted of relatives and when it managed a valuable estate (1952). Thus Radcliffe-Brown constructs a couple of ideal types, cultural patterns having a good deal in common in spite of superficial differences, starting from a very common problem of ensuring the continuity of a family corporation managing a family farm or herd or whatnot.

To manufacture a structuralist approach to the same problem, we set out a series of contrasts likely to be taken into account in the moral evaluation of a succession problem. People may be classified by:

1. Is the person dependent for support on the estate or not?
2. Is the person closely or distantly related to the deceased?
3. Is the relation created by marriage or by blood?
4. If by blood, was the deceased married to the mother or not?
5. Did the deceased have a substantial moral debt to the person for service or not?

6. Is the person competent to take over the authority of the deceased or not? (Both actual and ritual competence are relevant.)
7. Is there enough of an estate so that anybody really cares?
8. Is the potential heir a person who can be trusted to act honorably in cases where his self-interest conflicts with his obligations to others having an interest in the estate?
9. Was the relation of the deceased to the property in question that of 'owner' or not? (etc.)

A complete classification of all the people involved with the deceased in all his rôles by all the criteria above would be very complex. No doubt very few systems of succession use all of the distinctions, and when they do they do not use them in all cases. But already the above list of considerations looks as if it would describe the main brunt of conversations about succession problems in authors as diverse as Jane Austen, Fyodor Dostoyevsky, and Tsao Hsueh-chin (*The Dream of the Red Chamber*).

The structural method: a rough outline

When we turn to the analysis of a particular normative order, using either of these methods, we run a grave risk of oversimplification. It is clear, for example, that the categories king, clergyman, nobleman, and commoner were fundamental moral categories for eighteenth-century France. The king could never be treated as merely another nobleman, and although he was a very powerful official of the Church he could not be mistaken for a cardinal. King was a pervasive status, relating a man to all institutional areas in a distinctive way. So was 'nobleman' pervasive, carrying legal privileges, economic advantages, and career opportunities in both the royal bureaucracy and the Church. And of course the status 'clergyman' likewise pervaded family life, political life, legal privileges, etc.

But after some detail about the classification into four estates, and some internal legal differentiation of them, we shall have to discuss in some detail the enormous variation in status and privileges within them. When writing about American society we are much less likely to forget that one resident alien is a distinguished Visiting Professor of Anthropology, while another picks grapes in the Salinas Valley, than we are to forget that some noblemen were prime ministers and others petty landowners.

But even in the face of personal variations, this pervasive classification of people in many parts of the normative system determined the dominant status of people – that is, the classification decisively shapes the opportunities, rights, and obligations to which a given person is exposed. This in turn means that from a psychological point of view, classification shapes people's dominant conception of their identities, of the continuities in their own lives: continuities in the way they are treated by others, in the purposes which it is appropriate for them to pursue, in what they amount to in terms of the values and functions of the society as a whole.

Such pervasive classification also shapes the stratification systems and the rôle systems of the component institutions of the society. The line between minors and adults in the society as a whole decisively shapes families (adults always run them), schools (teachers and parents run them in all respects in elementary and secondary schools, in colleges only in areas connected to academic life), factories (minors are excluded), automobile and real estate markets (minors cannot get credit, so must have adult agreement), and so on.

Major moral categories and prejudice

Women, foreigners, children are all categories about which people have stereotypes. That is, at the same time that the category 'young woman' may be defined normatively as 'not capable of consequential actions and so not to be taken seriously; sexually attractive and fecund and so to be protected,' the same category also functions in a belief system, in such beliefs as 'women are more emotional than men; women can rarely achieve the highest peaks of aesthetic or intellecutal performance.' Likewise children are commonly believed to be less intelligent or worse informed than adults, and usually required or encouraged to go to school.

The actual institutional actions which cause women, children, foreigners, or black people to have different normative rights and duties are called 'discrimination' and the beliefs associated with those categories are called 'stereotypes' or 'prejudice.' The relation between prejudice and discrimination has been subject to acrimonious debate because it touches on the political questions of who is to blame and what is to be done. If prejudice causes discrimination, then a person who does not believe the stereotype is innocent, and what is needed is education. If the prejudiced beliefs are merely surface manifestations of pervasive categories in the whole normative order, 'institutional racism' or 'institutional sexism,' then it is not so easy for a person with liberal beliefs to hold himself innocent, and what is required is the use of power to stop discrimination rather than education to stop prejudice.

A person's first reaction to this causal question is likely to depend on his attitude toward the discrimination. For example, in the United States children up to about 16 are required to be in school and to be out of the labor market. This discrimination is much greater and more uniform than labor market discrimination against blacks or women. This has not always been the case, of course. Before 1865 most blacks were legally prohibited from selling their labor, and children were allowed and even encouraged to sell theirs. This discrimination against children is associated with a stereotyped belief that children are more ignorant than adults. Like other stereotypes, a few moments' examination of the evidence available in one's own experience is generally enough to show it to be false. All of us can certainly match, to the child's advantage, a youngster under 16 we know against some adult we know.

In this case hardly anyone would urge that it was their unexamined stereotype that makes them support discrimination against children in the labor market. A proposal to apply the criterion of ignorance 'fairly,' so that people of whatever age who failed a test were required to go to school, and those who passed it were free to get jobs, would strike them as preposterous. The idea that by educating people out of their stereotypes one could get them to support a 'fairer' system in which brilliant ten-year-olds could hold jobs and dull 50-year-olds had to learn algebra would not appeal to anyone.

Historically the logic of the inquiry in sociology usually has proceeded from stereotype to emotions. Sociologists have reasoned that if people do not decide how to treat others by reason of the explanations they give, then it must be emotions, irrationality. When one *favors* the discrimination the emotion postulated is often called love, love of children, love of country; when one opposes it it is often called hate, or a word ending in '-ism' (racism, sexism). It is clear from our daily experience that indeed a few people are passionate haters of blacks or women or foreigners, or passionate patriots, or always go squishy when children are around. It thus is fairly easy to imagine that pervasive normative categories are the result of a widespread *mild* infection of public opinion with the affect that we see in strong form among the virtuosi of emotions, among fanatic patriots or bigots.

But this will not do either. The virtuosi of emotional anti-communism hate American radicals worse than Southeast Asian ones. But the nation they 'love' kills Southeast Asian Communists, and makes speeches against American ones. That is, their discrimination does not fall where their hatred does. The emotional tone of a congressional debate on family property law, bearing on women, or the setting up of Civil Service qualifications which exclude many blacks, or of the negotiation in a firm of the retirement age, is not that of a lynch mob. People change their emotions nearly as fast as their stereotypes, loving the noble mysterious Russian peasant soul or hating the Asiatic barbarian posing as a European according to what emotion the State Department suggests this year. Survey studies show that most people, most of the time, hardly notice what emotion they have to abstract categories like 'young woman,' 'child,' 'foreigner,' or even 'black.' And when they do notice the emotion, it is quite often a generous one.

The problem is that reason and emotion are both individual causes, but the thing to be explained is a social construction. It is, to be sure, mental, as all moral systems are mental, from the grammar and phonology of a language to the highest flights of philosophical jurisprudence. But when we observe that the rule that 'passed' and 'past' be pronounced the same way in English must in some sense be in people's minds, we are not inclined to look either for a process by which the individual reasoned it out, nor for an emotion toward the 't' sound. The characteristics of the normative role of 'young woman' are much like the rules of phonology: socially established mental structures that people use to construct, on the one hand, the sounds of particular sentences, or on the other, the particular moral structures of a concrete family or a concrete office staff. To look for reason or emotion in the individual as a cause of such a moral category is therefore looking in the wrong place. Instead we have to look for principles of evolution and growth of (more or less) integrated structures of symbols, moral categories, and their manifestations in particular concrete institutions. The key symptom we use to determine when 'prejudice' is likely to be connected with 'discrimination' is when the prejudice is about a category which is a pervasive element of the institutional order in many areas of social life. For that will indicate that instead of being a random belief, it is a belief serving the function of making cognitive sense of the moral order. People may have a wild stereotype of, say, Turks, and never discriminate, but have moderate and changeable stereotypes of women, and discriminate in all areas of their social life. It is the structural function of the category woman in the normative order as a whole which accounts for the disproportionate effects of mild emotions and stereotypes.

We must think of the problem of the relations between prejudice (stereotypes or hatred) and moral categories in a much more complex way. In the first place, by the fact of being fundamental categories of social thought, moral categories form a catch basin for generalizing tendencies of beliefs, emotions, and moral injunctions. To some degree stereotypes of men and women, emotions of sexual solidarity and generalized interest in the opposite sex, and moral injunctions about the care of children or the responsibilities of child support are all organized around the distinction of men versus women because the distinction is there. Such a socially instituted category channels the generalizing impulse toward itself, as the most readily available reservoir for general ideas and feelings.

Second, a socially instituted category makes use of human mental capacities, whatever they are, to construct an ideology in its defense. Faculty with an interest in maintaining their authority, or plantation owners running a place whose basic moral category is racial, attach now beliefs, now emotions, now moral injunctions to the categories student or black. But the insistence with which faculty urge on parents that students are ignorant and should be educated, or plantation owners urge on hill farmers that blacks should not be uppity, comes from their dependence on a manifestation *in a particular moral order* (the plantation or university) of a pervasive social category. Of course, reproduction of the same dependence on a moral category in multiple areas of life, as in the pervasive interest of South African whites in the color bar, can make many groups ready to receive, amplify, and return each other's ideology; a feedback leading to an extraordinary ideological screech so difficult for moderate English and American racists to live with.

Third, the close relation of pervasive categories to identity, to the confidence that both you and others know who you are, renders all change of basic moral categories a soul-wrenching experience. When such a displacement is forced on a person by someone on the disadvantageous side of the boundary, a sudden growth of prejudice is more a protest of wounded vanity than a continuous repressive policy.

And finally, most of the time people are treated as women, or children, or blacks, or too old, because the possibility of treating them otherwise has never occurred to the discriminating person. Giving another person an individual identity, an individual place in the moral order, is an effort. The deep wound in a sensitive woman, child, black, or old person is often caused more by thousands of instances of cruel indifference, or minor thoughtless insult, than by the massive apparatus of systematic oppression.

That is, the relation of prejudice and discrimination to moral categories is one of overdetermination. Once the categories exist, different sorts of causes cumulate to produce both prejudice and discrimination organized around the same categories.

The legal philosophy of the system of privilege in the old régime

The legal organization of the old régime is nowadays generally viewed as a system of monopolistic corporate privileges, organized to favor the rich and oppress the poor. This view had its origin in the efforts of reformers like Turgot and publicists who wrote during the eighteenth century. It became the official view because it was the official ideology of the Revolution. The whole system looks queer and irrational to modern eyes, because it was based on different ideas about what law was for, what its relation to government should be, what the rôle of 'private' interests should be. The system as a whole was more similar to modern university administration than to modern law or modern corporations (a modern business-school eye has equal difficulty understanding the administration of a university).

There are four basic principles that make the old régime's legal philosophy different from the modern one:

The first is the idea that every important administrative official was basically a judge. An old régime official decided cases according to two principles simultaneously: the public purpose for which he was appointed, and the general body of legal doctrine to which citizens, 'corporations,' and the government itself were subject. His practical decisions about how his job should be done had the force of law, were subject to legal appeal, and constituted the jurisdiction of his court. The extensive conflict between royal officers, especially the *intendants* who were chief administrative officers of provinces, and other courts (seigneurial or baillage courts, *parlements*) reflects the fact that a royal officer's legal jurisdiction, as a judge, tended to expand into all areas for which he had practical responsibility. The legal device by which this was done in general was the king's right to withdraw any case from any court and to decide it himself; i.e. in a different 'court.' Thus every important shift in administrative organization simultaneously reorganized the legal system, and undermined the rights of some court or administrative body. We shall call this the principle of legalistic administration.

The second principle was that every socially important function in the society was a public function, a responsibility of the state. Supplying food to Paris, for example, was not merely a business that some people happened to be in; it was of the nature of a public office, and the wholesalers and navigators who did the work were responsible to the king and his officers for it. This meant in turn that they had to have judges and courts and special legal standing, so that they could be legally obliged to fulfill their offices, and legally defended in the profits and wages of that office. The extensive legal provisions about how work was to be done, and who could do it, represented an extension of the idea described above – the idea that a public administrative officer was basically a judge and an origin of law, in his area of competence, to 'private' social functions. A guild was therefore something like a court of law in an area of the economy, and simultaneously something like an administrative arm of the government. This identification of private and public functions was especially prevalent in the administration of the basic economic resource of the old régime, agricultural land, and much of what is called 'feudalism' has to do with the conception of land ownership as a public office, as a part of the government, and of a public office as a court of law and an origin of law. We shall call this the principle of mixture of civil law and public law.

The third principle, perhaps by the end of the old régime more of a contradiction in the system than a principle, was the legal unity of the individual. That is, the general presumption was that all of a man's life was devoted to a single public or social function, and that this single dominant status determined which courts and laws he was subject to. His taxes, for example, should be administered by the same law court (cum administrative apparatus) that determined his qualifications as, say, a goldsmith; the body of law, the court, and the administrative section of the state apparatus to which he was subject had to correspond to his overall status. Thus, theoretically, every social function and all the people who performed it had a distinct legal status, responded in their own courts, had their taxes determined by their own courts, and so on. We will call this the principle of an 'estate' legal system.

The final principle was that the people in a given legal niche, a given legally created status, had a legitimate right to respresentation in the law court (cum administrative apparatus) that governed them. This right of representation was not egalitarian, and did not extend to government as a whole but only to their own guild or estate. But, for example, the officers of a guild who served as a court of administration for the legal jurisdiction of the guild (the *jurés*) were almost invariably masters in the guild, and often were either elected by some class within the guild or (when the office was a venal office bought from the king) selected by the guild to buy the appointment. We shall call this the principle of corporate administration.

The principle of legalistic administration is analogous to two principles in university administration: that all important administrators should have scholarly qualifications so that they can be judges of the academic merits of decisions, and that many administrative decisions are reviewable by bodies of faculty. The principle of mixture of civil law and public law has only a distant analogy in a modern university, though the incorporation of student residences as teaching organizations in the more ancient 'college' organizations of Oxford and Cambridge is more closely analogous. That is, a residence was conceived of as a university institution devoted to public university purposes, rather than the private purposes of students. The principle of an 'estate' legal system is analogous to the university principle that a person's competence corresponds to his other discipline, and that he or she should be judged (in the first instance) by his or her peers (i.e., his or her superiors) in that discipline. He is to be judged by the *jurés* of his own guild. The principle of corporate administration is analogous to the rôle of departments as the lowest unit of the administrative hierarchy and simultaneously a body of colleagues who are responsible for the detailed regulation of their disciplinary jurisdiction.

The overall result of a legal system organized according to these principles is that everyone (or more practically, everyone important) has legal privileges which depend on his social function and are manifested by his being subject to a special court. But also his privileges depend on his status *within* the corporation which administers that court. From the point of view of political dynamics it also means that every (important) social interest group has a legal and administrative arm, embedded in the legal organization of society as a whole, which can be defended by appeal to the king's laws and regulations that legally 'create' that guild or estate. The politics of interest groups become, above all, matters of corporate litigation, in which the central issue is very often which court has jurisdiction over a given matter, or a given person.

The legal boundaries

The social functions of most interest to the government, and hence those which had the most solidly institutionalized positions of legal privilege, were the cosmopolitan functions – those which tied localities into the national and international system. These functions in turn were divided into two main sets: those of 'the court' (the king and *les grands* or 'the great'), and those of the cities and localities; the court controlled *all* the cosmopolitans, and some of those cosmopolitans controlled local areas directly. There were always great distinctions of wealth, prestige, organized deference, and power between people directly involved in royal policy and in contact with the king, and the rest of the nobility and privileged classes. The special legal status of the king himself extended, for many purposes, to his ministers and his household. All the top members of the royal administration were noblemen (except for a couple of foreign financiers), but by no means were all noblemen among *les grands*.

Below *les grands* were five basic types of cosmopolitan functions that usually either resulted in the conferment of nobility or were recruited from among nobles: taxation and internal administration (the *intendants* and various royal officials of municipalities and provinces); large-scale wholesale trade and the associated administration of taxes on commerce; law courts and judges above the local level and in the more important localities; the higher clergy (those with more than parish responsibility); and the military.

Each of these social functions, except the military, requires the person in charge to so manage the local system that he gets something from it which circulates in the society as a whole or, in the case of higher courts, defends the rights of those who circulate from local interference. The king's interest in these functions was straightforward: his fluid resources all came from these supra-local streams of money and goods. The majority of the tax money by the end of the old régime came from taxes on commerce, managed by the General Farms, a 'private' corporation that supervised the public officials who actually collected the taxes. The corporation advanced the money to be collected to the royal treasury. In rural areas, although the majority of the *taille* was used for local purposes, part of it, and most of the *capitation* and *dixième* or *vingtième* taxes went to the royal treasury. Part of the revenues of the Church, which came both from the tithe and from the returns of church lands, were given as a 'free gift' to the king, and of course they supported the Church itself, which was more like a government department than a private congregation. In earlier times the services of men in the army had been directly extracted from the local system by noblemen and brought to the front by them, a so-called 'feudal' army. The direct interest of the royal administration in cosmopolitan social functions was then a taxation interest. It spent resources that it could only get from local systems by cosmopolitan intervention in them.

In an old fashioned feudal system, of, say, around the year 1200, all these cosmopolitan functions were concentrated for a given area (in legal theory) in one person – the head of the local noble family. It is he who collected taxes, made and judged laws, recruited military resources from the local area and led them to battle, and saw to the support of the Church. The core governmental institution was, in the pure case, an assembly of noblemen, of all the people who could support supralocal functions (especially warfare and the Church) because they were the *origin* of all supralocal resources. The growing complexity of cosmopolitan relations in the areas of France with the most extensive commerce, the most bureaucratization of the royal administration, the most developed system of legal professionalism, and the most penetration of 'modern' monastic and episcopal religious organization undermined this monopoly of cosmopolitan functions by the local lord.

In the less cosmopolitan economies of Brittany, the *Massif Central*, the Alps, and the Pyrenees, the identification of the basic economic function of landlord and the basic cosmopolitan governmental functions was more nearly preserved. The government was run more by assemblies of landed nobles, taxation was both less productive and less complex, and there was less occasion to create new bureaucratic nobility. The legal organization of taxation, in the old régime the crucial aspect of the legal organization of government, required the consent of these assemblies. This was the main significance of the distinction between *pays d'états*, where the estates consented to taxation, and the *pays d'election*, where special local officials (*élus*) were appointed for judging taxation assessments and functioned under the supervision of royal officials (receivers, and ultimately the *intendant*). The ratio of what was ideologically 'new' nobility (the *noblesse du robe* of the law courts, noble merchants – almost entirely in large-scale wholesaling – and ennobled government officials) was therefore much higher on the plains, in the Seine, Loire, and Aquitaine basins (the jurisdiction of the Paris *Parlement*). In addition, of course, the landed nobility of highly commercialized agriculture developed many more commercial interests and moved more easily into commercial enterprises. And there were many more rich local bourgeois in such areas to buy noble estates. So the lord of a local area was himself often involved in commerce.

The legal boundary of noble privilege therefore was changing, with the increasing commercialization of the plains of France, and the increasing dependence of the royal government on commerce for taxes. The ideological ground for this change was royal favor. The king, in theory, created new nobles. The change was most rapid in the areas most subject to the royal bureaucracy and most commercialized. But the change had built-in lags, both because nobility was generally inheritable, and because once created it could not easily be destroyed, for it had formidable legal and political resources.

The system of legal privilege for the third estate was both more complex and more obscure. It is partly obscure because of Marxist misinterpretation of its nature. First, it is not true that large-scale businessmen were excluded from the nobility. This would have been very difficult in any case, since most of commerce dealt with agricultural goods. It is not within reason that a large-scale noble supplier of the main article of commerce should take no interest in its marketing, especially when large profits are to be made in marketing, and especially when wholesale commerce is intimately regulated by a government run by nobles. Not only is it not within reason – it is not true. Nobles engaged in commerce. Second it was not true that those businessmen who were not nobles had no legal privileges which they were interested in defending, and that they were therefore thrown willy-nilly, rich and poor alike, into alliance against the government. Third, it is not true that the philosophy of reorganization of the government (of taxation and monopoly of social functions, that is) was radically different between the nobles and the third estate in 1787–9. What they disagreed on was mainly which estate should run things. Finally it is not true that the third estate uniformly favored the 'capitalistic' freedom of commerce that was one of the main legal results of the Revolution, a result carried through, in large part, by the assembly of the third estate. In order to understand the skein of causes that ultimately led the third estate to carry through a revolution they had had no real intention to carry through, we need to address the problem of the legal organization of cities and guilds.

The eighteenth-century city as a productive system

What makes it so hard for a modern student to see what was going on in a medieval or early modern city is that he has to imagine away the bureaucratic control of production. *Nobody was there* to tell a baker, or a goldsmith, or a mason, or a shoemaker, what to do and how to do it. The 'company' that made wine did not have a national distribution system that relied on Gallo Burgundy always being, for better or worse, the same stuff. Instead production was organized in family firms with a few apprentices, and whatever was not sold directly by the artisan to consumers was bought by wholesalers to ship elsewhere. The key sources of non-local income to the city were people who could tap the flow of tax and rent money in the society – government officials, bishops and abbots, landowners – and people engaged in wholesale commerce. The people who functioned to relate a city to the economy of France were *not* manufacturing corporations.

The notion that a design or quality control engineer or marketing executive would decide what a man should produce was as foreign to the eighteenth-century city as the notion that a university president should specify what advances in linguistics the anthropology department should produce would be today. The bureaucratic superior was a legally trained official or a rich bourgeois who had bought an office, hardly anyone to consult on the quality of leather to make shoes.

As in modern cities, the great majority of work done (two-thirds or more) was for the local population. Only a small part was working in industries that 'exported' products or services from the city to the rest of the country or abroad. In the eighteenth century the 'export' goods were rarely manufactured goods. An artisan shoemaker in one city was no more efficient than an artisan shoemaker in another city, or in a village in the countryside, so there was no reason to concentrate artisan production in a single city in a 'factory.' Instead the 'exports' were higher government services, higher religious services, and wholesale trade. Within a given city, then, the *menu peuple* were mainly *artisans and retail traders working for the local market of the city*, with no particular national significance. Manufacturing and retail trade were not the big businesses of the society; government, religion, and wholesale trade were.

Thus within the city there was a sharp division between an élite of government officers, higher clergymen, wholesale traders, and large landowners of the region, on the one hand, and the retail, manufacturing and service workers that served the city population, on the other. The powerful guilds that ran 'municipal' governments were largely drawn from wholesale traders. They of course had some conflicts with the local royal representatives, the higher clergy, and local landowners, about who should really run the city, who should pay for local public services, and how much money should be sent to Paris. But this is quite a different conflict from the conflict of the *menu peuple* with the élite for representation of their interests (low food prices, higher prices for their products and services, control of competition in a given line of business, especially competition from shoddy work, reduction of their tax load, and so on).

Legal boundaries in cities

The legal boundaries that were central in cities were organized in the guild system. But there were very different kinds of guilds. They can be classified into three broad types: (1) guilds with representation in the municipal government, (2) guilds with royal charters but without significant representation in city government, and (3) guilds without autonomous legal powers. Broadly speaking, the guilds with representation were the merchant guilds engaged in wholesale trade and finance. The guilds with royal charters but no significant representation had a legally established monopoly over the provision of certain local goods and services (bakers, masons, shoemakers, and the like), with the legal right to challenge any other group who competed in the industry, and the right to admit apprentices, journeymen, and masters to the guild. Their economic regulations and taxation powers were reviewed by local royal officials and by the courts, and administered by sworn officials (*jurés*) of the guilds (who usually had to have approval both of the guild masters and of the royal or municipal officials).

But this system of craft guilds in its turn gave legal significance and monopoly value to the *internal* status of a man within his guild, as a master rather than a journeyman or apprentice. A general tendency of even the less privileged guilds to give rise to an oligarchy of masters with legal monopolies tended to set up a class conflict *within* the guild between masters and journeymen, and an interest group conflict over prices with the consuming public. Finally there were craft associations without royal charters, with precarious legal standing, and few monopolistic privileges, often trying to gain royal charters and monopolies.

Thus the early modern city in France was organized in a series of nested conflicts, each revolving around a legal boundary between corporately organized status groups. The first level was the conflict between the privileged wholesale bourgeoisie and rich rentiers, controlling 'municipal' government through representation of merchant guilds, with the royal bureaucracy, the clergy, and sometimes local landed rentier nobility, over taxation and other governmental powers. The second was between the citywide legally privileged cosmopolitan oligarchy of wholesalers, often together with the royal government, and the privileged élites of local service guild, masters in the artisan trades, over the latter's claim to representation and to monopoly powers. The third was the conflict between the local guild élites and the journeymen and apprentices who were excluded from opening their own shops by the legal monopoly power of the guild. And finally all local monopolies had price conflicts with the general population, and conflicts over status honor, taxation privileges, and legal rights.

This nested set of conflicts, as Max Weber argued extensively, (1968: 1301–68) have always tended to produce a revolutionary 'democratic' tendency in cities. But the more democratic the government that these conflicts produced (where cities have some legal authonomy), the more opposition it gets from national governmental institutions that depend on controlling tax flows through local privileged groups, so the more such a democratic government tends to be undermined by a drift of power back toward the merchant and rentier oligarchy that controls the flow of exports and imports to the city, the group that is rich and nationally powerful.

In times of religious excitement, bad harvests, famine, and food riots, or in military conflicts of the city with other cities or with rural or royal authorities, a rapid movement toward democratic constitution of the city tends to take place. But in times of peace, plenty, and ecclesiastical control, those democratic constitutions decay into systems of monopolistic privilege and oligarchical control. This drift is reinforced by a strong royal government interested in tax returns, though strong royal government also tends to bring about a substitution of royal power for local oligarchic control.

To put it another way, a social movement of city oligarchs to increase their powers relative to the royal government is faced with a dilemma. Such movement tends to ignite in a chain reaction the claims of craft guilds against the oligarchy, and then of the *menu peuple* against corporate privilege in general. This chain reaction happens especially when it is combined with a shortage of food (focusing resentment against wholesale merchants) or with popular religious enthusiasm (e.g., the Jansenist conflict). It is this ignition of nested conflicts that made the city of Paris such a revolutionary place, and forced the moderate constitutional demands of privileged cosmopolitans in the Estates General into a democratically revolutionary course.

Law, grace, and venality in the system of privilege

The system of legal privileges for classes of people described previously is a great oversimplification. From a legal point of view, the added complexity of the system depended on the rôle of the king's 'grace,' his capacity to make exceptions to the laws he had established or to any general administrative arrangement of the government. Concretely one of the most important manifestations of this 'grace' was the system of venal offices. For the crucial aspect of a venal office is that it is a privilege extended by the king to a particular person, not on the ground of some general principle of administration or general legal principle, but rather because that person was willing to pay for the privilege. Thus it created types of legal inequalities which were not rationalized by an overall public purpose (except the purpose of getting more money for public purposes), nor built into the system of law as whole, nor administered with control from the central authority subjecting them to overall shifts in public purposes. In the telling phrase, in the old régime 'even the inequality was unequal.'

The jurisdiction of a venal office became much like a right of private property, defended by the interest of its holder rather than by the public purpose it served. That jurisdiction in its turn had to be created by carving up the legal obligations created by the state into pieces that could be sold as private property. But this tended to set the interests of bureaucratic state administrators and the higher law courts (interested in legal uniformity) against those of venal officers. Further this competition of jurisdictions made the exact state of the law uncertain – whether or not a claim of a bureaucratic administrator of jurisdiction would hold up, or whether it would turn out to be in the jurisdiction of a venal officer, were matters to be decided each time a new special regulation was made creating a venal office.

Finally, the solidity of the value of a venal office depended on the reliability of enforcement of those legal obligations of citizens which brought in the fees. Insofar as that enforcement depended on the bureaucratic apparatus of the state, it tended to be uncertain. An *intendant* might well think he had better things to do with his small budget than to insure the fees of a venal officer by providing police when and where that officer said they were needed.

The most valuable venal offices tended to be of one of two kinds. First, offices which carried nobility with them, with the corresponding legal and social privileges, were valuable as means of social ascent, regardless, to some degree, of their value in money returns. Second, some venal offices were valuable because they settled 'constitutional' questions, especially in city and guild government. That is, the question of who should rule a guild or a city could be resolved by buying the offices that had jurisdiction over the guild or city. The corporate group, especially the wealthier members of it, could help insure their monopoly position in the economy by buying the offices through which the state regulated corporate matters.

Thus by the time of the meeting of the Estates General in 1789, questions of the distribution of privilege were intimately tied up with constitutional questions, especially questions of the powers of the king. And the queer phenomenon of the *parlements* (made up of nobles), and the noble estate itself in the Estates General, attacking many aspects of the system of privilege becomes much more understandable. One of the most common demands in the noble *cahiers* was, for example, that nobility should be granted only on the basis of merit. Aside from challenging the simple notion that people who inherit their status should be unequivocal supporters of ascription, this is representative of a great many demands by the nobility 'to make inequality more equal,' to ground privilege in generally understood laws and regulations rather than on arbitrary grace from the uncontrolled will of the king. A nobleman who got his status through buying an office that carried nobility with it was a nobleman only because he was rich, not because he was deserving.

In addition, of course, the king could only charge for the offices that established corporate self government of a guild or a city if he rendered the constitutional status of that group's corporate liberties precarious. He could not charge them for their constitutional status unless he was willing (and claimed the right) to take it from them if they did not pay.

And finally, the multiplication of jurisdictions, and the lack of bureaucratic and legislative control over those jurisdictions since the jurisdiction was private property, interfered with bureaucratic officials when they were discharging their duties. When we remember that the bureaucracy was a noble bureaucracy, in the sense that the people in positions of high responsibility for seeing to it that governmental and public objectives were achieved were virtually all noblemen, it is not surprising that there were powerful currents within the nobility for restricting and regularizing the system of privilege.

The legal reflection of this whole problem of irregular privilege was one part of a crucial legal privilege of the king, the right to withdraw any legal case from any jurisdiction in which it fell, and to allocate to it a court more to the king's liking, especially one more under his own thumb. Even though a rather similar right was granted to noblemen (the right of *commitimus*, which allowed all noblemen to bring their cases to the appropriate *parlement*), it divorced the control over the allocation of status so thoroughly from a regularly organized legal system that many noblemen objected to it. This is manifested in the high percentage of noble *cahiers* just before the Revolution which asked that courts of exceptional jurisdiction (courts to which the king committed certain matters which he did not want to have decided by the regular *parlements*, especially a good many tax matters) should be abolished. We shall not treat the constitutional conflicts involved. Our interest here is in what it implied for the system of legal distinctions whose rough outline is given above. Aside from the organized system of distinctions among estates, there was in the old régime a massive organization of purely personal privileges of a normative kind, reflected in treatment at law and in public policy, granted to individuals on the basis of a systematic administration of the king's grace, i.e., on the basis of 'exceptions to the law.' The principle that there should be, beside the normative system, an extensive system of *justice d'exception* rendered the scheme of normative boundaries much less regular and systematic than is implied by a schematic characterization of the old régime as a *Standestaat*, an estate society.

The language of moral categories in old régime stratification

Much of the language of the old régime has a feudal ring: king, noblemen, commoner, estates general, and the like. The point of the discussion above is that the feudal language was now a language for discussing quite a different stratification order, especially in the plains of northern France and of the Aquitaine basin, and most especially in the cities of those regions. That is, the system of distinctions between, say, nobleman and commoner, was used in the old régime and sounds like the distinctions of feudal society. But a great deal of legal activity, especially by the royal bureaucracy, had changed the moral obligations and the social rôle attached to the categories. One of *les grands* at the king's court or an *intendent* in charge of the royal bureaucracy in a province was not an ordinary nobleman – certainly not the same sort of nobleman as a landowner in Brittany or a wholesale merchant in Orleans was.

Thus in many ways the language of feudalism had enough distinctions in it to be able, with the aid of some centuries of ingenuity, to describe a moral order of a highly commercialized bureaucratic empire, governing an estate society in which there were multiple social functions in each estate. No strong functionalism connected the feudal language to a feudal mode of production. Instead the feudal language formed a structure of distinctions that could be utilized to block in a moral order of quite a different kind. In Brittany or in the Alps the language still described an older moral order.

That is, the system of basic moral categories was a 'deep structure,' in which moral paragraphs could be written to explain the obligations and rights of relatively traditional feudal lords, modern wholesale grain and wine merchants in cities, and ennobled royal officers.

This deep structure of common moral categories was a culture of stratification that unified a stratification system consisting of very disparate parts.

Probably eighteenth-century Frenchmen, as well as modern scholars, believed that they lived in a single stratification system. This is shown by the fact that the Parisian-based Revolution abolished the system throughout the country, substituting a new moral language: citizenship for status, liberties for privileges, representation in government for guild membership, landownership for seigneurial rights, and so on. One major consequence of the Revolution then was to treat disparate stratification systems, in cities, on the northern and Aquitaine plains, and in the peripheral *pays d'état*, as if they were the same, and to abolish the culture of stratification that had made them appear to be the same.

But this shows the power of the deep structure of the culture of stratification categories to assimilate and shape the views of people differently situated, people with different grievances in the old régime and different hopes for the new, so that they believe themselves governed by a common value system and a common moral order when they are not. The deep structure of moral categories shapes the prejudices of revolutionaries about what features of society are the source of their difficulties as well as the prejudices of racists.

PART II

ORGANIZATIONS

9. Bureaucratic and craft administration of production: a comparative study

Administration in the construction industry depends upon a highly professionalized manual labor force.[1] The thesis of this paper is that the professionalization of the labor force in the construction industry serves the same functions as bureaucratic administration in mass production industries and is more rational than bureaucratic administration in the face of economic and technical constraints on construction projects.

Specifically we maintain that the main alternative to professional socialization of workers is communicating work decisions and standards through an administrative apparatus. But such an apparatus requires stable and finely adjusted communications channels. It is dependent on the continuous functioning of administrators in official statuses. Such continuous functioning is uneconomical in construction work because of the instability in the volume and product mix and of the geographical distribution of the work. Consequently the control of pace, manual skill, and effective operative decision (the essential components of industrial discipline) is more economical if left to professionally maintained occupational standards.

After presenting evidence and argument for these assertions, we will try to show why work on large-scale tract construction of houses

[1] 'Professionalized' here means that workers get technical socialization to achieve a publicly recognized occupational competence. 'Public recognition' involves preferential hiring (ideally to the point of excluding all others) of workers who have proved their competence to an agency external to the hiring firm or consumer. Often this agency is a professional association composed exclusively of qualified persons and more or less exhaustive of the occupation. This professional association itself often enforced preferential hiring rights of its members. The professional's *permanent labor market status* is not to be confused with permanent firm status (preferential hiring or continued employment of the current employees of a firm). This definition therefore, differs somewhat from that of Nelson Foote (1953).

continues to be administered on a nonbureaucratic, craft basis. Tract housing turns out to be a major revision in the *marketing* of construction products, rather than a revision in the *administration of work*.

Our method will be to reanalyze certain published demographic and economic data for their administrative implications. Since the data were collected for other purposes, they fit the requirements of our problem only roughly. The gaps in the information and the gross character of the categories make it necessary, therefore, to use very rough statistical procedures and to limit the data to a suggestive role.

On the basis of the empirical findings, we will re-examine Max Weber's model of bureaucracy, showing that some elements of that model are not correlated with other elements. This will provide a basis for constructing a model of bureaucracy as a subtype of rational administration, with professionalization another main subtype. A general model of rational administration will be built out of the common elements of these subtypes.

Bureaucratic administration and craft administration

Craft institutions in construction are more than craft trade unions; they are also a method of administering work. They include special devices of legitimate communications to workers, special authority relations, and special principles of division of work, the 'jurisdictions' which form the areas of work defining labor market statuses. The distinctive features of craft administration may be outlined by contrasting it with mass production manufacturing administration.[2] The object of this section is to show that craft institutions provide a functional equivalent of bureaucracy.

Mass production may be defined by the criterion that *both* the product *and* the work process are planned in advance by *persons not on the work crew*. Among the elements of the work process planned are: (1) the location at which a particular task will be done, (2) the movement of tools, of materials, and of workers to this work place, and the most efficient arrangement of these work-place characteristics, (3) sometimes the particular movements to be performed in getting the task done, (4) the schedules and time allotments for

[2] This account of mass production institutions is derived from Peter Drucker, (1950 and 1954) along with the work of David Granick, (1954).

particular operations, and (5) inspection criteria for particular operations (as opposed to inspection criteria for final products).

In construction all these characteristics of the work process are governed by the worker in accordance with the empirical lore that makes up craft principles. These principles are the content of workers' socialization and apply to the jobs for which they have preferential hiring rights.

This concentration of the planning of work in manual rôles in construction results in a considerably simplified communications system in the industry; but the simplification does not markedly reduce the number of people in administrative statuses. Administrative statuses are roughly equivalent to occupations in census categories: proprietors, managers, and officials; professional, technical, and kindred workers; and clerical and kindred workers.

The proportion of administrative personnel in the labor force in various fabricating industries does not vary widely. In construction the proportion of the labor force in the three administrative occupations is 15.5 per cent; in manufacturing as a whole it is 20.6 per cent; in iron and steel primary extraction, 15.5 per cent; motor vehicles and motor vehicle equipment, 17.6 per cent; in chemicals and allied industries, 33.4 per cent (U.S. Bureau of Census, 1950: Table 134, pp. 290–1). But these rough similarities in proportion of administrative personnel conceal wide differences in the internal structure of the communications system.

To provide a rough index of one of these differences in the internal structure of the authority systems, we have computed the proportion of clerical positions in the administration. This should provide an index of the proportion of people in administration who do not legitimate by their status the communications they process (e.g., typists, filing clerks, bookkeepers). They file the communications; they do not initiate them. Authority structures with special communications-processing positions may be called 'bureaucratic' structures.[3] They provide for close control of the work process farther up the administrative hierarchy, and hence facilitate the control and planning of the work process in large enterprises. They decrease the depend-

---

[3] This takes one of Weber's criteria of bureaucratization as an empirical indicator, namely administration on the basis of files. I believe some of the other characteristics of bureaucracy named by Weber can be derived from this one, while some cannot. See Max Weber (1946b).

Table 1 *The proportion of administrative personnel* who are clerks in selected fabricating industries, U.S., 1950.*

Industry or industry group	Percent of administrators clerks
Manufacturing	53%
Motor vehicles and accessories	63%
Iron and steel primary extraction	60%
Chemicals and allied	45%
Construction	20%

*Proprietors, managers, and officials; professional, technical and kindred workers; and clerical and kindred workers. *Characteristics of the Population, Part 1, pp. 290–1.*

ence of the enterprise on empirical lore and self-discipline at the work level and allow technical and economic decisions to be concentrated. Finally, they allow the processing of information and communications from distant markets, enabling the enterprise to be less dependent on the geographical location of clients.

The proportion of administrative personnel who are clerks in various fabricating industries is presented in Table 1.

Clearly the proportion of all administrative personnel who are clerks is considerably greater in manufacturing generally than it is in construction, and the typical mass production industries tend to have even greater development of specialized communications processing structures. The centralized planning of work is associated with this development of filed communications, with specialized personnel processing them.

Another type of internal differentiation of authority structures (systems of originating and processing communications legitimately directing workers) concerns the status and training of the originators. In some authority structures in fabricating industries, people in authority are largely defined by ownership and contract institutions, while in others their status derives from professional institutions. That is, communications from a position in the authority system may be considered legitimate because of the special competence of the originator, a professional; or they may be legitimate because of the special responsibility of the originator, as owner or official, for economic decisions.

We may contrast administrations by the proportion of people in

Table 2 *The proportion of top administrators* who are professionals in various industries, U.S., 1950.*

Industry or industry group	Professional authority positions
Manufacturing	50%
Motor vehicles and accessories	63%
Iron and steel primary extraction	64%
Chemicals and allied	65%
Construction	31%

*Proprietors, managers, and officials; and professional, technical and kindred workers. *Characteristics of the population, part 1, pp. 290–1.*

authority whose status derives from special education. This may be denoted as 'the professionalization of authority.' The proportion of all 'top' administrative personnel (proprietors, managers, and officials; *and* professionals) who are professionals in the selected industries is presented in Table 2.

The contrast in the degree of professionalization of authority between manufacturing and construction, and more especially between mass production and construction, is just as clear as was the case with bureaucratization.

The engineering of work processes and the evaluation of work by economic and technical standards take place in mass production in specialized staff departments, far removed from the work crew in the communications system. In the construction industry these functions are decentralized to the work level, where entrepreneurs, foremen, and craftsmen carry the burden of technical and economic decision.

This decentralization of functions of the firm to the work level in construction, and the relative lack of information about and professional analysis of work processes at administrative centers, is accompanied by a difference in the types of legitimate communication.

In the construction industry, authoritative communications from administrative centers carry only specifications of the product desired and prices (and sometimes rough schedules). These two elements of the communication are contained in the contract; first, the contract between the client (with the advice of architects or engineers) and the

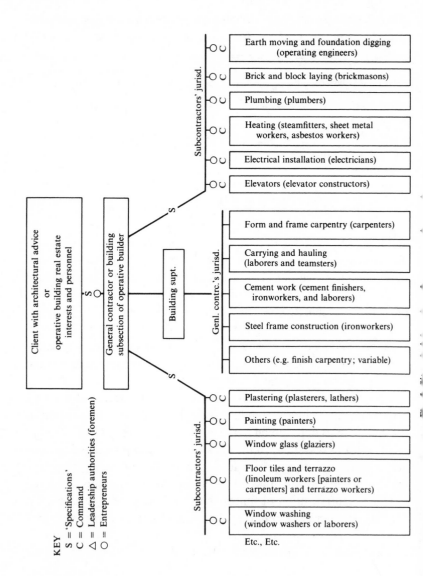

KEY

S = 'Specifications'
C = Command
△ = Leadership authorities (foremen)
O = Entrepreneurs

Client with architectural advice or operative building real estate interests and personnel

General contractor or building subsection of operative builder

Building supt.

Subcontractors' jurisd.

O C Earth moving and foundation digging (operating engineers)

O C Brick and block laying (brickmasons)

O C Plumbing (plumbers)

O C Heating (steamfitters, sheet metal workers, asbestos workers)

O C Electrical installation (electricians)

O C Elevators (elevator constructors)

Genl. contrc.'s jurisd.

Form and frame carpentry (carpenters)

Carrying and hauling (laborers and teamsters)

Cement work (cement finishers, ironworkers, and laborers)

Steel frame construction (ironworkers)

Others (e.g. finish carpentry; variable)

Subcontractors' jurisd.

O C Plastering (plasterers, lathers)

O C Painting (painters)

O C Window glass (glaziers)

O C Floor tiles and terrazzo (linoleum workers [painters or carpenters] and terrazzo workers)

O C Window washing (window washers or laborers)

Etc., Etc.

general contractor,[4] and, second, between the general contractor and subcontractors. Subcontractors do the work falling within the 'jurisdiction' of the trade they specialize in.

In mass production, where both the product and the work process are centrally planned, we find a system of legitimated advice on work and legitimate commands from line officials to foremen and workers to do particular work in particular ways. This more finely adjusted communications system depends on the development of specialized communications positions (clerks) and staff advice departments (professionals). These differences in administration are shown in Figs 1 and 2.

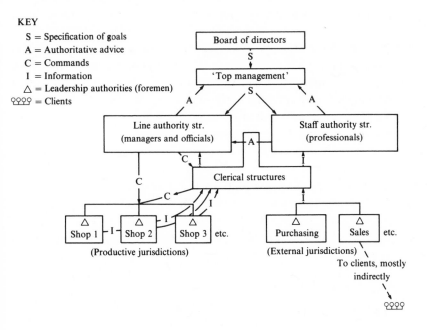

KEY
S = Specification of goals
A = Authoritative advice
C = Commands
I = Information
△ = Leadership authorities (foremen)
ⱷⱷⱷⱷ = Clients

Fig. 2. Administration of a mass production firm.

Craft administration, then, differs from bureaucratic administration by substituting professional training of manual workers for detailed centralized planning of work. This is reflected in the lack of clerical

[4] This step is omitted in the case of operative builders, but otherwise the authority structure is similar.

workers processing communications to administrative centers and less complex staffs of professionals planning work. It is also reflected in the simplification of authoritative communications from administrative centers.

Variability and bureaucratization

In this section we try to demonstrate that professionalization of manual labor is more efficient in construction because bureaucratic administration is dependent on stability of work flow and income, and the construction industry is economically unstable.

Bureaucratization of administration may be defined as a relatively permanent structuring of communications channels between continuously functioning officials. This permanent structuring of channels of legitimate communications, channels defined by the permanent official status of the originator of the communication and of its receiver, permits the development of routine methods of processing information upward and authoritative communication downward. That is, it permits administration on the basis of files and the economical employment of clerical workers.

Routine processing of administrative communications and information is economical only when the overhead cost of specialized information-processing structures is highly productive; this productivity will be high only if rules concerning the route of communication can be taught to clerks. Otherwise, if it is necessary to use discretion in the choice of the receiver of a communication, it is cheaper to rely on visual supervision and executive or professional discretion.

The case of mass production
Bureaucratization of administration depends therefore on the long-term stability of the administration. Of bureaucratic industrial administrations Peter Drucker says:

> The central fact of industrial economics is not 'profit' but 'loss' – not the expectation of ending up with a surplus ... but the inevitable and real risk of ending up with an impoverishing deficit, and the need, the absolute need, to avoid this loss by providing against the risks ... The economic activity of an industrial economy is not

'trade' taking place in the almost timeless instant of exchange, but production over a very long period. *Neither the organization* (the human resources) nor the capital investment (the material resources) *are productive in the 'here and now' of the present.* It will be years before the organization or the investment will begin to produce and many more years before they will have paid for themselves.[5]

It is clear that he cannot be talking about construction organizations, which have to be productive 'here and now.'

This association between orientation to stability and large-scale bureaucratized firms reflects the social requirements of complex communications systems between designated officials. Administrations faced with critical problems of instability and flexibility, such as those in the construction industry, will not find it economical to teach clerks rules for channeling communications. For it is impossible to hire a clerk on the labor market who will know the firm's communications channels, so clerks have to be kept on even when they are not productive.[6] And it is difficult to specify rules for channeling communications in advance when volume, product mix, and work-force composition change rapidly, as they do in construction.

The case of construction

The variability of the construction industry, its intimate dependence on variations in local markets, makes the development of bureaucrcy uneconomical. Table 3 shows the relationship between one type of variability and the employment of clerks.

Data are for some types of construction firms, for all firms in Ohio

5 Drucker, (1950: 52). Veblen said the same thing in a different moral vocabulary: 'Under the changed circumstance [the replacement of the "captain of industry"] the spirit of venturesome enterprise is more than likely to foot up as a hunting of trouble, and wisdom in business enterprise has more and more settled down to the wisdom of "watchful waiting." Doubtless this form of words, "watchful waiting," will have been employed in the first instance to describe the frame of mind of a toad who had reached years of discretion ... but by an easy turn of speech it has also been found suitable to describe the safe and sane strategy of that mature order of captains of industry who are governed by sound business principles' (Thorstein Veblen, 1948b: 385–6).

6 Also the class position of clerks makes it more difficult to hire temporary clerks.

large enough to have a report to the State Employment Office (those normally employing 3 or more persons). In the first column the mean size of firms in the branch is reported (computed here), and the branches are classified by mean size. In the second column is an index of seasonality of employment for the years 1926–36 (computed in the source).[7] In the last column the average proportion of the labor force who were clerks in 1939 is reported (computed here).

The relationship between the development of clerical statuses in administration and the stability of the work flow is clear from Table 3. The strength of the relationship within the industry can give us confidence in asserting that instability decreases bureaucratization. There are only two inversions, and these are of insignificant size: sheet metal and roofing should have been less bureaucratized than plumbing; and painters should have been less than brick, stone, and cement firms. This is a strong support for the hypothesis that the lack of bureaucratization in the construction industry is due to general instability.

We do not have space to document adequately the sources of variability in the work flow of construction administrations. The main elements may be outlined as follows:

---

[7] The index of seasonality was computed in the source in the following way: the monthly index of employment in firms reporting was computed for each year of the ten-year period, to the base of the mean employment of that year. Then the ten indices (one index for each of the ten years) for each month were arrayed, and the median taken. The 12 monthly medians give an over-all picture of seasonality for the category for the ten years. Scatter diagrams of these monthly indices, standardized for the general level of employment during the year as outlined above, are presented in Viva Boothe and Sam Arnold, (1944: Chart 16, pp. 83–6). Graphs of seasonality are presented by drawing lines through the median monthly indices. This procedure eliminates between-years (presumably cyclical) variations in employment level.

After this array of 12 monthly indices is found, the index of seasonality reported in Table 3 is computed by the formula:

$$\frac{\text{maximum} - \text{minimum}}{\text{maximum}} \times 100,$$

where the maximum is the largest median monthly index, and minimum the smallest. This gives an index ranging from zero (no seasonality) to 100, which would be the result of no employment at all in the minimum month. From the scatter diagrams, this might result in an under-estimation of the short-time instability only for electrical contracting firms. But other evidence indicates that electrical construction firms have very stable employment. See W. Haber and H. Levinson, (1956: 54). They rank construction occupations by percentage working a full year. Electricians work less than proprietors but more than any other occupation, including 'foremen, all trades.'

Table 3 *The relationship between mean size of firm, seasonality of employment, and the percentage of the labor force clerks, for branches of the construction industry.* *

Type of contractor	Mean size of firms (1939)	Index of seasonality of employment (1926–36)†	% of clerks in labor force‡ (1939)
More than 8 employees per contractor			
Street, road, and sewer	12.3	73	4.8
Sand, gravel, excavation	9.9	43	7.6
Ventilating and heating	8.2	29	11.7
4–8 employees per contractor			
Brick, stone, and cement	5.5	47	3.3
General contracting	6.9	43	5.2
Sheet metal and roofing	4.9	29	11.7
Plumbing	5.1	20	10.9
Electrical	6.3	13	12.5
Less than 4 employees per contractor			
Painting and decorating	2.5	59	3.9

*Taken from Viva Boothe and Sam Arnold (1944: Table 19, pp. 82–7). Plasterers are omitted from this table, because the number employed was not large enough to give a reliable figure on seasonality of clerks' work, the original purpose of the publication. There were less than 50 clerks in plastering enterprises in the state. Consequently the needed figure was not reported in the source. Plasterers' employment is very unstable, so the omission itself supports the trend.

†See footnote 7
‡Excluding sales clerks.

1. Variations in the volume of work and in product mix in the course of the business cycle.[8]

2. Seasonal variations in both volume and product mix.[9]

3. The limitation of most construction administrations, especially in the specialty trades, to a small geographical radius. This smaller market magnifies the variability facing particular firms according to well-known statistical principles (individual projects can form a large part of a local market).[10]

[8] Miles L. Colean and Robinson Newcomb, New York, (1952: 18–20, 49–50, and Appendix N, 219–42). Also Clarence Long (1940).

[9] The data reported from Boothe and Arnold show both great seasonality and differential seasonality by trade. Their data show construction to be one of the most seasonal industries (1944: 23–7).

[10] See Colean and Newcomb, (1952: 250–1), for the ecological limitations on administrative scope. For data on variations in volume in local areas, see U.S. Bureau of Labor Statistics, (1953: 22–5).

4. The organization of work at a particular site into stages (building 'from the ground up'), with the resulting variability in the productive purpose of any particular site administration (See Bertran and Maisel, 1955: 3–5).

Summary of empirical propositions

It now seems wise to review the argument thus far. We are trying to show that the professionalization of the manual work-force persists partly because it is a cheaper form of administration for construction enterprises than the bureaucratic form.

First we argued that bureaucracy and professionalized work-force were real alternataives, that: (a) decisions, which in mass production were made outside the work milieu and communicated bureaucratically, in construction work were actually part of the craftsman's culture and socialization, and were made at the level of the work crew, (b) the administrative status structure of construction showed signs of this difference in the communications structure by relative lack of clerks and professionals, and (c) the legitimate communications in construction (contracts and subcontracts) showed the expected differences in content from the orders and advice in a bureaucracy. Contracts contained specifications of the goals of work and prices; they did not contain the actual directives of work, which, it seemed to us, did not have to be there because they were already incorporated in the professionalized culture of the workers.

Secondly we argued that the bureaucratic alternative was too expensive and inefficient in construction because such administration requires continuous functioning in organizational statuses. But continuous functioning is prevented by the requirement that construction administrations adapt to variability in both volume and product mix. Using the employment of clerks as an index of bureaucratization, a close relation was found between seasonality in branches of construction and bureaucratization. This strong relationship was combined with knowledge of the general instability of construction to support the contention that bureaucracy was inefficient in construction.

The implications of marketing reform

There is a good deal of careless talk about the bureaucratization of construction and the introduction of mass production by operative building of tract homes (privately built housing estates). The central innovation of operative building is in the field of marketing and finance rather than in the administration of production. The similarity of productive administration in operative building and in other large-scale building is well summarized by Sherman Maisel:

> Many popular assumptions about subcontracting – that it lowers efficiency, raises costs, and leads to instability – are contradicted by our study in the Bay area of the reasons for subcontracting and its efficiency relative to its alternatives. Building appears to be one of the many industries where vertical disintegration increases efficiency and lowers costs without lessening stability. The fact that most large [operative housebuilding] firms have tried integrating various of the processes normally subcontracted but have usually returned to subcontracting them, is of great importance because it shows that the present prevalence of subcontracting is the result of a policy deliberately adopted by builders after testing alternative possibilities . . .
>
> The logic of trade contracting has developed as follows: (1) Efficiency reaches its maximum effectiveness under specialized labor. (2) Specialized labor reaches its maximum effectiveness when applied regularly on many units . . . (3) The problem of sustaining specialized jobs as well as the coordination of the movement of men among them requires special supervision, usually performed by trade contractors . . .
>
> Given the need for specialized mechanisms, the builder gains greater flexibility and a decrease in the problems of supervision through subcontracting (1953: 231–2).

The central limitation on supervision is the increase in overhead when mediated communication is introduced. 'A disproportionate increase takes place [in overhead in the largest construction firms] because production has spread beyond the area of simple visual control by the owner or owners [of the firm]' (Maisel, 1953: 102).

In fact, the characteristic of mass production administration, increased specialization of tools and other facilities at a planned work place, does not take place with increasing size. Most machinery added in large firms consists of hand power tools and materials-handling machinery (see Maisel, 1953: 103).

The low development of distinctively bureaucratic production-control mechanisms, such as cost accounting, detailed scheduling, regularized reporting of work progress, and standardized inspection of specific operations, is outlined by Maisel (1953: 123–30). What happens instead of centralized planning and bureaucratic control of work is an increase in the fineness of stages on which crews of workers are put. This results in the development of more efficient, but still quite diversified, skills. And most important, these skills still form a component of a labor market rather than an organizational status system.

Operative decisions are still very important at the work level, rather than being concentrated in production engineering and cost-accounting departments. Modification of tools for special purposes is done by workers (e.g., the making of templates which provide guides for standardized cutting operations, or the construction of special scaffolds for the crew.) There is no large element in the administration with the specialized task of planning technological innovation in the work process. And stable communications between work crews and decision centers are poorly developed.

The central consideration is that variability of work load for the administration is not very much reduced, if at all, by operative building. And it is not necessarily economical to take advantage of what reduction there is, when the subcontracting system and structured labor market are already in existence.

What is changed, what makes the economies possible, is the place of the goal-setting function. The productive goals in the past were set by clients with architectural advice, who quite naturally did not set goals in such a way as to maximize productive efficiency. In operative building productive goals are set autonomously by the administration. This means that they can choose, among the products they might produce, those which are technically easier. The main reduction of costs, of course, comes from the planning of the construction site so as to minimize transportation and set-up costs. Sites next to each other minimize costs of moving men, materials, and equipment to the site. Warehousing of materials can be planned to fit the individual site, rather than burdening builders' supply places. Uniformity of design reduces the complexity of materials distribution, reduces design costs, and so forth.

The main innovation, then, is the planning of the *product* for ease of production, rather than in the planning of the *productive process*. This is the introduction of the conceptions of Eli Whitney on *standardized parts* into construction, rather than of Henry Ford's innovation of *standardized tasks*.

Rational administration and bureaucracy

Since Weber, there has been a tendency to regard rational administration as identical with bureaucratic administration. This tendency has been especially strong among sociologists. We have chosen to define bureaucracy as a special type of rational administration and to discuss the social sources of an alternative method of institutionizing rationality, namely, professionalization.

The central point of this analysis is that the components of Weber's ideal type do not form an inherently connected set of variables. Some of the components of the ideal type are relatively uncorrelated with others, while some are highly correlated.

We have called craft production unbureaucratized, although it does involve 'the principle of fixed and official jurisdictional areas, which are generally ordered by rules.' (Weber, 1946: 196). The rules in this case are to be found in the jurisdictional provisions of trade unions, in the introductory sections of collective contracts, and in state licensing laws for contractors. The duties in construction are 'distributed in a fixed way as official duties' through legally binding contracts. 'The authority to give the commands required for the discharge of these duties is distributed in a stable way.' The sanctions, especially firing, are stably allocated to contractors and subcontractors on the particular project.

The principal difference comes in the criterion: 'Methodical provision is made for the *regular and continuous* fulfillment of these duties and for the execution of the corresponding rights." (Weber 1946: 196) It is not the rules governing jurisdiction and authority which we take to be characteristic of bureaucracy, but the regularity and continuity of work and status within an administrative system. We have shown that regularity and continuity are in fact correlated with our operational criterion of bureaucratization, the proportion of clerks among administrators.

Secondly, we have argued that 'the principles of office hierarchy . . . in which there is supervision of the lower office by the higher ones,' is dependent on stable communications structures, provided we differentiate *goal setting* from *supervision*. In construction there is no possibility of 'appealing the decision of a lower office [subcontractor] to its higher authority [the general contractor or client] (Weber, 1946b: 197). The goals of subcontractors are set by 'higher authorities.' But their work is not supervised, nor are their decisions appealable. Office hierarchy in the command-advice sense, then, is correlated with regularity and continuity in official statuses. Goal-setting arrangements can be changed drastically (e.g., from the client to the operative building corporation) without changing the administration of work in a bureaucratic direction.

The other main criterion Weber proposes concerns the stable structuring of communication (files), which we have taken as the empirical indicator of stable, rule-governed communication channels among official statuses.

These last three elements of Weber's ideal type (continuity, hierarchy, and files), then, are functionally interrelated; they are found together in mass-production administration but are absent in construction administration. But the first three elements (stable jurisdictions, official duties, and authority) are found in both construction and mass production, so they cannot be highly correlated with the elements of continuity, hierarchy, and files.

Weber draws from his ideal type certain implications concerning the position of the official. Some of these are derived from distinctive characteristics of bureaucracy as we have defined it, and some are derived from general requirements of rationality. Characteristics common to bureaucracies *and* nonbureaucratic rational administrations include:

1. Positions in the organization are separated from the household positions. Positions in construction as workers, foremen, and entrepreneurs involve the separation of work from home life, firm accounts from household accounts, firm and trade promotions from family ties.[11]

---

[11] Not that being a contractor's son doesn't give a competitive advantage; it is only that positions are not inherited, but awarded on a competitive basis. A contractor's son still has to meet occupational standards. On the advantage of sons of *Handwerker* in various trades in Germany, see Heinz Lamprecht, (1951: 42, 52).

2. Rational administration requires the allocation of work to those who are competent. This often involves hiring on the basis of formal training, certification, and examination. Not only civil servants, but also craftsmen, and private legal and medical practitioners, have to pass examinations or possess certificates of formal training. The main difference is that professional examinations allocate work throughout a labor market, while civil service examinations recruit only to organizational statuses.

3. To a large extent pecuniary compensation, regulated by the status of the worker, characterizes rational administration, as well as bureaucracy. At least, wage rates for each occupational status in construction are negotiated.

A characteristic of bureaucratic officials that is not found in construction is permanent appointment. Authorities on a construction project are appointed by subcontracts only for the duration of the project. The basis of responsibility for leadership duties is the contract for specific work (and the contractors' reputations) rather than generalized loyalty to the administration. Payment to authorities is not salary determined by the status of the official but payment for performance set by competitive bidding. Finally the career of the worker in construction is structured not by administrative regulation but by status in a structured labor market. These differences also distinguish private professional practice from bureaucratic administration.

We would construct an ideal type of functionally interrelated characteristics of bureaucracy as follows: The defining criterion would be stable, rule-ordered communications channels from and to continuously occupied statuses. This criterion implies: (1) development of files and employment of clerks, (2) hierarchical command-advice authority structures, and (3) career commitment to an *organizational* rather than a labor market or *occupational* status system.

Bureaucracy thus defined is a subtype of rational administration. Rational administration requires the government of work activity by economic and technical standards and hence requires:

1. Differentiation of the work rôle from home life (and other deep interpersonal commitments).

2. The organization of work statuses into some sort of career, in which future rights and duties depend on present performance according to specified standards.

3. A stable allocation of work to persons formally identified as able and willing to work and subject to discipline by understood work standards, and payment by the administration only when such workers are 'productive.'

4. A stable legitimate way of communicating at least the goals to be reached by subordinates and of seeing that these goals are accomplished.

This means that we take Weber's observations on the 'Presuppositions and causes of bureaucracy (1946: 204–9) to be mainly about the presuppositions and causes of any kind of rational administration. The presuppositions of bureaucracy are conditions facilitating continuous operation of an organizational status system, either continuity of work load and returns or institutionalized legitimacy of the status system itself (e.g., the military).

Continuity in status in a labor market, instead of an organization, we take to be the defining characteristic of professional institutions. Both the traditional professions and crafts in construction have professional institutions in this sense. These are characterized by (roughly) occupationally homogeneous organizations seeking control of the rights and duties associated with doing work within a defined jurisdiction. By this control they assure competence discipline. Both professions and crafts, then, guarantee labor market rights and enforce labor market duties which make up a professional status.

Conclusion

Concepts in organizational theory, such as bureaucracy, tend to take on a nebulous character because research in this area has consisted largely of case studies of particular organizations. An industrial firm engaged in mass production may certainly be bureaucratic, but not all the characteristics of the organization are distinctive of bureaucracy. Case studies cannot, ordinarily, sort out the inherent from the ephemeral connections among organizational characteristics. Systematic comparisons of different types of organizations, which we have attempted here, can refine our conceptual apparatus by defining complex concepts comprised of elements that hang together empirically.

The concept of bureaucracy developed here is not merely a descriptive one; it contains propositions about the connection between its elements. Such a concept cen be refined either by proving new elements to be necessarily connected to those already incorporated or by disproving the hypothesized connection between elements. Similar definition is needed for other complex concepts in the social sciences: the city, sovereignty, the firm.

A definition of the firm, for example, should include those characteristics inevitably found in social units producing goods for markets. Such a definition of the firm would be not merely a category to put concrete organizations into, but a set of propositions about the relations between markets and social groups. Such propositional definitions can be best derived from the systematic comparative study of organizations.

10. Social structure and the founding of organizations[1]

This essay will be concerned with the implications of the fact that organizational forms and types have a history, and that this history determines some aspects of the present structure of organizations of that type. The organizational inventions that can be made at a particular time in history depend on the social technology available at the time. Organizations which have purposes that can be efficiently reached with the socially possible organizational forms tend to be founded during the period in which they become possible. Then, both because they can function effectively with those organizational forms, and because the forms tend to become institutionalized, the basic structure of the organization tends to remain relatively stable.

For example, the present urban construction industry, with specialized craft workers, craft-specialized subcontractors, craft trade unions, and a relation of contract between the construction enterprise and the consumer, was developed in European cities before the industrial revolution. Such an organization requires relatively dense settlement, some detachment of socialization for occupational rôles from families to be vested in guild-like organizations of craftsmen, contracts enforceable in the law, free wage labor which can move to some extent from job to job and employer to employer, and so on. Such conditions do not normally exist in agrarian societies. This craft form of organization has persisted partly because it is well adapted to the problems of the building industry and partly because of the force

---

[1] The relation of the age of organizations to their social structure is one of several topics on which Robert Blauner and I have had extensive correspondence and discussion over several years. I can no longer sort out which ideas are his, which are mine, and which are my projections of what he would say if he considered some particular aspect of the problem. The responsibility of publishing these ideas before the difficulties are cleared up is, however, entirely mine.

of tradition and vested interest, except in certain circumstances. In the Soviet Union, which had a quite normal-looking construction industry in the cities before Revolution, a combination of forces (government being virtually the only consumer, industrial building being emphasized in contrast to residential and commercial building, the destruction of autonomous power of trade unions) has resulted in the thoroughgoing destruction of the craft system. During the 1930s there were actually fewer apprentices (a characteristic feature of craft systems) in construction than in the steel industry, even though the construction industry grew much faster during the period. Except in these circumstances (up to now, fortunately, exceptional cases), the basic craft organization has persisted and has distinguished construction from more 'modern' industries.

Looked at another way, an examination of the history of almost any type of organization shows that there are great spurts of foundation of organizations of the type, followed by periods of relatively slower growth, perhaps to be followed by new spurts, generally of a fundamentally different kind of organization in the same field. For instance, most men's national social fraternities were founded in one of three periods, 1840–50, 1865–70, and 1900–20. The first wave were founded mainly at northern colleges that later became liberal art colleges and seem to have had something to do with the secularization of student culture in reaction to previous evangelical currents, and perhaps also functioned as a defense against the high tide of Jacksonian democracy. Fraternities in the second wave were founded in the South, later spreading to the North, and clearly had something to do with the difficulties of Northerners and Southerners being 'brothers' right after the Civil War. Several were founded in Lexington, Virginia, where Robert E. Lee headed Washington College, which is suggestive of the symbolic conditions surrounding their founding. The third wave was of 'anti-fraternity fraternities,' especially of Jews, Negroes, Catholics, and students at teachers' colleges, with a heavy outpouring of anti-discrimination statements and praise of poor college students in the chartering documents. (These observations are based on my own tabulations from fraternity handbooks.)

Our interest in these spurts derives from the fact that organizations formed at one time typically have a different social structure from those formed at another time. Further the slow rate of growth after the spurts generally indicates that few organizational restructurings are taking place, hence the *date of the spurts* is highly correlated with the *present social structure* of the organization whose type originates in one of these spurts. These spurts are best documented in the field of economic organizations, largely because of the influence of Schumpeter (1934; 1939; 1951; Conrad, 1961), who thought they were fundamental to the explanation of business cycles. But the history of virtually any type of organization suggests the same pattern.

Thus, there was a rash of savings bank formations in the 1830s. The first factory industry, textiles, developed in its factory form in England mainly between 1800 and 1830, and was imported pretty much in that form to the United States toward the end of that period. Railroads, and consequently new communities and counties, and, of course, great steel companies, had their great period of organization in the 1850s and again in the 1870s. Organized socialist parties spread throughout western Europe after the organization of the Second International. New universities were founded in the United States mainly from 1870 to 1900, and the universities 'founded' before or after that time are mainly other types of schools (especially liberal arts colleges or land grant colleges) on their way up. Practically no private liberal arts colleges, and very few liberal arts colleges of any kind, have been founded since 1900. At present, junior colleges are being organized at a high rate.

Most of the national (or 'International') craft trade unions were founded between the Civil War and the beginning of the twentieth century. They had great growth in local organizations and membership in the World War I decade. The next great spurt of union foundation was, of course, the organization of CIO unions in the 1930s, especially 1937. Streetcar companies and electricity-producing companies were all the rage from 1887 to 1910. The combination of the streetcar and the railroad was at the back of the great reorganization of retail trade by department stores (Macy's, 1858; Marshall Field's, 1852), chain stores (A & P, 1901; Woolworth's, 1879), and mail-order houses (Sears, Roebuck, 1886; Montgomery Ward, 1872). (All dates are from *Moody's Industrial Manual*.) The automobile revolution, and consequently the foundation of the great automobile companies and the rapid growth of the oil and rubber industries, came in the 1920s. Roughly concomitant was the rise of the industrial chemicals industry and (shortly following the reorganization of medical education in the first decade of the twentieth century) the reorganization and centralization of the pharmaceutical trade. Mass production of airplanes and regular air transportation became important during and after World War II. The data processing industries are still going through the throes of organization. The mass communications industries were mostly organized in the 1920s, although the fundamental mass communications industry, printing and publishing, derives from before the factory production period. Retail trade and many of the service industries derive mainly from the preindustrial city and farming is obviously a prefactory industry.

Stability of types over time

All this would be merely an interesting facet of social history, if it could not be shown that certain structural characteristics of a type of organization are remarkably stable over time. But Hoselitz, for example, has provided data on the proportion of workers in enterprises with more than 200 persons in different industries in Germany in 1882 and 1956 (1961, p. 545). Even though the average size of enterprise in all industries (except printing, which seems to be due to changes in census coverage with the partition of Germany) increased steadily throughout the period, the Spearman rank correlation of proportions of firms with more than 200 employees in 1882 and 1956 is 0.74. That is, if an industry was a small firm industry in 1882, it was very probably still a small firm industry in 1956, though the absolute size of a 'small' firm was likely to be somewhat higher.

An even more direct indication of the power of persistence of organizational forms comes from a study of Japanese manufacturing (Rosovsky & Ohkawa, 1961). The authors classified branches of industry into those making products in general use before the Meiji Restoration in 1868, when Japan's rapid modernization of the economy started (but apparently there had been relatively rapid economic growth in the previous period, particularly a great increase in the productivity of land). Manufacturing enterprises in the traditional sector are much smaller, much less capital-intensive, less oriented to a luxury market. For instance, among all manufacturing industries, only 35.0% of the labor force was employed by firms of size

4–29; among indigenous industries, the proportion was 74.4%. The unweighted mean of urban expenditure elasticities (cross-section) for indigenous commodities was only .401; for modern commodities it was 1.022.[2]

In general, in Japan, as in other industrialized countries, unpaid family labor is most prevalent in agriculture, somewhat less prevalent in retail and personal service industries, less yet in urban construction (apparently the heavily male character of the industry somewhat overcomes the normal expectation that this industry should be highly involved in families), and much less in the thoroughly modern economic sectors. *Within* manufacturing, 8.7% of the workers in 55 indigenous industries were unpaid family workers, while the national average for all industry included in the Census of Manufacturers is 3.2%.

For the United States, Table 1 presents statistics on various aspects of the social structure of industries by a rough age-of-industry classification.[3] I have had to leave many industries out because of my ignorance of their history, and at best the age classification represents my impressions from a casual reading of economic history. Some better criterion of the 'age' of a product (such as that used by Rosovsky & Ohkawa) is needed, but this would necessitate a much finer industrial classification than is available, and a separate research project in the history of American technology.

The first two columns are proportions of the labor force involved in the kinship sector of the labor market, of self-employed and unpaid family workers. The third column is the proportion of clerical workers in the 'middle-class administrative personnel' group made up of clerical workers, professionals, proprietors, managers, and officials.

---

[2] Expenditure elasticities are low when a smaller proportion of higher incomes is spent on a commodity, high when higher incomes lead to increased proportional expenditures on the commodity (i.e., high for 'luxuries,' low for 'necessities'). An elasticity of 1.00 would mean that the proportion spent on the commodity was the same for all ranges of income. Later industries were, of course, started when income was higher, so their current higher elasticities are probably an indication of preservation of organizational characteristics, in the sense that they are oriented to the same markets which had newly appeared when they were founded, while older industries are still oriented to markets that existed long ago.

[3] It is unnecessary to say that the age of an industry is not the average age of firms in the industry. Very few construction firms are as old as almost any railroad firm, although rails are clearly a newer industry. Most retail firms showing a highly 'traditional' organization are much younger than Sears, Roebuck, with a 'modern' organization.

Two industries, telecommunications and the Post Office, are not reported in this column because their operative personnel are classified by the census as clerical workers, so the proportion reported is not a good index of 'bureaucratization.' The fourth column reports the proportion of all 'top status people,' i.e., professionals and proprietors, managers, and officials who are professionals, thus providing an index of the development of staff structures.

The first column shows that the pre-factory industries still involve unpaid family workers to a greater extent than any of the industries developed after that time. There are three cells in the column that deviate from this pattern (deviant cells are starred for ease in locating them). Two of these come from industries which are deviant in *all* cells, namely Ship and Boat Building and Automobile Repair. Ship and Boat Building is much more modern on all criteria than would be anticipated on the basis of its age, and Automobile Repair is a twentieth-century traditional industry. The other exception in the first column is Water Transportation. (Clearly the introduction of the steamship, diesel propulsion, and the steel hull reorganized the shipbuilding and water-transportation industries much more than I had anticipated). With these exceptions, all the pre-factory industries are above 0.15% in the proportion of unpaid family workers, and all those whose organizational forms were determined after the beginning of the nineteenth century are below 0.15%. On this basis, we can hazard the historical guess that the first stage of 'bureaucratization of industry' was the differentiation of the work rôle from family life. Note also that the level of unpaid family labor in all United States industries except agriculture is below that of manufacturing as a whole in Japan, as reported above. This suggests that unpaid family labor declines with time and modernization in both the traditional and modern sectors, but the difference between these two sectors remains even in advanced industrial countries.

In the second column there are indications of a slightly different relation of kinship institutions to the organization. 'Self-employment' is an indication of the 'employment' of 'unpaid family labor' in the work of *managing* the enterprise. Thus, the two breaks in the column indicate the present results of the historical process of differentiating managerial rôles from kinship rôles. Prefactory industries are at 5.9 per cent or above in the proportion in the kinship sector (two exceptions), early nineteenth-century industries between 3.0 and 6.0 per cent (one exception), railroad age and later industries are below 3.0 per cent (two exceptions). Before commenting on this, we will treat the closely related third column.

In the third column, the decisive break is again between prefactory industries and all later ones, the former running below 45 per cent clerical workers among administrators, the later above (five exceptions). Since the proportion of clerical workers among administrators is a good indication of the development of files, regularized communications channels using written communication between designated officials, the origin of 'bureaucratic' administration of production (in this sense) can be roughly located in the early nineteenth century.

Combining these results, we see two crucial stages of the 'bureaucratization of industry.' The first took place at the beginning of the factory age and involved the introduction of written and filed communication into factory administration and the differentiation of both work rôles and lower management from family institutions. But the top administration was still in the hands of owners, and the factory was still an element in the family estate of the top management. Authority can become more hierarchical, can have more levels, with impersonal written communications and filed records. The superior efficiency of a bureaucratic communications apparatus for large-scale administration allows the size of the enterprise to expand somewhat, resulting in fewer top administrators (reflected in fewer 'self-employed' than in the prefactory period). But top management is still not a normal career stage in the life plan of a subordinate official, for the top managers are still 'self-employed', and their positions depend on their success (or the success of their ancestors) in building up a family estate.

Later, in the railroad age, top managerial positions were differentiated from kinship institutions and made into 'occupations' of employed career officials. Capital was now frequently recruited by the sale of corporate securities on the open market, and the size of the business did not depend on the size of the family estate inherited by top management. Top managerial positions became a career stage in the life of employed officials, rather than a prerogative of sons and husbands. The same process apparently took place in the old industries of Ship and Boat Building and Water Transportation, while in

Table 1[a] *Characteristics of the labor force of industries classified by age*

Industry	% Unpaid family workers	% Self-employed & family workers	Clerical as % administrative workers	Professionals as % authority
Pre-factory				
Agriculture	13.3	76.3	0.4	0.7
Forestry, fisheries	0.5	33.2	14	79*
Retail trade	1.4	23.7	26	7
Construction	0.2	19.2	20	31
Hotels, lodging	1.0	17.8	37	9
Logging	0.5	15.4	18	21
Wholesale trade	0.2	13.3	47*	11
Printing, publishing	0.2	5.9	51*	54*
Ship, boat building	0.1*	2.9*	55*	64*
Water transportation	0.0*	1.7*	36	12
Early nineteenth century				
Woodworking industries	0.1	6.0	45	14
Stone, clay, glass	0.1	5.4	48	45*
Leather, except footwear	0.1	3.0	52	22
Apparel	0.0	3.4	53	18
Textile industries	0.0	1.2*	62	36
Banking, Finance	0.0	4.2	69	15
Railroad age				
Post Office	–	–	not relevant (mail carriers)	3
Railroads, railway express	0.0	0.1	70	17
Street, railroads, buses	0.1	2.0	68	28
Coal mining	0.1	2.7	45	31
Metal extraction and fabrication	0.0	1.6	54	54*
Railroad and miscellaneous Transportation equipment	0.1	0.9	58	66*
Modern				
Automobile repair	0.5*	23.7*	23*	4*
Telecommunications	0.1	0.4	not relevant (operators)	51
Crude petroleum, Natural gas	0.0	5.7*	35*	55
Rubber products	0.0	0.6	59	60
Motor vehicles and equipment	0.0	0.5	63	63
Electrical and gas utilities	0.0	0.3	62	65
Chemicals and allied	0.1	2.5	49	69
Air transport	0.1	2.5	49	69
Petroleum, coal production	0.0	0.9	48	71
Electrical machinery and equipment	0.0	1.0	53	73
Aircraft and parts	0.0	0.4	46	89

*Cells deviant from hypotheses.

Automobile Repair and Crude Petroleum and Natural Gas Extraction traditional forms have been introduced into new industries.

The fourth column represents roughly the development of staff departments. In organizations originating before the modern age, less than 35% of the top status people (those who occupy positions of authority either by virtue of their office of proprietorship or by virtue of professional training) are made up of professional people (six exceptions). After the beginning of the twentieth century, at least half of the authority positions are occupied in new industries by professionals (one exception). Two of the exceptions are accidental features of the data. The government departments concerned with forestry and conservation (which are relatively new) are disproportionately made up of professionals, and account for a large share of the professionals found in these industries. So here the index does not represent the development of staff departments, but the dominance of new departments of the government. Second, writers and editors are counted as professionals, but are not generally in staff departments, so the misplacement of printing and publishing is not really meaningful.

Discounting 'accidental' exceptions which reflect inadequacies in the data we have used, the main exceptions to the generalizations are in the 'machine-building' industries. These industries, whether building ships, locomotives and railroad cars, machine tools, automobiles,

---

*Based on my computations from U.S. Bureau of the Census, 1952, pp. 290–1. Comparison with figures for 1960, for those industries in which comparable data are available, shows a virtually identical ranking of industries by criteria of professionalization of authority and the proportion of clerical workers among all administrative workers. All industries but one (out of 14 where comparable data are available) have become more professionalized in authority. All prefactory industries but one (out of the five where data are available) have become more 'bureaucratic,' in the sense that a higher proportion of administrators are clerks in 1960 than in 1950. All but one of the early nineteenth-century, railroad age, and modern industries have become less 'bureaucratic' by this criterion. The drifts over a decade within industries are small compared with the differences among industries at the starting point, which accounts for the preservation of relative positions.

(Note: I have combined 'Sawmills and Planing Mills,' 'Furniture,' and 'Miscellaneous Wood Products' into a general caterogy of 'Woodworking Industries.' Also I have combined 'Primary Iron and Steel Extraction,' 'Non-ferrous Metal Extraction,' and 'Metal Fabrication' into a general category of 'Metal Extraction and Fabrication.' The individual subindustries in these cases are similar on all the indices computed here and generally originated at about the same periods, so no confusion in the general picture should result from these combinations.)

aircraft, electrical machinery, or other machinery, all have modern forms of organization, whatever their age.

For economic organizations where the data are fairly readily available, structural characteristics of a type of organization tend to persist, and consequently there is a strong correlation between the age at which industries were developed and their structure at the present time.

Probably other organizations as well still have traces of their time of origin. It seems very unlikely that national social fraternities being organized now [1964] would have racial and religious exclusion clauses. The representatives of national fraternities or sororities who visit campuses during rushing seasons (the periods when new fraternity members are recruited) are sometimes provided with printed instructions and arguments to help them deal with chapters that want to pledge a minority-group member. If the unprejudiced forces are so strong as to require special efforts of national officers to overcome them, newly founded groups without a tradition to defend would probably save themselves the trouble.[4] If working-class parties in Europe were organized without reference to tradition now, the overhanging revolutionary mood of Marxist ideology would probably be dispensed with. If universities were just being organized now, the federal government and its research arms would undoubtedly play more of a rôle in university government. If the YMCA were organized now, it would very likely be a secular agency more similar to the mental health movement. And so on.

Developing a theory of the correlation of age and structure

A theory which seeks to explain this observed correlation type and its structure must deal with at least three questions. (a) Why are organizational forms originated at different times different at the time of their foundation? (b) What kinds of forces internal to the dynamics of passing on an organizational tradition tend to maintain the form in

---

[4] The fact that almost all fraternities founded between 1900 and 1920 were 'anti-fraternity' fraternities of ethnic or nonsectarian groups, without exclusion clauses, is only slight support for this guess, if any, for these fraternities were reacting to previously established fraternity systems, not starting anew.

more or less its original shape? and (c) Why are such traditional organizational forms not eliminated by the competition of new organizational forms which become possible in succeeding periods?

The second and third questions are partly unnecessary, to the degree that the technical and economic conditions of a particular enterprise determine its appropriate organizational form. For example, I have argued (Stinchcombe, 1959; also reprinted here) that the unbureaucratized craft-subcontracting structure of the construction industry is particularly suited to the highly variable work load of the industry, the varied nature of its products, and to the fact that the work that has to be done at a particular site varies a great deal depending on the stage of the process of building which has been reached. These conditions have been relatively uniform in urban construction in capitalist societies for a long time. As soon as the social structure of early modern cities was appropriate for the development of this form, special-purpose organizations for construction were 'invented.' Since the technical innovations in building did not appreciably affect the conditions which made the form appropriate (unlike the effect of technical innovations, in, for instance, shipbuilding or the construction of wheeled vehicles), the form persisted. In other words, if we considered building skyscrapers a 'new industry' as we consider automobiles a 'new industry,' then simply because certain of the economic and technical characteristics crucial in determining the socio-technical system did not change with the invention of steel frame construction and elevators, the 'new industry' of skyscraper construction has a traditional form and violates our main hypothesis.

On the other hand, railroads perhaps could not be 'invented' until the social forms appropriate to an inherently very large-scale enterprise had been invented, and railroads still being inherently a large-scale enterprise (unlike those technical systems that had been already incorporated into economic life before it was possible to construct such large organizations), they still show the characteristics inevitably associated with size.

In short, by a combination of the postulate that economic and technical conditions determine the appropriate organizational form for a given organizational purpose and the postulate that certain kinds of organizations (and consequently the technical systems which require them) could not be invented before the social structure was appropriate to them, a complete theory of the correlation between age and structure of organizations could be developed, with no recourse at all to special 'traditionalizing' forces.

Such a theory would be particularly appropriate to deal with certain of the deviant cases in the analysis, such as the automobile repair industry. This industry is clearly 'new' because it is dependent on the existence of the automobile industry; we might hold that the automobile industry itself could not be invented until organizational forms appropriate to large-scale factories and nationwide distribution systems had been invented. The industries that are dependent on the automobile industry could not develop until the age of modern bureaucratic enterprise, yet their own technical systems need not be those that require modern forms of organization. We can suspect that this is exactly the case with the automobile repair industry. This is supported by the observation that many underdeveloped countries which find it impossible to introduce automobile manufacturing have no difficulty whatever developing a very vigorous and effective repair industry. But both because I believe there is direct evidence of traditionalizing forces, and because the evidence is not at hand for judging the alternative theories, I will develop the extant answers to all three of the questions posed above.

(a) Why are organizational forms developed at different times systematically structurally different? Two of the fundamental problems in starting new types of organization are to concentrate sufficient resources in the hands of an innovating élite and to recruit, train, motivate, and organize personnel in a structure that will function more or less continuously. Or, to rephrase these requirements in terms of the structure of the organization, an organization must have an élite structure of such a form and character that those people in the society who control resources essential to the organization's success will be satisfied that their interests are represented in the goal-setting apparatus of the enterprise, and the body of the organizational structure must have such relations to the labor market that an adequate quality of motivated work gets done.

Three of the most important resources are power (in the sense of capacity to coerce if necessary, e.g., the right of eminent domain for railroads), wealth, and moral commitment or legitimacy. With these resources it is possible to achieve discipline within the organization and the consent of those outside whose consent is essential. Different organizations of course make use of different 'mixes' of these resources (Etzioni, 1961). Railroads and other 'natural monopolies' must have more political legitimacy than more competitive industries. Character-forming organizations need more capacity for moral suasion than economic organizations. Large corporations must be granted by law more capacity to act in spite of objections by minority owners than small partnerships.

But different societies, and the same societies at different times, have different devices for distributing these resources to innovators, and have different 'qualities' of such resources. A classic analysis of the quality of resources and their availability to innovators, with consequent effects on the form of organization of production, is Weber's analysis of the social sources of consent to the authority of entrepreneurs starting factories. Urban land, at least, had been alienable, and hence available to entrepreneurs, during the European Middle Ages. Commercial institutions for transferring the control of money were also fairly well developed long before factory industry became important. One of the main resources that was problematic, according to Weber, was whether entrepreneurs could 'recruit the obedience' of labor. His argument on the relation of the Protestant ethic to obedience to impersonal technical norms rather than to personal authority is too well known to bear repeating.[5] But somewhat less attention has been paid to his analysis of the impact of formally free labor. Clearly, if obedience is owed to traditional lords or to conquerors, it cannot freely pass to innovators whose resources come through peaceful pursuit of market advantage, upstarts from the common people. In an extended analysis of slavery, Weber tried to show that the *quality* of labor under a system is inadequate for factory enterprise. He gave at least four reasons for its inappropriateness: (a)

---

[5] This part of the argument, however, has often been lost in the concentration on the rôle of religion in the recruitment of entrepreneurs. As Weber argued, entrepeneurship is both a matter of innovation and a matter of nontraditional authority, and a flow of innovations without nontraditional authority does not revolutionize a productive system. The definition of entrepreneurship purely as innovation probably accounts for the ignoring in the literature of Weber's more complete argument on why state churches and free professional magicians discourage the passing of authority to those not hallowed by tradition. An excellent study of the effect of a powerful priesthood on the development of one type of capitalist authority is Elkins (1959, pp. 52–80).

it eats up capital, already likely to be in short supply; (b) it makes labor into a fixed cost (the subsistence of slaves, who are too valuable to let starve in bad times, unlike free labor); (c) the slave market is intimately dependent on the fortunes of war, so the price of labor is not calculable and the only sure, stable supply (by raising slaves) is risky in an unsteady market because of the long period between investment and payoff; (d) most important, the degree of responsible initiative required in factory work cannot be achieved by application of force or legal constraint. This last is also an objection against traditional forced labor. In sum, authority in plantation agriculture may pass to entrepreneurs efficiently enough with slavery, but entrepreneurs in factory production cannot get the kind of obedience they need under the economic conditions they can meet by any other system than formally free labor, preferably paid in money wages.[6]

We can say something quite similar of free wage labor in a modern economy. It seems that wage labor is inappropriate for providing the kind of discipline of workers appropriate for a modern economy, and wage labor is disappearing in the more rapidly growing segments of the economy, being replaced by salaried career labor, recruited from schools and colleges. The process is slow and takes place largely at the growing edge of the economy, just as was the case with wage labor. Basically this is due to the fact that 'labor' is more and more the production, dissemination and application of knowledge rather than energy. Particularly in the very rapidly growing industries, such as education, weapons design, computer production and sales, advertising, and research, production varies much more with the amount of knowledge and intelligence than with the amount of energy applied. To an increasing extent, the exports of the richer countries reflect the fact that they can produce, disseminate, and apply knowledge much more cheaply than poorer countries, where human energy is cheaper. Natural resources are becoming less important in determining the flow

---

[6] The reasons for inefficiency in systems of payment in kind are too complex to go into here, where the purpose is to illustrate the problem of passing resources to new organizations. Briefly, payment in kind tends to traditionalize and stereotype authority relations, to orient exchange to the normatively defined 'needs' of the exchanging parties, and consequently to make the reward system within the organization less flexible. Compare Weber's analysis of the significance of money.

of international trade, and educational systems are becoming more important.

The system of rewards and punishments appropriate for maximizing the amount of knowledge and intelligence that will be applied in a work rôle are likely to be quite different from those appropriate for maximizing the amount of energy applied. In particular, the organization of work rôles into a *career* is much more important, and the necessity for rewarding performance from minute to minute is less important. A man's knowledge and intelligence do not vary much from one hour to the next, but vary greatly over his lifetime. Thus, the motivational devices for organizing labor have to be directed toward rewarding variation over lifetimes, rather than over hours.

This means that salaries are a more appropriate form of payment than wages, and the organization of a series of salaries over a course of years – in order to encourage further learning as a qualification for future jobs – is crucial. Thus knowledge-producing and disseminating industries, and those commodity-producing industries whose productivity depends on the application of knowledge more than on the application of energy, are likely to provide stable salaried employment, with salaries organized into a differentiated system so that a man's earnings vary markedly between years but very little in shorter time periods, a salary system in which income is relatively highly correlated with age, and a system of ranks or salary levels supposedly representing different levels of intellectual competence.

Where for economic reasons an enterprise cannot guarantee a complete career line for the people whose knowledge it needs – for instance, if it is too small to support an operations research group or an adequately diversified legal staff – the appropriate arrangement is not to employ such workers in an explicitly insecure job. The appropriate arrangement is similar to the client and free-professional relation, by which industries applying knowledge to laymen's problems have traditionally been organized. Fee-for-service consulting relations are more likely to arise, in the absence of salaried career specialists, than are wage-labor arrangements.

Thus, as the crucial factor of production obtained from 'labor' changes from energy to knowledge, the appropriate organization of the labor market changes from wage labor to salaried labor or free professional practice. This new organization of the labor market has its focus in the university, whose labor force is organized exactly according to the principles outlined above. The university is not only a model of what knowledge-producing industries need to look like, it also plays a vital rôle in the larger system of labor market organization, for it provides the prospective professional with the initial knowledge on which a future career is based and also provides extensive consulting and research services on a fee-for-service basis. The fees, incidentally, are very steep.

More and more of the labor market of the society at large can be expected to approach the organization of the labor market in higher education. This reorganization of the labor market around the university started, in a significant way, toward the end of the nineteenth century. The 'modern' industries of the above analysis have already reorganized their administrative apparatus until it looks very much like a university, and the very modern industries at the edge of current growth have as much as half of their labor force in university-type labor market structures (e.g., the business of building rockets has about that proportion).

The picture of the United States economy in the year 2500 could probably be approximated fairly well by expanding the social structure of a major university to a population of two or three hundred million. Clearly, there are many kinds of structures which can be built to be oriented to this type of labor market which could not be built before. Thus, both the early capitalist forms of enterprise and certain modern forms depend on reorganization of the labor market.

The creation of institutions appropriate to a formally free labor market, then, are a structural precondition of one type of organization according to Weber's argument. Something of the same sort goes on with other resources for organization-building. For instance, the number of people committed to the systematic advance of secular knowledge, and hence available as faculties for universities, obviously differs among societies, and differs over time as a heavily rural frontier society concerned with practical problems and the salvation of souls turns into an urban secular society. With the invention of social devices to 'capitalize' this resource into going concerns – land grants, boards of regents made up of rich men rather than clergymen, norms imported from Germany (for research degrees, faculty government, teaching loads, and salaried faculties) – modern universities could be founded. Or to take another example, socialization in professional schools can make staff departments a paying operation, both by supplying knowledge on the labor market and by giving professionals a definition of their mission in industry. Or the development of savings banks means that capital need not come out of the family estates of friends and relatives, both increasing the amount of wealth available for investment and depersonalizing the process of laying one's hands on it.

The organizations formed at any given time must obtain the resources essential to their purpose by the devices developed at the time. Since these devices differ, the structures of organizations differ.

An example of the effect of changing devices for mobilizing strategic resources on elite structure is suggested by Duverger's analysis (1954, pp. 1–60) of the different structure of the egalitarian political parties, depending on whether they were organized before or after trade unions became strong. In England, the Labour Party was formed in the first decade of this century, after trade unions had become strong. In the United States, the Democratic party was a strong functioning organization before any important national unions were formed. In the formal constitution of leadership in the Labour Party, the election units and the interests represented are trade unions; in the Democratic party they are state party apparatuses. Examples of the historical determination of the available alternatives of elite structure of organizations could be multiplied. The legal development of boards of directors who could act in the name of stockholders, or the development of the legal definition of the rôle of trustees so that the resources of the dead or of non-profit enterprises could be administered with a practical degree of discretion, fundamentally changed the possibilities of corporate and institutional élite structure. The development of stock exchanges and of the variety of investment instruments changed the possibilities for recruiting capital. The regularization of the grant of government powers (such as the right of eminent domain) to 'private' organizations such as canal companies and railroads again opened up new alternatives. The net result is the tremendous range of alternative ways of organizing an elite available in modern society, documented by Dahl and Lindblom (1953, esp. pp. 10, 12, 14–15, 17).

The structure of labor markets

The structure of labor markets, or institutions and practices by which men are distributed among organizations (the analysis to follow of the current American labor market is deeply indebted to Phelps, 1957) changes over the course of history. This means that the nature of the norms governing workers, the quality of the competence which can be recruited, and the bases of the motivation to work which an organization has to deal with and adapt its structure to, change. For purposes of comparing labor market structures, one can specify the elements of labor market structure as: (a) the nature and quality of preparation for work rôles outside employing organizations, particularly in schools, (b) the organization of licensing agencies and practices, (c) the nature of organized groups which determine the norms of the employment contract, such as unions and professional associations, (d) the manner in which particular jobs are (or are not) integrated into careers in which the quality of current performance affects future statuses, and (e) the structure of competition for labor, or looking at it from the point of view of the individual, the range of alternatives open to people occupying particular organizational statuses. I will first discuss in these particulars the variety of ways that sectors of the labor market of the United States are socially structured at present, then consider briefly the historical development of the labor market context in which organizations have had to be founded.

Labor may in the first place be committed to particular jobs by family ownership in the organization itself, as is quite typical of most American farming, much of retail and service employment, and the top echelons in middle-sized business. About a sixth or a fifth of the total civilian labor force, and perhaps a tenth of the urban labor force, are proprietors, self-employed (which of course includes many professionals), and unpaid family labor. These people fail (very generally those who fail enter the manual work force) when the enterprise fails. The successful urban small-business population is quite heavily recruited from ethnic groups whose family structure and attitudes toward work achievement provide the kind of disciplined performance necessary to build a business – Jews (Lenski, 1961, pp. 91–3),

Greeks,[7] and Japanese are especially prominent examples. Most farmers are sons of farmers.[8] This section of the labor market, then, is intimately tied up with kinship institutions, and it is impossible to understand the organizational structure and functioning without analyzing the interpenetration of kinship and economic activities. On the five points: (a) workers are prepared either within the family or in empirical socialization in other business organizations, (b) no licensing or educational qualifications hold, (c) organized groups mediating between family members do not exist, (d) career motivation depends on tieing the fate of the individual to the development of the family estate in the business, and not on occupational promotion, and (e) skills and estates are rarely completely transferable to other enterprises, so that a person's fate is closely tied to the fate of the particular enterprise rather than to the general labor-market status of his kind of skill.

The labor markets for employed middle class people are generally organized according to bureaucratic principles, more or less mixed with professional principles (the difference being that professionals have a labor-market status which applies to a wide range of organizations, defined by professional associations, while bureaucrats are more oriented to particular organizations). That is, employment is conceived to be permanent and not to respond to short-run market variations; most higher officials are recruited from among lower officials; selection and promotion are on grounds of competence and seniority as determined by standard procedures (unilaterally set up by management). Recruitment is from schools, and generally based on an evaluation of school performance. All these characteristics tend to make the job a stage in a career within the same organization, with the criteria of promotion at each career stage determined by superiors (Caplow, 1954, pp. 149–56). The 'career' begins before employment in schools which provide relevant training.[9] Roughly speaking, such bureaucratic labor markets include civil servants, employees of large

---

[7] Hutchinson (1956, p. 225) reports that Greeks are about 29 times as frequently proprietors of eating and drinking palces as would be expected on the basis of their proportion in the population.

[8] As a representative datum, Lipset and Bendix (1959, p. 21) report a 1947 study in the United States showing that about 83% of farmers are sons of farmers.

[9] I have analyzed the impact of the structure of different parts of the labor market on those students in high school headed for those parts in Stinchcombe (1964).

unorganized firms (mostly in the 'white-collar industries' of trade, finance, insurance, etc.), and employees outside bargaining units in large unionized firms. About a quarter of the civilian labor force is in this sort of labor market structure. In summary: (a) preparation for work is in schools; (b) qualifications are generally judged by the employer, rather than by the government through licensing (there are some exceptions, as in employed medical practitioners); (c) employees are unorganized; (d) the career is within a particular organization, but not tied to it by ownership; (e) the range of alternatives for ranks above the bottom is generally limited by the stake built up in the career within the organization, but the more their qualifications for a job partake of a 'professional' character, the more cosmopolitan their careers.

About a tenth of the civilian labor force are unionized employees of small firms, mostly organized by craft, especially in the construction, maritime, entertainment, and printing trades, and some service trades in large cities. Mobility between firms is generally high, but occupation and union membership are relatively stable, and careers are organized by unions and union membership. Unions generally set conditions of employment more or less unilaterally and control access to jobs. The internal administration of work in firms or projects is heavily determined by craft organizational principles (see Stinchcombe, 1959). In sum: (a) union-supervised apprenticeship outside of schools is carried on in firms of the crafts; (b) unions certify competence and control access to work; (c) unions set the conditions of employment within wide limits, (d) careers are within the occupation, rather than being limited to one firm, and (e) there is generally an alternative job under the same wages and working conditions available to the craftsman, who is thus rarely dependent on a particular enterprise.

Manual labor under union contract in large firms is not generally conceived of as a career for two reasons: higher positions are not generally achieved by older hourly-rated workers, and employment responds to short-run adjustments in the product market. Wages rather than salaries are paid, and the 'generalized loyalty' to the organization expected of bureaucratic employees (mentioned by Weber) is not effectively expected of most wage workers. Recruitment is generally controlled by management rather than by unions, but is not generally oriented to getting special qualifications in the workers, either educational or craft; skilled workers under such labor-market arrangements are very often trained within the factory. Counting employees who are not union members but are covered by union contracts, something like a fifth of the labor force is in such labor market structures. In summary: (a) the preparation for work is generally not organized outside the firm, either in schools or in unions, but training is for particular jobs in particular firms, (b) workers are not licensed or certified except by the employer himself; (c) employment conditions are determined by bargaining between unions and managements; (d) particular jobs generally do not form part of a career and management does not undertake to promise permanent employment, steady progression in pay and prestige, or the opportunity for growth; and (e) there is much movement among factories by workers seeking better conditions, and some from factories to the other sectors of the labor market.

This leaves the unorganized employees of small firms and (unorganized) private employees outside the business population. Farm labor, clerks in small retail trade, waitresses, service workers such as gasoline station attendants, domestic servants, and the like, fall in this class. A little over a fourth of the labor force is in such employment, which quite generally does not form a career in any sense, has uncertain tenure wages and working conditions determined *ad hoc* by employers, no protection for workers by many of the laws governing the labor contract with larger firms. In short, this part of the labor market conforms very well to the classical economist's picture of a 'free' labor market. The concentration of misery in this sector of the labor market is proverbial. In summary: (a) no special institutions for training workers generally exist; (b) workers are not licensed; (c) no organized groups interfere in the employer–employee relationship; (d) careers generally do not exist; and (e) labor moves freely from one employer to another.

In a general and all too sketchy way, we can describe the evolution of the British and American labor markets historically as follows: in feudal times kinship and political obligation to particular lords organized the labor force (political obligation is largely confined to military service now). Early modern cities, and, with the enclosure movement, the countryside also, saw the evolution of 'free' labor markets and the origins of craft organization. Bureaucratic organization of 'organizational enclaves' in the labor market, within which the control of careers gave added power to discipline the middle-class labor force, was by and large the development of the nineteenth century. Extensive organization of professional schools and the gaining of control over large segments of the middle-class labor market by middle-class 'craft' organizations based on control of professional education, though traditional in a few professions, received its major impetus in the twentieth century.

These two kinds of social structural variables, the terms on which wealth and power are available and the structure of labor markets, partly explain why organizations set up at different times have different forms at the beginning. It is considerably more difficult to explain why many types of organizations retain structural peculiarities after their foundation without falling into tautologous statements about 'tradition,' 'vested interests,' or 'folkways' not being changeable by formal regulation. The problem is to specify who it is that carries 'tradition' and why they carry it, whose 'interests' become 'vested,' under what conditions, by what devices, whose 'folkways' cannot be changed by regulation, and why. This problem is at the very center of sociological theory. Unfortunately, we are not much closer to an answer to the problem now than we were in Sumner's day. Some elements which may move us along a little way for the particular field of organizational analysis have been suggested by Selznick (1957).

The basic process that Selznick sees is one in which an organization in order to solve its problems has to make commitments to outside and internal social forces. In order to ensure the preservation of some precarious value within the organization, for instance, people have to be socialized, careers molded, and power allocated to defend the value. Or in order to get political support, the TVA must make some permanent commitments to agricultural extension services and farmers' organizations. During both of these processes, ideologies are elaborated to explain the power structure, to teach people their responsibilities, and to justify the stable relations between the organization and the outside. But to mold careers, to allow outside organizations permanent control over some aspects of policy, to create and justify power distributions, is not only to mobilize social forces for present purposes. It is also to infuse the resulting structure with value, to make it an 'institution' rather than a dispensable technical device. 'Interests' become 'vested' because it is possible to defend the interests by appeal to the value the organization was set up to serve (the connection is spelled out in the ideology developed to explain the power distribution), and to use in their defense the powers originally allocated to enable people to serve the values.[10]

Thus, in craft-organized industries, unions can and do appeal to the norms of craftsmanship – the value of the industrial discipline they provide – to defend the closed shop. The powers they use to defend their monopoly in the local labor market they obtained originally because they could in fact provide a skilled labor force on predictable terms. The current effectiveness of their strikes is a function of the degree to which craftsmen are in fact superior to untrained men for the work.

Besides these internal traditionalizing processes, we must also explain why new organizations, making use of newly created means of harnessing wealth, power, and moral commitment to organizational purposes, do not destroy the old forms of organization by competition. But, of course, they often do. The family farm and the family retail business are in a long-term decline in the face of newer organizational forms. Socialist parties have lost heavily in some places (e.g., France, Italy) to the combination of devices for mobilizing the workers and poor peasantry used by Communist parties; in other places (especially Germany, but also Italy and France) to new devices for combining religious loyalties and desires for democratic government in Christian-Democratic parties. Armies that do not adapt are defeated in war. When university medical schools really organized to destroy proprietary medical schools, after the Flexner Report, the latter disappeared except in the medical cults.

In other words, it is problematic whether the advantage of new organizational forms over the old will be sufficient to destroy the old. But also the character of the Darwinian process, the form of the

---

[10] If the term 'vested interest' is to mean anything more than an interest in opposition to one's own values, then we need some definition of the term 'vested.' In the law, a 'vested' interest is one judged legitimate by recognized legal procedure according to legal norms. Before a will is taken to court, the heirs have 'interests' in the estate. When the decision on the validity of the will has been made, their 'interests' become 'vested,' and they can start to 'enjoy' (e.g., sell or lease, destroy, consume) their interests. In organizations, interests would be 'vested' analogically if they were recognized as legitimate according to the norms and values of the organization.

struggle for existence, differs for different kinds of organizations. If resources for current operations come from endowments rather than either from sales or from legislative appropriation, the organization may last much past the time when its structure was truly competitive. This is merely a particular case of a 'sunk cost,' which generally gives older organizations an advantage. An endowment is a permanent investment in a particular organization, and being permanent is free as far as current costs are concerned. The flow of benefits from the resources invested in an endowment have to be obtained from the organization or not at all. Unless an internal reconstruction of the old organization takes place new organization of a new form has to be beneficial enough to be able to compete even without the advantage of free services from sunk costs.

Natural monopolies, like railroads before airlines, streetcars before automobiles, armies under stable governments, are much different types of Darwinian process than competitive business or armies in time of revolution. Prestige competition as between universities, allows much more room for self-deception than market competition in which revenues decline.

That is, besides the degree of advantage of newer over older forms of organization which helps determine whether the old form continues or is replaced, a basic determinant of persistence of organizational forms is the degree to which the existence of an organization depends on its being better than its possible competitors.

To recapitulate the argument of this section, organizational types generally originate rapidly in a relatively short historical period, to grow and change slowly after that period. The time at which this period of rapid growth took place is highly correlated with the present characteristics of organizations of the type. For instance prefactory industries still use more unpaid family labor, early factory industries are still family firms but bureaucratized below the top, railroad age industries have career officials at the very top, but do not generally have staff departments of professionals well developed, while modern industries have no family labor, no family management, and extensive staff departments.

The explanation is that organizations which are founded at a particular time must construct their social systems with the social resources available. Particularly, they have to build their élites so that they can recruit necessary resources from the society and to build the structure of the organization so that in the historically given labor market they can recruit skills and motivation of workers. Once such going concerns are set up in a particular area, they may preserve their structures for long enough to yield the correlations we observe by any one of three processes: (a) they may still be the most efficient form of organization for a given purpose; (b) traditionalizing forces, the vesting of interests, and the working out of ideologies may tend to preserve the structure; and (c) the organization may not be in a competitive structure in which it has to be better than alternative forms of organization in order to survive.

11. On social factors in administrative innovation

The basic postulate of this presentation is that resistance to administrative innovations is mostly due to (more or less) rational anticipation that concrete interests (career prospects, risks of failure, chance for exceptional success, etc.) are endangered. Consequently what we want to do is to classify administrative innovations simultaneously by the interests they advance (generally collective interests or goals of some corporate group) and interests they damage (generally interests 'vested in,' *i.e.* protected by the normative structure embedded in, the old régime). In general the idea is that in order to advance some corporate interest in higher efficiency, one has to sacrifice the career or authority interests of some people who are advantaged by the old régime. If we can connect together sources of higher efficiency with *types of damage* to 'vested interests,' we will have the basis for a differentiated theory of resistance to administrative innovation.

The general reasons that this is a special problem are that: (1) a general way to reward administrative responsibility is by the promotions – and administrative reorganization reorganizes promotion chances; (2) a sign of one's future career chances, and a symbol that can be used in interpersonal prestige seeking, is the weight of the decisions one is responsible for – and administrative reorganization redistributes authority; (3) administration is a matter of the relations between information and decisions, but the right to take a decision is a property right, because different decisions give profits to different people – in order to reorganize information processing for decisions, therefore one often must reorganize property rights, and such reorganization often involves therefore top levels of the organization and property, rather than technical, considerations.

So in order to invent a classification of administrative innovations that will lead to productive analyses, we have to locate connections between sources of efficiency and impact on promotions, authority and responsibility, or property rights.

(1) Elementary administrative reorganizations

The least problematic type of innovation is clearly one which merely reorganizes communication for greater effectiveness within a fixed status structure. Even such trivial rearrangements may create tensions or resistance. For example, reorganizing a flow of information that must be acted on in such a way that a low status person transmits information that has the character of a command to a higher status person creates tension. An example given by William Foote Whyte is the client's order for food in a restaurant, transmitted by a waitress to a male cook. In one case he solved the tension by having the waitress put the order on a spindle, which the cook removed at his own discretion (Whyte, 1948).

A second general problem with even minor reorganization for greater efficiency of communication is that, as Crozier (1964) has analyzed at length, uncertainty creates interpersonal power. The informal organization of power is therefore often destroyed if, for example, anyone can get the information from a computer through a terminal instead of having to ask the person in charge of that information.

Generally speaking these status consequences of elementary administrative reorganization are invasions of status rights that were not legitimate in the first place. Consequently the opposition to them usually does not have any effect politically, but rather works by bad temper, tears of frustration, unexplained sulking, and the like.

(2) Reorganization of symbols of status

The chief case of reorganization of symbols of status is the allocation of space. Space, and the characteristics of offices, symbolize status and authority, and allocate rights to include or exclude people in an activity or a bit of information. That is, they function both as symbols of status and also as 'property,' as the right to control one's own fate and arrange one's work to suit oneself. At the time I was at Johns

Hopkins University, one right which was maintained in the office of the President of the University rather than delegated was the allocation of space. Ordinarily when space is reorganized people invent all sort of reasons why their future plans involve the use of all the unused space, why secretaries need private offices, and the like. When low status people like students are originators of demands on higher status people like secretaries, or even worse professors, you generally find strong arguments, first, in favor of installing counters, windows, doors, or other barriers to communication, second to restrict the hours in which such demands can be initiated, and third to put the lowest status person at the window or counter. Any plan to reorganize the space so as to provide freer access for lower status people also sets off a burst of rationalizations for the restrictions. As long as one maintains the restriction one has to then provide for a caste system so that high status people can originate demands in spite of the barriers.

Privileges that are explicitly allocated by the organization on the basis of rank are also hard to reorganize. I recall a professor of sociology at Berkeley who seriously maintained that letting students park in a parking structure previously reserved for faculty and staff was 'unconstitutional.'

Because these symbols are recognized by the organization as having a serious connection to authority and rank, their reorganization tends to produce serious political efforts with legitimate arguments (if not always true or organizationally rational arguments) to hinder the innovation. It takes a serious mobilization of political power in an organization to reallocate space, or to change the rules by which parking privileges are given out. Authority over space allocations should always be concentrated at the highest practical level.

(3) Decentralization of authority

Reorganization of authority systems presents very different problems when authority is to be decentralized, that is, when lower status people are to be given more discretion or looser controls, than when authority is to be centralized. For example, the problem of allowing students a choice between courses is a lot different than the problem of imposing a new course requirement. The main problems with decentralization are: (a) the chance that lower participants have different utility functions, so that decentralization implies a change in policy, (b) the invention of new, more abstract flows of control information so that details can be delegated without delegating overall control of policy, and (c) motivation of the intermediate authorities to conform to the decentralization.

(a) A common feature of debates about decentralization is the 'myth of the happy-go-lucky slave.' The basic notion is that the underclass do not know what is good for themselves, will not take the time and energy to investigate things thoroughly, or are inherently incompetent to maximize what needs to be maximized. For example, the myth would say that if allowed to choose courses for themselves students would take only easy courses or only interesting courses or only politicized courses, certainly never statistics, that they would not listen to advice of the faculty about what they should take, and that they do not know enough about the structure of the field as a whole to choose wisely. That is, the arguments urge that if one decentralizes decisions then the utility function that will be maximized will be altered. The difference between advising students that they will probably need and want to have had statistics, and requiring statistics, is that it is the students utilities that are maximized in the first case, the faculty's idea of student utilities in the other. Conservative or 'radical planning' arguments generally oppose 'classical liberal' arguments (say John Stuart Mill) by some such assertion of the ignorance or evil qualities of the underclass.

Sometimes the debate on this question takes the form of asking whose utilities ought to be maximized. In such cases the success of the decentralization often depends on the constellation of political power. A well organized and powerful underclass like the proletariat often gets liberties that a poorly organized and weak underclass like students cannot get. Sometimes the debate takes the form of investigating the factual pattern of preferences of the underclass, for example, by experimentation and new monitoring. Sometimes the debate takes the form of proposals to add new substitute controls for the ones that are being taken off, such as personal advising of students in place of requirements.

(b) A common reason for decentralizing is simply that the flow of tactical decisions to the top of the hierarchy prevents that top from paying enough attention to strategic considerations. When the decentralization takes place there is a technical problem of inventing a flow of more abstract information, so that strategic decisions are not also decentralized. The crucial feature of this process from a social point of view is that lower levels of the organization must perform this abstraction process (if the higher level performs the abstraction, then they will be as burdened with details about tactics as before). But lower level people have many other motives in talking to their superiors than conveying exactly correct information. Particularly when the abstracted information is used to evaluate the subordinate unit (e.g. cost accounts or performance statistics), there are reasons to expect new flows of information to lead to new ways to evade accurate performance measurement.

Quite often the solution to this problem is to create a police force with a separate hierarchy, and particularly a separate career structure. One of the reasons the chief cost accountant is often of very high rank, and often has his people (or her people, if chief accountants are ever women – I do not know of any female chief accountants) detached in various departments, so that the chief source of performance statistics will not be corrupted near its source. Obviously setting up a new policing apparatus, and solving all the problems of mutual trust and distrust that have to be dealt with, can create political and trade union conflicts and is generally a tension-filled process.

(c) Quite often decentralization decisions are taken by central authorities, who want to redistribute authority from the middle levels to lower levels. For example, usually the rules enforced by lifeguards in swimming pools are more restrictive than the rules set down by the directorate in charge of the athletic facility as a whole – this generalization is based only on seventeen pools in four countries, but seventeen out of seventeen is quite a statistic. Suppose for example that a pool is open for adults from 20.00 to 22.00 hours, and the lifeguards rule that no one can enter after 21.00 hours (because that makes it harder to persuade them to leave at 22.00 hours). If the central directorate did not want to make such a restriction, they would have to persuade the lifeguards to let people in after 21.00 hours, unless of course they wanted to come down to the pool to let people in themselves. The central directorate may have as much trust in the utility function of the lowest level as of the intermediate level, and it already has a readymade police force for new control information in the former intermediate level, but the intermediate level has no real motive for destroying its own authority.

In particular intermediate level authorities have all kinds of ways for using the power of interpretation of the rules, and the power to explore in networks of mutual trust at the intermediate level to find solutions for problems of lower participants, so as to recreate the authority relations. If we study the telephone traffic of a department in an American university, most of the calls will be to one or another minor official elsewhere in the bureaucracy, often asking for an exception to a rule or asking for the way to formulate a particular decision so that it is in conformity with the rules. Since everything sensible is always a violation of the rules – I think it was the railroad magnate Hill in the U.S. who said, 'you can't build a railroad within the law' – this means that rule manipulators have power. For example, I once had a Dean confess to me that he could not permit me to carry out a collective bargain I had made with my office staff – which was formally within my powers as a Department chairman – because his administrative assistant did not agree that it was a good idea. The reason his administrative assistant knew about it was because my administrative assistant opposed it, and told him.

(4) Imposition of hierarchical relations

The distinctive problem I want to point to here is subordinating people to new authorities. That is, decentralization involves freeing subordinates. What I want to analyse under (4) is creating new bonds on subordinates. This may take the form of (a) governing a new area of subordinate behavior, by extending the jurisdiction of the superior, (b) adding new, more complex, control information or sanctions so that a finer tuning of control becomes possible, (c) adding an intermediate level in a hierarchy or other special control structures such as an inspector's department, or (d) increasing the punitiveness of sanctions for violating orders or regulations. We will deal with the case of abolishing an independent jurisdiction in the next section.

The general problem here is the reaction of subordinates to the reduction of their discretion. Some of the best studies of this type of innovation are those by James Q. Wilson (1968) of reform police administrations. The usual reason why one has reform administrations in American municipal police departments is that lower level police discretion is being used to allow prostitution or gambling to go on, or to allow violation of building codes, evasion of special taxes, special patrolling of private functions at public expence, in return for bribes. All the devices mentioned above are used by reform police administrations, because the general problem is that *any* discretion in a police department with a culture of corruption can be turned to corrupt purposes. The lower policemen enter into a sort of originality competition with the police chief, to see whether they can invent evasions as fast as the chief can invent new controls.

What is distinctive of these innovations is that, in the Dahrendorf sense, they are class conflicts. They pit people who are dominated against people who dominate them, who now propose to dominate them in a new way. Ordinarily trade unions and other class conflict organizations will get involved in such conflicts, if these organizations exist. Passive resistance, 'conscientious withdrawal of efficiency,' grievances, and other informal equivalents of open class conflicts are likely when there are no trade unions. As Gouldner (1954) found in his study of a wildcat strike, if the formal union apparatus cannot legitimate conflict under these circumstances (the withdrawal of the 'indulgency pattern' is a clear case of increasing hierarchical control, which involved all four processes above), the conflict is likely to break out of the collective bargaining framework.

(5) Destruction of career chances

A common problem in administrative reform is the 'Buy or make?' decision. Formally one should go on the market to buy a component or service whenever there are economies of scale, accidental variations between organizations in abilities of personnel, inefficiencies in one's own organization, or other competitive advantages in competing firms. In fact we hardly ever find the destruction of a department in one organization in order to buy the same service in another, but if no such department exists we do find organizations failing to create one. The difference is that it is much harder to destroy the jobs and career chances of people already in the organization than of those not yet hired.

The capacity to destroy subunits, or to drastically reorganize career chances, can generally be legitimated only by reference to outside contingencies. That is, unless an organization as a whole is going bankrupt, it is very hard to legitimate internal reorganization to save money. Consequently business organizations are much more likely than other kinds to carry out 'buy or make' administrative reforms, and to do those only in hard times. Ordinarily a competitive disadvantage of a section of an organization is regarded as temporary and remediable, and as a good investment of slack resources from the rest of the organization.

One circumstance in which this is not so true is when a merger takes place. What happens in a merger is that the 'constitution' of the organization is being rewritten, and consequently legitimacy is reconcentrated toward the very top of the organization's political system. Drastic pruning of relatively unprofitable parts of an organization is therefore one of the implicit profits of mergers. Succession crises and other occasions for regarding the 'constitution' as problematic also make the destruction of career chances possible. Machiavelli somewhere urges in a rather similar context that the Prince should appoint a prime minister to carry through such punitive policies, then 'discover' what the prime minister has been doing and execute him.

(6) Reorganization of property rights

Administrative reorganization may involve the relocation of decision powers which carry with them rights to benefits. For example, long-term contracts for ships for dry bulk goods or oil redistributes the risks of rising or falling rates for rental of ships, and also enables both the shipping company and the client to design the ship for the particular trade envisaged. So the administrative advantages of long-term contracts carry with them redistribution of risks of profit and loss, i.e. contingent redistributions of property rights. If the price of ships goes down the long-term contract is a valuable property of the shipowner; if the price of ships goes up, the long-term contract is a valuable property of the client, say the oil company. When an administrative reform requires a redistribution of property rights, the owners of those rights are likely to be concerned.

The general solution here is exchange, that if one requires property rights for an administrative reform, one has to buy them. Such administrative reforms therefore tend to be easier in the private sector (as one President of the University of Chicago once observed, 'there is not much market for a used university campus'), but to require the attention of top authorities in the organization. The previous comment on mergers legitimating destroying parts of the organization is a particular application of the general relation between the non-routine exchange of property and centralization of decisions.

Quite often informal property rights within organizations are dealt with in the same way. For example an implicit property right to the promotion chances that inhere in a certain position of authority may be bought off by 'kicking him upstairs,' by paying the promotion cost in order to get the authority back to reallocate a new way.

Generalizations about administrative reform

The classification above is roughly in the order of seriousness of the opposition to administrative reorganization, and consequently in the order of the concentrations of political power required to carry them through. We can therefore state some tentative generalizations about the relations between political structures of organizations and the probability of different sorts of reform. Some of these have been suggested above.

(1). The more difficult the administrative reorganization (the higher its number in the classification above), the more it must be legitimated by pressures from outside the organization, such as bankruptcy, legislative requirement, merger or ownership change, etc.

(2). The more difficult a reform, the more concentration of power toward the center of the organization will facilitate it, and so the more it will be found only in highly hierarchical organizations like armies or business firms, and not in less hierarchical ones like universities or trade unions.

(3). The more difficult a reform, the more it matters whether the central authorities in the organization favor that reform, the more the initiative for such reform will come from the top, and in other ways the higher the hierarchical level that will be involved in the reform.

(4). The more difficult a reform, the higher the cost in political turmoil, strikes, personnel loss, and other social disruption one will have to be willing to pay, and perhaps the higher the money cost for buying off the opposition.

(5). The more difficult the reform, the more selection there will be for what Selznick (1957) calls 'institutional leadership,' and the more likely it is that routine bureaucratic leadership will fail – serious administrative reforms are entrepreneurial, *not* administrative, matters.

12. Norms of exchange

A basic typology of exchange relations

People enter into exchanges in modern economies to get what they want. Consequently norms about exchanges are mainly norms to see to it that they get what they want. To analyze the variations in exchange norms, then, we have to start with a typology of what people want in exchanges. I propose that the main dimensions of wants that affect the norms of exchanges are *continuity of exchange* (continuous to intermittent), *productive purpose* (from satisfaction directly from the object or service exchanged to use of the object or service in a productive system), and *conditionality or adaptiveness* (from wanting something unconditionally to wanting it under some conditions, which in turn may be 'on demand' – e.g. wanting the money in one's checking account (i.e. current account) – or specified – e.g. on the death of the insured).

For example, the subcontracting system in the construction industry is in part designed to handle the variability in the wish to exchange by a general contractor, caused by variations in the work flow he must handle. Rather than hiring a crew of painters permanently, he exchanges when convenient. But the exchange, like a permanent hiring exchange, is for the purpose of incorporating them into a productive system, the site crew for a building, and so involves specifying technical standards and scheduling constraints. The exchange is unconditional, in the sense that when the contract is signed the general contractor knows he wants the building painted, except for acts of God or riot. The intermittency changes the norms as compared to those characterizing, for example, hiring a worker in an oil refinery. The involvement in a productive system changes the norms as compared, for example, to buying a household appliance, requiring some system of technical and coordinating communication between buyer and seller. The uncontingent character of the exchange means that, for example, there are runs on banks but a painting contractor rarely finds himself committed to paint more than he is able.

Perhaps the extreme values on this set of variables are the marriage contract and shopping in stores. A marriage contract is continuous ('till death us do part'). It is contingent in a wide variety of areas. That is, what is to be exchanged varies with what the partners need in various circumstances ('for better or for worse, in sickness and in health'). The contract normally establishes a household for the continuous production of shelter, food, children, and other goods and services. Shopping is intermittent, the goods are bought as they stand rather than as adapted to the productive system, and once bought a change in circumstances does not change the terms of the exchange. Employment or exchange in the labor market is toward the marriage end of the set of variables. Partnership in a firm is nearer to marriage than common stock ownership in the capital market. Fiduciary exchanges, as with banks or insurance companies, are more marriage-like than, for example, changing dollars into foreign currency at an airport exchange office. A landlord–tenant exchange has more of the tension of a family than a hotel–guest relation.

Briefly, continuity versus intermittency influences the presence of norms about *status*. By status we mean rights and duties with respect to a *flow of rewards* which continuously provide advantages to be divided up. Psychologically the advantage of having status with respect to a flow of rewards is *security*, that a person knows what he will owe and what he will earn. Norms about the division of risks caused by variations in the flow are central. Relation to a productive purpose influences the presence of norms about *authority*. That is, a productive system depends on adapting the actions of a person or a piece of capital equipment to an integrated system of action. The adaptation of action (or the installation and maintenance of a complex piece of capital equipment) requires a flow of commands, cost criteria, specifications, through the exchange. The legitimacy of these communications about changes in activity is secured by authority norms. Conditionality influences the presence of norms about *responsibility*, or *fiduciary obligation*. Specifying the obligations of a trustee of an estate, for example, involves specifying the range of environmental variation that the trustee is responsible for adapting to.

Obviously in general productive systems will be a combination of fiduciary relations (e.g. board of directors to stockholders) and authority relations (directors to employees). The difference between an employee who adapts his activity to a change in demand between two product lines because he is told, and a director who calls an executive to account for excess inventory in a declining product line, does not reside in the market contingencies that cause a change in behavior. Instead the difference is in the major norms of exchange that specify two contrasting obligations. An employee is hired to accept authority in the workplace; a director is elected to be responsible for stockholder interests.

Family law, which governs exchanges which are continuous, productive, and conditional or adaptive, has all three aspects. The right to 'support' for a wife or child is a status right. The disciplinary rights of parents over children are authority rights. Fiduciary responsibilities are more diffuse, but are indicated for example by divorced husbands paying 'child support' to the child's mother, who is then responsible for supporting the child, or by various standards of being a fit mother in child custody cases, the fitness being a requirement of fiduciary responsibility.

The deviant behavior that challenges a particular exchange relation varies with its requirements, and with the norms that correspond to the requirements. The critical deviant behavior for a continuous exchange is running away (e.g. observe the indignation of the New England textile unions to 'runaway plants,' or the provisions in family law for 'desertion.') The most indicative deviant behavior for productive purpose exchanges is the method of slowdown used by some unions, 'working to rule.' Unless there is adaptation of the subordinate to changing conditions, adaptation specified by a superior, the technical system will not work. 'Working to rule' is applying the norms appropriate to exchange in which the buyer specifies exactly what he wants in standard terms to an exchange in which the wants of the buyers are governed by a productive purpose. 'Working to rule' is especially deviant (and hence especially effective as a labor relations weapon) in skilled work, which depends most on adaptive adjustment.

Deviance in fiduciary relations in which the fiduciary is 'responsible' for adapting to a changing environment is 'irresponsibility,' departure from the standard of what 'a reasonable person' would do under the circumstances. Deviance in fiduciary relations is thus situationally variable. The moral accompaniments of fiduciary exchanges are particularly salient in strikes by professional people, such as professors or physicians. Professional strikers refuse to do things that are organizational conveniences (meeting classes on campus, billing hospital patients) while continuing to be responsible to their clients (teaching, writing references, treating diseases, etc.). That is, strikers recognize their fiduciary obligations but not their authority obligations.

Our discussion of the norms of exchange will therefore be organized in three main sections: continuity and status norms; productive purpose and authority norms; conditionality and fiduciary norms. In each of these sections we have three intellectual tasks. One is to specify the conditions under which people want continuous exchange, or productive exchange, or conditional exchange. A second is to describe the moral phenomenology, the subjective viewpoint, associated with the varieties of exchange wants. The third is to discuss the varieties of social patterns, especially norms and enforcement apparatuses, that can provide the moral prerequisites for people to get what they want from exchanges.

Status norms and continuous exchange

Commitment to exchange

When an exchange relationship is continuous, such as bureaucratic employment, marriage, the exchanges among subsidiaries of the same corporation, current exchange is modified by the expectation of future exchange. That is, in the future there will be a flow of valuable goods if the exchange *relationship* is not destroyed by the current exchange. The rule of *caveat emptor*, let the buyer beware, is not appropriate to the current exchange because the person who commits fraud or renders a poor performance gains only a small amount in the current exchange, but sacrifices the whole (discounted) value of the flow of future exchanges. Norms about 'fair' exchange thus serve the interests of both parties, in that whatever disadvantage they may sustain from unfair norms of fairness, those norms protect them from the destruction of the relationship, and hence protect the capitalized value of future exchanges. Further, a general reputation for fairness may advantage one of the parties, so that, for example, an employer may keep on a high seniority worker who no longer pulls his load because firing him would undermine his profitable exchanges with young workers who hope someday to have seniority themselves.

The first requirement of such a system is that the future exchanges should in fact be secure, so that the future advantages for which one sacrifices his or her current interest will in fact be there. That is, the first requirement is for norms of *commitment*. Further, in general, these have to be norms that distinguish particular others as people (or organizations) to whom and from whom one has a commitment. It is not much good for a person to have the status of autoworker in a society unless some particular firm is willing to employ that person. Statuses may be more or less generalized, to be sure. A physician has a status with respect to many potential clients, secured by the monopoly of licensed physicians. But it is from particular client bank accounts that the rewards of holding the status come, and those particular bank accounts have to be committed in a continuous exchange. The difference between a license to practice and the labor contract with a particular auto manufacturer is one of the potential number of clients for a person's services, not that the commitment does not have to be concretized into a practice involving particular clients who do the paying.

Norms of commitment seem to take four main forms: (1) the giving of hostages, (2) leaving the market for alternative exchanges, (3) the passage of control over one's own resources to the exchange partner, and (4) reputability in the market as a whole. For example, traditionally the commitment to a marriage was shown by a woman by (1) having children (fathered by the husband), (2) rules against adultery, stronger than those against fornication among the unmarried, (3) the husband's control of the property of the pair, or in more modern times community property, and (4) the sacrifice of one's reputation in case of divorce or separation. Children are hostages; sexual monopoly is leaving the marriage market; community property binds resources to the marriage; concern for reputability solidifies a precarious commitment.

Some continuous exchanges use one of these commitment techniques more than others. For example, stable exchanges among firms are very often set up by a subsidiary–parent corporation transfer of ownership control (3). A physician is constrained to come when the patient needs him, rather than at his own convenience, by the damage to his reputation if he lets a patient die in order to go to a party (4). The norms of commitment in the labor market are shown by the frequent appearance of advertisements announcing that the present employer will not know of the inquiry; this clearly indicates that many employees think they will gain advantages from an employer by (appearing to) grant the employer a monopoly position (2). The cementing of alliances by marriage among royal houses in premodern Europe standardized the giving of hostages as a device for increasing the continuity of exchanges of military and diplomatic support (1).

The basic phenomenon in an effective commitment is that each party be satisfied that at all relevant points in the future, the value sacrificed by the partner by stopping the exchange will be greater than the advantage that partner can get by stopping unexpectedly. Hostages do this by being more valuable to the partner who gives them than to the partner that receives them. Evidence of giving the partner a monopoly position by leaving the market shows that one intends to sacrifice the whole value of the relationship in case of rupture, rather than only sacrificing the difference between the value of this stable exchange and the alternative stable exchanges. This explains why wives used to tolerate the husband's breaking their monopoly with a prostitute, but not with a mistress. Passing control to a partner, for instance by selling out and becoming a subsidiary to a parent corporation, transfers the interest in future profits directly to the partner in return for an immediate capitalization of that value, and transfers control over the fulfillment of the selling partner's continuous obligations to the parent. This method of getting commitment, of course, depends on the solidity of authority norms giving the parent control of the subsidiary, or fiduciary norms making the old management of the subsidiary responsible to the parent. The notion of reputability is that the partner will lose more than the value sacrificed by continuity, at least psychologically if not in concrete advantages in the market, if he gets a reputation for shady dealing.

In each case at the time of the establishment of a relation, both partners conceive that there is positive value for them in continuity, or at least that the disadvantages of continuity are less than they will gain from establishing the relation. But there are usually circumstances that can be easily imagined, often circumstances that are inevitable, when it will be to the advantage of one of the parties to break it off.

An important concrete manifestation of commitment norms are norms of seniority. We have been talking as if the contract of commitment were established in a timeless instant, on the model of a marriage that starts at the wedding and lasts 'till death us do part.' But even in this situation, a person who jilts his or her fiancé(e) after a five year engagement is violating something very like a marriage commitment. And in the employment relation the growth of seniority rules, or security of tenure in an agricultural tenancy, or tenure in a university, is so universal that its absence is a sure sign of merciless exploitation. Commitments are negotiated in a gradual increasing fashion, rather than in a timeless instant.

The risk of making a sudden commitment is that if a person is mistaken about the commitment of the other, he has sold himself into bondage. A one-sided holding of hostages, a one-sided monopoly, a one-sided transfer of control over one's resources, a one-side staking of one's reputation, all lead to slavery. One general solution to this is to move the commitment by small stages, so that at each point (if all goes well) the partner would lose more by bugging out than is being risked with increased commitment. Where commitments are psychological, as in courtship, this results in delicate jockeying and frequent tests of the degree of commitment. But one way to regularize the process in a bureaucratic enterprise is, for example, to only provide expensive training to those who have shown six years of commitment, and conversely to only grant job security after six years. Seniority also has the advantage of being a continuous variable allowing different degrees of commitment, and of the differential commitment seeming fair to the workers. I don't know why it seems fair to the workers.

Fair rates of exchange and exploitation

If a commitment is effective, it establishes a bilateral monopoly for the two parties. The skilled autoworker has seniority only in Packard Motors, and the workers who know Packard's production process are the workers with seniority. Within the range between price of labor at which Packard is willing to go out of business, and that at which the workers will quit in spite of their seniority rights, any price is possible. A bilateral monopoly does not have a unique equilibrium rate of exchange, and the range of possible rates is set by the degree of commitment.

If the degree of commitment is unequal, clearly, the 'principle of lesser interest' analyzed by Willard Waller (1938) for marriage obtains. That is, if one of the parties is heavily committed, while the other is in a free market, the free partner can push the rate of exchange *below* the going market rate, can 'exploit' the commitment of the other. For the committed person will stay in the relation as long as the value of the hostages he has given, *plus* what he gets in the exchange, exceed the market rate. If, for example, a wife would just as soon be married to any of several other men, while the husband is in love, or worried about his reputation, she can take him for all he's worth.

The first set of norms governing bilateral monopoly created by commitment are therefore often equality-of-commitment norms. It is both partners who get married, not one married and one still engaged. Of course these norms often provide an 'unequal equality,' as in the difference between 'love, honor, and cherish' *versus* 'love, honor, and obey.' But especially when the exchange rate cannot be directly administered by normative agencies, an attempt is made to prevent the worst excess of the 'principle of lesser interest' by equalizing commitments.

But supposing there are two committed partners, the exchange rate cannot be determined by market considerations. Further, the continuity of the relation means that the exchange rate needs to be continually negotiated, and it means that the whole lives of the partners are affected by the exchanges. Moral forces tend to be mobilized when people are disposing of their whole lives, and they have time to operate. Moral forces tend to be slow and clumsy, while rational situational adaptation tends to be fast and precise. Hence moral forces are stronger in status markets such as the labor or marriage market than in commodity markets. (Capital markets tend to be dominated by fiduciary relations, analyzed below.)

There are two broad classes of regulation of the exchange rate in continuous, bilateral monopoly situations: substantive norms that determine standards of fairness directly, and procedural norms that provide that standards of fairness will be applied. Substantive norms may specify the exchange rate directly, as in sharecropping rents, controlled rents, minimum wage legislation, comparison groups specified in advance in collective bargaining, and the like. Or they may provide the decision criteria by which the exchange rate is to be determined. The two main forms of the determination of decision criteria are protections of the standard of living (e.g. pension programs, unemployment insurance, child support and alimony provisions, escalator clauses to protect against inflation, productivity allowances) and protection of markets (e.g. exclusive franchises to protect marketing investments of car dealers, or the frequent provisions in selling a firm to a parent corporation that the seller will not enter the same business in the same market for a period of years).

Procedural norms have two main forms, those providing for arbitration, and those providing for limitation of the means of conflict. The object of arbitration is to provide an external source and validation of norms of fairness by a third party without an interest in the outcome. Examples of the limitation of the means of conflict are legislation on strikes and lockouts, complex and subtle norms requiring 'bargaining in good faith,' collective agreements providing that there will be no strikes over management reorganizations to improve productivity, informal norms in marriages that prevent calling in one's parents in internal conflicts (or at least providing that both sets of in-laws will be called in).

Power, time, and function
The argument above has a basically functional form. That is, we have argued that continuous exchanges 'need' status norms, in particular commitment norms, protection against the 'principle of lesser interest,' substantive regulation of the fairness of exchange rates, or procedural regulation of the fairness of the process by which exchange rates are established. Our examples are directed at showing the simple functional correlation: the more an exchange is a continuous exchange, the more status norms of commitment, protection against exploitation, fairness of exchange rates, fairness of bargaining procedures tend to appear. But of course societies do not always get what they need: American society needs honest used car dealers; the Middle East needs effective structures of international bargaining.

Further even societies that need and get, say, effective regulation of collective bargaining in the labor market, do not usually get it until quite a while after they need it. If marriage laws result in factual inequality of the commitment of men and women, with the consequent opportunities for husbands' exploitation of wives, a very long time may pass before easy divorce norms equalize the situation by reducing the socially enforced commitment of wives.

In functional arguments there are two main mechanisms by which needs get fulfilled by appropriate structures, power mechanisms and evolutionary mechanisms. Low political and normative power of women, historically, would tend to produce a normative system that was ineffective in providing for the needs of women. An increase in women's power would tend to produce more functional norms, in the sense of the argument above. This is because a normative system is created by a political process, and the power determines whose needs a political process serves.

But also, needs only encourage those functional structures that are around to be encouraged. Mammals might have replaced dinosaurs much faster if there had been any mammals around to exploit their advantages. The species complexity of the family of mammals, the variety of ecological niches for which there were mammals of an appropriate functional structure, increases with evolutionary time, because the genetic process does not provide an unlimited variety of structures for ecological niches to choose among, but rather provides only structures closely related to the species composition of the previous generation. Likewise, if a change in the power position of women changes the selective pressures on normative structures, the normative results of the changed situation tend to appear over a relatively extended historical period rather than immediately, because each generation of norms is closely related to the norms available in the previous generation.

There are two sorts of power situations that affect the normative terms of continuous or status exchanges. The first is the power situation at the time of establishing the relation, which affects the normative provisions of the bargain about the terms of continuity. The tendency of such relations to remain stable over times means that a change in the power situation over history produces *cohorts* of relationships. That is, those relations 'born' or established at different times will tend to have different terms at birth, because of the changing power relations in the original bargains, and will tend to preserve those different terms throughout the life of the relation. At any particular time, then, a classification of relationships by their birthdates will be an implicit classification of them by the power situation at their birth, and their terms should vary with their birthdate. Especially drastic changes in power or emancipation proclamations in areas of former slavery would tend to create sharp differences in the terms of (say) landlord–tenant contracts in agriculture, according to whether the area was developed agriculturally before or after independence or emancipation. For example, while similar in inherent tendencies, the terms of race relations in the plantation South and the irrigated plantation Southwest should tend to be different; after the Civil War we would expect tenancy contracts of older men to be different from those of young men, and this difference should be greater if the tenant remains on the plantation on which he was a slave.

The second sort of power is influence on the normative system itself. Worker influence on the political system has, for example, changed the conditions for negotiating exchange rates (collective bargaining legislation), increased security of pension plans, required contributions to unemployment insurance and health insurance schemes, provided for the government to act as a third party enforcing norms in representation elections, and the like.

The development of interests in the normative order by a social group depends on the continuity of exchange, on the development of markets into status systems. A bazaar economy consisting of a multitude of individual unique nonrepetitive exchanges, in which individuals change the business they are in from day to day as chance and market opportunities make it advantageous, does not create a steady interest in the norms protecting the condition of the buyer, or the seller, or the wholesaler, or retailer, or the jobber who contracts for production and the retailer who transmits it to the public. The lack of elaboration of the normative order in such bazaar structures throws each man on his wits; and conversely of course, a man who trusts the weak normative order rather than his wits comes to a bad end (see Geertz, 1963).

The above considerations show why keen students of the evolution of capitalism focus so strongly on the existence of firms, that is, organizations producing continuously for a market.[1] Firms are both more efficient, shaping their organizations and competence to a continuous place in the division of labor, and also more capable of elaborating the moral and legal order of modern capitalism, an order based on making the status system responsive to the market (see especially Polanyi, 1944).

Productive purpose and authority

The employment relation

Herbert Simon, in a fundamental paper on 'A formal theory of the employment relation,' (1957b) showed how the central phenomena of authority can be generated in exchange relations. Briefly the argument is this. The central phenomena of authority are related to a 'zone of indifference' of the subordinate (the term was invented by Chester Bernard, 1946). By a 'zone of indifference' we mean a *set* of activities, *all* of which it would be rational for the worker to exchange at his wage rate. The higher the wage rate (as compared to alternatives available to the worker), the more costs (in terms of unpleasant and dangerous jobs) the worker would be willing to pay to retain the advantage of his wages. That is, the higher the wage rate in a given job as compared to the competitive wage rate, the larger, in general, is the zone of indifference of the worker. Conversely, as the competitive wage rate goes down, e.g. by unemployment during a recession, the size of the zone of indifference at a given wage rate goes up. Authority is strengthened by paying high wages, and by bad times outside the firm.

The zone of indifference is also increased if the tastes of the workers do not make a less desirable activity much more costly to him than another activity. The more equal different activities are in the minds

[1] Three from very different intellectual traditions are Max Weber, who described the 'bourgeois enterprise' in a phrase very similar to that given above as a definition of a firm; Clifford Geertz, whose anthropological study of markets in Indonesia was just cited, contrasts the bazaar economy to an economy of firms; John R. Commons (1924) focuses on, for example, the development of property rights, defensible in the courts, in 'goodwill,' i.e. the interest of the firm in maintaining and continuing to benefit from continuous exchanges with clients – when such goodwill can be bought and sold, it provides the legal foundation for operating an economy of firms rather than a bazaar economy.

of the workers, the more flexibility authorities have. For example, if the work life of the worker is permeated with family considerations, then some activities (those that reward his family) are much more desirable than others (those that reward strangers). The worker is therefore not indifferent between activities, and the amount of effort required by authorities to get the worker to do the unpleasant activity of rewarding strangers increases. Detaching the worker's work life from all possibility of rewarding family members would not make sense, of course, because it would mean giving up a central motivation of workers. What does make sense is to make sure that all possible activities reward family members equally, i.e. only through the wage paid, not through tieing activities directly to family rewards. The substitution of bureaucratic administration for patrimonial administration means, among other things, giving up the opportunity to reward *particular* activities by tieing them to strong family motivations, for the sake of equalizing the value of activities for the worker, and hence strengthening authority by extending the zone of indifference.

Under what conditions will an employer prefer to buy a zone of indifference rather than particular activities? According to the argument above, if the employer knew he wanted particular activities in advance, he or she could buy them on the labor market at the competitive wage rate, or get them effectively cheaper by tying the activity directly to family welfare. And clearly this is often done. Rather than run automobile sales bureaucratically, car manufacturers allow families or corporations to own the 'job' of selling cars through a franchise system. This allows car dealers to use their business power to reward their children and relatives, and produces a small aristocracy with inheritable status in the core of the most modern bureaucracy. Presumably car manufacturers do this for rational reasons, since they know perfectly well how to run bureaucracies of employed people, with nepotism rules, orderly careers, and all the rest. Thus it is not true that bureaucracy is always preferable to patrimonial administration, for people who have the choice sometimes choose patrimonial administration.

Clearly the central question of rationality from the point of view of an employer is the distribution of uncertainty between different kinds of risk. An exchange partner is likely to want authority when he or she *does not know* which *particular activity* he or she is likely to want, but is *reasonably sure* he or she will want *some* activity. Under these conditions it is rational to become an employer, to buy a zone of indifference rather than a set of particular activities.

The basic argument of this section is that these considerations of Simon predict the circumstances under which authority norms will grow out of exchange relations, and also predict much about the content of these norms. Briefly I will argue that the *continuous pursuit of a productive purpose* produces an employer interest in authority rather than in particular activities, and that the central additions to status norms (which are derived from the continuity of the exchange) will be *norms preserving the zone of indifference.* Pure status norms tend to rigidify an exchange system. Thus in particular we will expect a series of norms that specify the relations between authority and status, to preserve the flexibility of authority, whenever an exchange relation is established in order to pursue continuously a productive purpose.

Aristocracies in modern administration

Since there is a widespread idea that bureaucracy is pervasive in modern society, that all important exchange relations in the labor market are authority exchanges, in the next two sections I want to demonstrate that I have something to explain. If all activities are exchanged in a context of bureaucratic authority, then the thing to be explained is the general superiority of bureaucracy to every other form of administration. Perhaps the central mistake of Max Weber was to conceive his problem as one of explaining the general superiority of bureaucracy. The two sections will treat the rational origins of aristocracy by exchange partners that have a choice of not creating an aristocracy, and subcontracting, that is, establishing a temporary contractual exchange of money for specified activities rather than a general exchange of wages for authority. These alternatives lap over into the previous section (subcontracting is related to discontinuous exchange) and the following section (aristocracy is related to fiduciary exchange). They are discussed here, rather than where they really belong, because it is essential to destroy the previous mind set of pervasive bureaucracy before one can see the nature of the problem of this section.

By an aristocracy, I mean a group of people granted roughly equal status (a 'peerage') in a continuous flow of goods (a 'tenure'), under a proviso of loyalty to an ethic attached to that status (an 'oath of fealty'), who are given extensive rights of self government ('independence' and 'representation' in a 'parliament') in an area of activity in which their monopoly is guaranteed by higher, generally political, authority (a 'fief'). The language in parentheses is intended to suggest that this definition is closely related to the classicial definition of aristocracies in the early modern states of Western Europe, the 'feudal' aristocracy in the 'Ständestaaten' or 'estate societies' of the sixteenth to eighteenth centuries. But the exact correspondence of this definition, in all its elements, to the status of professors in the most productive modern universities (and its lesser applicability to less distinguished, 'teaching,' schools) suggests that the form of administration has not disappeared, and that some of the most modern activities are well administered by such a system. The principal difference of modern university faculties from feudal aristocracy is that status is not (directly) inheritable.

In fact, the main modern form of aristocracy, the 'classical' professions of the law, medicine, and university teaching, only achieved organized aristocratic status in America in the middle of the late nineteenth century, and did so *under the pressures of modernization*. (See Larson, 1977.) Until medicine was a science, until law was rationalized, until colleges turned into universities, there was no need of a professional aristocracy.

Why should the pressures of modernization tend to *create* aristocratic administration, and the peculiar structure of exchange relations with tenure and self government? The argument must start, I believe, with the postulate that authorities give up the rights of government only when they cannot themselves govern. This tends to happen whenever the information or competence required for policy-making is not available to the ultimate power holders. Rational judgement in medicine requires both extensive medical education and information on each particular case, strategically organized in the light of that case's peculiarities, rather than routinely organized by standard operating procedures. Likewise judgement about research directions can only be made by people who know enough about the research to form an educated judgement. Thus we find that the budget of the National Science Foundation is much more aristocratically determined by bodies of peers than are university budgets, although NSF is larger and embedded in government bureaucracy. The reason is that buildings and curricula are much more manageable by non-experts than are research expenditures. Aristocratic administration in early modern times was grounded primarily on the incapacity of the central government to get information about people and production on a distant fief, and perhaps even more its incapacity to collect information on the actions of lower officials.

A 'modern aristocracy' with inheritable status has been created in automobile dealerships for new cars. The key difference between this system and universities is also the key difference between universities and the traditional 'free professions' of the private practice of law and medicine. This is that the rational administration of the system requires that two forms of *property* be managed under the influence of information not available at the center. The most important is probably the goodwill of a clientele, a reputation for honesty, reliable repairs, and the like, that create stable exchange relations between the clientele and a local enterprise. The second is the physical property required for local operations, the physician's surgery or the car dealer's display rooms and repair shops. University property for research (libraries and computers being most crucial) are not so specialized to the local situation, not adapted to the local clientele of the research scientist, and so do not require local holding of property rights. The idea of a research scientist 'selling his practice' would be ridiculous in a way not at all true of a car dealer or a physician.

In short, aristocratic administration tends to be used when bureaucratic authority is impossible or inefficient for the tasks at hand. It also tends to occur when the exchange is of a fiduciary kind, to be analyzed in the following section.

Subcontracting
The great modern world wide corporations are highly bureaucratized administrative systems. Their crucial resources are physical capital and a technical and marketing tradition that works.[2] Furthermore the

---

[2] Incidentally, the problem of the correct measure of *size* is crucial in studying multinational corporations. The American giants are not much larger than the largest European corporations, as measured by their *numbers of employees*. They are much larger by the criterion of *total production and sales*, and somewhat, though not proportionately, larger in amount of capital invested. That is, what makes them giants

most advanced, presumably the most bureaucratized, modern societies get their trading advantage in international trade largely by exporting capital goods (and the accompanying technical advice). Thus it might seem natural to predict that the capital goods industries would be among the most bureaucratic, that the advantage of the great corporations and the most developed countries was in their superior bureaucratic capacity in managing such a complex bureaucratic system for producing their core advantages on the world market, for producing capital goods.

But in fact the capital goods industry, especially construction but also other heavy capital goods production, is characterized by small firms, highly specialized firms dominated by craftsmen and professionals. The core of bureaucratic capitalism, the capital goods industry, is run by subcontracting and professionalized authority in specialist firms, rather than by bureaucratic authority.

The key reason for this is the great instability of the market for capital goods. Investment generally is much more influenced by the business cycle than is consumption. Further much construction of capital goods is carried on outside rather than inside buildings, so is much affected by the seasons. Capital goods have to be adapted to the productive purpose of the particular enterprise, to the size of the investment being made, to innovations in the productive process. A new steel plant or bridge or airport is not exactly like the last one (see Stinchcombe, 1959). This instability of the market and of the technical processes of production requires each new productive enterprise in the capital goods industry to be especially constructed for the job. Subcontracting to specialized firms is a method of tailoring the organization to fit the task. Productive goals are specified in the *specifications* of the subcontract, rather than by continuously exercised authority over the activities of the workers by a long hierarchy of bureaucratic officials.

Just as modernization of medicine or research created new aristocracies, so the modernization involved in substituting capital for labor in production created new systems of *ad hoc* administration in the capital goods industries. Bureaucracy is not a good thing for all the most modern tasks.

are the factors mentioned above, physical capital and effective technical and marketing traditions, not their population size.

Conditions of continuous exchange of authority and compliance

From the above considerations we can summarize the conditions under which it will be rational for a buyer of activities to buy a zone of indifference rather than contract for specific activities. These can be summarized by the catchwords: continuity, uncertainty, wisdom, and institutional differentiation.

By continuity we mean that the buyer (employer) expects to be continuously engaged in producing the same thing, and so to exclude subcontracting in the capital goods industry. By uncertainty we mean that the employer expects to have to adjust the activities he buys to changing conditions of supply or to technical change, and so to exclude what might be called continuous subcontracting in which a flow of activities is prespecified in a pure status exchange. By wisdom we mean that the employer must be in a position to choose rationally what activities he or she will specify by the use of authority, and so to exclude the modern aristocracies of medicine or university teaching. By institutional differentiation we mean that the employer has the capacity to screen off work activities from family, religion, politics, or other sets of norms and rewards which might destroy workers' indifference between the various activities the employer might choose.

Given these functional predictors of the rationality of exchanges of compliance for authority, we want to ask under what concrete conditions they are likely to come about. The first such condition is clearly the expectation of the continuous availability of rewards if the activities are continuously carried out, or more simply, a stable market. I might like to manage a thousand men or women to satisfy my whims, but I do not have the flow of rewards necessary to buy their zones of indifference (besides which following my whims is, under modern conditions, a sufficiently demeaning job that potential employees would not be indifferent between whims). Stable markets of monopolies, stable tax flows to governments, and statistically stable demand for mass consumption goods, all can satisfy the requirement for continuity. Demand for capital goods cannot. Thus we expect to find continuous authority systems in public utilities (monopolies), modern governments (stable tax flows in modern times), and in mass production industries and modern mass retail trade.

But if quick coordinated changes in response to technical changes or to changed models or to changed relative prices of factors of production are not required, activities do not need to be coordinated. After the complicated interdependencies of producing an automobile have been coordinated, there is a very simple flow of a few models of finished automobiles to the dealers, and the dealers' activities in Schenectady do not have to be coordinated with dealers' activities in Fresno. Interdependence of activities means that variations in any one are sources of uncertainty for the others. Thus high variance of technical conditions combined with interdependence of activities puts a high premium on adjustability of each activity. Constancy of demand and uncertainty of technical conditions makes it rational for an employer to buy a zone of indifference rather than specified activities.

But universities are supported out of a stable flow of taxes and research has rapidly changing technical conditions. The reason it does not produce close authoritative supervision of research by Deans is that Deans lack the wisdom to choose research wisely. Only if the information and competence required to choose activities can be concentrated at higher hierarchical levels can a choice made by supervisors be as wise as a choice made by a worker. This is not really a question of inherent complexity of the task. It is not inherently easier to machine a valve to a tolerance of .001 inch than to repair a blood vessel in the neck by surgery. Instead wisdom can be concentrated above the level of the workplace if the elements of the work process are routinized and standardized, so that a few pieces of information about the operation (its cost, scheduling, required materials) are sufficient to make a rational decision about it.

This in turn depends on the inherent characteristics of the technology and work flow (whether it *can* be accurately enough described by a few abstractions), and the organizational technology of information flows (cost accounting, performance statistics, timing information for the stage of production of each product type). Thus for example the work operations of the chemical industry require Ph.D. chemists to design, and are inherently complex. But the complexity is routinized, and the high proportion of accountants in the labor force of the industry shows that a routine abstraction of cost features of these processes is sufficient for bureaucratic planning. That is, chemical production is inherently as complex as chemical research, but can be routinized.

But if we examine the broad pattern of history, we find that many Kings who 'need' a bureaucratic army and bureaucratic tax collection do not get it. One common pattern is that attempts to set up such chains of authority dominated by 'the King in his council' are subverted by the development of an aristocracy, by 'feudalization' or 'confucianization' of the administration. A gentleman does not do as he is told, but as he thinks right. As officials turn into gentlemen, the King in his council loses control and norms of honor are substituted for norms of authority.

Norms of honor are partly a rhetoric in which the pursuit of self interest is rationalized. But they are structurally an invasion of the administration by norms appropriate to other institutional spheres, especially family, religion, and self defense of corporate status groups. Conceptions of honor that go beyond obedience are ordinarily, partly at least, notions that an official is responsible for the general health of the social system, for charity and mercy toward its members, for respect for its cultural and religious ideals, for the proper dignity of aristocrats as individuals and families. That is, norms of honor are reflections of the lack of institutional differentiation, so that officials become responsible in the eyes of their peers for norms beyond those of the authority system.

Lack of institutional differentiation of course creates difficulties in the development of all specialized normative systems, difficulties for all systems uniquely dedicated to a single purpose. A university cannot devote itself entirely to research because then no one will take care of teaching, nor can it create norms that professors should spend all day in tender loving care of students because then no one will take care of research. But norms of authority are more thoroughly specialized than other kinds, because they ask that workers be indifferent to all other considerations than the purposes of authorities; authority norms are harder to write in such a way that they always balance properly different normative considerations. Consequently the larger the range of relevant normative considerations (the lower the degree of institutional differentiation), the smaller the zone of indifference, and the more activities instead are specified in advance by traditional norms that ensure a balancing of normative considerations from different institutional spheres.

Subsidiaries and takeovers

A uniform result of comparative studies of administration in modern economies is that firms which are subsidiaries are more centralized internally than firms not owned by other companies. That is, more of the decisions in a subsidiary are the responsibility of the chief officer than in a free standing firm. This suggests that creating or buying a subsidiary involves creating or buying authority over a firm. Is it possible to extend the Barnard-Simon zone of indifference reasoning to this situation; is there any realistic sense in which the parent corporation would want to buy a zone of indifference in a subsidiary corporation?

The crucial considerations here are 'organizational slack' and 'capital rationing' in the potential subsidiary. By 'organizational slack' we mean that the flow of revenue to a firm is great enough so that it can support activities that do not pay their way. By 'capital rationing' we mean that there are resources of goodwill or technical competence or physical capital which cannot be efficiently utilized without further capitalization, capitalization that is impossible with the present organization and ownership structure. The reason we classify these together is that they are both situations in which the activities of the potential subsidiary are below the optimum because of organizational constraints. The argument will be that by buying authority over the firm, the parent corporation becomes able to choose a mix of activities nearer the optimum, and that therefore the creation of new authority norms in subsidiaries reflects the reasons for such exchanges. One main purpose of takeovers, then, is to buy a zone of indifference of the subsidiary in order to choose activities nearer the optimum.

There are two main sources of organizational slack, the internal politics of the firm and the competitive situation. One of the activities of a firm (say textbook publication) may provide a flow of revenue sufficient to support another activity (say monograph publication). A firm with a craftsmanlike appreciation for the fact that textbooks are based ultimately on monographs may have powerful editors who defend the losing list of monographs, who have developed stable exchange relations with monograph authors who vaguely promise textbooks, and who are otherwise committed to the present product mix. The internal politics of the firm may make it impossible to choose those activities yielding maximum profits, namely sacrificing the monographs.

The competitive situation produces organizational slack when the technical or marketing systems of the firm are interdependent so that every viable firm needs all the elements of the system. For example, a publisher needs both a list of books to sell and a sales organization to sell them. Two publishers in the same market may therefore have to maintain two sales organizations, neither of which makes a profit as such, but both of which are necessary to make the lists profitable. If one buys the other and imposes enough authority to abolish one of the sales organizations, the larger combined list may make the remaining sales organization more profitable.

Feeder lines for airlines and other transportation businesses may have the same character, that two systems of feeders may not pay while one integrated system would.

In this case the organizational slack arises from technical indivisibilities in parts of the technical or marketing system that require firms to build overcapacity in parts of their system for competitive reasons. This overcapacity in one system can be used as a 'free good' in the other system, increasing the joint profit rate. But this can only come about if the present authority over the division of profits can be restructured by a shift of ownership, and authority over the abolition of parts of the new combined system can be located in a place in which the joint rate of return is the decision criterion.

A particular case of this joint productivity complex is especially interesting from the point of view of exchange norms. One great difficulty in international trade is to obtain an agent one can trust in another country. A firm needs an agent because collecting information on, say, the market for agricultural machinery in Australia from a factory in Birmingham, England, is very difficult. Yet the Birmingham firm needs to trust the agent because that information, once paid for in pounds, is equally useful for International Harvester, who might buy it for dollars. International marketing information from the importing country is thus technically interdependent with production or wholesale buying for export, yet the norms of international trade are often not solid enough to ensure control from Birmingham over a commercial agent in Sydney.

One rather surprising adaptation to this problem is the tiny international conglomerate. A small wholesale buyer of agricultural machinery for export from England may own a firm with seven employees in Australia, another with three employees in New Zealand, another with five employees in Argentina, and one responsible for East Africa at Nairobi. Owning one's agents allows sure ownership of the marketing information and goodwill built up with the resources (both money and costly cooperation) of the parent company. It also allows a choice of activities by the agent which maximizes the joint profit rather than the agent's profit. But most generally, it allows enforcement of norms through the *authority system* which, within a country, would be enforced through a common civil law of contracts or a common orientation to good business ethics as conceived in a single business community.

The problem of competition is reversed here. Exactly because a competitor also needs an agent in Australia, and the loyalties and norms of an agent in a foreign business community are problematic, ownership of the agent is rational self-protection. These tiny international conglomerates are often created by buying out small family firms in the country where one needs an agent. Usually it seems that the authority system is not so extensively transformed in such take-overs, if only because a Birmingham businessman does not know very well how to operate in Australia.

Capital rationing seems to come about in the following way. A firm with a valuable resource (a patent, or goodwill in a certain city) has an ownership structure such that all the profits (over the interest rate) will go to the present owners, and even more crucially risks other than unprofitability of that resource are borne by the general budget to which the resource contributes. This is especially likely to happen in family firms, where the overall welfare of the family, with all the risks of all the activities in which they are all engaged, is built into the utility function of the firm by family ownership. What that means is that *in* the present ownership structure, the flow of income from the resource is more uncertain than it would be if owned by someone else. Other mechanisms that can produce such increases of uncertainty, such as management instability in a small firm, small capacity of a firm to insure risks in a new business, which a larger firm can do more easily, or lack of secure access to complementary factors of production (e.g. a sales force, a cost accounting system, etc.), may also produce capital rationing.

Further, capital rationing can be produced by organizational slack, as analyzed above. That is, because a valuable resource is embedded in an organization that eats up the returns to support non-paying activities, an investment in expanding that resource has a lower expected rate of return than it would have if it were divorced from the slack system.

When a firm is confronted with a capital rationing situation, that means that bankers and other investors will not invest in utilization of resources up to the level that would be rational in the market, *if* the market could be divorced from the firm's organization. From the point of view of the present owners of the resource, this means that the resource pays less than it could because its exploitation is underfinanced. From the point of view of a potential buyer of the firm, it means that the resource in his reorganized ownership makes substantial further investments in that resource profitable. If the potential parent has money lying around in low yield investments, or can itself get money at a good rate in the market (not being faced with capital rationing itself), then it can pay more for the firm confronted with capital rationing than the firm is worth to its present owners. But when it gets that firm, the parent had better make sure the administration of it is no longer devoted to family welfare in many businesses or to supporting organizational slack. That is, it needs to centralize authority in order to change the firm's utility function to make the resource pay.

Let us recapitulate this argument, relating it to the theory of the employment relation. There are situations in which it is rational for a parent corporation to buy a zone of indifference of a potential subsidiary, rather than to subcontract with the firm, to prefer an exchange of authority to an exchange for particular activities. These conditions are those of organizational slack and capital rationing to the potential subsidiary. Both of these come about because the ownership structure of the potential subsidiary leads it to choose a non-optimum line of activity. In buying out the owners, the purpose then is to change the decision criteria of the subsidiary. In order to change those criteria, a reorganization of the subsidiary which centralizes authority is necessary to ensure that the changed decision criteria are actually applied. Hence subsidiaries, because of the purposes that make parent–subsidiary exchanges rational, tend to have more centralized internal authority than do free-standing firms.

The basic logic of the exchange of money for authority is the same for takeovers as for the employment relation. Hence the variables of continuity, interdependence and technical uncertainty, wisdom in the parent, and institutional differentiation should also apply to takeovers and mergers. The extension of these principles to this new case will not be carried out here, but is a direction of research suggested by the argument above. Likewise the norms of parent–subsidiary relations should have the same general content as bureaucratic authority norms, shaped by the purpose of preserving the zone of indifference of the subsidiary so that the parent can choose activities for the subsidiary.

Fiduciary exchange

Trusts, agents, and corporation law

Historically the law of corporations developed out of the law of trusts and the law of agency, rather than out of the law of the master–servant relation. That is, boards of directors are also employees of the stockholders, but they are *mainly* legally trustees. And operating executives of a corporation are also employees of the board of directors, but *mainly* legally agents of the board. Stockholders, like the minor children for whom a trust is created, cannot legally exercise the 'ownership' of the firm's goods by disposing of them or using them. Only the board, like the trustee, has operating legal control ('possession') over the resources of the firm. Likewise an officer of the corporation is bound legally to exercise his agency in good faith, not to exceed the authority granted him, but his acts (if legal within the law of agency) commit the corporation and its resources.

What the stockholders buy in hiring a board, and what the board buys in hiring officers, is not so much a zone of indifference, as a promise of responsibility, a promise to carry out a fiduciary rôle as a trustee or as an agent. The capital market is shot through with these fiduciary exchanges, and the ponderous conservatism of bankers and stockbrokers and corporation lawyers is more an ethical imperative of fiduciary exchanges than a character type of the very rich.

What this means is that the character of the norms that define bureaucratic hierarchies change as one gets toward the top, change from authority norms to fiduciary norms. It is stupid to apply concepts appropriate to authority (e.g. span of control) to the top of the hierarchy. What sense does it make to say that the span of control of the board of directors, a committee, is one, namely of president of the company? The origin of the law about the top of the hierarchy in the law of trusts and the law of agency suggests the direction of analysis.

The purpose of trusts and agency

Inheritance law provides for trusts because the heir is often not trusted (either by the court or by the person who died) to administer the estate rationally. Children were always presumed incompetent to manage their own affairs, and women were often presumed incompetent. So the basic purpose of a trust was to provide wisdom in the management of an estate when wisdom was presumed lacking.

The choice of a trustee generally required not only wisdom, but also either disinterestedness and identification with the interests of the heir.

The first of these, wisdom, is reflected in the legal provision for trustees and agents that both must act as 'a reasonable man' would act in the circumstances. That is, the norms do not specify what specific actions the trustee or agent should carry out. Nor is it any excuse in the law that the action taken is not forbidden in the document creating the trust or the agency; if that action was not one that a reasonable man would have taken under the circumstances, the trustee or agent can be held liable. It is a defense for an agent, but not a trustee, that he or she was specifically instructed to carry out unreasonable actions. Specific instructions of a trust document can be violated if changed circumstances make those instructions an unreasonable way to achieve the purposes of the trust, though of course the courts are cautious about violating the specific provisions of the document.

The second of these, disinterestedness, is reflected in 'conflict of interest' norms, which try to ensure that the trust or agency is used in the interest of the beneficiary or principal rather than in the interest of the trustee or agent. Identification with the interests of the beneficiary or principal is often achieved by norms of election and dismissal, as in the case of boards of directors, or precarious or discretionary tenure, as in the case of cabinet officers, officers of corporations, or commercial agents.

The problem with both of these normative provisions is that they are easily corruptible, and that the law is a very inefficient way to prevent corruption. Hence the norms of wisdom and disinterested service are often supported by structural devices providing for continual review of performance of these central normative provisions. The most common of these are collegiality (a committee as trustee), publicity, especially periodic reports, and auditing, in the sense of having disinterested investigators periodically reviewing the performance of the trustee or agent.

In its full development, the norms of a trust or agency provide for six features (besides the obvious one that the trustee or agent should be paid, usually well paid, for his trouble, responsibility, and competence): (1) reasonableness or wisdom; (2) disinterestedness; (3) election or precarious discretionary tenure; (4) collegiality; (5) publicity; (6) audit. In general large transfers of capital to new enterprises take place in the context of exchange relations with all these features. Further, professional aristocracies in medicine or universities have many of these features. And of course the whole theory of representative government is based on these provisions for the legislature and the cabinet.

Status groups and fiduciary exchange

By a status group we mean a group whose claim to a high position in the stratification system is based on prestige, defended by an ideology of status honor, by an ideology of loyalty to an ethical system that applies peculiarly within the group. This does not mean, of course, that aristocrats or bankers or university professors sacrifice money for prestige. They may occasionally do so for the sake of the ethical system on which their honor is based, but the honor of poverty is not eagerly sought by grandees or investment bankers or university professors. In fact the process is exactly the reverse – the claim of special wisdom governed by an ethical system organized around status honor is the basis for claiming high incomes, control of wealth, and power in the social system. Conceiving of honor and wealth, or honor and power, as alternative utilities with socially established preference exchange rates, such that aristocrats and college professors are socialized to a noble preference for honor over wealth, is a remarkable psychologizing of a social process. It suggests that professors of sociology would like to distract public attention from their high incomes.

The argument of this section is that status groups generally derive their functional health (when they have it) from their capacity to facilitate fiduciary exchanges. That is, the argument holds that the capacity of a status group to hold its members to an ethical standard above that legally required (specifically, a standard of a 'reasonable' and 'disinterested' person) allows the group to monitor the difficult normative problems of obtaining trustworthy trustees and agents. All sorts of social functions that require fiduciary exchanges become more possible to such groups, so the groups tend to dominate capital and investment markets, politics in representative governments, and often the professions.

Consider the common observation that groups showing no particular capacity for capitalist organization in their home country often dominate the commercial and industrial sectors of countries they migrate to, just as do traditionally commercial guest peoples. Not only Jews in Medieval and Early Modern Christian and Muslim societies, but also Chinese in Southest Asia, Indians and Arabs in Africa South of the Sahara, Southern Italians and Levantines in South America, all are disproportionately represented in commerce, and disproportionately successful. Yet China, India, or Southern Italy are not noted metropolitan centers of capitalist advance. The argument above implies that when such small immigrant groups become status groups in a new society, with devices of social control and conceptions of status honor more strict than those applying to the native population, they become capable of establishing fiduciary exchanges within the group which facilitate the movement of credit, investment, and commercial agency relations. This advantage in fiduciary exchange produces dominance in social structures that functionally depend on fiduciary exchange, such as banking, commerce, and generally areas needing new investment.

A key characteristic that Weber noted of status groups is that their solidarity is based on sharing a style of life. That is, a status group usually has a distinctive style of dress and grooming, a shared pattern of recreation (for example hunting, golf, polo), a standard of conspicuous consumption, common memberships in associations, a distinctive pattern of gentlemanly education isolated from that of society, a distinctive, often aristocratic, theology, a complex of ladylike 'accomplishments' for the women, often of an artistic kind, patterns of courtesy, a distinctive accent or sometimes a distinct language. The whole round of life is dominated by a shared and distinctive culture, by which members of the status group show 'breeding,' and by a 'friendly but firm' manner of dealing with other orders, of such a kind that can make the exclamation of Sheridan's *School for Scandal* (c 1779), 'Such condescension!' a compliment. In most status groups uniformity of style of life is protected by a practice of within-group endogamy; this protective function of endogamy is what gives the notion of a 'bad marriage' moral fire. Jane Austen's novels portray the pattern in all its subtlety.

The relation between the style of life of a status group and its capacity to sustain fiduciary exchanges is straightforward. First, the degree of social control necessary to sustain a morally imperative style of life, penetrating to matters of artistic taste, taste in wives and husbands, and friendly but firm manners toward lower orders, is also *sufficient* social control to sustain the ethics of fiduciary relations. Dishonor for an ungentlemanly breaking of one's word is not only a problem of conscience for an individual, but a sanction of being expelled from the social circle of gentlemen. Ungentlemanly behavior in other areas of life is therefore an accurate measure of who can be trusted to be a gentleman as a trustee or agent. The dominance of aristocrats in diplomacy long after republicans have taken over the labor ministry is related to the confidence of aristocrats that they can trust each other. A person (in aristocratic circles, a man) who pays his gambling debts can be trusted to represent the republic in foreign lands. A person ('man') who is 'too smart by half,' too original in manner and substance, shows that his responsiveness to the ethics of trust and agency is also likely to be precarious.

Second, the status ethic itself is built into a style of life. The display of affluence is an earnest of disinterestedness; surely a man of such substance need not cheat to make a living. A 'friendly but firm' disregard of the welfare of, or affection for, members of other orders protects obligations within the group from competitive obligations out of the group. The other side of a 'friendly but firm' manner is paying gambling debts before paying the tailor, or charging usury to outgroup members but reasonable interest to the people one would dine with. Particularly the obligation to be a 'reasonable man' in caring for the interests of others is built into the gentlemanly code.

A more general way to state these points is that a status group extends to the group as a whole certain aspects of family solidarity: mutual trust backed by mutual inspection and mutual social control, all oriented to an ethical system that is built around the collective welfare and status of the group. And just as extended kinship groups facilitate the movement of credit among kinsmen, so the attenuated kinship of a status group facilitates the movement of credit in relations of trust and agency.

The rationality of fiduciary exchange

The two sources of corporation law in trusteeship and agency suggest the two conditions that make fiduciary exchanges rational. One traditionally appointed trustees whenever the beneficiary of the resources held in trust was thought to be incompetent. One had agents whenever the information required to make a rational decision was available to the agent but not to the principal. One appoints captains of finance to boards of directors on the general ground that those who have made themselves rich probably know how to make us small stockholders rich.[3] One has an ambassador in a foreign capital because the president cannot go there himself.

An investment banker has control of a good deal of money that requires an immense amount of competence and information to use at its highest rate of return. He (or she, if the banking industry were different than it is) is therefore in the position of an incompetent heir

---

[3] Thorstein Velben's classic *A Theory of Business Enterprise* (1921) is organized in large measure around this proposition. Veblen is the only student of the investment market that I know of, save Weber's treatment of the stock market in Hamburg and Berlin, who understood the basic rôle of fiduciary exchanges in the system. The combination of his ironic humor about the style of life of big businessmen, and his conviction that they trusted each other in order to milk the rest of us more effectively, prevented the profound insights of this study from contributing to economics. I agree with Veblen both about the ridiculousness of the very rich, and their pernicious effect on society. But not having his literary gifts may be an advantage to me, because in the absence of powerfully communicated prejudices the reader may carry away a stronger sense of Veblen's logic. The Weber study is summarized in Bendix (1960).

to a fortune, from a structural point of view. He or she needs a trustee who knows the steel business, or the electronics business, or the department store business, sufficiently well to control investments rationally. The trustee is likely to be a board of directors, on which the investment banker puts an agent. The exchange (investment) is embedded in a fiduciary relation of a fully developed kind, with norms of reasonableness, disinterestedness, election or precarious tenure in an agency, collegiality, publicity, and audit. The board of directors in its turn needs to invest these resources in concrete activities, which they cannot (rationally) supervise themselves because the detailed flows of information about the activities would tell them more than they need to know to discharge their trustee functions. The Board then appoints agents for the crucial links in the flow of detailed information, usually at least a President and a Treasurer who have direct agency relations to the Board rather than a hierarchical relation between themselves. Often, probably because the organized mind does not like gaps in a hierarchy, there will be a fictional hierarchy in which the President supervises the Treasurer. But the President had better not really try. A Spanish phrase for this set of key agents of the Board, 'hombres de confianza,' ('men of [in whom we have] confidence') communicates much better than our organizational charts what is going on. The phrase in American organizational discussions that most nearly represents fiduciary relations is 'to take responsibility for,' often used in board meetings of all kinds of organizations (or collegial meetings of professionals) in discussing the division of labor.

Fiduciary relationships and getting one's money back
The usual reason one entrusts money to an enterprise one does not care about enough to administer oneself is not that one has a great passion for producing cars or having a department store in his or her home town. The purpose instead is to get the profits or interest back out, and perhaps to withdraw the principal. But it is hard to take an automobile assembly line down to the pawnbroker when the money is needed. The central role of fiduciary institutions (banks, insurance companies, pension funds, brokerage houses) is to redistribute income streams in time, so that the automobile company has a positive flow (from the savers) during investment and a negative flow (to the savers) when they want the money. Under conditions of certainty this

would be a job of arithmetic, and while a saver would have to trust his banker to add and subtract correctly, there would be no deeper function to relations of mutual trust.

There are three general kinds of uncertainty that these institutions have to deal with: aggregate uncertainty of total income flows, such as the business cycle or inflation creates; uncertainty about the size and temporal distribution of income flows from investments, such as that created by mining finds, or fads, or incompetent management; and uncertainty about the temporal distribution of demands by savers, such as is created for insurance companies by an epidemic or for banks by a run on demand deposits. From the point of view of an individual saver or investor, the distribution he wants of his total income flow among flows with different amounts of these kinds of uncertainty is his *liquidity preference function.* At one extreme a saver may want no uncertainty about the amount of money in the flow, only uncertainty about inflation or deflation. His or her preference will be for currency or demand deposits, i.e. a high degree of liquidity. At the opposite extreme the saver may want the highest rate of return and protection against inflation by sinking his total assets in productive investments, that the saver chooses on the basis of his or her own detailed information. That is, the saver prefers low liquidity with its attendant returns.

The functional problem of fiduciary institutions is that the liquidity preference functions of savers do not add in a natural way to a flow of investment that fits the liquidity requirements of productive enterprises. Much of business cycle economics is organized around that agonizing fact. While I think the contributions of organization theory to the aggregate economic problem have only begun, and show great promise (especially, but not exclusively, for socialist investment policy), I am not competent to deal with that problem. But the key to the continuous balancing of the books of a bank or insurance company is to be able to sell savers and productive enterprises the temporal distribution of income flows they need, at the liquidities or risk functions they can take, and have the amount that can be called in at any time equal the demands at that time. It is the rôle of fiduciary relations with productive enterprises to collect accurate information about the liquidity and profitability of the investment-generated flow of income, and to impose the (often more conservative) liquidity preference function of the investment banker. It is the rôle of the bank or insurance company as trustee of the savers' fund to give them the liquidity and risks they have demanded, at a price (in return below the market profit rate) they are willing to pay. That is, the central rôle of fiduciary exchanges in the economy is the certification of risk levels in flows of income.

While the certification of risk levels requires information the depositors do not have about the risks of investments, the imbalance between the aggregate of high demand for liquidity by depositors or policy holders (they want their money when they die, not when Boeing's new investments start to pay off) and the low supply of liquidity in productive enterprises (the high degree of uncertainty in the flow of business profits) is dealt with by pooling risks, and by banks and insurors holding reserves. That is, the rôle of the representative of the bank on the board of directors cannot be predicted from a naïve theory that he is an agent of demand depositors. His is an agent of the bank, which because of pooling and reserves has a different liquidity preference from depositors, though also (often), a different preference for liquidity than the rest of the directors.

More generally, fiduciary exchanges between organizations have the function of transferring resources from one organization to another, but so modifying the policy-making procedures of the receiving organization that a preference function (e.g. among risk levels) of the sending organization is satisfied. 'Having a good credit rating' is an accrued confidence by potential sources of the necessary resources that policies compatible with their interests can be followed (e.g. that a debt will have the agreed liquidity). Ordinary trusts provide that the trustee will follow a policy reflecting a preference function of the beneficiary (or one the beneficiary 'would have if he or she were competent'). That is, fiduciary relations generally arise whenever the *values* or *preferences* or utilities of one person or organization, the beneficiary or principal, are supposed to govern the policies of another person or organization (the trustee or agent). Fiduciary institutions generally arise when a large-scale transfer of resources governed by preferences of one group (e.g. savers) have to be satisfied by the aggregate of policies followed by another group (e.g. productive enterprises), especially where there are substantial increases for both sets getting what they want from pooling

(e.g. pooling risks and pooling reserves that back demand deposits, etc.)

We note briefly that many exchanges between professional and client are of a kind that functionally require fiduciary exchanges. Medicine, law, teaching, are shot through with norms and institutions similar in kind to trustee-beneficiary relations; these norms tend to evolve into committees of trustees, with audit procedures; they tend to get embedded in a status group with a distinct style of life, and so on.

Exchanges and organizations

The reason for bringing the norms of exchange up is, of course, that organizations are systems of continuous exchange. Hence their normative systems are systems of norms governing continuous exchange. The amazing capacity of the sociology of organizations to continuously reforget this fundamental point each time it is rediscovered (by Marx, Weber, Simon, Gouldner) is due, I think, to what I like to call the Durkheimian fallacy, cleverly reprapogated as the Durkheim-Weber-Pareto fallacy in Parsons' persuasive *Structure of Social Action* (1949). In order to analyze the problem it will be convenient to restate Parsons' analysis of utilitarianism in abbreviated form, in order to see where sociology as a whole has gone wrong in spite of its geniuses.

Parsons' basic argument is that exchanges require norms, for example, norms of commitment (the L cell), of authority to adapt activities (the A cell), of responsibility for goals (the G cell), of the permanent status division of rights and duties (the I cell). The elaboration of the required norms for exchanges has been the focus of his work since the *Structure of Social Action*. The core problem of utilitarianism, according to Parsons, is that it had no place to get norms from, theoretically, except various *ad hoc* constructions like a social contract with a leviathan. The basic postulate then was that such norms cannot come out of rational consideration of one's own advantage, and therefore that continuous systems of exchange (i.e. all social systems) could not sustain themselves without pre-existing commitment to the norms.

The Durkheimian solution to this problem is that such commitment to norms, making society possible, is derived from irrational commitments to society, manifested in pure form in primitive religion, and in attenuated form in the 'precontractual elements of contracts' in modern society. As primitive and naive social solidarity wanes, and rationally oriented exchanges and rationally organized culture advance, therefore, the moral requirements of social organization decay. Briefly, if commitment, authority, responsibility, and status-system fairness are not grounded in an irrational commitment to the sacred, they have no ground at all.

This is a remarkable argument, that in order to be rational one has to have a solid foundation of irrationality. Little wonder then that Parsons seized on the *Protestant Ethic* thesis, that an irrational search for salvation was required for the origin of bourgeois capitalism, and Pareto's argument that socialism was irrational solidarity much like religion. For these likewise were arguments that good sense was not enough to lead people to make profits by continuous production of cotton textiles in factories, or to lead workers to think that if the rich had less, they would probably have more.

But the argument is empirically suspicious. The law of trusts and the law of agency are hardly direct offshoots of primitive religion; collective bargaining in situations of bilateral monopoly to create stable status norms has at best an indirect relation to the New Testament; the worker need not believe that the foreman is an agent of the supernatural in order to switch from the '86 to the '87 model Impala. That is, the new norms of corporate organization were created and made valid considerably after their moral foundation had been thoroughly undermined by the progress of rationality. And the argument that Australian primitives could probably manage investment banking better because of their close relations to the supernatural origins of mutual trust has a certain air of unreality.

If we look at the origins of the normative system of the great corporations,[4] we find that people are perfectly capable of making a social contract to set up a normative system to make cars. When it does not work too well, they do not pray for supernatural guidance in reorganizing the authority system. Or rather, if they do, there is no evidence that it makes the new system work better.[5] Instead they

---

[4] The best analysis I know is of Alfred D. Chandler (1962).
[5] We need not maintain people are *always* collectively rational in order to maintain that they are *capable* of collective rationality.

figure out whether authority or agency relations are better ways of controlling the operating divisions, and if agency is better, they decentralize. And if that does not work, they may try subcontracting. In fact, the history looks more like evolution in the crude sense, of keeping norms that make profit, than evolution in the Parsonian sense of differentiating progressively more specific and rational norms from a primitive bud of irrational commitment to General Motors.[6]

The requirement for the rational origin of a social contract is simply that at all points in the growth of the normative system, moving to the next step is Pareto rational (pays somebody and, perhaps after side payments, costs nobody). Once commitment is secured to a certain degree, moving to greater mutual commitment by elaborating norms takes place *with the resources of previous commitment.* Many status exchanges that would be unduly risky, too much Hobbesian temptation to cash in the other's commitment and run, are rational when both of us are already in this together.

My argument is that the dominance of new norms in organizational exchanges, norms with no appreciable grounding in Medieval Christianity, shows that there are a lot of paths to complex normative developments in which an evolutionary sequence of Pareto-rational movements exists. In short, the precontractual element of contract can perfectly well be a previous contract. Regardless of the ultimate origin of royal authority in the eighteenth century in religious ideology (I don't believe that either, but it is not essential to my argument), the authority of the corporate charter and the board of directors under that charter is the result of the piecewise Pareto-rational evolution of the law of trusts into corporation law, and of devices rationally evolved by investment bankers (election and audit and publicity) so that they could trust their money to somebody else without losing it. Leviathan did not get there in a cataclysmic deal for security, but by a slow rational process of watchful waiting until one finds a system one can trust. The sobriety of investment bankers, their positive lack of Australian primitives' enthusiastic religious solidarity, is exactly

---

[6] Parsons was never very enthusiastic about Weber's essay on the 'Protestant Sects in America' (1946) in which the basic argument was that commitment to Methodism was quite likely to be a rational device to improve one's credit rating. Again there is a parallel in substance, if not in style, between Weber's essay and Veblen's brilliant 'Salesmanship and the Christian Churches,' (1948).

attuned to the slow construction of trustworthy normative systems in which all of us (all of us on the inside, that is) can make a mint.

This argument implies that normative systems of organizations grow out of the more general matrix of continuous rational exchange, and tend to disappear when they are no longer rational. Most people managed to control their grief when the Edsel Division collapsed.

This means that the basic explanatory task for organizational sociology is the explanation of the rationality of norms of organizations in terms of exchange theory. Commitment, seniority-status systems, authority, trust, and responsibility are not impositions of human emotion on rationally engineered social devices, but rather (often, at least) the essence of the rationality of the organization.

This argument also means that organizational relations are not different in kind from contracts in the market. Every contract is an organization in miniature, a normatively controlled exchange relation that lasts a finite amount of time. And every organization is a system of contracts. Organizational sociology is a branch of the sociology of markets.

PART III

SOCIOLOGY AS A PROFESSION

13. On getting 'hung-up' and other assorted illnesses

A discourse concerning Researchers, wherein the nature of their mental health problems is discussed and illustrated

All of us involved in graduate education have watched the agony of many students choosing a dissertation topic, getting 'hung up' in the middle of the project, stopping work in black despair. And we have watched either ourselves or our colleagues refusing to send a paper to a journal editor in order to 'perfect' it – and then sitting for days in front of the paper doing no perfecting, in an impotent anxiety stupor.

Most of us also have had bright daydreams of universal acclaim, of the non-existent book review that starts: 'this is a great book, which will revolutionize the discipline . . .' And we have had the conviction, in dark moments, that all our efforts are play-acting for the petty rewards that universities dispose. We have known people, or are people, who are excellent scholars who never manage to finish anything. We have seen brilliant cocktail-party sociologists or biologists be let go for 'not producing.'

In short, we have seen every conceivable neurotic symptom interfere with our own or others' research. In hardly any other profession do neurotic problems incapacitate so many people such a large part of the time. I would guess that such mental health problems add an average of a year to the Ph.D. program, mostly in the dissertation 'hang-up.' Even among those who get a research degree and are recommended for scholarly promise to leading universities, a very large percentage of assistant professors fail to do enough to justify keeping them on. Those who have already done research quite often cannot do it again.

What is it that a person has to do to produce new knowledge? The crucial peculiarity of research is that one has to choose an objective for oneself, and motivate oneself by that objective alone. Only rarely does someone else choose the objective, and even more rarely is there a series of definite obligations to deliver results by specified dates. Creative scholarship would not give the desired results if arranged as a job with specified obligations. But this means that only a person's own conviction that the result will be worthwhile is available as a motivation.

The conviction of intrinsic value of work is a weak reed to sustain a year or two of drudgery. There is little daily accomplishment, little short-term reward – beyond the conversations with people who do not understand what one is about – to sustain the effort.

Aside from the motivational weakness of one's own convictions, this freedom of choice poses, in stark form, what psychologists call an 'identity problem.' Most people can explain what they do by appeal to the requirements of the job, or to the orders of the boss, or to the custom of the manor. But perfectly free choices reflect what kind of people we are. One who designs cigarette-lighter mechanisms may never call their work 'creative engineering,' but because their job is specified and circumscribed, one need never ask oneself whether one is, in fact, a creative person. In contrast, if my research project is not creative scholarship, it's because I'm not creative. For the scholar, each choice of a research topic or strategy is a choice of what kind of person to be.

The motivational rub here is that every scholarly work, whatever its size, changes in the research process. A project that ends up after a year or two of work with results that the investigator could have foreseen in considerable detail probably is not worth doing. Thus the investigator has built his or her identity on a shifting foundation. Each adaptation of his/her bright visions to the practical realities of unclear results, and error, and ignorance of related work, poses the question again: 'Do I want to be the kind of person who does that kind of sloppy work?' The courage to answer 'yes' is hard to come by.

Momentary depressions get magnified by this process. The passing doubt that the new cigarette-lighter mechanisms are worth all the effort passes as the person with the designing job goes back to it. But passing doubt that a line of scholarly work is worthwhile stops the work, which in turn creates doubt what kind of person one is, which keeps the work stopped. The academic slang for this is 'hung up.' This sort of problem is more severe in dissertation projects for several reasons.

First, the dissertation comes at the time in a person's life when he is choosing an intellectual identity, often for the first time. 'Am I more an intellectual or more a sociologist?' Put another way: 'Do I want to be judged by the body of cultured people in our society or by a body of specialists?' 'Is a refinement of econometric technique worth doing,' She or he may ask, 'when we are in Vietnam? 'Is the philosophy of science as worthwhile as doing science?'

These choices are always latent in the choice of a manageable piece of scholarly work, but the first choice not to be an intellectual (or not to be a sociologist) is the hardest.

Second, at most other times during a person's life he or she has multiple activities. A mature scholar is usually working on several research problems simultaneously. As one of them turns to dust, another shows progress. Professors also have teaching obligations, conferences and congresses, rewriting or lecturing on old work, interminable committee work, and – if worst comes to worst – helping out a student who is 'hung up.' The fluctuations of her or his self-respect are not likely to be so wide. In the first years of graduate school, also, the multiplicity of courses, examinations, experiments, papers, and conversations give a large enough pool of alternatives to provide insurance against total collapse.

But the dissertation tends to become the sole preoccupation of the student. This means that normal oscillations of conviction, normal adaptations to ruined hopes, occupy the whole life-space of the student. It may reflect an already high level of maturity for dissertation students to carry other scholarly enterprises at the same time. But my experience is that those students who are also writing something besides the dissertation do not get 'hung up' as often, and usually finish sooner. The more work one does at the same time, the greater the efficiency of each. (This suggests that a good screening question for prospective professional scholars might be: 'What else were you writing while you worked on your dissertation?')

Then there is the reverse problem. It often turns out that a line of research goes dry, or a particular style of research turns out not to provide adequate data to decide the crucial questions. Perhaps a technique does not work sufficiently well, or perhaps the world just is not as the researcher thought. Then the rational solution is to throw it over and switch lines of research, or perfect quite different techniques, or even perhaps sit and think. But a person throws out work on which her or his identity is based only a little more easily than she or he throws out a baby to try again.

The dependence of people's identities on what kind of work they have chosen to do helps explain one of the most peculiar phenomena of academic life. Often we see a work that looks complete, or nearly complete. For the next year or two we hear that the man is revising it. Then, after applying some pressure perhaps, we see the final product – with no substantial changes. From any economic or prestige calculation, or from considerations of priority, or from consideration of how much new work could have been done meanwhile, it should have stood or fallen as it was. Usually it would have been better to throw it away than to perfect it for so long.

This 'publication shyness' or refusal to finish is clearly related to the problem of putting one's identity on the block. But the peculiar circumstances under which a scholar has to expose himself making 'bearing witness' more difficult than usual. In a revival meeting, when one bears witness to what manner of man he has become, there is a man paid to welcome him into the fellowship of Christ. When a scholar does the same, men are paid to tell what is wrong with it, judge whether it was worth doing, and decide whether he is to enter the communion.

This is accentuated when the academic labor market is highly active, as at present [1966]. Each author knows that no one of consequence reads a piece of research without considering whether he should hire the author. Not only is the scholar taking his or her own measure with the product; he or she knows their colleagues are as well. It is partly this knowledge that sustained their motivation when it seemed not worth the while. But when both one's self-respect and public standing ride on the throw, it is hard to make the cast.

A crucial difference between research and other activities is that the scheduling is under the control of the person to be judged. A surgeon probably feels more anxiety in a precarious operation, but the patient's needs and hospital routine enjoin a scheduling. People who work for someone else, someone who wants a report at a given time, cannot hold it up indefinitely perfecting it. But the scholar decides when he or she is ready.

One of the peculiar distortions of the research process that this causes is concentration on scheduled activities. One activity that is highly scheduled, for example, is the research-grant application. If the application is to pay salaries next year, it has to be in by a certain date. Papers for research journals do not have such deadlines, except perhaps in fields where establishing priority is a common problem.

Many scholars attempt to overcome the finishing problem by systematically hunting up people to promise completion to, such as an organizer of a conference, or an editor of a book, or a publisher. But such deadline-creating opportunities are not as open to graduate students and young persons, for no one is interested in pinning them down.

An additional source of anxiety in scholarly work derives from the biographies of scholars. A scholar at a leading university has ordinarily been the brightest boy or girl in the class for most of their life – else they would not have got in either as a graduate student or as a professor. They are very likely to have based their self-respect on their brightness.

Going into research or scholarly writing is often the first time they have to associate with a body of people who have also always been the brightest boys or girls in class. Besides, they are for the first time compared across all age-groups; it is no longer sufficient to be the best 24-year-old mathematician around. One has to be the best mathematician around if one is still to base one's self-respect on comparative brightness.

It is extremely unlikely that any given scholar will be the best around. Even after stretching the human capacity for self-deception, at least 75% of all scholars must recognize that someone they know could do their work better than they. (Fortunately, that someone has chosen to do something else.) The discovery comes as a rude shock to a person who has learned to respect themself for being the only one who could get all the problems right.

This accounts for much of the bitter back-biting, the denigration of others' work, the conspiracy theories of how leading scholars publish work of members of their clique, the close attention to rank and precedence, the sneaky comparative counting of numbers of foot-notes, the explosive priority conflicts, the equation by the envious of a high publication rate with sloppy work, and other seamy aspects of academic life. They are defense mechanisms to protect a challenged self-conception, a conception learned in long years of getting rewards for being pretty good for a boy or girl of that age.

But if it produced only meanness and petty bickering, it would be unpleasant but not crucial. It also plays into the anxiety created by the identity-choice aspects of research itself. When research must bear the burden, not only of being worthwhile, but also of showing that the researcher is the brightest student in class, the load becomes too much. It is too much to require of a piece of work that it not only incarnate an intellectual identity, but that it also prove something false about the author. (A very illuminating case may be found in Norbert Wiener's autobiography, *Ex-Prodigy* (1953): Wiener left mathematics completely after graduate school, retreating into writing for an encyclopedia, when it was no longer sufficient to be the best 19-year-old mathematician in the country).

This problem is particularly intense the first time it is confronted, most often in graduate school. Graduate students are often more interested in their work for what it tells them about themselves, about whether they are 'brilliant' or not, than for what it tells them about the world. Generally in the process of maturation, this disturbance calms down somewhat, and they aim to have it said of themselves, '—does good work.' But we all see the slightly megalomanic symptoms in our colleagues, so irritating because it undermines our own megalamania.

Research is necessarily a social process. Rarely is the interaction with others solely by way of the printed page; in the United States at least, such isolation is never characteristic of graduate students. Instead they are involved in a social system of advice and criticism, of oral examinations and thesis supervision, of research assistantships and co-authorships, of seminars and conferences, of cocktail party conversation and marginal comments on manuscripts, of review editors' comments and grant review committees.

This web of social-intellectual relations around a research project is quite sufficient to immobilize it. The relatively new rôle of research entrepreneur is reserved for those who can keep research moving through the web. A graduate student who is not something of an entrepreneur, not a manager of promises and commitments, of emphasizing the different aspects of the product for different faculty and foundation 'clients,' may possibly win through by sheer intellectual power. Then again, they may not.

One difficulty with the social system in which research is embedded is that the various members of the system cannot imagine how good work can be done in ignorance of their specialties. As a research project comes up against a new source of advice and criticism, it, and the person carrying it, become loaded with a new burden of 'I don't think you've sufficiently thought about ...' The ellipses stand for whatever the special competence of the adviser is. There is no way of avoiding this, because the chances are very good that the researcher has indeed not thought about ..., and that it is indeed important.

This derives from the inherent purpose of research, which is to extend a *body* of knowledge. The more places a given finding can be hooked to that body of knowledge, the more important it is. And the modification of research to take account of something else may save it from being either trivial or outright mistaken.

But from a human point of view, this means that students are constantly confronted with their own incompetence to carry out their own research. But being incompetent, he or she is also usually more competent than anyone else by the the time they have gone any distance in the work. With maturation, most people either become slick in covering the gaps in their knowledge, or get used to being incompetent.

A second sort of difficulty is that one's advisers always forget the previous papers, or do not listen when one tries to explain what it's all about (thinking they already know), or forget what they advised last time, or honestly change their minds. About half of the things one 'has not thought about' were the topics of previous papers, or things one was told not to worry about, or useful comments on quite a different research project which the adviser would have done had it been *their* topic.

Particularly when one is dependent on the recommendation of the adviser, this normal half-communication leads to frustration and discouragement. It would be hard enough to bear if all the criticism and advice were well conceived. When much of it is off the point, under circumstances where the listener knows their intelligence is being judged by the enthusiasm with which they receive the mistaken advice, it requires great strength of character to bull through.

In general, distortions of reality from psychological forces are most prevalent in areas of ambiguity and in areas of 'expressive' behavior. Neurotic manifestations are most easily detected in a person's religious behavior and thought, in the 'style' of their dealings with other people, in the way they perceive inherently ambiguous realities (such as the sentiments of others toward them), and in free associations and dreams.

Of all kinds of work dealing with 'reality,' research is one of the most 'expressive,' and it deals with the inherently ambiguous 'reality' of knowledge that does not yet exist. Neurotic problems from other areas of personality, therefore, are likely to be manifested in research. Research in process is very like a dream, and 'dream work' (the phrase is Freud's) or distortion is characteristic.

Because of its very close relation to identity, research tends to be infused with other sorts of identity problems besides intellectual. Women researchers are likely to infuse their research behaviour with problems of feminine identity. They are faced with a constant danger of being brighter than their husbands, present or potential. The suppression of the hard intellectual bite of the work, of intellectual aggressiveness when it is called for, is perhaps the most serious such identity difficulty. Excessive pliancy to male advice is perhaps another. (Conversely, young men often seem to be attacking papa pretty aggressively.)

Particularly in the social sciences and humanities, ethnic, national, and sex identities usually become involved in the choice of research topics. It is a relatively rare Negro sociologist who does not study 'race relations' – but this almost never means Indians or Chinese. Few economists from underdeveloped countries specialize in the dynamics of rich economies, while many more economists of rich and self-confident nations study underdevelopment. Jews are considerably overrepresented in Judaic studies, farmers' sons in agricultural economics, and ministers in comparative religion.

This is by no means an inherently bad phenomenon, but it often limits the vision of scholars. For instance, the comparative study of ethnic relations in different societies is in a parlous state, partly because Jews have studied only anti-Semitism, Negroes have studied black ghettos, French Canadians have studied French–English relations, and colonial intellectuals have studied imperialism. The names of leading comparative scholars generally have a majority-group ring, as Karl Deutsch, or E. H. Carr.

Such distortions as these do not usually stop work, unless the identity demands a kind of work which the environment will not accept. Radical identities in conservative environments, identities as general intellectuals in specialized environments or as specialists in intellectual environments, identities as poets in critical environments or as critics in (rare) creative environments – such incompatibilities may emasculate a student's work because their own strength of character is not enough to carry it through in the face of hostility.

Other neurotic distortions of research remind one of hysterical paralysis. The powers of a well-tested intellect are immobilized and atrophied, accompanied by symptoms of disturbance in other areas of life. I do not pretend to understand such matters, and most diagnoses I have heard sound fanciful to me. They do, however, indicate the peculiar vulnerability of research to neurotic disturbance.

Obviously, a good many people overcome all these difficulties and lead happy, productive lives in research. And a good many get research degrees, though often somewhat delayed. Can we say anything about how they arrange things so that work can go on?

Many of the anxiety-inducing characteristics of research are essential to its proper functioning, and are the source of its attraction as a life work. Individual freedom and responsibility for research decisions is necessary for two reasons. First, it guarantees the necessary pluralism of the scientific community. The main line of advance always peters out after a while, and without new starts a discipline dies. New starts depend on individual autonomy. Second, the decentralization is necessary because within six months or a year, a competent student who has pursued the work usually has better judgement than a genius who has not.

Furthermore, many of us chose a research career because we wanted to choose our own intellectual identities, and would quit if we could not. Invasions of academic freedom which threaten to remove this source of anxiety are more vigorously protested in research institutions than elsewhere, because they touch sacred values. The freedom to choose an intellectual identity, with all its anxiety-producing consequences, is an inherent part of scholarly endeavor.

The same is true of the criticism that newly published work meets. And it would be a poor scholarly enterprise that did not have a lot of the brightest students in their classes. Descriptions of work never done before are always less clear and reliable than other descriptions, and advice during research has to depend on such descriptions. These are inherent dilemmas of the research process: eliminate the causes and one eliminates the research as well as research anxiety. Clearly what is called for is symptomatic relief.

There are various games one can play with oneself to alleviate some of the distress. Some of them are quite irritating to colleagues and are probably damaging to the system as a whole, but they preserve research capability. One of these is monomania, the conviction that only one's own work is worthwhile. This can be supported by carrying on intellectual relations only with disciples, sycophants, and former graduate school peers who will tolerate your insanity for old times' sake.

A functionally similar solution is always to talk and never to listen. This is hard to get away with as a graduate student, but the professor who gives the same answer to every question, usually in the first-person singular, is a familiar academic figure.

A prodigy syndrome can quite often be assuaged by a slashing attack on incompetent or routine pieces of work. In the social sciences and the humanities, reviews are generally a safe place for this. The more distinguished the author, the more satisfying a demonstration of two pages of superiority. It would be quite a different matter to be superior for 300 pages.

As long as people with such adaptations are not too powerful, the value of the research this enables them to do probably outweighs the damage. The damage is also lessened in larger departments, where a pluralistic structure enables students to slip out from under the oppression.

Less noxious adaptations can be made both by individuals and by departmental administration. As far as possible, students should keep themselves from being too narrowly focused on one project. Working on a couple of promising term papers or reports of previous research while doing a dissertation is useful. This also helps carry one over the period immediately after the dissertation, where others usually have nothing in the pipeline. I think most scholars naturally make the adaptation of several simultaneous projects later in their careers. With three or four projects going at once, they are unlikely to get 'hung up' on all of them at the same time.

Setting intermediate deadlines for partial objectives, somewhat flexible but with definite expectations, also tends to suppress getting 'hung up' and to reduce publication shyness. Preferably, the commitments will be made by the researcher, and to someone who is close to the project – certainly no farther away than the immediate supervisor. But they should be commitments to a rather forbidding, non-indulgent figure who will make it unpleasant if he or she does not come through. If graduate students had to promise a conference presentation of something from the dissertation after about a year – or face the prospect of backing down in semi-public form if they were not ready – it might speed things along. (Mature scholars usually do this for themselves.) Formal, obligatory departmental seminars with finished papers to be presented every x weeks might work.

For the professors, there ought to be a set of norms about how long one should work on a grant proposal, for the proposals do have natural deadlines and form a refuge from anxiety-provoking research. In the case of the social sciences, for example, this might be a week for each $10,000 up to $30,000, and then a rapidly declining additional time allowance up to a maximum of three months for a million or more dollars. I suppose we would lose some grants that way, but gain some papers. Knowledge is harder to come by than money.

It seems to me that the only solution to the problem of not being the brightest student in class is to shift one's basis of self-respect to ultimate values. If one organizes one's life around the advance of science, or social justice, or artistic excellence, another's greater contribution does not lessen one's own. I do not believe that the values and purposes of academic institutions are counters in a zero-sum game, where I lose what you win.

But even if they were, it would be good for the scholar's mental health to be able to feel joy in the 'shock of recognition' of someone else's good work. After all, if he or she appreciates others' good work they are more likely to read his with charity.

14. Max Weber's *Economy and Society*

Shortly after getting out of graduate school, I put a good deal of effort into reading the untranslated parts of Max Weber's *magnum opus* with my graduate school German, living with the fear that the effort would be wasted because the part I was reading would be translated soon, but with the hope that if it were translated I would at least be sure I had got it straight. Re-reading it now, entirely in my native language and in a continuous fashion, provides an occasion to comment on whether people starting out at this time to be sociologists should start as I did. Is *Economy and Society* a good place to start an intellectual biography now? What is there about this work that is of continuing value to the discipline?

There are clearly some parts of the book that have become archaic. The discussion of meaning at the beginning of the book, for instance, would be written quite differently by a modern scientist of Weber's quality, incorporating the recent advances in cognitive psychology and linguistics. Much of what Weber discussed philosophically has been investigated empirically.

Likewise Weber's treatment of calculation in economic enterprises is oriented to an old-fashioned financial balances calculation rather than to the representation of a causal system with monetary measures of the variables as in modern cost accounting, or to the devices of operations research and linear programming for rational calculation in the case of unpriced inputs or outputs. We know a good deal about rational planning of physical production quantities (rather than market price quantities) from detailed studies of the Soviet system (for instance, the recent brilliant study by David Granick, 1967).

Weber's discussion of the direct relation of the state to the economy considers mainly the problem of the creation of money rather than treating the nation as a whole as a 'household,' as in modern national income theory, with combinations of fiscal and monetary controls.

Weber ignores the impact of the high rate of technical change in the economy on the definition of rationality. If an economy is advancing technically at between two and three percent per year, then technical stagnation will cut a firm's efficiency almost in half in a period of twenty years, as compared with other firms in the economy. Technical stagnation is, therefore, more irrational than almost anything that stupidity, sentimentality, or family ties might lead to a businessman to do at any particular time. Keeping up with science and technology is more fundamental to rationality in the economy than Weber's treatment implies. Rationality should not be defined as a quality of decisions at a particular time but rather as a pattern of systematic improvement over time.

These examples of archaisms come mainly from Weber's analysis of the economy because that is what I know most about. I presume that there are similar substantial deficiencies in his analysis of politics, religion, law, or cities. Though the *best* of modern analyses are generally better than Weber in the details, we could eliminate a lot of tiresome reading by cutting out modern analyses that are substantially worse. But the main value of the work is not in the details – it is in the architecture of the work as a whole.

Talcott Parson's analysis of the architecture of the work as a whole is, roughly speaking, that the book is mainly about values and their influence on social organization. Reinhard Bendix's analysis is, again roughly, that the book is mainly about domination and authority. My analysis is that is is mainly about economy and society. I think Weber's main contribution was the way he used the model of classical economics to construct a theory of economic progress. Since much of the technique for this architecture is obscured by the brilliance of the detail, I will outline briefly the strategy of theory building I think Weber was using and describe briefly how some of the specific parts of the book relate to this basic structure. This will show why *Economy and Society* is a much better book on economic development than all but a very few books on that subject written today. In my opinion, only Clifford Geertz sometimes approaches Weber's quality of intellectual construction in this field, and that usually in short spurts.

Each of the sections of the book can be thought of as an attempt to detail a given area of social life, which organization of that area of life comes closest to being compatible with the growth of rational bourgeois capitalism by most closely satisfying the postulates of classical economic theory? What are the main alternative, nonpropitious forms of organization in that area of life? How do these alternative forms undermine rational calculation and exchange in the economy? In what ways was the development of that area of life different from other approximations to the propitious organization in the western European Middle Ages, Renaissance, and absolutist periods? The last question is important because such differences in the West might explain the growth there of a classical economic reality.

The areas of life to which these questions are applied are: (1) the structure of economic enterprises themselves, especially their accounting mechanisms and their embedding in markets (pt. 1, chap. 2); (2) kinship institutions in relation to the economy, especially the forms of appropriation and inheritance of economic opportunities with the resulting kin structuring of economic enterprise (pt. 2, chaps. 2, 3, and 4); (3) more or less solidary suprafamilial interest groups, with a common dependence on some kind of economic opportunity or valuable social status, such as social classes, estates, and ethnic groups (pt. 1, chap. 4; and pt. 2, chap. 5; and mixed with political considerations, pt. 2 chaps. 11–16); (4) religious groups, and particularly religious suprafamilial ethical socialization for economic life organized by a society's ethical and religious leaders (pt. 2, chap. 6, and mixed with politics again, chaps. 14 and 15); (5) courts, judges, lawyers, and other structures for resolving civil disputes, especially in their aspect of making economic obligations predictable and calculable (pt. 2, chaps. 1 and 8); (6) the structure of local government and its relation to the central powers of government and also its relation to the military risks and opportunities of the society with special attention to the government of commercial and manufacturing cities (pt. 2, chap. 16); and finally (7) the institutions for the application and control of violence, and the resulting institutions of taxation, of slavery and other politically enforced labor, of conquest, of public office holding, of politically induced disturbances in the system of civil law and property ownership, and generally other violence-backed exactions from the economically active population (pt. 1, chap. 3; and pt. 2, chaps. 10–15).

For instance, the kinship institutions of a society facilitate economic rationality (in the limited sense of approximating the situation in which people will act as they are postulated to act in classical economics): (1) if families can own property without political and religious encumbrances and if most economic property is owned without such encumbrances; (2) if other kinds of bodies as well as kin groups can corporately own and control property; (3) if no legal restraints on sales of property in the interests of future heirs exist; (4) if families do not own public offices or places in a craft guild or otherwise have property rights which restrict free mobility of labor; and so forth.

As another instance, the central government is most favorable to economic rationality of a capitalist sort when the conditions under which violence will be used are strictly predictable from rationally organized laws and administrative regulations. Hence, various features of bureaucratic administration that prevent an official from using state power for his own benefit (as he typically does under patrimonial administrative systems) facilitate economic rationality. The first achievement of bureaucratic government, then, is to render lower officials controllable by higher officials. But if these higher officials, in turn, are despots with 'irrational' political objectives, official actions are still unpredictable. Lower officials controlled by higher officials, who are controlled, in their turn, by rationally organized law and rational technical training, provide the best governmental situation for satisfying the postulates of the classical economic model of the economy.

The reason we sometimes get lost in a wealth of detail in Weber's treatment of each of these areas of life is that he insists on telling us how some fifteen or twenty major cases look, superficially, like rational-legal bureaucratic authority but, in fact, are not. He then details how these cases work, how they might be grouped into *types* of nonpropitious circumstances, and how the appropriate institutional forms grew up in the late medieval Occident. Sometimes one gets exasperated with being brought almost to the climax of propitious circumstances for capitalistic rationality only to have some *differentia specifica* turn him aside at the last moment. I still do not really see why the ancient Greeks did not make it, but that is probably because, of all the historical blank spaces in my mind, ancient history is the most massively blank. But at other times Weber is so movingly brilliant, so reorganizes the average sociologist's fragmentary knowledge of inter-mediate-level ('feudal') societies into meaningful patterns that the reader loses interest in capitalism and starts wondering what will happen to the lords, ladies, monks, and peasants.

For instance, chapter 15 of part 2 is about the relation between the state and the priesthood and the consequent interpenetration of state administration and religious interests. The separation of church and state and the secularization of law and administration are good for capitalism. So far, we are in the main part of the architecture of the work. But Weber gets carried away with the distinction between caesaropapism (appointment of bishops by the king) and hierocracy (subjection of the king to appointment and confirmation by the priesthood) and its working out in religious and political structures. Many of the differences between English caesaropapist history (after the break with the Roman Church) and, say, French history, have interesting similarities to the differences between the Eastern Chris-tian caesaropapist empires of medieval times and Western develop-ments. Even if this were not part of a larger architecture, translating this chapter alone might justify producing a very expensive book.

The chief value of having the entire book in English is, I think, that it allows us to suppress our inclination to get caught up in the cornucopia of alternative forms, sometimes brilliantly outlined in a chapter. When we suppress that inclination, we see that the book is a detailed statement of the conditions under which the classical model of the economy works. It is therefore a statement, in general theoreti-cal terms, of the specific social phenomena to which the discipline of economics as we know it applies. I think that it is a correct statement for the most part. Most of the criticisms made of Weber's economic sociology are irrelevant to the main problem because the architecture of the work has not been understood: the critics have perhaps reshaped the noses of some of the decorative gargoyles on the edifice.

The annotations to different parts of the book were done by different people. This gives us the opportunity to compare types of rationalization of scholarship. Max Rheinstein, who annotated the section on the sociology of law, is clearly a mind of the same order of magnitude as Weber himself. He has treated Weber's text as a statement about the world, and in his footnotes has compared the text with the world. He is the only annotator who sometimes says, 'Here Weber seems to be mistaken,' and then goes on to say what the facts of the case are and what it means for the theoretical point under discussion.

Talcott Parsons annotated the section which gives descriptive concepts about the types of economic organization. Parsons treats the text as a system of concepts rather than as a theory about the world. When he finds Weber in error, the authorities quoted against him are other theorists – for instance, he quotes Oscar Lange in his criticism of Weber's old-fashioned treatment of pricing under socialism. Parsons is much inclined to fuzzy discussions of the relation between the meanings of words in English and those in German, and between common German meanings and Weber's neologisms. The tendency of sociological theorists to discuss social life in an autistic language apparently has ancient and honorable roots.

The highest level of theoretical discussion that the other annotators reach in discussion of the fuzz of translation. They treat the text as a reflection of Weber's mind rather than of the world and only document things that indicate what Weber's thought rather than using the footnotes to tell us what is true. The annotations are scholastic in the bad sense, of staying within the sacred tradition itself without relating the tradition to the world.

In contrast, I would give Rheinstein about the amount of credit I give Weber for writing the sociology of law section. The section is about twice as valuable with the notes as it was when Weber wrote it. Parsons I would give considerably less credit than Weber, while the others should get credit for the drudge work of translation and cross-referencing within the sacred tradition itself. Much more recognition should be given for this type of work. (But I hope I someday write a book that seems worth annotating to a man of Rheinstein's caliber.)

The footnotes are in the worst possible place. Before I tell you where they are (you would never guess), I want to say a few words about footnotes and publishers. Only by understanding the dynamics of footnote publishing will you be able to believe what they have done with the footnotes. Like tables and graphs of data, footnotes are designed for readers who want to know whether the statements in the text are true. Thus, footnotes, like tables and graphs of data, are used in journals and books intended to be read by scholars and by practitioners in fields where it matters whether the professional is right, such as, law, medicine, engineering, and so forth. They are not used where the reader needs material that is 'interesting' or 'relevant,' but in which they hardly care whether it is true. Thus, in journals of applied social science, in introductory textbooks, in psychiatric journals and monographs, in advertising copy, there are few footnotes.

The problem of a publisher of Weber is that he judges, correctly I imagine, that the average reader will be a graduate student who will have to answer questions on his prelims of the form: 'Discuss the relations between Quakerism and this-worldly asceticism in Weber's theory of the origins of enterprises oriented to capital accounting.' The student will not have to know whether Quakerism actually did produce a rational ascetic life in this world as frequently as did Calvinism (as Weber argued). Nor will he be asked whether it is true or not that the legal, economic, and technical preconditions of capital accounting were created before the Reformation in countries which never became Protestant. He gets a high pass for not making the common mistake of identifying the Protestant ethic with Calvinism, and the mistake of associating capitalistic enterprise with the spirit of capitalism. For the majority of readers, then, this will be a text, rather than a scientific work. So the publisher does not want to spend the money to put footnotes where the reader can easily consult them, namely, at the bottom of the page.

But the publishers have a hard time getting 'interesting' and 'relevant' work without footnotes, evidence, and other 'scholarly apparatus.' Most people who are smart enough to write (or translate and edit) a book care about whether it is true and hope to write for readers who also care. While the author or editor fights to keep the footnotes and the evidence near the text which they support, publishers push for eliminating or hiding them. In this book, the classical conflict between editor and publisher has been resolved by splitting the difference. The footnotes are separated from the text, but printed not in the back where the reader might find them but rather about halfway between. Then, in a glorious exercise of idiocy, the reader is not told in the text where the footnotes are. The reader must find the footnotes as follows: first observe the top right of the left-hand page you are reading to obtain the chapter number; then consult the 'analytical table of contents' for the pages of the notes. Or you can leaf through the pages rapidly until the number on the upper right of the left-hand page changes, and then leaf slowly back until you run into the notes. This works unless the chapter is a long one. If the chapter is long, the number you have to use is a lowercase roman numeral on the upper left of the right-hand page. If an arabic numeral appears there, use the chapter number.

So my answer to the question of whether people should still start their sociological intellectual biographies with *Economy and Society* is yes. It would be a much more enthusiastic yes if Max Rheinstein had annotated the rest of it and if the annotations were somewhere where they could be found.

15. Merton's theory of social structure

Of all contemporary theorists of social structure, Merton has had the greatest impact on empirical research. Investigators find it easy to understand how Merton's general ideas about social structure imply hypotheses about the pattern of behavior and the pattern of associations between variables in the setting in which their research is conducted. The argument of this essay is that this is due to the common logical and substantive character of all of Merton's theories of social structure. I would further argue, though I will not defend it in detail here, that this logical and substantive character of Merton's theories distinguishes him from almost all the other contemporary currents of social theory: Parsonian, symbolic interactionist, the Linton-Nadel kind of rôle theory, functionalism of the non-Mertonian kind. The main exceptions seem to me to be Homans and the exchange theory tradition, and to some degree the balance theory tradition, which have a similar logical structure and similar empirical fruitfulness.

What I will be trying to do, then, is to codify Merton's codifications, to outline the principles behind the choice of those elements in a theoretical tradition that he chose as central and worth codifying and those he ignored. The test case for the success of my effort is his approach to the social structure of science, where he was choosing freely what to pay attention to because there was not much to codify.

Briefly, I will argue that the core process that Merton conceives as central to social structure is *the choice between socially structured alternatives*. This differs from the choice process of economic theory, in which the alternatives are conceived to have inherent utilities. It differs from the choice process of learning theory, in which the alternatives are conceived to emit reinforcing or extinguishing stimuli.

290

It differs from both of these in that for Merton the utility or reinforcement of a particular alternative choice is thought of as socially established, as part of the institutional order.

For example, the choice of illegitimate means to socially established goals is *defined* in terms of the institutional definitions of legitimacy and of worthwhile goals. The choice between the alternative 'innovation' and another alternative, say, of 'ritualism' (legitimate means, lack of commitment to socially approved goals) is a choice between alternatives whose utilities or capacities for reinforcement are institutionally structured (Merton, 1968: 185–214). Because the alternatives are socially structured, the resulting choice behavior has institutional consequences.

But the focus of Merton's theory of these 'choices with institutional consequence' is on variations in the rates of choice by people differently located in the social order. For example, when he discusses the choice of political loyalties between the machine that gives 'help, not justice' and the reform parties that give formal justice, he wants to know which social groups (for example, new ethnic groups) will be structurally induced to prefer help to justice and which to prefer justice to help. That is, the core variable to be explained is different rates of choice in different social positions in a structure, or in different structures, between these institutionally consequential alternatives (Merton, 1968: 73–138).

The reason that I have chosen the term 'core process' for rates of choice between structured alternatives, rather than independent or dependent variable, is that the causal chain goes both ways from this patterned choice. When scientists for example choose early publication as a method of claiming rights in a finding, rather than choosing secrecy, the high rate of early publication has the consequence of supporting the communism of science, supporting equal access to all scientists to past achievements regardless of intellectual property. This is using the rate of choice for early publication as an independent or causal variable to explain how an institutional pattern is maintained (Merton, 1968: 604–15). When Merton explains the difference in frequency of felt rôle conflict in a rôle-set by the degree of visibility (the degree of segregation of audiences to which the different rôles connected to a status are played), he is explaining a difference in rates of types of solutions to rôle conflict by the structure of relations among audiences and between audiences and rôle performance (Merton, 1968: 428–31). That is, in the case of priority as a motivation for communism of knowledge, he is tracing the consequences of a high rate of choice of early publication. In the case of choice between segregation of audiences and other resolutions of rôle strain, he is asking the structural causes of different rates of choices.

The reason the causal chain goes forward from the rates of choice is that the alternatives are socially structured exactly because they are institutionally consequential. The reason the causal chain goes backward is that many details of structural position determine the exact nature of the structuring of those alternatives for particular people.

To this basic linking process which connects structural forces to institutionally consequential choices, and thence to institutional patterns, Merton adds two kinds of causal loops. The first is the one for which he is perhaps best known: namely, the recasting of the nature of functional analysis so that institutional consequences of action act back to shape the nature of the alternatives that people are posed with. The consequence of a group choosing help, not justice, is the viability of the political machine, which then provides alternative ways for businessmen to serve illegal but profitable markets, alternative career opportunities for lawyers to become judges when they are good at giving help and not so good at giving justice, and so on (Merton, 1968: 73–138).

The second kind of loop is in the historical development of a social character out of a systematic biographical patterning of choices. For example, a cosmopolitan is structurally induced to choose nonlocal patterns of information collection, and corresponding areas and styles of influence, which differ from the behavior patterns of locals. These styles become imprinted as basic character orientations toward information and influence which lead people to have consistent biographies as local and cosmopolitan influentials, so that the patterns of behavior do not change with each change in particular situational circumstances (Merton, 1968: 441–74). Thus, the second loop is a feedback through character formation which produces personal continuities in *the kind of link a given person is* between structural pressures and patterns of choice behavior. The figure below gives a schematic outline of the structure that I will argue is common to Merton's theorizing.

The remainder of this essay is directed at fleshing out this alleged

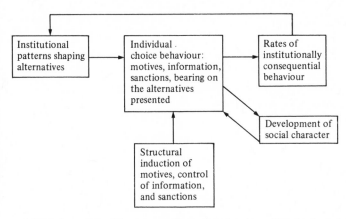

Schematic outline of the common theoretical structure of Merton's analyses.

common logical form of Merton's theorizing about social structure with illustrations chosen from many of his theoretical essays. I will try to suggest at the end why this pattern of theorizing has lent itself better than most others to the derivation of empirical hypotheses about social strctures.

Before doing that, however, I would like to make a brief comment about the relation of this theoretical structure to the historical tradition of sociological theory. The striking thing about it is how many elements of different traditions there are in it, traditions that have thought themselves opposed. The core process of choice between socially structured alternatives owes a great deal (explicitly acknowledged) to the W. I. Thomas–G. H. Mead analysis of definitions of situations and self-conceptions. Where it differs from much contemporary work derived from that tradition is *not* adding to it the hopeless proposition, 'God only knows what definitions people will give to situations.' The focus on institutional consequences of choices owes a great deal to the functionalist tradition, again thoroughly acknowledged. But Merton does not add the untrue proposition that institutions will always manage to get people to behave in the way required for their effective functioning. The analyses of character and biography clearly owe a good deal to Freud and the neo-Freudians, to Thomas' typology of character types, and many other sources. But Merton adds neither theories of the limited variety of characters that might be produced, nor theories of the indelibility of early experience, to the core perception of socially formed character structure.

What we find repeatedly is a free willingness to borrow and a free willingness to shear off from the borrowings the grandiosity and sectarianism of the originals, which made them fit uncomfortably with other processes in an overall theory. We will each be well served in the history of social theory if our successors consistently behave like Merton and refuse to adopt our dogmatisms while adopting our virutes.

1. Individual choice of structurally patterned alternatives

If it is true that Merton has focused his theories around processes of individual choice, why do his theories look so different from those of people who proclaim they study choice? There are four main traditions in the social sciences that make that proclamation: economic decision theory and its relatives;[1] reinforcement theory and its exchange extension in Homans;[2] symbolic interactionism with choice determined by definitions of the situation;[3] and Parsonian theory with choices about inherent value dilemmas determined by cultural values.[4] It will therefore be useful to contrast Merton's strategy with each of these.

Consider, for example, the choice between legitimate and illegitimate means in the essay 'Social structure and anomie.' In the first place, Merton is trying to explain different rates of crime, that is, different rates of choice to do behavior well known to land people in prison if they get caught. I presume he would agree with what I take to be the main point of new criminology: if theft or running a numbers game or peddling heroin were not defined as crimes, people would not go to prison for them. But, of course, that is not the situation of choice

---

[1] Economic decision theory is outlined in any intermediate level text in microeconomic theory; for example Stonier and Hague, (1972).

[2] For reinforcement theories of social choice, see George C. Homans, (1961).

[3] For the symbolic interactionist tradition, a fine outline is the first and last part of David Matza, (1969).

[4] The attribution to Parsons of a social choice theory is genetic in the sense that he has never renounced the orientation of *Structure of Social Action* (1937), especially the introductory essay. People have become much less active choosers of what to value and what to do about those values as Parsonian theory has 'matured.' It would be hard to tell from recent Parsonian writings that this was a theory of socially conditioned choices of the meanings of actions. See Talcott Parsons (1949).

that slum dwellers are confronted with. There are connections between the choice of a career running a numbers game and the likelihood of going to prison, the likelihood of social opprobrium, the likelihood of involvement in groups with other criminal enterprises. These connections are set up by 'the society.' That is, the character of the criminal alternative to a regular career is socially structured and, by virtue of that structuring, entails multiple simultaneous consequences for the individual.

In contrast to the basic postulates of microeconomic theory, the different aspects of this alternative are not separate commodities, so that a person can take the money but not the likelihood of a prison sentence, nor can he take as much of each as he most prefers within his budget constraints.

In reinforcement theory, the argument would be that people choose a pattern of socially structured flows of reward and punishment. No doubt, once in the numbers business, people avoid as far as possible those acts that lead to prison or to obloquy. But their own control over not 'emitting' the behavior that brings prison, *but* emitting that which brings money, is preempted (as far as it can be) by the society.

Because the laws and sanctions of the larger society and its officials have a coercive power to define the situation, criminals cannot simply make up their minds that numbers games are O.K. People define situations, but do not define them as they please. I do not know which value dilemma policemen are resolving when they decide that numbers people are a bunch of crooks, nor the one resolved by a person who decides then to be a crook. But it is hard to imagine that value orientations at the most general level have much to do with choosing a criminal career.

That is, in each alternative theory of choice there is theoretical awkwardness about the society putting together bundles of predictable social reactions to acts, so that an innovative career outside the law is the choice of a social status, a choice of the schedule of reinforcements, a choice of a complex of determinate definitions of the situation, a choice of the values one will live by. This theoretical attention to bundling of choices is the distinctive feature of Merton's analysis.

To take another example, the essay on the intellectual in a public bureaucracy is principally organized around the choice by the intellectual between investigating all alternative policies and improving that policy that has already been decided upon. This choice comes in a socially structured form. Policy-makers tend to listen to intelligence about how to do what they want to do and tend not to listen to intelligence about why what they are doing is all wrong. The choice between having a broad and accurate assessment while being unheard in policy councils and having the right answer to the wrong problem while being heard is structured by the place of intellectual activity along the 'continuum of decision' (Merton, 1968: 269). Presumably, many intellectuals find both having the right problem *and* having their right answer heard rewarding, or in keeping with their basic value premises. They would like to define their situation as involving both.

But they are not free to choose the combined alternative bundle of wide-ranging consideration of alternatives and of having the cabinet's ear. The eminently practical answer I once heard a college professor give to the question, 'But how can we get out of Viet Nam?' 'By getting on ships,' is socially structured as woolly thinking, while the most fantastic theories of the effects of bombing or of the possibility of the South Vietnamese government becoming a revolutionary force in the countryside are socially structured as hardheaded realism. This is because the fantastic theories bear on the policy options in consideration by the cabinet, while the theory that one could come home on ships does not.

The point, then, is that the social process presents a socially structured choice between alternative cognitive styles. People do choose among cognitive styles in order to make history, but again they do not make history as they please.

Perhaps the most straightforward case of the social structuring of choice is in reference group theory. Out of the whole field of gestalt analysis of how frames of reference determine perception and evaluation, the most theoretically and methodologically intractable must be the process of comparison of oneself with abstract ideas about groups. We know a great deal about how judgements of oneself are shaped by motivated distortion. We know that sociologists themselves can hardly figure out what a given group's norms or status are. Out of all the choices of comparison processes to study, then, the choice of reference group psychology is the least likely to yield clean and powerful theories. But Merton insists, and correctly.

We take as an example of how he proceeds his analysis of the 'completeness: ratio of actual to potential members' of a group (see Merton, 1968: 368–9). He uses the example of the AMA ('about 65 percent of all licensed physicians') and the American Nurses' Association ('about 41 per cent of all employed professional nurses'). The point of the analysis is the relation of completeness to 'social standing and power.' But social standing and power are important because in normative judgements about medical matters, or comparison of oneself as a medical student with the status of the physician one hopes to become, the social standing and power of a group socially structure the choice. It is much harder to choose to be another kind of physician than the AMA normatively defines than to be another kind of nurse from that which the ANA defines. Thus the variable at the core of the analysis is the degree to which the choice of reference groups is socially structured.

This approach to society through individual choice between socially structured alternatives is the opposite of either psychological or sociological reductionism. There is, to be sure, consistent attention to the fact that people have to do all social actions. And there is close empirical analysis of norms, structures, collective representations, and so on. But Merton is engaged in understanding the world, not in drawing university department lines' projections onto the world. Externally constraining social facts have to get into people's minds in order to constrain them. But people are clever about getting what they want out of a constraining social structure. The whole question of whether social action is 'really' psychological or 'really' social appears as a fake problem.

2. Structural causes of variations in patterns of choice

The patterning of alternatives

The first strategic consideration in explaining patterns of choice between structured alternatives is of course that structuring itself. If quick publication of a scientific finding secures priority, while secrecy does not with any certainty do so, then quick publication becomes a more common pattern. The development of institutions (scientific journals, citation norms) which structure the choice so that priority can be reliably established by publication itself changes the motivational field of the choice. Before this development, publication would not reliably reach the relevant audience, each author could defend his own false claim to priority by mobilizing friends to use minor distinguishing features of his writing to claim priority (for example, using Newton's clumsy notation for the derivative rather than Leibnitz' elegant one as a symbol of loyalty to Newton's priority claims), people were not negatively sanctioned for failing to cite sources or parallel developments, and so on. Thus priority could better be established by attaching a finding to a 'system' to make a major splash than by getting it published quickly (Merton, 1968: 610–12; see also Zuckerman and Merton, 1971; Merton 1969). The change from one system of structured alternatives ('system' publishing) to another (journal article publishing) increases the frequencies of the choice to publish quickly.

Or consider the explanation for the hypothesis that ritualistic adaptations to high success goals and limited means will be more common in the lower-middle-class. In this class ' . . . parents typically exert continuous pressure upon children to abide by the moral mandates of the society . . . ' (Merton, 1968: 205). The hypothesis is then that moral constraints structure the alternatives of the lower middle class into two of the possible five adaptations: success within the norms or failure within the norms. The possible alternatives of crime ('innovation') or vagrancy ('retreatism') are excluded by the moral environment of this class (Merton, 1968: 205–7). Thus, the rate of ritualism as a choice should increase in this class because the alternatives to ritualism are bundled together with dishonor, personal rejection, and nagging by lower-middle-class parents. The increase of the costs of the alternatives to ritualism leaves ritualism as the only likely reaction to lack of success for that class.

In both these cases we have the same pattern of explanation. The attachment of specified rewards (for example, priorities) or punishments (for example, parental disapproval) to the structured bundles among which people must choose, by specific social structures (modern scientific publication structures, lower-middle-class families), determines the motivational potential attached to the bundles. As these structurings of choice change (by institutional development of science, by moving from one class to another), the rates of choice change. They may change either by increasing the reward attached to one alternative or by increasing the punishments associated with the others.

Structurally induced motivation

In 'Social structure and anomie,' Merton talks about American social structure as inducing a high motivation for success in all parts of the class system. In the sociology of science, he talks about the special motivation induced by the social structure of science for prestige, especially prestige by publication. In the analysis of 'Reference group theory and social mobility,' (Merton, 1968: 316–25) motivation is treated in two different ways; on the one hand, attachments to nonmembership groups are structurally motivated by the prospect of social mobility; on the other, conformity to the norms of a nonmembership group is motivated by positive attachment to it.

In each of these cases, we have social influences on people's goals, which in turn affect their rates of social choice. These are exogenous to the formation of the alternatives themselves, in some sense. That is, the sources of motivation to succeed are not the same as the sources of the bundling together of innovation (crime) and prison by the criminal justice system. Promotion in university based on publication, or the public validation of arduous scientific work by publication, is not the same as the institutionalization of priority rights through publication. Nor in fact is the induction of the goal of establishing priority among scientists directly due to the bundling of priority with publication. Let us discuss the distinction between social structuring of alternatives and structurally induced motivation further, because the distinction is subtle.

Exogenous variation in the different components of a social theory of choice is, as econometricians have pointed out much more sharply since these essays, an essential element in untangling causes that go around in circles. Since people making choices analyze the situation as a whole, the causes in theories of choice almost always go around in circles. This logical point about the structure of Merton's theories is therefore crucial, and needs further elaboration.

Consider the fact that in order for ordinary people to establish priority for a scientific discovery they would have to publish. Ordinary people do not publish, at least not very often, and do not worry about it. Scientists publish a great deal in journals that do not pay them – in fact, in some one may pay the costs. And they worry about it a good deal.

The systemic quality of the high rate of publication therefore incorporates two elements. In the first place, there is the institution of scientific journals, citation practices, and so on, which ties together priority and publication. Second, there is the passion for priority among scientists, which Merton's historical studies of science evoke so well.

The institution that bundles the alternatives varies over historical time. At any given point in time, the passion for priority (the structurally induced motivation) varies over individuals, with scientists being far more passionate than ordinary people, university scientists much more than industrial scientists, scientists in fields in which one can tell whether something has been discovered or not (for example, physics) much more than scientists in fields in which one cannot (for example, sociology). The leisurely pace of publication in sociology is not to be explained entirely by different publication institutions (though the preference for books about the system of sociology as a whole over articles reminds one of ancient times in the physical sciences). Rather, it is to be explained by the different induction of the goal of establishing priority in the social structure of sociology.

Thus, the distinction between the structural sources of motivation and the structuring of alternatives allows us to untangle the motivational aspect of the structured alternatives from the goals people are trying to reach by choosing those alternatives. The two forces cause variations over different sorts of observations: historical in one case and cross-sectional in the other. That rare quality in sociological writing, of wandering easily from history to survey research without giving the feeling that one is lost, is due to Merton's preeconometric instinct for the problem of identification in systems of interacting causal forces.

With the same logical structure, adopted from 'Social structure and anomie,' I tried to identify the interaction of motivation and structured alternatives in producing high school rebellion (see Stinchcombe, 1964: 134–69). The argument took the form that young men were more exposed to success ideology than young women, and middle-class men more than working-class men. When the school tells some of *each* group that they will not get into the middle class by legitimate means (for example, tells them by giving them low grades), then the middle-class failed men should react with most rebellion, working-class failed men with somewhat less, and failed women with least. I am not as sure as when I wrote the book that the data support this. The point here, however, is that the logical structure of theory permits a test of a complex interactive model of how motivation and constraints on alternatives produce differential rates of choices of those alternatives.

There are four main kinds of sources of variation in structurally induced motives in Merton's work: socialization into a culture, reward systems, self-affirmation in a social role, and structurally induced needs.

Thus, American children are taught (socialized) that people ought to succeed and that success is a measure of personal worth. There may be cultures that stress success but have alternative standards of personal worth as well. The first structural source of variable induction of motives, then, is differential socialization (Merton, 1968: 185–214).

Besides being socialized to value scientific discovery, university scientists in modern societies are involved in reward systems (status systems) which make money, power, freedom at work, and social honor all dependent on priority of scientific discovery. Such a status system cumulates motivations of diverse people around the same goal. Whether one wants to be rich, powerful, free, or honored, if one is a scientist in a university he or she satisfies his or her motives by establishing priority. Thus the dependence of all rewards on one performance criterion in a status system induces the cumulation of motives around that performance (Merton, 1969).

In the social psychology of reference group behavior, the generalization from wanting to be an officer to wanting to be like an officer involves a motivational postulate of the kind now often discussed as 'ego identity.' Conforming attitudes in the military, and anticipatory socialization for becoming an officer, are partly motivated by affirming one's (potential) social rôle as an officer (Merton, 1968: 319–22). The intellectual in a public bureaucracy who wants to do as he thinks is right rather than as he is told does so partly because he wants to affirm his identity as an intellectual and as a person with an ideological commitment to effective public policy (Merton, 1968: 261–78).

A fourth source of differential motivation is illustrated by the special need of immigrant ethnic groups for help, not justice, from the political machine. Many motives in people's lives (jobs, getting out of difficulties with the law, special food for ritual occasions like Christmas) require manipulation of the social structure. When people are unskilled, legally disadvantaged, or poor, this manipulation poses special difficulties (Merton, 1968: 73–138). A set of structurally induced special problems in satisfying the motives of everyday life creates in turn in a person a special motive to have trusted friends in high places who can manipulate for him. That is, ordinary motives create special motives under conditions of need, under conditions in which those ordinary motives can only be satisfied through a single channel.

Thus, there are four main structural sources of goals or motives in Merton's theories: socialization, reward systems, affirmation of identities, and needs. As structures vary in the degree to which they induce relevant motives in individuals, they will vary in the rates of choice of alternatives to which those motives are relevant.

Structural governance of information
Many of Merton's central concepts have to do with information. Among the distinguishing features of science is its communism, but this does not refer to salaries or research grants or monopolies over the teaching function. Instead it refers to information. A central concept in his rôle theory is visibility. Influentials are distinguished as cosmopolitans or locals in the first instance by their readership of newsmagazines. Self-fulfilling prophecies start on their spiral course by the communication to a public. Manifest functions and latent functions are distinguished by the information of the relevant public about them. Clearly, then, information is crucial to the whole of Merton's structural analysis.

There seem to be three major mechanisms by which information flows affect the pattern of structured choice behavior. First, sanctions depend on information. One person cannot sanction another for something he or she does not know the other has done. Second, information affects people's ideas about what choices they are confronted with. People do not choose alternatives they do not know about. Third, people use information in the concrete construction of successful activities, and success in an activity makes the activity more likely to continue. The collective competence of a science to solve scientific problems would be impossible if scientists could not find out the answers of other scientists to their questions. Most of what we teach or use in our research is the wisdom of others – our competence consists of others' wisdom.

Information and sanctions

... Social groups so differ in organization that some promote efficient 'feed-back' of 'information' to those who primarily regulate the behavior of members, while others provide little by way of efficient feed-back. The structural conditions which make for ready observability or visibility of role-performance will of course provide appropriate feed-back when role-performance departs from the patterned expectations of the group (Merton, 1968: 374)

The probability of rewards and punishments is, of course, a central feature of the motivational situation in structured choices, and this probability is centrally affected by information. For example, the rate of choice to speak frankly to physicians, lawyers, and priests is affected by the confidentiality of those communications. The rate of choice of a professor saying what he thinks, instead of what he thinks socially acceptable, is affected by the low observability of the college classroom (Merton, 1968: 427). The troublesomeness of an intellectual in a public bureaucracy is partly that he is likely to publish the arguments for a rejected alternative (Merton, 1968: 277, by implication). Although I do not find the argument explicit, it is clear that one of the reasons the functions of a political machine for the rackets are latent rather than manifest is that if they were manifest the whole group would be in jail.

Information and alternatives

The core of the argument in 'The self-fulfilling prophecy' is that information about what collectively is likely to happen (whether it is a priori false or true) affects the rate of choice of individuals, which affects the probability of the collective outcome. Before depositors' insurance, runs on banks destroyed many banks. The 'knowledge' that there was a run on the bank therefore caused depositors to want to get their money out. As more banks failed because of runs, it took less information on a run to start one. Thus, there was a cumulation *within* each bank of information on a run causing rates of choice that produced a run, and a cumulation of collective consequences producing still further information on runs *in the banking system as a whole*, so that there was an acceleration in the number of bank failures up to the banking reform of the New Deal (Merton, 1968: 476–7).

Information on what is going to happen puts a future-oriented animal such as man into a different choice situation. One behaves differently toward a bank that will be solvent than toward a bank that will not be. One behaves differently in providing educational opportunities for black people when he or she 'knows' black people will fail than when he or she 'knows' they will succeed. In general, what we mean by 'reality' is what *will* happen, and what has already happened is of very little interest unless it influences the future.

In some ways, these observations are very closely related to the discussion of social structuring of alternatives above. That is, the social alternative with which a bank depositor is confronted 'really' changes if he or she 'knows' the bank will fail, in much the same way that the method of establishing priority really changes with the institution of scientific journals. But what differs is that the alternatives change with only an input of socially established information, instead of with changes in the true situation. Either type of change in the alternatives changes the rates of socially structured choice.

Information and success
Merton has spent much effort on the one institution in which collective success is almost purely determined by information, namely, science. In some ways, therefore, it is no sign of extraordinary acumen that he should notice that the flow of information determines the success of activities. The communism of information in science is vitally relevant to the success of each scientist in solving his or her own puzzles. The exponential growth of knowledge in physics had a sharp downturn during World War II, a downturn not made up by a spurt of accumulated creativity after the war (Hamblin, et al., 1973: Fig. 8.6,

p. 143). Presumably, this is directly related to the destruction of the communism of physics by secrecy in the interests of national security (whether it is a good idea to preserve national security by maiming physics is, of course, an infinitely debatable question). No one with any experience in scientific work would be likely to doubt that upwards of nine-tenths of what he or she knows is due to the giants from whom he has learned. And Merton's central contributions to the sociology of science do not consist in repeating the obvious.

What is more relevant is that he has generalized this function of information in other structural processes. The cosmopolitan influential plays a different rôle in the local social system presumably because he or she can perform some leadership functions better than the local (and vice versa, of course). The central thing he or she can do is to mediate between the problems of the local system and the larger institutional and cultural system within which many local problems have their solution. The reason he or she can do this is that he or she routinely collects information from, and about, the larger system (Merton, 1968: 460–3). That is, the peculiar information of cosmopolitans makes them more successful at tasks that use that information.

Though the main subject of Merton's work on seventeenth-century science is the development of science itself, he was forced to construct a theory of the information needs of practical activity. The compass was only really useful when the error of measurement of direction at different points (due to the displacement of the magnetic poles from the geographical poles) was known (Merton, 1968: 673–4). Clearly, knowing which direction is north contributes to one's success in arriving where one wants to arrive. And success in navigation was important to the social support of astronomical and magnetic investigations.

The social patterning of information flows thus influences rates of socially significant choices by influencing the sanctions attached to choices, by influencing the perceived alternatives between which people choose, and by influencing the rate of success of the alternative chosen.

Structural patterns of sanctioning power
Besides knowing whom to reward and punish, a person or group has to be *able* to reward and punish in order to control behavior. The rate at

which a person will choose to behave in a way that offends or helps another depends on whether the other can punish or reward that person. The two central mechanisms that Merton discusses are *power* and *usefulness*. These are not conceptually radically distinct, but their connotations are quite diverse. Roughly speaking 'power' connotes the capacity to get another person something (or to deny him or her something) from society at large. Thus the capacity of a bureaucratic superior to allocate blame for mistakes to his or her subordinates rests on his or her special access to organizational blame-allocating centers. This is organizationally generated 'power,' which produces fearful ritualism in subordinates (Merton, 1968: 249–60). The cosmopolitan's 'influence' is interpreted primarily in terms of his or her 'usefulness' for, for example, managing the cultural life of Rovere (Merton, 1968: 461). The distinction could be described as a strategic place in the *social flow* of rewards and punishments ('power') versus a strategic place in the *social production* of rewards and punishments ('usefulness').

Aside from information determinants of this placement in the flow of rewards and punishments, discussed above, Merton has not systematically analyzed power systems and their implications. Consequently, I will leave the topic with the note that a systematic account of the implicit theories of power in the variety of Merton's structural essays would repay the effort.

3. Structural outputs of patterned choice

Latent and manifest outputs
The output of one of these systems of patterned choice is socially organized behavior. But Merton's crucial interest is how such patterns fold back on themselves to maintain or undermine the pattern, or otherwise to affect the structure as a whole. As a rough scheme, not to be taken too seriously, I would distinguish five types of structural implication for this causal folding back: manifest and latent functions, manifest and latent structural locations of an output; and deviant 'symptoms' of these four realities. This is all very abstract, so let me carry through an example.

When analyzing the place of publication in science, Merton talks about at least five different kinds of things. First, he speaks of the manifest function of speeding information. Since most research workers in a field read important results before they are published, and many volumes of journals are never checked out even in leading research libraries, this manifest function cannot be the whole story. Second, there are at least two latent functions of publication, namely, establishing priority for scientific discoveries and the validation to oneself that the discovery (and hence the life that went into making such a discovery) is important. This was analyzed above. Third, there is the structural place of the manifest function in the norm of the communism of science. Publication is one of many institutional devices (university education is another) that manifest the norm of communism in science, that people ought not to be excluded from ideas for one's personal benefit. The latent structural place of the output is on the vita of the individual scientist, and consequently in the promotion system of universities and the interuniversity competition for prestige and resources. That is, the latent social processing of the output is processing in scientific status systems, and it is the fact that there is a firm social structure processing the latent output (priority claims) that makes the system hang together. This is what makes the latent function of establishing priority by publication a critical one – one that makes it likely that the latent function will maintain the practice even when the manifest function is hollow. The solid social location of the latent function then produces pressures for 'deviant' behavior according to the manifest institution of communism, namely, bitter fights over priority, over 'private property' rights in ideas. Fights over priority are *not* latent functions (perhaps latent dysfunctions), but rather symptoms that all is not as it seems. Sensitivity to socially patterned deviance is one of the skills Merton repeatedly uses to locate these systems of intertwined manifest and latent functions with their corresponding structural location. (See Zuckerman and Merton, 1971; Merton, 1969; and Merton, 1968: 604–15).

We see the same pattern in the analysis of the political machine. The diagnostic symptom is patterned behavior deviant from good government democratic norms (though obviously dependent on democratic norms). The latent functions include 'help, not justice,' service to illegitimate business, decision-making capacity in a system of decentralized formal powers, and so on. The manifest structural place of the output is the institution of democratically elected local government. The latent structural place is an organized system of ethnic groups, big businesses, illegitimate businesses and their markets, and so on, which turns the latent functions into a reliable supply of social capital for the machine. Just as the tenure decision has no formal structural place in the communism of science, so the whorehouse has no formal provision in the City Charter (Merton, 1968: 73–138).

The crucial point here is that latent functions are not merely outputs of a pattern of choice that happen to come about but *strategic inputs* for other structures in the system as a whole. This strategic quality in turn makes them into effective causes of the maintenance of the pattern. Happenstance outputs that some people happen to like and others not to like will not effectively fold back casually to maintain the pattern.

A second type of output of a patterned choice is a social distribution of life chances. The differential risk of different social classes for ending up in prison is an example. The point of the 'Social structure and anomie' paper is that these differential risks are built into the structure of the society and are characteristics of the structural position rather than of the individual in it. The point to note, then, is that a subtle psychological mechanism of strain in people's reactions to ends and means produces a characteristic of a social position. Such subtle transformation of levels is a specialty of Merton's. It serves the latent function for a discipline unsure of its identity of allowing us to be psychologically subtle while proclaiming our nonpsychological character – nothing here but social class, the most eminently socio-logical of all ways to get psychology into the discipline.

Let us take, for an example, the most difficult case for this – the mapping of complex products of extended activities of the mind on social structure – the sociology of knowledge. In the midst of an astringent account of the massive confusion of the sociology of knowledge at the time (1945) comes a passage of Merton's own commitments:

> A basic concept which serves to differentiate generalizations about the thought and knowledge of an entire society or culture is that of the 'audience' or 'public,' or what Znaniecki calls 'the social circle.' Men of knowledge do not orient themselves exclusively toward their data nor toward the entire society, but to special segments of

that society with their special demands, criteria of validity, of significant knowledge, of pertinent problems, etc. It is through the anticipation of these demands and expectations of particular audiences, which can be effectively located in the social structure, that men of knowledge organize their own work, define their data, seize upon problems (Merton, 1968: 536)

Note how the structural position has been defined in terms of a subtle set of psychological considerations, of how to organize work, define data, seize upon problems. The audience becomes a force on the man of knowledge by his expectations about it, and these expectations are a complex mental construction on his part.

The example that follows is a contrast between the audience of newly established scientific societies ('plain, sober, empirical') and the universities ('speculative, unexperimental') (Merton, 1968: 537). Of course, it is true that these audiences are mentioned as being located in different structures ('societies' versus 'universities'), but it is not the structural position that explains the rate of choice of the individual (of experimental versus speculative science). Instead, it is the social psychological dynamics of that structural position. The degree of determinacy relating the structural characteristics to the social psychological processes can be left undecided (in fact, of course, experimental science took over the university structures a century or two after the example, which Merton dated in the seventeenth century). But the social mapping of these processes does two things. First, it allows sociologists to study complex psychological patterns without butchering the complex reality. Second, it produces a discriminating social map of rates of social choice, without having to resort to residual categories like 'false consciousness,' or 'degrees of autonomy from the substructure,' or 'ultimately always asserts itself,' or petty bourgeois determination of thought because 'in their minds they do not exceed the limits which [the petty bourgeoisie] do not exceed in their life activities' which clutter up the sociology of knowledge.

Thus, one set of outputs of choice between socially structured alternatives is different rates of different psychological outcomes mapped onto different structural positions in a social order. These range in social determinacy from inherent in the structure (social class and crime [innovation], for example, are inherently connected in

American social structure) to 'accidentally' connected with the structure (for example, empirical science and nonuniversity audiences).

Socially patterned character development

These different socially induced rates of patterned choice socialize people exposed to them. The timidity of a bureaucrat and the systematically narrowed view of the intellectual in a public bureaucracy are not merely situational adaptations. Repetitive situational adaptations form character. Thus the timidity and narrow-mindedness of a bureaucracy are not only maintained because the situations that produce timidity and narrowness are continuously present. They are also maintained because over time the people in them become timid and narrow (Merton, 1968: 249–60, 261–78).

Likewise, a person in a structural position in the flow of communication that makes him or her specialize in translating cosmopolitan information into local influence works out a pattern of life to do that translation regularly. He or she becomes a cosmopolitan, rather than happening to serve in the situation at hand as a cosmopolitan (Merton, 1968: 441–70).

The promotable person becomes a future noncom in many areas of life; the innovator becomes a professional criminal; the discoverer becomes a career scientist. Social patterns maintain themselves then not only because they shape the situations of people. The situations then shape characters which fit them and contribute added stability to the system.

4. Why it works

Let me now suppose both that I have correctly identified the paradigm behind the paradigms in Merton's work on social structure and that I am right that his work has started more (and more penetrating) traditions of empirical research than that of other contemporary theorists. How might we explain this superiority?

First, I do not agree with Merton's implicit diagnosis that it is because he works on 'theories of the middle range' (Merton, 1968: 39–72). It seems to me that in the dialectic between Parsons and Merton, generality has been confused with woolliness. Merton, in taking up the correct position on woolliness, has tricked himself into taking up the incorrect position on general theory. The true situation is precisely the opposite. It is because Merton has a better general theory than Parsons that his work has been more empirically fruitful. I will try to discuss this under the traditional general virtues of theories: elegance, power or fruitfulness, economy, and precision.

Elegance

Making consensual esthetic judgements of theories is harder than making other kinds of judgements. In the first place, there are major differences in esthetic style; spare classical styles which use simple material to create complex effects – Merton or James S. Coleman are examples; embellished rococo in which an immense variety of beautiful theoretical detail is more or less integrated by thematic means – Claude Lévi-Strauss provides an example; romantic in which concepts are evoked with incantations and words heavy in connotations – Edward Shils is a good example. Only a few people can make an esthetic impact in all three styles: Clifford Geertz maybe. My own taste is classical; in the extreme I like geometry with a complex theoretical structure made up of only points and lines.

But I think two aspects of esthetic experience in sociological theory would get wide assent. The most fundamental is the capacity of a theory to say with the same set of statements something complex and realistic about individual people and what they are up to and something complex and realistic about a social pattern. The impact of George Herbert Mead or Max Weber is partly explained by the fact that they make both people and structures real. Much of the sparely classical beauty of economics comes from the easy translation between market equilibria and striving individuals.

The central intractable problem for sociology has been the relation of individuals to the social order. The drive to 'bring men back in,' (Homans, 1961) to develop a 'naturalistic sociology,' (Matza, 1969) reflects dissatisfaction with the crude picture of individuals that structural explanations tend to give. And although the defense of professional monopoly has altogether too much to do with objections to explanations as being 'too psychological,' there is also a flat obvious quality to explanations of social behavior that come down to 'they did it because they wanted to' or 'they did it because of their thalamus.'

Merton's theoretical structure provides multiple opportunities to move back and forth from striving or thalamic men to social structural outcomes. Sometimes the psychology is obvious, as when people do not react to what they do not know about. Sometimes, as the case of audiences as central structural units in the sociology of knowledge, the connection between the behavior of individuals and the structure is extraordinarily complex.

Merton gains this esthetic effect principally by modifying the structural concepts so that people fit as natural parts of them. A rôle-set is a much easier thing into which to fit one's experience of trying to figure out what a professor is supposed to do than is a Linton rôle. A notion of deviance that says there is something wrong with ritualistic overconformity, that the rule-bound petty office tyrant was not what we had in mind when we passed the rules, rings truer to our experience of conformity and deviance.

If the kernel of esthetic experience in sociological theory is the unity of social and psychological statement, the outer covering is irony. Good comes from evil, complexity from simplicity, crime from morality; saints stink while whores smell good; trade unions and strikes lead to industrial peace under a rule of law and a collective contract; law and order candidates are fond of burglary. Merton clearly loves irony. He is most pleased to find motives of advancing knowledge creating priority conflicts among scientists, and hardly interested in the fact that such motives also advance knowledge. He likes to find political bosses helping people while good government types turn a cold shoulder. He likes to find Sorokin offering statistics on ideas to attack the empiricist bent on modern culture and to urge an idealistic logico-meaningful analysis of ideas. He likes to range Engels and functionalists down parallel columns to show them to be really the same. The immediate subjective feeling that one has learned something from reading Merton is probably mainly due to the taste for irony.

A third esthetic advantage is closely related to irony: the onion-like layers of the theories. That is, like Lévi-Strauss or Freud or Marx, the esthetic effects of Merton's theory have to do with the process of moving from a more superficial view of a matter to a deeper underlying view. The onion looks brown, then light tan, then white but coarse, then white but fine-grained. Just as some of the finest effects in novels consist of shifts in point of view, so in social theory a layered structure gives an impression of movement, of learning, of an active social scientist figuring things out. There is more feeling of motion in Merton's essays than in most social theorizing.

Esthetic qualities of theory make it more useful in two ways. First, it makes it easier to persuade yourself to work with it, makes it fun to read and fun to play with. There is nothing duller to think about than 'Is social class really related to delinquency?' We would not have the right answer now (yes, but not strongly related) if we had not had something interesting to think about in the tedium of collecting the data.

The second is that esthetic experience encourages a shift in perspective, breaks up and reforms the molds in the mind. I do not know a good analysis of the relation between esthetic experience and creativity, but I offer the empirical generalization that people who cannot experience a thrill at a beautiful idea hardly ever amount to anything in a science.

Power or fruitfulness

In some ways, the body of this essay is directed at showing, first, that there is a general theory of social action in Merton's work and, second, that it is fruitful in many different empirical problems. I have commented about how, for example, the power of the theory allows diverse evidence from history to survey research to be brought to bear on the same empirical problem. The power has its most obvious (because easiest) manifestation in the apparent effortlessness of the destructive criticism of other theorists in his essays on functionalism and on the sociology of knowledge. If it were really as easy as it looks, brilliant minds like Malinowski or Sorokin could have done it.

But though the power of the general theory leads to quick perception of the holes in other theories, being one up on Malinowski or Sorokin is a trivial accomplishment. The crucial benefits in explanatory power come from two general characteristics of the theory. First, it combines attention to stability and maintenance of social patterns with attention to disruption of them. In the nature of things, if there is an equilibrium or self-maintaining state of a system, the state one is most likely to observe is that equilibrium state. If in a given setting a political machine is a self-maintaining state, then one common structure that will be found there is a machine. As in a Markov process with absorbing states, eventually everything ends up absorbed. This means that Merton's equilibrium theory has an inherent tendency to be about states of the system that are most commonly observed. But further, it focuses on the sources of variation and tension that explain deviations from these most commonly observed states. Whenever an equilibrium theory is something more than a vague notion that things will probably all work out for the best, it has an inherent advantage in explanatory power.

The second main explanatory power advantage of Merton's general theory is that it focuses attention on social magnification processes. For example, racketeers want to make money. But by being organized into a system together with legitimate business and with ethnic groups with precarious citizenship, both their capacity to make money is increased and the canalization of that impulse and the money by the machine produces a large impact on, for example, the judicial system. By canalizing the impulse to establish priority into early publication, scientific journals magnify the impulse to gain prestige from communicating results and maximize its impact on the speed of communication and on the norm of communism of knowledge. By monopolizing medical licensing and access to hospitals, and enrolling most of the profession, the AMA increases the power of consensual norms in the profession about what a physician should be and becomes a stronger reference group for aspiring physicians. Magnification and canalization of causes create discriminating impacts, thus increasing the information content of a theory of causes.

The crucial feature of the theorizing that does this job of focusing on magnification is the constant attention to the structural location of a given pattern of choice. It is the structural location of corruption in the machine that makes it more than random temptation of public officials. It is the institutionalization of priority in the communication process itself that magnifies the impulse to publish. It is the location of a reference group in the power system that makes it a crucial channel for transmitting ideals.

Economy

There is one trivial kind of economy in social theorizing which many of us could learn with profit: the willingness to write about one thing at a time. The brunt of one version of 'scholarly' norms in social theorizing is that one should always introduce distinctions that might be useful in some other situation, but do not bear on the problem at hand, in order to show awareness of the tradition of the discipline. The frequent experience of not quite knowing the subject of a theoretical essay is partly due to our penchant for writing books to be entitled 'The Social System' or 'Economy and Society,' 'The Rules of Sociological Method' or 'Constructing Social Theories,' which give a cover for introducing bright ideas in the order they occur to the author. A book with a pretentious title like 'Social Theory and Social Structure' is much more palatable if made up of essays making one argument at a time. It is easy in Merton to figure out which idea is being talked about at which time and what is the relevance of a conceptual distinction to that idea. Besides being an epistemological principle, Occam's razor is also a principle of rhetoric – not to clutter an argument with multiplied conceptual entities.

But I have tried to show above that the great variety of Merton's empirical theories is generated from a small set of common elements, organized around a core theory of rates of choice among socially structured alternatives. A half dozen or so major elements, in two or three major varieties each, generate structurally similar theories in a wide variety of empirical situations.

Precision

Perhaps the main epistemological mistake of sociologists is to confuse generality with lack of specificity. Newton in generalizing the theory of gravitation did *not* say the Earth goes sort of around the Sun, and Mars goes sort of around slower and farther out, and this is the same general kind of thing as rolling balls down an inclined plane. The theory of gravitation is simultaneously very general and very specific about exactly what will happen under various exactly described circumstances. The sociological tradition that defines a theorist by the absence of exact empirical description and prediction is completely foreign to the tradition of theorizing in the mature sciences.

Merton's theory is set up to explain variations, specifically variations in rates of choice. It is a perfectly answerable empirical question whether the establishment of scientific journals decreased the time between major discoveries and the use of those discoveries in further scientific work. The generality of the notion of socially structured alternatives is no bar to precise predictions about the rate of scientific communication. The generality of latent functions is no bar to a precise prediction about which kinds of political structures will collect higher rates of contributions from rackets. The structural distribution of delinquency and hyperconformity is precisely predictable from the argument of social structure and anomie.

There are two main elements to this precision. The first is that Merton never loses sight of the fact that the only thing that can be explained is variation. This means that no scientific theory can ever be about less than four things: two states of the effect and two states of the cause. The frequency with which this elementary matter is left implicit in sociological theorizing is little short of astounding. Whatever, for example, causes rôle conformity, its absence has to cause something else. That something else is a phenomenon out in the world, which has to be described before one knows what rôle conformity is and, consequently, what has to be explained. An entirely fictional portrayal of a Hobbesian state of nature will not do for the other end of the variable of conformity. Merton puts various phenomena at the other end, depending on his purpose – concealment or rôle audience segregation, having a bad attitude toward the army, hyperconformity of a ritualistic kind, solving problems by political machine methods, and so on. Contextually, then, rôle conformity becomes a number of different things, resulting in greater conceptual precision. Further, a distance between two people or two structures along one of these conceptual scales becomes an intractable fact to be explained. Because it is conformity as opposed to ritualism, *or* as opposed to rôle segregation, *or* as opposed to something else, the distance between a more conforming and a less conforming person means something precise. Distances along different scales then have different explanations, but one is not reduced to 'multiple causation' or 'failure of a system to meet its functional requisites' to explain deviance.

Yet this precision is not lack of generality. Visibility occupies a stable place in the general conceptual scheme, bearing the same relation to other concepts in a wide variety of empirical circumstances. Hollow conformity likewise, at least ideally, occupies the same place when it is pretending to pursue a manifest function while really being after a latent one as it does when it is a kind of behavior especially characteristic of the lower-middle-class or of the bureaucratic personality.

Critique

This last example, however, illustrates the main difficulty of Merton's way of proceeding. Because the general theory is nowhere extracted and systematized, we are not quite sure that hollow conformity to a manifest function is exactly the same as hollow ritualism of the lower middle class, bearing the same relation to other major concepts in the system. The piecemeal presentation of the theory makes a primary virtue of its power, its extensibility into many empirical areas. Taken as a whole, the structure of the corpus of theoretical work does not forcefully communicate the elegance, economy, and precision of the theory. And this makes it hard to work on the lacunae.

16. A structural analysis of sociology

The fundamental observation of structural analysis in Lévi-Strauss[1] is that institutionalized systems of exchange (of women, material goods, symbols) rest on a double system of distinctions. On the one hand, those who can or must exchange according to the norms of the system must be distinguished from those who cannot – for instance, a kinship system must define the boundaries of endogamy within which the system is institutionalized (e.g. the tribe). On the other hand, the units which can or must exchange must be distinguished from each other, at least so that one can be defined as lacking something that the other can furnish – for example, in kinship systems the exogamous unit that needs a wife must be distinguished from the unit eligible to supply a wife. It is this peculiar irony of the central forms of solidarity being defined by a system of differentiation that has captured Lévi-Strauss' imagination.

The second part of Lévi-Strauss' argument is that in order to talk about society and solidarity, the mythical system must have symbolic distinctions in it corresponding to the distinctions between subgroups that need each other in the system of exchange. Moieties or sections or lineages that are exogamous need to be contrasted symbolically with the moieties or sections or lineages with which they exchange. But these contrasts must be 'mediated' by other contrasts that distinguish the exchanging partners from the rest of the world.

In particular, Lévi-Strauss is interested in the system of mythical distinctions that contrasts objects in the natural world from those that

---

[1] The following account of what Lévi-Strauss was up to is mainly based on his early work on kinship (Lévi-Strauss, 1963, 1969a), modified in the light of the argument about symbols in his discussion of primitive cognitive psychology (Lévi-Strauss, 1966). I have borrowed a few things from his analysis of mythology (Lévi-Strauss, 1969b), but have been able to use very little of it because I do not understand it.

can enter into a specific exchange system as cultural objects with an agreed cultural definition. Material goods in the form of food, for example, occur in the form 'raw' in nature. By being cooked *by a social unit of the exchange system*, they become food that can be used in ritual exchanges in the system. Thus the mythical symbols having to do with the raw/cooked distinction can be used to discuss the transformation of socially insignificant objects into socially significant objects in an exchange system.

Likewise, women when they come into the world are merely children born to a certain mother. By a mythological as well as a social process, they become women descended from a certain social group, such that they can be exchanged in marriage, and that marriage can be distinguished from incest, rape, or seduction. The social meaning of exchanges of women between kin groups is discussed mythologically in terms of myths of descent, of 'blood,' and the like.

Finally a symbolic object is created by rituals, by social work performed to lend meaning to the symbol, a meaning in terms of the exchanges to take place. The bread and wine become symbols of the body and blood, to be exchanged by the Church for symbols of subjection (e.g. kneeling) by the rituals of the communion service.

The structure of scientific exchange systems

Clearly the discipline of sociology (especially within a country) is a system of exchange, in which students correspond to women as being people of low status and power who must be 'placed' in other departments, job offers correspond to material goods which are exchanged partly to show mutual respect, partly to improve each others' material positions, and scientific papers are symbols exchanged. The units corresponding to exogamous groups in kinship systems are departments, which therefore must be normatively defined as being incompetent in some respect or other, and consequently in need of exchange.

A student must be socially defined as a student of a certain descent, or as we say 'specialization,' by an apprenticeship and sponsorship system involving dissertation committees and the like. Raw creativity in a wide variety of fields does not produce a social object which can 'fill a slot' in the normatively defined needs of other departments. The discomfort of students who find they have to be *either* a theorist *or* a sociologist of education *or* a social psychologist *or* a methodologist is a reflection of this need for them to be related to the normative definition of the needs of other exogamous groups.

The ritual method of producing a student is called 'training' or 'education,' and its purpose in the exchange system is to establish lines of descent, 'lineages,' which can then have something to offer other lineages that is distinct from what they already have. The mythology of 'specialization' and 'training' then is the fundamental form in which a raw brain becomes an exchangeable student. The personnel committee is the core of the departmental ritual system, which defines needs of the exogamous group, by declaring the department to be incompetent in the following x fields (by ideologies of 'balance' or 'coverage'), and consequently in need of students from other descent lines.

The exchange of job offers is closely related to the exchange of students, except that people are hardly ever in fact exchanged. At least the ratio of offers to acceptances is very high as compared to the situation in student exchange. Instead the production of a job offer is like cooking a ritual meal, in which reciprocation is expected to be in the long run rather than immediately, especially by a reciprocal job offer when the time comes. The core of the meaning of the system is that it represents a way for a department to reaffirm the value of other departments, to recognize what kind of lineage they are, and to express a normatively valid need for the lineage to which the offer is made. The required immediate ritual exchange is that the person to whom the offer is made must show 'seriousness,' i.e. that he would find it worthwhile also to be in the other lineage.

The ritual process by which a scientific paper is produced is, of course, the refereeing process. This is a certification that an intellectual product may be put on a vita as a serious symbol of the worth of the person and of his lineage. It can then be exchanged as scientific knowledge and its previous exchange as a mimeographed paper is ritually validated. This ritual system is discussed in terms of distinctions of 'competence' or 'talent' and is especially crucial for defining the boundaries around the discipline, in contrast to anthropologists or political scientists or statisticians, from whom we learn but with whom we do not exchange.

Thus the crucial managers of the exchange system are: dissertation committees, which produce students of a certain lineage; personnel committees which produce job offers to members of other senior faculties and the people who show seriousness in response to such a show of respect; and referees of scientific journals or of book publishers, who produce certified symbols of science for the vita.

The central structural fact about the system of exchange overall is that it is rather strongly bounded, in all three exchanges, by disciplinary boundaries, and moderately strongly bounded by national labor markets. If I were to name the ten most interesting students of social structure in the world, maybe two or three would be officially sociologists, and maybe four or five North Americans. The list is of course personal to me, and I would not be so ritually gauche as to provide the list, but the experience is probably common. But the historians, economists, psychologists, anthropologists, and political scientists are not in the same exchange system, nor are most of the non-North-Americans. That is, we do not exchange students, do not exchange job offers (when I was young and naive, I used to propose to hire whomever I thought was the best person for a given set of intellectual tasks, regardless of discipline or nationality; I learned better), and do not referee each others' papers.

The structure of the sociological myth

The core of ritual for asserting the boundaries around the discipline as a whole is the annual convention. It is based on two basic mythical postulates: that we are interested in what each other have to say, and that we are competent judges of each others' work. There is attached to this ritual a formal representation of both the system for exchange of students (a placement service) and of exchanging certification of scientific papers (the sessions). There is also formal representation of the two sorts of lineages, namely specialists and departments. The governing bodies of the exchange ritual are carefully balanced by specialty and by what is euphemistically called regional representation, but is actually departmental. Sub-systems of exchange of scientific papers ('sessions') are set up along the lines of specialties, and the lineages have 'Chicago breakfasts,' 'Hopkins parties,' 'Berkeley dinners' and so on. The exchange of job offers is partly set up at the convention as well, as people who meet in the powerful committees politely inquire of each other whether they might be willing to move.

But overlaid on this are some master rituals of disciplinary solidarity, the Presidential address (which is ritually non-specialized), the open cocktail party, the 'business' meeting at which there is no business, and so on. Further we notice various informal rituals of lineage heads (who structurally conflict for the allocation of positions for students, job offers, and space in the journals) meeting for drinks and carrying out rituals of mutual respect. Further there will be participation of the integrating figures of the discipline – almost always former chairmen of leading departments and experienced in 'balance' – visiting to participate in specialty meetings and showing up to grace lineage parties of other departments.

The central myth then is that for all the internal distinctions, we are engaged in a common intellectual enterprise whose collective purpose is different from that of anthropology, political science, economics, or history. There is therefore an attempt to create the sense of a distinctive competence, a 'sociological theory,' as the common (and foolish) criticism of theoretical papers as being 'too psychological' or 'just economics' shows. This is backed by a set of myths about having acted in common – through some famous fathers of the discipline – to do a set of things no one else can do.

The converse of this process takes place in university bargaining over faculty posts. That is, it might offhand seem more rational to hire a distinguished social historian like E. J. Hobsbawm or Alfred Chandler, who are better sociologists than most of us, to fill sociological needs by a person in the history department. But the history department has to agree to be incompetent in sociology – whatever the facts, and so avoid wasting their posts to further the sociological enterprise – in order to claim that sociology is incompetent in history – whatever the facts. Thus the definition of the boundaries is an agreement to exchange students, job offers, and papers within the boundaries, and to agree to be incompetent across the boundaries to preserve the integrity of disciplinary exchange systems.

The central rôle of figures of historical origin of disciplines in this mythical system is illustrated by the comment of a history professor at Johns Hopkins shortly after a sociology department was established there. 'We have been reading Weber in the History Department since the 1920s. I don't see why now we need a whole department to read Weber.' The first barb in this is the use of the verb 'to read' in place of 'to do research like.' The implicit argument is that sociology's relation to Weber is mythical, that one is more likely to learn to do comparative history in a history department. (The correctness of this attribution of the mythical character of our commitment to comparative history may be shown by the fact that, of the three sociologists I can think of who do Weber's kind of research, Reinhard Bendix, Barrington Moore, and S. N. Eisenstadt, one has divorced the discipline, one has been divorced by the discipline, and the third has his satrapy on the periphery.) The second barb is the denial of monopoly over the mythical figure, and hence implicitly over the competences supposedly distinguishing the discipline.

But once the distinction between sociology and the scholarly world at large is established mythically by discussions of the 'sociological approach,' and consequently the distinction of sociological student exchange, job-offer exchange, and refereeing processes is justified, then the exogamous subunits must by mythically defined. As in kinship systems, this has two aspects: locality and descent. Each exogamous unit at a certain locality is supposed to have ties and alliances with others in the system ('affinal relations'), by representing the other lineages in the locality group. The central device by which this is supposed to be achieved is the exchange of students. In order for the system to work, each department must be willing to define itself as in need of students from another lineage.

There are two overlapping systems for doing this, a primitive one of 'specialties' and a sophisticated one of 'approaches.' When one is explaining 'needs' to an administration, one uses the language of specialties. We need someone in African studies, or juvenile delinquency, or organizational sociology. Some people inside departments actually take that rhetoric seriously, I suppose on the Lewis Carroll principle that what I say three times is true, and I am forced to say it to the administration. But the sophisticated version is that one will look for someone in an approach or academic tradition that is making another department famous. One wants the best student of Robert K. Merton or Otis Dudley Duncan or Talcott Parsons, rather than a sociology of science student or a quantitative stratification student or a theorist at the *most* general level. Or one wants to represent the ethnomethodological approach or the structural approach or the mathematical models approach. (The verb 'represent' is actually often used).

This tension has to do with the different character of the exchange system of the university (which I am mainly ignoring here) and that of the discipline. The university exchanges control over recruitment (making disciplines possible) for the predictable performance of some set of teaching tasks in courses that have names and, more important, numbers. The Registrar depends on Sociology 107 always being the sociology of deviance, substitutable from year to year and never something a person might take six times. Of course, a university knows substantively that it's a pretty poor department in which that is literally true, and that particularly, over the course of 20 years, it is a failure if it is the same course at all. Further they do not really care whether the person who teaches it is primarily famous for contributions to the symbolic interactional sublineage, or to the quantitative sociology sublineage, or to the Marxist sublineage in which the criminals are the oppressed. Thus every appointment has to be clothed in two rhetorics, one about 'needs' for 'specialties' for the university and one about 'representation' of 'approaches' for 'diversity' in the departmental faculty.

Both of these distinctions are largely mythical. For instance, one of the more interesting papers in the symbolic interactionist tradition is James S. Coleman's (1957) much ignored paper on multidimensional scaling about 20 years ago. By formalizing mathematically the symbolic interactionist postulate that an attitude was an action tendency toward a socially defined object he derived an interesting series of consequences about how attitude items might be related statistically. Now such an achievement ought to make him a candidate for a job where a department 'needs' a symbolic interactionist. Of course it does not, because in the mythical system symbolic interactionism and mathematical sociology (especially scale construction) are different lineages, and a bastard child is not of much use in the exchange system until he or she has been ritually accepted as descended from the lineage. In this case, most of the official mathematical lineage from which Coleman ritually descended did not understand G. H. Mead, and the symbolic interactionist lineage did not understand the statistics, so the paper was aborted (this very often happens to bastards).

The point is that the paper was fighting the solidly entrenched mythology that symbolic interactionism and mathematical sociology were different 'approaches,' and it has the same mythical difficulty as would be shown by having a mythical elephant as clever and deceptive as the mythical deermouse. How would you know whom to hire if symbolic interactionists could be the same thing as mathematical sociologists?

Thus the mythical system has to have crosscutting distinctions between 'specialties' and 'approaches' on the one hand, and 'departments' on the other. Departments have to be locality groups, and consequently a delicate balanced network representing the system as a whole; they must also be lineages, and consequently dominated by one 'approach' rather than another.

From the point of view of the individual, one is confronted with having to agree with one's department that one is incompetent in enough fields and approaches so that the department as a collectivity has 'needs.' Considering yourself (and your students, by a kind of feudal generosity) to be competent at everything in the discipline is the same sort of crime as incest, for it is a normative betrayal of the exchange system.

Suppose that we tried in fact to hire the smartest people, regardless of 'specialty' or 'approach.' Since there is nothing very difficult about sociology, such a group of people could satisfy the university by teaching everything. They could presumably replace themselves, by 'training' people to be flexible about 'approaches' and 'specialties.' But then like a kinship group with no incest taboo and no exogamy, they would have no ground for exchange, no necessity to be members of a 'discipline.' And that means they would have few grounds to urge *their* students on other departments. There would be a unidimensional prestige ranking instead of a partial ordering by 'specialties' and 'approaches,' more like the Oxford–Cambridge axis in England than like the system in the U.S., with the consequent relative weakening of 'disciplines' as opposed to 'colleges' as the guiding integrative institutions. That is, the master of rituals would be élite rituals rather than specialty rituals, and the central mythical distinctions would be to distinguish the elite from the mass, rather than lineages from each other. But you can only get away with such a claim if you are actually as good as Oxford and Cambridge, far better than the rest of the universities. No university in the U.S. is that much better than another five or six, so unilateral exchange with the élite giving their students to the mass is not a structural possibility.[2]

Thus we get the multiplication of fake controversies over 'approaches,' usually formulated in lineage terms, organized around the founder of the lineage. The question is whether one is in the true descent of G. H. Mead or Karl Marx or Paul Lazarsfeld or Max Weber, not whether what one has to say makes sense. The tiny philosophical differences between Mead and Parsons have to be blown up into contrasting approaches; when you add a simple notion like unconscious norms, similar to grammatical norms, to the symbolic interactionist tradition, you get a full blown sect of ethnomethodology. A convenience in presenting quantitative results has to be blown up into a full blown revolution, in path analysis and dependence coefficients, so as to create a Duncan and Boudon lineage.

I am not arguing of course that path analysis is not a substantial convenience, nor that the place of unconscious norms in social interaction was not greatly underplayed before Garfinkel. These are both real advances. What I am arguing instead is that there is a tremendous rush to create new 'approaches' which can only be explained by the necessity to create new needs. Otherwise we would just learn path analysis and about unconscious norms and go on about our business. A person who likes Karl Marx would not be expected to agree to be incompetent in the work of Howard Becker or James S. Coleman.

Besides these distinctions based on needs, we must have a mythical set of devices for justifying the national closure of labor markets. The most amusing difficulty with this is the Canadian system, which is required to try to hire Canadians from United States graduate departments. Their recruitment letters are models of the universalism–particularism dilemma. But we all want to go abroad, and to have somebody else pay for it because it is a public service. There are only two ways for it to be a public service – either we are incompetent and have to learn, or they are incompetent and we have to teach. Now obviously the decent thing to do from the point of view of inter-

---

[2] In England it is very precarious in sociology; at least three universities compete seriously with the big two (the big two are not very good in sociology) and a system much more like the American disciplinary one is developing, a system unlike the unilateral system in the humanities and some of the sciences.

national scientific solidarity is to assert both at once, i.e. to treat national scholarly traditions as lineages.

But if one asserts international differences in competences, why are we not exchanging students and job offers and refereeing articles across the boundaries? I would argue that most of the international differences are about as mythical as most of the differences between departments and approaches within a given nation. That is, there are some minor intellectual differences. I would judge that on the average it would take a competent English sociologist about six months to become a competent North American sociologist; a little less for Israel, Scandinavia, and Japan; more for West Germany and the communist countries. The reverse process is about of the same order of magnitude. That is, it would take about six months for a competent North American sociologist to become a competent English sociologist, a little less for Israel, Scandanavia, and Japan, a little more for West Germany and the communist countries. I would say this is about the distance between specialties and approaches in the United States. It takes about six months to become an ethnomethodologist or a path analysis expert or a specialist in race relations or deviant behavior.

But that is like saying it would only take six months to learn the norms and rituals of the Clan of the Elk. It is true enough, and if all we were really up to were honoring the Elk and advancing the science respectively, that would be enough. But as Lévi-Strauss has pointed out, the purpose of having totems is to make people who are all basically the same into fundamentally different *kinds* of people, so there is some excuse for passing women, gifts, and ritual performances among them. The triviality of learning to be of the Clan of the Elk has nothing to do with the matter. The point is that an Elk is a different beast than a Cougar, and is competent to produce women that a Cougar can marry, feasts to which a Cougar can be invited, and ritual symbols that a Cougar is not in a sufficiently sacred position to produce.

In particular what we have to establish internationally is that these are a different breed of people with whom it is useful to exchange visits, but not students, job offers, and scientific papers. This is a very uncomfortable business in academic life, and goes far to explain why visiting fellows from abroad are so systematically, if selectively, ignored. Having been on both sides of this process, in Chile, England,

and the Netherlands as a visitor and here as a host, I have some experience of the dilemma. A foreigner may possibly get taken seriously *until* some serious decision has to be made. But a foreigner does not normatively prevent my student from being hired, my United States peers from getting job offers, and my papers from being published. Fellows from abroad are interesting enough men and women, but after all these are serious matters. This non-seriousness of the way foreigners are treated is of course difficult to justify on universalistic grounds.

The mythology of becoming in sociology

On the basis of the structural requirements of the system of exchange, Lévi-Strauss argues that there must be a mythology about the transformation of the world of nature into the world of culture, which turns innocent people, food, and natural objects into clan members, ritual feasts, and sacred symbols. Thus every mythological system must have a system of distinctions which distinguishes the natural world according to its potentiality in terms of the social world. A child as a natural object has to be distinguished according to his or her potentiality to become a member of a certain lineage; a raw piece of meat has to be distinguished as appropriate for Thanksgiving or Easter, or for a feast of the Clan of the Elk; places (or a wafer and wine) have to be distinguished as potential churches (or potential body and blood of Christ).

Furthermore on top of this detailed definition of nature in terms of its cultural potentialities, there must be a mythology of becoming, in terms of which children become wives, the raw becomes cooked, the bread and wine become a sacrament.

Thus there is a double mapping mythologically of the natural world on the social world. In the first place, distinctions in the natural world have to correspond in a rough way with the distinctions needed for the society, though they are arbitrary from the point of view of a scientific description of nature (Lévi-Strauss goes to great lengths to show that the 'unscientific' descriptions of nature by primitive people do not indicate lack of powers of observation, but rather the uses to which the description is to be put culturally.) In the second place, there has to be a system of mapping of distinctions, of the transformative process, so that one knows when a natural child becomes a marriageable woman, a piece of meat becomes a feast, a piece of bread becomes the body of Christ. That is, there is a mythical representation of the productive process by which natural objects become social objects. This interest in production and its ideological representation is what allows Lévi-Strauss to talk in pseudo-Marxist terms about what he is doing, for the central symbol that represents French national intellectual solidarity is that the most diverse sorts of people should claim to be Marxists.

The associated mythology in sociology is that which describes what turns a bright person into a competent person, a young person of promise into a senior faculty member and lineage head, and a research result into a scientific paper. These involve on the one hand distinctions among events in nature. Some undergraduates are bright and some are not. Some young scholars have promise and some do not. Some research results are original and solid and some are not. But in each case there is also an overlaid distinction about the cultural process. Some bright people are educated or trained to be sociologists and some are not. Some young people of promise have not 'done anything since' and some have. Some research results have been responsibly interpreted for the discipline and some have not. In short, some of nature is edible and some is not, but overlaid on that, some is cooked and some is not. (And even when natural foods are not cooked, when we eat raw ground beef or crisp fruits and vegetables, they have to be seasoned and served in special dishes or cut into elegant strips or taken together with very highly cultured cheese; eating apples picked in an orchard is not 'having a meal.' Raw creativity likewise has to be cultured, or at least taken along with a good dose of cultured learning).

The mythology of turning a bright person into a competent person is a combined one of testing the distinction in nature – was he really bright? – and transforming the nature into a cultured product. The transformation process is 'training,' and involves demanding that the person be ready to participate in the exchange system of his 'specialties.' This involves especially being ready to reproduce, for the locality group, the network of lineages of ideas that constitutes the exchange system as a whole. You cannot be a certified competent stratification person unless you can acknowledge (knowledgeably) the contributions of the lineage of Marx and that of O. D. Duncan. That is, you must be cultured so that the mythology that we are all interested in each others' work is a viable myth. You need not be required to reproduce the lineage of thought on stratification of, say, Clifford Geertz, because that is protected behind the two barriers of his being an anthropologist and his being a specialist in religion. The crucial part of Ph.D. specialty examinations is that they certify that you are allowed to be incompetent for the rest of your life in areas not covered in the examination, because they are not in your specialty.

The 'training' part of the mythology, which involves establishing that somebody needs you, is organized around research apprenticeship and the dissertation. This is the process by which, although solidly standardized as a specialist, a competent person is established as distinctive, as a woman some particular other exogamous unit ought to want to have in marriage. The neuroses of the dissertation are essentially similar to the neuroses of coquetry, in which the person needs to establish that he or she is uniquely desirable, though also a good solid person by the standards of general eligibility.

The process by which a young person of promise is turned into a lineage head (a 'senior professor') has the same mixture of components of testing nature and 'maturation.' But there is the additional problem that appointing a new lineage head changes the character of the locality group. There are some strong patrilocal patrilineal systems in academia in which the exchange of young people of promise is the only respect that is paid to other lineages, and those few young people of promise actually promoted are those that reinforce the distinctiveness of the lineage. Such irresponsibility to the exchange system is called 'inbreeding' in polite conversation, 'incestuous' policy in private. But usually there is a compromise between local rule and respect for the exchange system, and distinguished outside members of the profession are consulted about the promotion to prevent 'inbreeding.' And in fact it is a pretty doubtful transformation process if it is not validated by a job offer from the outside. The transformation of the Clan of the Elk into the Clan of the Cougar by transforming foreign elements into lineage heads is what makes gossip about departments one of the core elements of the mythical system of sociology.

That is, part of the myth has to do with the production of a senior professor from a young person of promise, with tenure corresponding to initiation into a lineage. But the second part of the mythology has no exact counterpart in lineage systems, for the new professor transforms the character of the lineage. Rather than generational succession of essentially the same kind of men, the women (students exchanged) become men (professors), making the lineage itself a product of the exchange system, just as the true genetic, as opposed to social, lineage system is in marriage systems. This makes the question of what is happening to a particular department an interesting subject of gossip.

Myth and reality

Lévi-Strauss does not, of course, maintain that there is no substantive distinction between raw and cooked food. Likewise it would be foolish to equate a competent sociological paper to the raw creativity of a sophomore bull session. The sociological competence of historians, anthropologists, or political scientists is indistinguishable in general from that of sociologists, but like the cooking of women of the wrong lineage, it can be hard work, and can be well or badly done.

Whatever its other social functions, a myth gets some of its vigor from its relation to reality. As the practical household units of a primitive tribe change, by ecological changes or by warfare or by the failure of descent lines to reproduce, the mythical system of kinship either loses its vigor or changes to correspond to the new reality.

The sect-forming tendency in sociology is likewise grounded in the reality that no one can do everything (though perhaps some can do anything), just as exogamous clans linked in exchange rings are grounded in the reality that it would be exhausting, if perhaps fun, to marry everybody. The petty chauvinism of sociological sects results in destructive feuding just as overweening clan loyalty does; it is not only a betrayal of the exchange system but also a Bad Thing. The social supports of the universalism of scientific standards, the dominance of competence over sect loyalty in the scientific status system, are derived from the exchange system.

The tendency for the Oxford–Cambridge axis to award status for Common Room wit and for the entertainment value of scholarly findings may seem a pleasant contrast to the deadly dullness of the average refereed paper, but jokes are, after all, often mistaken observations about the world. In particular the jokes of an incestuous élite ingroup also form a mythical system, shaped by the social requirement *not* to exchange on the basis of equality. Mythical inequality is as likely to produce distortions of reality as the mythical substitutability of Sociology 107 from year to year. The incest of the Pharaohs was grounded in a distinction among superior and inferior lineages every bit as mythical as that between Cougars and Elk, and considerably less amusing in its consequences. But the mythology of inequality is a topic not relevant to many of Lévi-Strauss' societies, and not well developed by him.

If sociology's relation to Weber is as mythical as the relation of the Church to Christ, we must take what comfort we can from the fact that at least both chose first class myths.

17. On journal editing as a probabilistic process
(with Richard Ofshe)

The process of evaluating papers for journal publication is a measurement process, similar to the other measurement processes of qualitative material in the social sciences. Let us assume that there are no biases in this process, and that it has about the same level of measurement efficiency as other measurement processes based on coding qualitative materials.

A good qualitative measurement technique rarely has a reliability coefficient of more than about .50 (i.e., a correlation of .50 of one measurement with another measurement by the same technique). Let us assume that *all* the covariation between two measures is due to the true variable we are trying to measure. Then the square root of the reliability of a measure is the upper limit of its validity. If we assume that journal editing as a measurement process is as good as good qualitative measurement can possibly be, given our experience in the social sciences, we would estimate the validity of a judgement of article quality to be about .70.

Then the situation would be about as diagramed in the accompanying figure. The two major journals in sociology accept about 16 per cent of the papers submitted to them. If the quality of papers judged is approximately normal, we can say that papers *judged* to be 1 standard deviation or more above the mean of papers submitted will be accepted. Assuming a correlation of .70 between the true quality of the paper and the judged quality, we can estimate the proportion of acceptances of papers of different quality. That is, for papers at different points on the abscissa we want to calculate what proportion will be judged to be above the acceptance level of 1 standard deviation above the mean. We will assume that our figure represents a bivariate normal distribution.

To solve the problem we need to compute the conditional distribution of judged quality (in normalized form) for a given value of true quality (in normalized form). For a given value of true quality, X_i, the distribution of judged quality would be normal, with a mean equal to

$$\mu_{y|x} = \rho_{xy}X_i$$

and a standard deviation equal to

$$\sigma_{y|x} = \sqrt{1-\rho_{xy}{}^2}$$

where y is the measure of quality (see Hald, 1952: 593). If we assume that $\rho_{xy} = .70$, then this gives

$$\mu_{y|x} = .7X_i$$
$$\sigma_{y|x} = \sqrt{.51} \simeq .7$$

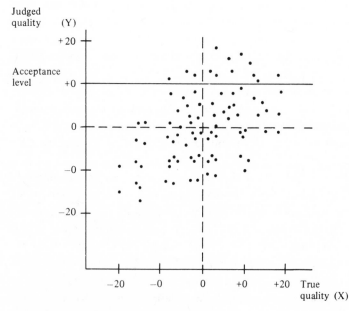

Scatter diagram of judged quality on true quality

Table 1 gives the hypothetical percentage of acceptances for papers at different levels of true quality, if the measurement efficiency of the

Table 1 *True quality and proportion of papers accepted*

True quality interval in standard deviations	Mid-point	Per cent accepted
−3.0 to −2.0	−2.5	.005
−2.0 to −1.0	−1.5	.18
−1.0 to 0	− .5	2.8
0 to +1.0	+ .5	18.0
	Supposed acceptance level	
+1.0 to +2.0	+1.5	50.3
+2.0 to +3.0	+2.5	84.3
+3.0 to +4.0	+3.5	97.8

refereeing process is represented by a correlation of .70 between judged quality and true quality.

In order to clarify the model's predictions, consider the application of the model to a set of 100 papers submitted for publication. By retaining the assumption that the distribution of true quality of papers is normal, it is possible to estimate the frequency that papers within a given interval of true quality will be submitted. Given the frequency of papers of a certain quality being submitted and the probability of their being judged to be above the acceptance level, it is an elementary problem to calculate the result. Table 2 presents the expected fate for papers of different true qualities.

Table 2 *Life and death of 100 papers*

Interval in standard deviations	Probability of acceptance at mid-point	Expected number of papers of this true quality	Expected acceptances	Expected rejections
−3.0 to −2.0	.00005	2	0	2
−2.0 to −1.0	.0018	14	0	14
−1.0 to 0	.028	34	1	33
0 +1.0	.180	34	6	28
		Supposed acceptance level		
+1.0 to +2.0	.503	14	7	7
+2.0 to +3.0	.843	2	2	0
Total		100	16	84

On the surface, the model's predictions do not appear too distressing. Of the 84 submitted papers that were truly below the acceptance level, 77 (92 per cent) are rejected and only 7 (8 per cent) are accepted. For the 16 papers truly above the cut-off point, 9 (56 per cent) are accepted and 7 (44 per cent) are rejected. In terms of numbers of papers, there are about equal numbers of distinguished papers being mistakenly rejected and mediocre papers mistakenly accepted.

When one considers the effects of the evaluation procedures on the final composition of a journal, the results are as follows. Manuscripts of truly distinguished quality account for only 56 per cent of the papers published, while fully 44 per cent of the papers should have been rejected. Although the average probability of a good paper (one in the class that is between 1 and 2 standard deviations above the mean) being accepted is about .50 and that of a mediocre paper (one within 1 standard deviation above the mean) is about .18, the mediocre quality of the journals is accounted for by the differences in the frequencies with which papers of various qualities are submited. Note (see Table 2) that there are enough good papers being submitted to fill the journal, but they are simply being rejected in favor of papers of lesser quality.

To get some idea of what this means from the point of view of an author, it may be illuminating to consider what would happen if everyone's work reflected only his IQ. The mean sociologist, from the data on IQ's in graduate school, probably has an IQ of about 130. The standard deviation of the IQ distribution is about 15 points. This would mean, under the assumptions, that people of between 130 and 144 IQ's should expect an acceptance ratio of their papers of about 1 in 5. People of between 145 and 159 IQ's should expect about one-half their papers to be accepted. For those between 160 and 174, the expected acceptance is about 17 out of 20. People in the IQ range between 175 and 189 – say somewhere near that of Isaac Newton – should expect rejection of about 2 out of 100 papers.

The impressive thing about the model above is that it does not take a conspiracy theory of journal editing to account for the rejection of a great many good papers and the publishing of a large number of mediocre papers. Even if social scientists as editors are as accurate as people ever are in coding qualitative material, nearly half the good papers will be rejected and the journals filled with mediocrity.

18. The mathematical biology of survey research centers

The hive or colony of social insects is divided into workers who go out to collect honey from the environment, and queens who eat disproportionate amounts of honey they did not collect, and produce eggs. The central question of hive viability is the ratio of queens to workers. The central question of species viability is whether enough new hives are created by new queens to replace hives that get destroyed by predators, that die out from too many queens and not enough workers, or that die out after the death of the queen keeps the workers from producing either workers or queens. It takes at least one queen to produce a hive.

In each of these respects the relations between researchers who write and professionals who do the work in survey research organizations is smiliar. It takes roughly one paid Ph.D. level professional worker to support sufficient data collection for a professor who uses survey research and his advanced students. The other analogies are obvious. Consequently the models that population biologists have worked out to study the growth of hives and species viability of social insects may be useful in analyzing the fate of survey research. In historical or participant observation or fact free research, each professor can be his own queen and his own worker, and hive viability is not a problem.

The queen's rôle in a hive is to produce workers (in survey research organizations, jobs for workers by making grant proposals believable) by producing eggs. The workers' rôle is to produce from the environment the materials for turning the eggs into more workers and more queens. The more of the growth of the hive that takes the form of queens, the fewer of the future eggs will be able to grow into workers and queens because the queens do not forage. The hive, so to speak, makes an investment of present worker productivity either in

337

producing more workers or in producing and supporting more queens. The following development is modified from Edward O. Wilson, (1970: 432–4). If we let

λ = the birth rate of the worker population, i.e., the number of workers that could be fed if all worker effort went into workers

μ = death rate of the worker population

N_w = the number of workers in the colony

N_j = the number of queen larvae in the colony, so that the change per unit time in the number of queens will be a constant times N_j – the constant will depend on the time it takes to raise a queen.

If we let the number of queens be Q, then we can guess that

$$\frac{dQ}{dt} = KN_j = bN_w \tag{1}$$

This says that the number of queen larvae that can be supported by a colony increases as a linear function of the number of workers.

But since the more workers there are, the more they interfere with each other in raising new workers, and perhaps the less likely any of them is to have a queen lay an egg for him to tend which will result in a new worker in the next time period, the rate of growth of the worker population may be a logarithmic function of the worker population. These would be diseconomies of scale due to the worse fit and worse contact between workers and queens in a larger hive. It might be then that in the absence of queen larvae taking up the foraged food, you would have

$$\frac{dW}{dt} = \lambda N^s - \text{(queen factor)} \quad {}_{(s<1)} \tag{2}$$

where s is a measure of the diseconomies of scale. But the total number of workers will be decreased by the number of queens that live off them but do not produce eggs, who are virgin queens who will go out and start new colonies. So the 'queen factor' in equation (2) is the number of queen larvae in equation (1), multiplied by some constant which says how many worker larvae have to be sacrificd to grow each virgin queen. Since the number of virgin queens produced in a given time period is dQ/dt, or bN_w, we can simply modify the b coefficient by this sacrifice rate to obtain a law of growth of the worker population.

$$\frac{dN_w}{dt} = \lambda N^s - cNw - \mu Nw \tag{3}$$

If c is very large, either because the queens are very greedy and do not help produce workers, or because the number of virgin queens produced increases with the number of workers very rapidly, the colony will have what Edward O. Wilson calls 'explosive' growth. The colony grows along all right until it starts producing too many, or too greedy, virgin queens. Then these start to eat up the resources that might produce new workers, and extinguish the colony except for the virgin queens who go out into the world trying to start new colonies. From an evolutionary point of view this is a good adaptation to a short foraging season and a winter which can only be overwintered by fat queens. It is exemplified by the hornet *Vespa orientalis*. As the National Science Foundation or National Institute of Mental Health turn cold, for example, fat tenured professors are more likely to overwinter than interviewing, coding, or programming staff, ready to start a new colony in Spring.

If the value of c, the greediness and number of virgin queens as a function of colony size, is in the intermediate range, colony size settles down to an oscillatory equilibrium. The mathematical structure of this solution is the same as the famous Lotka problem of the foxes and the rabbits, in which a generation of foxes that is too big eats up the rabbits that should have supported their children, so that the number of foxes in the next generation goes down allowing the rabbits to grow again.

If the value of c is low enough, the colony undergoes a steady growth to a large size with a stable (and low) ratio of queens.

The policy of the old Bureau of Applied Social Research under Lazarsfeld exemplifies the high production of virgin queens, producing a large number of new colonies throughout the country after a short but meteoric growth of the colony, and a process of colony extinction as there are not enough workers to tend the eggs. The low ratio of queens to workers and growth to large stable size is more characteristic of Michigan's Survey Research Center. The intermediate oscillatory equilibrium in which the growth of the queen population constantly threatens the workers' food supply is perhaps the most common situation elsewhere. The National Opinion Research Center grew more queens under Rossi then went through a Michigan-like period of growing workers again, and now (early 1970s) seems to be starting in the queen-growing business once more.

New colonies and stunted workers

There are two basic evolutionary devices in the social insects for starting new hives, swarming as among the honeybees and the lonely fertilized queens as among the overwintering hornets. In swarming insects the queen takes along a group of workers from the old hive, so that the new hive from the first has foraging workers and laying queens. In general in such swarming species the queen is more differentiated from the workers and is more monofunctional in egg laying.

If we examine the structure of, say, the Detroit Area Survey or the traditional academic department with some survey researchers, however, the lonely queen without workers is the core of the new hive. A typical accompaniment of this situation is that the first generation of workers tend to be stunted, while as the summer wears on the workers approach their normal size. The foraging efficiency of the hive therefore goes up over the first part of the season.

The mathematical structure of this process is quite straightforward. We assumed above that each worker larva required the same amount of foraging activity to bring him to maturity. Now the lonely queen's problem is to get enough workers quickly to start foraging, in the face of a lack of foragers to support them.

The lonely queen has to raise the first brood out of the accumulated stored energy of her own body. She generally does this by feeding them part of her egg production. She needs quick production of workers because there is a net drain of resources from the hive as long as no foraging is going on, and the reserves of the hive are going into the growth of workers. By adjusting both the time to maturity (the first generation is shorter), and the gross size of the mature worker, she can balance the accounts of the hive earlier in the Spring, and start a normal process of hive growth.

The quickly-raised underfed worker larvae of the first generation are stunted and not such good foragers. Consequently the overall balance of the accounts of the hive is still problematical, and the evolutionary process at the hive level works with special intensity at this period. Further, with a low, or even declining, balance in the hive food budget from foraging, there are no extra resources to produce virgin queens. The output for the hive is at best a set of workers who might, in the future, if the hive persists, be in a condition to be able to grow new queens.

Thus a continuing policy of starting new hives, exemplified by the Detroit Area Survey, has the consequence of low hive viability, dependency on the supply of fat queens who can raise a brood of stunted workers out of their accumulated resources, low production of virgin queens who are ready to start their own hives, and a relatively low level of foraging efficiency. If there is migration among hives, the stunted workers may help grow more queens in a viable hive – for example in the Survey Research Center. By the end of the first stunted generation's foraging, the lonely queen may be fatter than she was after the overwintering, and more ready to lay productive eggs in the future.

The process of swarming, with a fertilized queen taking her workers along to start a new hive, decreases these processes. But in many social insects it appears that a single queen in a relatively small new hive depresses the production of new virgin queens. Sometimes, it seems, she eats them. This might be called charismatic leadership, in which the exceptional quality of a single individual determines the growth patterns of alternative leadership, and the smaller the compass over which the leadership exercises sway, the more her exceptional qualities discourage those same qualities in others. The problem of succession then is maximized in the early charismatic days of the new hive.

The evolutionary problem of swarming is that the new hive needs a niche in the environment big enough and rich enough to support the hive from the beginning, and another hive cannot produce as many swarms to go find such a niche as it can single fat queens. Apparently a particular problem is finding a nest big enough to hold the swarm so it can start raising its own new generations of workers and eventually queens. Having found a nest big enough to hold the swarm, the next problem is to find a field to forage in without too much competition so that the large hive requirements can be met.

The contrast between spreading by fat queens and spreading by swarming is perhaps illustrated by the colonization of Berkeley by the Bureau of Applied Social Research, and the colonization of Johns Hopkins by NORC (with some workers stolen from the Columbia hive). The Berkeley workers seem to have been more local talent grown by the colonizing queen, while a large Chicago swarm descended on Baltimore. It is notable that the Baltimore swarm entered a relatively unoccupied niche in educational sociology, and studies requiring fancy study designs, where the creation of jobs to support a large number of workers was less difficult. The smaller virgin queen setup at Berkeley did not need such a non-competitive environment, so penetrated more traditional areas open to more conventional study designs.

The growth of queens and soldiers

If we turn our attention away from the development of populations to the growth of individuals, we need to explain the morphological and functional differences between queens and workers, and within the group of workers those who compete with other colonies and predators in the foraging area (soldiers) and those who do the foraging (workers).

The simplest process of morphological differentiation is called 'allometric growth,' which has been investigated by J. B. S. Haldane (Wilson, 1970; 139–46). It may be illustrated by the growth of a population in which the poor have a higher reproductive rate than the rich. In that case the genetic stock represented by the poor will grow at a faster proportional rate than the genetic stock of the rich, with a possible change in the genetic structure of the population.[1] But a more

---

[1] The application of the allometric growth model to this problem is what led Haldane to his famous proposal to overcome the possible dysgenic effects of the poor having more children than the rich. His proposal was to make the rich poor and the poor richer, so as to equalize their reproduction rates.

direct example is the disproportionate growth of the parts of the body whose function is reproductive in the (larger) queens of social insects.

An allometric growth pattern is defined by the equation

$$\ln y = \ln b + a \ln x \tag{4}$$

where x and y are two measurements on the body of an organism. Equivalently, equation (4) may be rewritten as

$$y = bx^a \tag{4a}$$

If a is greater than 1, then y grows faster relatively to x, and larger animals (e.g. queens) will relatively speaking have much bigger y's compared to their x's than will smaller animals.

Another way to put the same equation would be to take θ to be the overall growth (e.g. the weight) of the animal, and let $\theta(t)$ be the weight of the animal at time t. Then if the percentage growth per small time period in y is a direct function of size, and the same for x, we get the system

$$\frac{\frac{dy}{dt}}{y} = \alpha\theta(t) \tag{4b}$$

and

$$\frac{\frac{dx}{dt}}{x} = \beta\theta(t) \tag{4c}$$

This leads to the solution that

$$\log y = \frac{\alpha}{\beta}\log x \tag{4d}$$

with the other parameters determined by the birth weight of the animal $\theta(0)$, and the relative sizes of x and y at birth. Hence a in equation (4) equals α/β in the system (4b, 4c).

Now if we imagine that what distinguishes a queen from a worker in a survey research center is the ratio of arcane to mundane knowledge and thought processes, we can imagine that the same sort of thing goes on in an individual biography. As a worker grows weightier, more richly fed with a larger variety of partially predigested data, the proportion of his mental operations that take mathematical form, or theoretical form, or answering the question, 'what does it all mean,' increases. The arcane/mundane ratio then will be exactly the kind of thing that grows with an increasing number of workers, as postulated in the first section above. If we let y be the predisposition at a given time to arcane thought, and x the tendency to mundane thought, then a coefficient a great than 1.0 will lead to a relative growth of arcane thought with increasing intellectual weight, i.e. with increasing numbers of foraging and predigesting workers.

Thus we generally find a career development of future queens in which there is a systematic pattern of doubt about their deserts. Early in their careers when their mundane thought level is largest (relatively), they are generally doubted most by their non-survey colleagues. Comments like 'no doubt extremely competent, but after all the ideas are not very original or profound' are the typical fate of the early survey worker in a heterogeneous department. Later on the workers in the survey research center start to doubt whether it might not have been too many years since he did an interview, or that fancy study designs like that hardly ever work. If the interview does not go or the specialized study design to test a complex hypothesis cannot be rescued when (as always happens) the complex hypothesis is not quite true, and the fanciness prevents a reasonable test of any less complex alternative, then the queen can live on accumulated fat while the workers go hungry.

There are undoubtedly personal variations in the α/β ratio at a given level of foraging and predigestion. At one extreme is the scholar who would just as soon work with simulated data to develop models or estimating procedures, with an essential infinite arcane/mundane ratio. At the opposite extreme is the convinced empiricist who, no matter how fat he gets, insists on thinking about what people actually say in the interview. As nearly as I can judge, these biases in growth are completely orthogonal to ability, and do not affect the population pattern of allometric growth of the two styles of thought. Those who remain at a high level of mundane thought at heavier intellectual weights can substitute for an undersupply of workers or stunted workers at an early stage of hive growth. Those who start out arcane may become queens in a hive with many workers, or start a generally sterile colony of their own with no foraging capacity. A particular difficulty is the lightweight queen who does not manage arcane thought but insists on doing it anyway. Among the social insects such intermediate animals may lay trophic eggs, which can be fed to the larvae in place of foraged food in times of dearth. The internal mimeographed arcane discussion paper which never gets published has some analogies to this. The infamous 'invisible college' of people on the inside who get to see mimeographed papers mainly see papers that do not advance knowledge enough to be published.

Except for a few parasitic and exploitative insects, the soldier workers are engaged in the defense of colonies against competitive colonies trying to take over the ecological niche of a given colony, and against predatory insects and animals that try to steal the food accumulated by the workers or the larvae. The niches of survey research centers are of course allocated in Washington. As in ant and termite colonies, only a small proportion of the workers are specialized in intercolony competition. Among ants and termites the crucial developments are a disproportionate development of the mandibles for chewing up the opposition, and the development of large hard heads for blocking the entrance of predators into the hive or colony. The disproportionate development of the bony exoskeleton of the head and the chewing hostile mandibles generally comes about by an allometric growth mechanism among workers who are overfed, but not enough to become queens.

Clearly the disproportionate growth of the arcane/profane ratio in the mind of the soldier who goes to Washington is not generally serviceable. What is needed is a diphasic growth process in which the hard bony head needed to deal with intercolony competition in Washington grows first, so that middle sized animals can run the center and get money, allowing queens and workers to reproduce behind the shield. The general patterning of universities which favors the growth of queens but not soldiers tends to undermine the competitive position of survey research organizations. In the center of intercolony competition in Washington itself we find such soldier-dominated survey research organizations, run more by workers halfway between workers and queens in size and characterized by a thick exoskeleton. The arcane/mundane mix of such colonies specialized in intercolony competition is of course lower, and they produce a small contingent of fertile queens. Organizationally they are quite often not located in a larger organizational environment favoring queen production, but rather in the Bureau of the Census, the Labor Department, the Agriculture Department, the CIA, or American University. They tend to be characterized by large colony size and low fertility in producing new colonies elsewhere. The pattern of diphasic allometric growth that can produce middle-sized soldiers and fat queens in the same colony is a late evolutionary development among the social insects.

19. Should sociologists forget their mothers and fathers

The uses of classic books or papers

I would like to discuss separately a number of uses of the classics. It is quite possible, for example, that one would not extract hypotheses about Australian religion from Durkheim's *Elementary Forms* (c 1976), and yet might read it for some other purpose. Let me specify these functions with the catchwords: (1) touchstones, (2) developmental tasks, (3) intellectual small coinage, (4) fundamental ideas, (5) routine science, (6) rituals. Let me specify briefly what I mean by each before analyzing them separately.

By a 'touchstone' function I mean the sort of thing Claude Lévi-Strauss was talking about in his autobiography (1965) when he said he read a few pages of *The 18th Brumaire* (Marx, 1963) before sitting down to write something himself. *The 18th Brumaire* was an example of excellence, showing the way a sociological study ought to sound.

I used to advise students to think of ten books in sociology they would most like to have written, then to analyze those ten to figure out what virtues they would have to develop in order to do the kind of work they admired. Classics as models of good work is the original sense of Thomas Kuhn's much-abused notion of a 'paradigm.' A paradigm is a case of a beautiful *and* possible way of doing one's scientific work. A touchstone then is a *concrete* example of the virtues a scientific work might have, in a combination that shows what work should look like in order to contribute to the discipline.

By a 'developmental task' I mean that advanced students need something more complicated than the clichés of elementary textbooks, in order to persuade them to make their minds more complex. For example, before people are ready to tackle the question of what is

347

the most strategic way to study how spiritual goals affect earthly goals, they need to have gotten used to thinking that people can want spiritual objectives in different ways. Reading Weber's *Protestant Ethic* (1958) will not teach graduate students much about the causes of capitalism, because they rarely know enough economic history to have any judgement of their own. But the notion that how one pursues salvation may affect how one pursues savings is a source of complexity of thought. I might mention here that the fashion of giving people just enough of Weber so that they come away with the notion, 'Religion is also important,' undermines rather than encourages this mind-complexifying function.

The 'small coinage' function is that of using a few citations to the appropriate literature to indicate generally in what tradition one is working. A paper may have a general innocuous title, mainly consisting of the word 'deviance,' for example. (There are some half dozen sessions at the annual sociological meetings with such a title, and a stranger cannot tell them apart.) But if the first footnote to a paper with a vague title cites Parsons, or George Herbert Mead, (1934), or Thrasher (1936), or Wolfgang (1972), or R. D. Laing (1959), or Lemert (1951), one soon knows what general sort of beast is being tracked on this particular hunt. Our mystification with the half dozen sections on deviance could be cleared up if the title of the section had to give two references in a footnote. Classics, then, serve shorthand functions, for communicating with knowledgeable people what sort of thing one is up to, and, therefore, what standards should be applied. No doubt some of the work that cites Laing would be improved by Wolfgang's cohort analysis, but one would only write that on a referee's report for a journal for the sake of contentiousness. For the small-coinage function one wants simplification, so the little snippet which says 'George Herbert Mead is interested in definitions of the self' is good enough. If we really kept in mind *all* of *Mind, Self and Society* (1934) it might indicate that Mead also was interested in gangs, like Thrasher (1936) and in the relation of means and ends like Parsons, and so on.

The fourth function, 'fundamental ideas,' is the one we usually emphasize in theory courses. It is this which explains the Coles' finding that heavily cited papers in the real sciences are more likely themselves to cite heavily cited papers, and the classics to cite other classics, than are lesser papers by the same distinguished authors (see Cole and Cole, 1973). If in a paper one modifies an idea nearer to the main trunk of a science, one is more likely to be addressing questions that the great minds of the past also have addressed, and to find their orientation useful. In the case of Einstein's first paper on relativity, this tendency went so far that Einstein simply ignored experimental results that flatly contradicted his theory, because they made it all too messy. (It turned out some years later that the experimental results were the result of a leak in the experimental instrument, but Einstein didn't know that.) Einstein wanted to show how Newton and Lorenz could be unified, not how some messy little fact could be explained. In this case we praise the classics for being both unique and fundamental, rather than for being fine work as in the touchstone function, for being complex as in the developmental tasks function, or for being symbols with agreed-on meanings for the small coinage function.

The 'routine science' function of classics is the same as the routine science function of ordinary papers and books. Besides being a touchstone of quantitative reasoning, more complex than Soc. 1, small coinage to show one is a pure sociologist, and a source of fundamental thought on how normlessness works, Durkheim's *Suicide* (1951) also has a bunch of hypotheses about suicide. One could easily imagine asking whether crack troops in the Israeli army kill themselves more than reserves, the same way it happened in France and Italy. One can think of a lot of differences in what it means to be an élite soldier in the two circumstances that might alter the self-destructive propensity. Classic scientists could usually still get promoted nowadays for their routine science. When Marx, for example, tells us about how piece-work wages work, we still imagine he could teach a lot of industrial sociologists something. It is this function which accounts for the famous advice, I believe of Thurstone, that if you wanted to write a classic you should build into the center of it a fundamental, but subtle, flaw. Then hordes of graduate students for generations would write dissertations refuting it, and some of them would find out new things to contribute to the discipline. Only if the classic also serves as a source of puzzles for daily scientific work would this advice be true.

The 'ritual function' of classical writers is typified by the advice Jim Davis used to give to graduate students, that they had to find a dead German who said it first before they could publish a finding (positive or negative) on the subject. We define what holds us together as sociologists in part by having a common history. So ritual myths about Max Weber's staring at a wall in nervous prostration, Georg Simmel being kept from a professorship for being Jewish, Thorstein Veblen refusing the Presidency of the Economics Association because it wasn't offered when he needed it (it is perhaps worthwhile to point out that he wasn't offered the Presidency of the Sociological Society), Parsons's dissertation on some obscure German's ideas about capitalism, all serve the functions that the cherry tree and the Gettysburg address written on the back of an envelope do in American history. And like the cherry tree and envelope myths, the fact that I don't really know whether any of them are true indicates less about the quality of my scholarship than it does about the ritual function of these classics.

So what I propose is that the question of the uses of the classics is really six questions, which all can have separate and contradictory answers. We can ask: (1) Are old models of excellence in sociological craftsmanship still close enough to what we do, so that *The 18th Brumaire*, for example, can show us what political sociology really should look like? (2) Are classics of sociology tough enough for advanced students to cut their teeth on, to replace clichés in the student's mind with complex and flexible patterns of thought, or is their complexity too obscure, too irrelevant to the science as it is practiced, to be useful? (3) Are the classic symbols of style of work in sociology really producers of sectarianism rather than division of labor – does the use of classics as small change debase the currency, so we fight over simple symbols rather than the real intellectual issues? (4) Is there still creative theoretical work to be done in developing the fundamental ideas of a Tocqueville, a Trotsky, a Weber, or even maybe Durkheim? (5) Is there a fund of unexplored important hypotheses in the classics to turn graduate students loose on, or to fill out the first paragraphs of empirical papers in *ASR*, *AJS*, *Social Forces*, and *Social Problems*? (6) Does the fact that you and I cite the same dead Germans (namely the ones who have been translated) hold us together in a common solidarity so that we can monopolize jobs in sociology departments, make people pay their dues to ASA in order to come to the convention to give papers to each other, and otherwise to serve as an intellectual community for each other?

The touchstone function

If one is looking just for intellectual excellence, to remind oneself or students what the real thing looks like, I think one does as well with Erving Goffman as with Georg Simmel, with Paul Veyne's *Le pain et le cirque* (1976) on ancient patterns of charity as with Max Weber's *The Protestant Ethic*, (1958) with Lipset, Trow, and Coleman's *Union Democracy*, (1956) as with Emile Durkheim's *Suicide*, (1951) with Immanuel Wallerstein's Volume I of sixteenth-century history (1974) as with Volume I of Pitrim Sorokin's *Social and Cultural Dynamics* (1957).

That is, there are several ways of being excellent in sociology, from exact description of interpersonal processes in Goffman and Simmel, brilliantly sharp theory illuminating rather disjoint historical processes in Veyne and Weber, quantitative exploration of social psychological processes producing structural patterns in *Union Demcoracy* and *Suicide*, and massive learning held together with a suspicious theoretical superstructure in Wallerstein and Sorokin. The scale is one of excellence of a particular kind, rather than one of historical origins.

The only reason we tend to use older works as touchstones of excellence is that our geniuses are rare, and have to be made to last at least until we get the next one. Now that we have Paul Veyne, I guess it is O.K. to forget Max Weber, at least for those who read French. But in the meantime we needed an example of theoretical precision and fertility in a disorganized field of historical particularity: the particularity disappears into a simplified theory in Durkheim's historical work; and the theoretical precision in Sorokin is not what I would advoctate imitating. That is, the touchstones of one kind of excellence cannot serve for the other kinds, so not every contemporary genius replaces all the originals. Even if we all agree that Erving Goffman is genius enough so that it doesn't matter whether we read Simmel or Goffman, we all, I believe, have the intuition that it matters whether we read Goffman or Weber. Similarly it matters among contemporaries; it matters whether we read Paul Veyne or Erving Goffman.

But what exactly is the function of those touchstones? When Claude Lévi-Strauss says in his autobiography that he reads a few pages of *The 18th Brumaire* before sitting down to write, it clearly is not to derive hypotheses from Marx's theory. Hardly anyone who reads Simmel's essay on the stranger (1950) then writes a survey questionnaire about the last five strangers you've met. The touchstone function is to furnish the mind with intellectual standards, not to furnish it with hypotheses.

I believe that the reason we need such touchstones is that first class science functions with aesthetic standards as well as with logical and empirical standards. These standards are not defensible by the positivist or the Marxist or the symbolic interactionist philosophies of science. No philosophy of science tells you where the chill of excitement at the beauty of the thing comes from. We may not ourselves know how to produce the beauty we admire, which is why we cannot really write a philosophy of science to tell us why Weber was great, Sombart only first class. But if we embed the examples of excellence in our minds, as concrete manifestations of aesthetic principles we want to respect in our own work, and use them as touchstones to filter out that part we throw away and that part we keep, we may very well manage to work at a level higher than we can teach. For we work by the standards embedded in the touchstone, standards we cannot formulate but can perceive if we use a paired comparison – is this piece as good as Simmel?

And if we cannot formulate and teach the aesthetic principles embedded in the touchstones, we can at least expose students to a leisurely inspection of what constitutes excellence. If students are exposed to *The Protestant Ethic* only as a causal problem: 'Which came first, capitalism or Calvinism?' they are deprived of its main value. As a hypothesis it's kind of dull, and probably wrong. But as a piece of work it is beautiful. If we can persuade students to combine good philosophy of science (so our hypotheses will be true) and the standards of intellectual beauty of *The Protestant Ethic*, we will have taught them to do better than ourselves.

Let me now make a brief aside on conflicting aesthetic principles. I was criticized recently by Wally Goldfrank for not writing a conclusion to my book, *Theoretical Methods in Social History* (1978), and by Theda Skocpol for being a Weberian. Both of these are true observations, and I would like to argue that they are connected. Let me use the touchstone method to analyze a bit why Weber and I do not write conclusions. A conclusion is a short essay version of the meaning of world history as a whole, which Sorokin and Wallerstein, for example, write, while Weber does not. I really agree with the Sorokin/Wallerstein aesthetic principle at stake here; if you really understand something you should be able to state the central thesis in a sentence, or if you are a little more prolix, in a short essay on altruism, or on the world system. I have affirmed that aesthetic principle, by quoting Selznick to that effect, in the preface to my *Constructing Social Theories* (1968).

But obviously I do not follow it as well as Sorokin or Wallerstein do. And while Weber had the excuse of dying before he was finished, I dare any of you to draft a conclusion for *Economy and Society* (1968). While I am well aware of how far I fall short of Weber's standard, I. would like to argue that I fall short along the same dimension, and that Sorokin and Wallerstein are working with a different aesthetic standard, along a different dimension.

No doubt it would be more satisfactory if we had a short essay of what *Economy and Society* all added up to. Parsons and Bendix have tried to write such essays, and it is an illuminating fact *both* that they felt pushed to do so, *and* that they wrote two completely different essays, Bendix on authority and Parsons on values. Roth wrote still a third essay as an introduction to the English translation, in which the book was mainly an essay on the nature of constitutional law, and I wrote a brief review essay in *AJS* (see above pp. 282–9) saying it was a book about historical approximations to the assumptions of classical economics. So we have at least four radically different summary chapters for *Economy and Society*. This shows that even Weberians, in their weak moments at least, respect the aesthetic impulse that led Sorokin and Wallerstein to give brief summaries of world history. Note however that nothing in any of our philosophies of science leads us to expect that history can be summarized in a few principles, with the possible exception of Marxism.

But I would argue that the summarizing standard really is inappropriate to the material we are working with. If Sorokin and Wallerstein were as lucky as the Greek sculptors, and had the gilding and paint of the grand theory washed off by centuries as the gilding and paint were washed off the statues, we would be left with their massive scholarship. As it is, poor Sorokin is remembered for a rather foolish summary about cycles of values, and I suppose Wallerstein, an equal time after his retirement, will be reduced to a slogan about world systems. Because they wrote their summaries themselves, there will not be four different ones.

And the reason is that all of world history, or even all the origin of capitalism, really cannot be summarized in twenty pages or four graphs. If you try, you get your book translated into lots of languages quickly, and then you are forgotten. I believe the forgetting is unfair, because the detailed interpretation of masses of evidence gets lost as well. But it comes from following an aesthetic standard, that of writing conclusions to historical works, which is inherently unattainable. And like the gilt and paint on Greek statues, a conclusion ruins the beauty of good historical work.

My general point here is that this all has nothing to do with any substantive disagreement between Weber and Wallerstein. I see nothing in Wallerstein that contradicts Weber, though I suppose if Weber addressed the question he would give a different interpretation of the failure of North Italian capitalism to industrialize. Instead, the difference is in where they locate the 'Aha!' experience, the feeling of aesthetic completion. Weber locates it in clean analyses of historical configurations, Wallerstein in summaries of the main historical drift of a given period. I would like to believe that the aesthetic experience sought by Wallerstein was possible to achieve without intellectual sloppiness. I do not believe it is.

Classics as developmental tasks

Perhaps the best way to pose the question of the contribution of classics to making one's mind complex is to try to imagine Max Weber or Claude Lévi-Strauss writing an introductory textbook. One can sort of imagine fitting Durkheim's *Rules* (1938) into the mind of an intelligent sophomore, but even when Weber tries, as in the first section of *Economy and Society*, he is just too complicated. One might use the clean elegance of Durkheim's *Division of Labor* (1933) as a touchstone of simple unified treatment – I would say of false simplicity and unity – but one would not use it to increase the variety in the mind of the student.

What one wants, to induce complexity and flexibility into the mind, is found in those thinkers where we suspect we are getting only half the argument the first time through. Clifford Geertz, John Dewey (in the original rather than in the symbolic interactionist cutdown version), the Karl Marx of the part of *Capital* that analyzes nineteenth-century England, Paul Veyne whose *Bread and Circuses* I mentioned earlier, Jon Elster's *Logic and Society* (1978), Parsons' *Social System* (1951) all stretch the mind, show a new way of looking at things and then another new way a few pages later.

This all is fairly autonomous from the question of whether the work is scientifically valuable. For example, when I, at 20, read John Dewey's *Logic: A Theory of Inquiry* (1938), I thought it fundamentally misconceived. I am somewhat less confident of that now, with all the advances in ethnomethodology that tend to support Dewey, but I still think it basically starts from the wrong end. But I think I came out of reading it with a deeper grasp of the problem, so that, compared with most positivists at least, I was better prepared for ethnomethodology. The point then is that even not agreeing with Dewey, the book stretched my 20-year-old mind, tempered a bit the sophomoric dogmatism of that mind, opened it to new sorts of evidence on cognitive social psychology. Similarly I think much of Lévi-Strauss is flawed in the middle, that he has no real causal mechanisms in the mind, demonstrable by other means than mythical analysis, to make the whole thing go. But, in the first place, I'm not sure, because I'm not sure I understand him. And, in the second place, I think if I could grasp what he saw as the problem, I would stretch my 48-year-old mind [1981].

While excellence and complexity of mind probably are correlated, we would no doubt give different ranks to different classics on the two dimensions. Geertz for example clearly is more challenging than imitable. I suspect even Lévi-Strauss might start writing with a sense of inferiority and bewilderment if he read a few pages of 'Deep Play' (1973), rather than a few pages of *The 18th Brumaire*. But even if the same pieces serve both functions, the functions are different, teaching aesthetic standards in the first case, teaching variety in the mind in the second case. And again there is no reason to prefer ancient to modern examples of complexity of mind.

Classics as intellectual small change

Now we come to a function which can better be served by older pieces than newer ones, that of serving as intellectual badges. Imagine if our badges for the convention had our names, our institutions, and our favorite classic writer. So mine might read 'Stinchcombe, University of Arizona, Max Weber.' Suppose now, in a fit of preciousness, I write instead, 'Stinchcombe, University of Arizona, Paul Veyne.' He is right now the person I am most intellectually excited about, and embodies the same virtues as Max Weber. But 90-odd percent of the people I met would not know who I was talking about so would not learn anything about the set of prejudices and intuitions to which I was declaring my loyalty.

But what do we need to know about the classics for this function to be served? If you know about Weber that he emphasized subjective phenomena, that he was interested in the economy and in governmental authority, and that he did historical research, you probably would know enough to identify me, to know whether you wanted to talk to me. Similarly Herbert Blumer's cutdown version of the pragmatist philosophers is perhaps better than the originals for the purpose of identifying a symbolic interactionist, and rather vague reference to Chomsky suffices to update it.

The important point to note about this function is that it serves to differentiate us. By choosing Max Weber I am, most obviously, *not* choosing Marx. This does not mean, of course, that I am not an admirer of Marx (as was Weber). But it means that I am unlikely to be interested in the tortuous paths of Marxist epistemology or explications of the Marxist texts; it means that I will enjoy reading those Marxists who rarely quote Marx, like Gramsci or Trotsky, rather than those like Lenin or Cohen who are always trying to be textually accurate (rather than historically accurate, if necessary). And in fact it means I will look with interest rather than with dismay at a theory of why the profit rate and the capital intensity of industry tend to remain the same rather than the profit rate to fall and intensity to rise.

Thus, by saying Weber, I enter into contention, generally at a childish level, I'm afraid, with those who would write Marx on their name tags.

The problem here is that we really need simple guidelines to choose people we want to read and to talk to. There are far too many things written for us to keep track of them all, and no one would seriously propose to enter into serious dialogue with all 14,000 members of ASA.

But just as those bibliographies from librarians never tell us which are the good books, and just as the index of a book does not tell us which of its arguments are coherent, so the small change use of the classics is *nearly* as deceptive as the use of session titles at ASA conventions. Even if we had the first three footnotes of all the papers in the deviance sections, we could not reliably find the session with the good papers. Our prejudices are not good guides to intellectual quality. The use of classics as identifying badges tends to produce sects rather than open intellectual communities. The badges tend to become boundaries rather than guides.

Fundamental ideas and where to find them

These are not the usual reasons we are given in graduate school for studying our intellectual parents. Instead the rationale is in the form of a genealogy of ideas. Certain fundamental ideas about, say, social causation of rates of voluntary behavior were formulated first in *Suicide*. Within the masterpiece itself there are certain first branches. Some of these branches have been fruitful, such as the anomie branch, and some have died, such as the branch about women committing suicide less because they are such simple souls. But the fundamental notions that norms regulate and tame personal goals, that some social commitments are so intense as to efface the personality and reduce its value to nullity, are first expressed clearly and brought into contact with the facts in Durkheim.

So when we run into a problem of how norms and social commitments influence personal psychology, it's logical to return to the source. In general, then, the deeper the ideas in any particular piece of work, the more relevant the classical work, the genitor of the whole line of work, will be.

This picture of the relation between the basic nature of a thing and its historical origin is deeply embedded in human thought, and has been analyzed in philosophy in Kenneth Burke's *A Grammar of Motive* (1952). The pattern found in the sciences, mentioned in the introduction, that much cited or classic papers themselves are more likely to cite other classic papers (as measured by *their* citations), indicates that in intellectual life this identification of fundamental ideas and classical origins has some truth to it.

If we imagine a developed science as looking like the evolutionary trees we used to see when we were in the tenth grade, we can see this function more clearly. Ordinarily we are working on the tip of some twig, and when we get into trouble we go back only to the first branching point to reconstruct. But if we are Einstein, we go clear back to the trunk, to Lorenz and Newton, and even flatly ignore experimental results on one of the twigs. Maybe something will show up between the trunk and the twig to explain away the contradiction. And for Einstein it did – a leak in the apparatus. Not all of us can depend on being able to ignore the facts like Einstein. But Einstein's achievement perfectly illustrates the process of ignoring the twigs for the trunk, because it is so extreme.

Of course it is true, as Kuhn has shown for several sciences (Kuhn, 1962), that the occasional reshaping of the trunk is a lot more important, and creates more discontinuities, than a lot of work on the twigs. So the obvious question comes up, why not work directly on the trunk, say by writing critiques of Weber, Durkheim, and Pareto or by writing a book to be called *The Structure of Social Action*? (Parsons, 1949). Why not work on theory itself, rather than on the twigs far removed from the theory?

But anyone who has read a pile of preliminary exams in theory knows why not – not many of us are Parsons, and it is not clear that even Parsons brought it off. The basic positivist stance, which is my stance, is that you can do something useful to the trunk of theory only if you approach it from the twigs.

To move to a more minor scale than *The Structure of Social Action*, it seems to me that a lot of essays on Michels' 'Iron Law of Oligarchy' were of very little use, while *Union Democracy* made the theory more precise, more solidly supported, more empirically relevant, more useful in every way. This is because it approached the problem of the distribution of power in a voluntary assocation from the twigs of facts about typographers, not from the general theory. What *Union Democracy* says about the possibility of democracy in working class organizations has to be addressed by any serious socialist. What thousands of prelim answers have said on the subject does not have to be addressed.

Thus I think that the true fact that classics deal with more fundamental ideas, and so are more fruitful to think about, appears in practice mainly as a mortal temptation to skip the empirical work. Certain easy literary tricks that turn thoughts about Simmel or Durkheim into a publishable essay tend to deceive us.

As Erving Goffman once said about Parsons, at that time the chief practitioner of working directly on the trunk instead of on the twigs, 'I wish social theory was as easy as Parsons thinks it is.'

Classics as underexploited normal science

But if it is not always wise to work only on the trunk of social knowledge, on the most general theories, the classics contain a lot of twigs as well as the trunk. Part of the way we recognize theoretical classics is by their empirical fruitfulness. Let me elaborate a couple of examples, the first of a very direct sort, the second somewhat indirect.

We recall that the main place in modern societies where Durkheim located altruistic suicide was in élite units in the military. The idea was that the society became so strong as to obliterate the value of the personality. In the first place, it would be interesting to know for more armies whether the suicide rate of élite troops was higher than that of regular troops. But clearly it is not a very big step to imagine that élite troops with a great deal of ideological dedication might be expected to evaluate individuality even lower than 'secular' élite troops. So perhaps the Nazi weaponed SS, crack Israeli commandoes, the survivors of the long march in the Chinese communist army, should have even higher suicide rates, while troops that are élite only by being near an unprincipled dictator, like the Shah of Iran's guard or Idi Amin's secret police, might not be distinct from the mass of soldiery. With only a slight extension of Durkheim's theory, we should be able to measure the social-psychological intervening variable, the devaluation of individuality, in élite troops.

These are examples at the level that Durkheim himself worked at. Now let me take an example from Max Weber's *Protestant Ethic* that requires just a bit of thought, but still would be within the range I would call 'normal science.' We already have had the very normal science of seeing whether Protestants did indeed start capitalist industries, and whether they did indeed avoid adventure capitalism in the form of the slave trade or of conquering gold mines or whatnot. Now I would like to show what happens when we stretch Weber a little.

One part of Weber's argument says that *whatever* the ethical system of a religious group, it will be more powerful in governing the behavior of laymen if the religion is organized as a sect. Perhaps the crucial sect feature for Weber was adult baptism, that one chooses sect membership only with an adult conversion. But various other features include the lack of monks and monasteries, lack of magical practices or rituals of any kind for the forgiveness of individual sin, congregational control of appointment of pastors, the institution of lay preaching by those who felt the call, and so on. The general idea was that all these features call upon all the faithful to be saints, while leaving them to live a secular life within this world.

It seems to me that it would not take a very great deal of ingenuity to develop measures of whether the *different* ethics preached by *different* religious groups were more salient to members if the group were organized as a sect than if it were organized as a church.

That is, Weber was interested in a particular ethic, that of popular Calvinism. He held that that a particular ethic was more likely to govern the behavior of members when a Calvinist-type religious current maintained a sect-like organization, than when it had become a state church or a tamed American denomination.

But suppose we take instead socialist ethics, which show some variety, but which surely always include donating time to working class organizations, writing socialist pamphlets, egalitarian behavior toward women and toward minority races and ethnic groups, trying to make sense of conflicts between socialists and others in such countries as Afghanistan, and of conflicts between variants of socialism in places like Cambodia, reading socialist classics, attending meetings of socialist groups, and so on.

It does not seem to me to be stretching Weber very far to predict that socialist morality should be more characteristic of members of socialist sects – defined the way Weber defined sects, as far as this is possible – than of social *ecclesiae*.

The general point here is that the puzzles one can find in classic works often are more interesting than the puzzle of entering another variable in a model of status attainment. The twigs we investigate in routine science can be nearer to or farther from the trunk. One way to find twigs nearer to the trunk is to examine the puzzles that still have not been investigated in classic works.

Ritual use of classics

It is the fact that we have all read these classics, or at least answered preliminary examination questions on them, that binds us together into an intellectual community.

But that brings up the question of how far the classics still sing to us, how far they symbolize what we are really all about. It seems to me that there is a broad correlation between a quantitative style in sociology and a cynical attitude toward the classics.

I think this is because there is teachable innovation in the quantitative branches of social science. That is, there are quite a few things that a run-of-the-mill quantitative social scientist can do now that Ogburn (1933) or Chapin (1935) or Durkheim could not do. There are not many things that a run-of-the-mill historical sociologist can do that Weber could not.

But there is a more serious problem. The classics of quantitative or mathematical social science are hard for nonquantitative types to read, while the reverse is not really true. Or perhaps better, it is harder to *show* that someone really has not been able to read Simmel than to show that they have not been able to read von Neumann and Morgenstern (1944), so people of the most variable command of Simmel can participate in the ritual. The impatience of quantitative people with classics is perhaps the central challenge to our feeling of being a moral community.

My own opinion is that a lot of the supermodernism of quantitative sociologists is beside the point. For example, I have never found a difference between the decisions I make on a cross-classification table when I use the method of my youth, which involves treating combinations of proportions as combinations of normal variables after the manner of Goodman in his Dorn-Stouffer-Tibbets (1961) paper, and decisions based on the log linear method now in fashion. It would, of course, seriously challenge our confidence in Goodman's current opinion if he had been radically wrong in *his* youth. But you can hardly be respectable and analyze percentage tables by non-log linear methods nowadays. What has happened here, I would say, is that the ideology that a science always uses the most modern methods has caused us to exaggerate greatly the virtues of the advances we have made lately.

It is still true that with all our advances in statistical methods, the main determinant of the value of a table is whether you have measured the right variables in a study with a good sample of the relevant population. If you have done that, then statistical efficiency does not matter much. That does not mean that I favor statistical inefficiency, of course, any more than I favor mistranslating Weber from the German. It just means that I think the ritual emphasis on modern methods has got out of hand, leading to a species of methodological scholasticism that is as bad as all the scholasticism of the textual analyses of Marx, Lenin, and Mao that we also have been burdened with.

But I do think that the quantitative cynicism toward the classics has one very strong healthy element in it. A central feature of any symbol of solidarity for sociologists should be, I think, that we be concerned for whether it is true or not. One of the things we tend to lose sight of, given all the other uses of classics, is that our central symbols ought to be tested for truth, as well as for intellectual beauty, complexity of thought, recognizability as intellectual small change, empirical fruitfulness, and the other virtues I have discussed.

When Dudley Duncan many years ago criticized me for using Durkheim's *Suicide* as a methodological example in *Constructing Social Theories*, he said something like, 'We can surely do better than that now.' Whitney Pope has shown in some detail that we *could* do better now (1976), and that is is quite doubtful whether Durkheim's theory is true or not. It surely is a bad thing for sociology to have false gods to symoblize the search for truth.

Moral

I suppose the moral of all this is that it is destructive to mix up the different functions that a classic can serve. We may believe that students' minds are expanded by reading Durkheim without our having to believe Durkheim has many true generalizations about the causes of suicide. George Herbert Mead can symbolize what is distinctive in symbolic interactionism even if we cannot quite figure out how to test the hypothesis of the independence of the 'I' from the 'me,' and to turn it into a puzzle for routine science. And one can enjoy the taste of Marx's famous passage in *The 18th Brumaire* about

French peasants forming a vast mass, without that beauty being undermined when we find some regions of modern France where the peasants vote Communist.

What is destructive about admiration of the classics, then, is the halo effect, the belief that because a book or article is useful for one purpose, it must have all the virtues.

Bibliography

Adorno, T. W. 1950 *The Authoritarian Personality*. New York: Harper.

Aristotle, *Politics*.

Becker, Gary 1957 *The Economics of Discrimination*. Chicago: University of Chicago Press.

1971 2nd edition of above.

Bendix, Reinhard 1960 *Max Weber: An Intellectual Portrait*. Berkeley: University of California Press.

Bernard, Chester I. 1946 'Functions and pathology of status systems in formal organizations.' Reprinted in his *Organizations and Management*, Cambridge, Mass., Harvard University Press.

Bertran, Gordon W., and Sherman J. Maisel 1955 *Industrial Relations in the Construction Industry*. Berkeley: University of California Press.

Bettleheim, Bruno 1943 'Individual and mass behavior in extreme situations.' *Journal of Abnormal Psychology* 38:417–52.

Blau, Peter 1957 'Formal organization: dimensions of analysis.' *American Journal of Sociology* 63 (July):58–69.

1964 *Exchange and Power in Social Life*. New York: Wiley.

Blauner, Robert 1960 'Industrial differences in work attitudes and work institutions.' Paper delivered at the 1960 meeting of the American Sociological Association. The main conclusions of this paper were published in Blauner, 1964.

1964 *Alienation and Freedom: The Factory Worker and His Industry*. Chicago: University of Chicago Press.

1972 *Racial Oppression in America*. New York: Harper & Row.

Blum, Jerome 1948 *Noble Landowners and Agriculture in Austria, 1815–1848*. Baltimore: Johns Hopkins Press.

Boothe, Viva, and Sam Arnold 1944 *Seasonal Employment in Ohio*. Columbus: Ohio State University Press.

Breton, Raymond 1964 'Institutional completeness of ethnic communities and the personal relations of immigrants.' *American Journal of Sociology* 70:193–205.

Burke, Kenneth 1952 *A Grammar of Motive*. New York: Prentice-Hall.

364

Caplow, T. 1954 *The Sociology of Work*. Minneapolis: University of Minnesota Press.

Chandler, Alfred 1962 *Strategy and Structure*. Cambridge, MA: M.I.T. Press.

Chapin, F. Stuart 1935 'Measurement in sociology.' *American Journal of Sociology* 40 (January):476–80

Cole, Jonathan R., and Stephen Cole 1973 *Social Stratification in Science*. Chicago: University of Chicago Press.

Colean, Miles J., and Robinson Newcomb 1952 *Stabilizing Construction*. New York: McGraw-Hill.

Coleman, James S. 1957. Multidimensional scale analysis.' *American Journal of Sociology* 63 (November):253–63.

1973 *The Mathematics of Collective Action*, Chicago: Aldine.

Commons, John R. 1924 *The Legal Foundations of Capitalism*. New York: Macmillan.

Conrad, A. H. 1961 'Income growth and structural change.' Pp. 26–64 in S. E. Harris (ed.), *American Economic History*. New York: McGraw-Hill.

Crozier, Michael 1964 *The Bureaucratic Phenomenon*. Chicago: University of Chicago Press.

Dahl, R. A. and C. E. Lindblom 1953 *Politics, Economics and Welfare*. New York: Harper.

Davis, Kingsley and Wilbert E. Moore 1945 'Some principles of stratification.' *American Sociological Review* 10 (April) 242–9.

Deutsch, Karl 1953 *Nationalism and Social Communication*. New York: Wiley; Cambridge, MA: Technology Press of M. I. T.

Dewey, John c.1938 *Logic: The Theory of Inquiry*. New York: H. Holt.

Dore, Ronald P. 1959 *Land Reform in Japan*. London: Oxford University Press.

Dovring, Folke 1956 *Land and Labor in Europe, 1900–1950*. The Hague: Martinus Nijhoff.

Drucker, Peter 1950 *The New Society*. New York: Harper.

1954 *The Practice of Management*. New York: Harper.

Duncan, Otis Dudley 1966 'Path analysis: sociological examples.' *American Journal of Sociology* 72:1–16.

Durkheim, Émile 1933 *On the Division of Labor in Society*. George Simpson (trans. and ed.). New York: Macmillan.

1938 *The Rules of Sociological Method*. Sarah A. Solovay and John H. Meuller (trans. and ed.). Glencoe, Il: The Free Press.

1951 *Suicide*. George Simpson (trans.and ed.). Glencoe, Il: The Free Press.

c.1976 *The Elementary Forms of the Religious Life*. London: Allen & Unwin.

Duverger, M. 1954 *Political Parties*. New York: Wiley.

Dyson-Hudson, Neville 1966 *Karimojong Politics*. Oxford: Clarendon Press.

Elkins, S. 1959 *Slavery*. Chicago: University of Chicago Press.

Elster, Jon 1979 *Logic and Society*. New York: Wiley.

　　1983 *Explaining Technical Change*. Cambridge: Cambridge University Press; Oslo: Universitetsforlaget.

Erikson, Eric 1950 *Childhood and Society*. New York: Norton.

　　1959 'The problem of ego identity.' *American Psychoanalytic Journal* 4:56–121.

Etzioni, A. 1961 *Complex Organizations*. New York: Free Press.

Foote, Nelson 1953 'The professionalization of labor in Detroit.' *American Journal of Sociology* 58:371–80.

Ford, Thomas R. 1955 *Man and Land in Peru*. Gainesville: University of Florida Press.

Geertz, Clifford 1963 *Peddlers and Princes*. Chicago: University of Chicago Press.

　　1973 'Deep Play.' Pp. 412–54 in Clifford Geertz, *The Interpretation of Cultures*. New York: Basic Books.

Glock, Charles Y., and Rodney Stark 1970 *Christian Beliefs and Anti-Semitism*. New York: Harper & Row.

Goffman, Erving 1963 *Stigma: Notes on the Management of Spoiled Identity*. Englewood Cliffs, N.J.: Prentice-Hall.

Goodman, Leo A. 1961 'Modifications of the Dorn-Stouffer-Tibbets method for "Testing the Significance of Comparisons in Social Data".' *American Journal of Sociology* 66 (January):355–63.

Gordon, Robert A., et al. 1963 'Values and gang delinquency: a study of street corner groups.' *American Journal of Sociology* 69:109–28.

Gouldner, Alvin 1954 *Wildcat Strike*. Yellow Springs, Oh: Antioch Press.

Gramsci, Antonio 1973 *Letters From Prison*. New York: Harper & Row.

Granick, David 1954 *Management of the Industrial Firm in the USSR*. New York: Columbia University Press.

　　1967 *Soviet Metal Fabricating and Economic Development*. Madison: University of Wisconsin Press.

Greenstein, Fred, and Nelson Polsby c.1975 *Handbook of Political Science*. Reading, Ma: Addison-Wesley Publishing Co.

Grodzins, Martin 1956 *The Loyal and the Disloyal: Social Boundaries of Patriotism and Treason*. Chicago: University of Chicago Press.

Haber, William, and Harold M. Levinson 1956 *Labor Relations and Productivity in the Building Trades*. Ann Arbor: Bureau of Industrial Relations, University of Michigan.

Hald, Anders 1952 *Statistical Theory with Engineering Applications*. New York: Wiley.

Hamblin, Robert L., R. Brooke Jacobsen, and Jerry L. Miller 1973 *A Mathematical Theory of Social Change*. New York: Wiley.

Hamsun, Knut 1920 *Hunger*. New York: Knopf.

　　1921 *Growth of the Soil*. New York: Modern Library.

Chen, Han-seng 1935 *Landlord and Peasant in China*. New York: International Publishers.

Heberle, Rudolf 1951 *Social Movements*. New York: Appleton-Century-Crofts Inc.

Heimer, Carol A., and Arthur L. Stinchcombe 1980 'Love and irrationality: it's got to be rational to love you because it makes me so happy.' *Social Science Information* 19 No. 4/5:697–754.

Hernes, Gudmund and Knud Knudsen 1976 *Utdanning og Ulikhet, NOU 1976:46*. Oslo: Univertetsforlaget.

Higham, John 1965 *Strangers in the Land*. New Brunswick, NJ: Rutgers University Press.

Homans, George 1941 *English Villagers of the Thirteenth Century*. Cambridge MA: Harvard University Press.

　1950 *The Human Group*. New York: Harcourt Brace, and World.

　1961 *Social Behaviour: Its Elementary Forms*. New York: Harcourt Brace & World.

Hoselitz, B. F. 1951 'Some problems in the quantitative study of industrialization.' *Economic Development and Cultural Change* 9:537–546.

House, Albert V. 1954 *Planter Management and Capitalism in Ante-bellum Georgia*. New York: Columbia University Press.

Hutchinson, E. P. 1956 *Immigrants and Their Children*. New York: Wiley.

Jacoby, E. H. 1949 *Agrarian Unrest in Southeast Asia*. New York: Columbia University Press.

Jahoda, Marie, et al. 1933 *Die Arbeitslosen von Marienthal*. Leipzig: S. Hirzel.

Kahler, Wilfried 1958 *Das Agrarproblem in den Industrieländern*. Göttingen: Vandenhoeck & Ruprecht.

Kerr, Clark 1954, The balkanization of labor markets.' in E. Wight Bakke (ed.), *Labor Mobility and Economic Opportunity*. Cambridge, MA: M. I. T. Press; New York: Wiley.

Klein, Sidney 1958 *The Pattern of Land Tenure Reform in East Asia*. New York: Bookman Associates.

Kohn, Hans 1951 *The Idea of Nationalism*. New York: Macmillan.

Kuhn, Thomas S. 1962 *The Structure of Scientific Revolutions*. Chicago: University of Chicago Press.

Kunkel, John 1961 'Economic autonomy and social change in Mexican villages.' *Economic Development and Cultural Change* 10:51–63.

Laing, R. D. 1959 *The Divided Self*. Baltimore: Penguin Books.

Lamprecht, Heinz 1951 'Über die soziale Herkunft der Handwerder.' *Soziale Welt* 3 (October):42, 52.

Larson, Magali Sarfatti 1977 *The Rise of Professionalism*. Berkeley: University of California Press.

Lazarsfeld, Paul F. 1955 'Interpretation of statistical relations as a research operation.' Pp. 115–24 in Paul F. Lazarsfeld and Morris Rosenberg (eds.), *The Language of Social Research*. New York: The Free Press.

Lemert, Edwin M. 1951 *Social Pathology: A Systematic Approach to the Theory of Sociopathic Behavior*. New York: McGraw-Hill.

Lenski, G. 1961 *The Religious Factor*. Garden City, NY: Doubleday.

Lerner, Daniel 1958 *The Passing of Traditional Society*. Glencoe, Il: Free Press.

Lesniewski, Victor, and Waclaw Ponikowski 1933 'Polish agriculture.' Pp. 260–77 in Ora S. Morgan (ed.), *Agricultural Systems of Middle Europe*. New York: Macmillan Co.

Lévi-Strauss, Claude 1963 *Totemism*. R. Needham (trans.). Boston: Beacon Press.

   1965 *Tristes Tropiques*. John Russell (trans.). New York: Atheneum.

   1966 *The Savage Mind*. Chicago: University of Chicago Press.

   1969a *Elementary Structures of Kinship*. J. H. Bell, J. R. Sturmer, and R. Needham (trans. and eds.). Boston: Beacon Press.

   1969b *The Raw and the Cooked*. J. and D. Weightman (trans.). New York: Harper & Row.

Lewis, Oscar 1964 *Pedro Martinez*. New York: Random House.

   1965 *La Vida*. New York: Random House.

Lipset, Seymour Martin 1950 *Agrarian Socialism*. Berkeley, CA: University of California Press.

   1959 *Political Man*. Garden City, NY: Doubleday.

Lipset, Seymour Martin, and Reinhard Bendix 1959 *Social Mobility in Industrial Society*. Berkeley: University of California Press.

Lipset, Seymour Martin, Martin A. Trow, and James S. Coleman 1956 *Union Democracy*. Glencoe, Il: The Free Press.

Long, Clarence 1940 *Building Cycles and the Theory of Investment*. Princeton: Princeton University Press.

McBride, George M. 1935 *Chile: Land and Society*. New York: American Geographical Society.

McCloskey, Herbert 1963 'Conservatism and personality.' In Nelson Polsby, R. A. Dentler, and P. A. Smith (eds.), *Politics and Social Life*. Boston: Houghton Mifflin.

Maisel, Sherman 1953 *Housebuilding in Transition*. Berkeley and Los Angeles: University of California Press.

Marshall, T. H. 1950 *Citizenship and Social Class*. London: Cambridge University Press.

Marx, Karl c.1963 *The 18th Brumaire of Louis Bonaparte*. New York: International Publishers.

   c.1967 *Capital*. New York: International Publishers.

Matza, David 1969 *Becoming Deviant*. Englewood Cliffs, NJ: Prentice-Hall.

Mead, George Herbert 1934 *Mind, Self, and Society*. Chicago: University of Chicago Press.

Merton, Robert K. 1952 *Reader in Bureaucracy*. Glencoe, Il: The Free Press.

   1968 *Social Theory and Social Structure*. enl. ed. New York: Free Press.

   1969 'Behavior patterns of scientists.' *American Scientist* 57, No. 1:1–23.

Michels, Robert 1949 *Political Parties: A Sociological Study of Oligarchical Tendencies of Modern Democracy*. Glencoe, Il: Free Press.

Norbeck, Edward 1959 *Pineapple town: Hawaii.* Berkeley: University of California Press.

Ogburn, William Fielding 1933 *Recent Social Trends in the United States.* New York: McGraw-Hill.

Olson, Mancur 1965 *The Logic of Collective Action.* Cambridge, Mass.: Harvard University Press.

Orwell, George 1933 *Down and Out in Paris and London.* New York and London: Harper and Brothers.

Paige, Jeffery 1975 *Agrarian Revolution.* New York: Free Press.

Parsons, Talcott 1949 *The Structure of Social Action.* Glencoe, Il: Free Press.

1951 *The Social System.* New York: The Free Press.

Phelps, O. 1957 'A structural model of the U.S. labor market.' Industrial Labor Relations Review 10:402–423.

Polanyi, Karl 1944 *The Great Transformation.* New York: Farrar & Rinehart.

Pope, Whitney 1976 *Durkheim's SUICIDE: A Classic Analyzed.* Chicago: University of Chicago Press.

Radcliffe-Brown, A. R. 1952 *Structure and Function in Primitive Society.* Glencoe, Il: Free Press.

Roberts, David R. 1956 'A general theory of executive compensation based on statistically tested propositions.' *Quarterly Journal of Economics* 70 (May):270–294.

Roberts, Henry L. 1969 [1951] *Rumania: Political Problems of an Agrarian State.* Hamden, Conn., Shoe String.

Rogoff Ramsøy, Natalie 1977 *Sosial Mobilitet i Norge.* Oslo: Tiden Norsk Forlag.

Rosovsky, H. and K. Ohkawa 1961 'The indigenous components in the modern Japanese economy.' *Economic Development and Cultural Change* 9:476–97.

Royal Institute of International Affairs 1939 *Nationalism.* London: Oxford University Press.

Scherer, Frederic M. 1980 *Industrial Market Structure and Economic Performance.* Boston: Houghton-Mifflin.

Schumpeter, J. A. 1934 *Theory of Economic Development.* Cambridge, Mass.: Harvard University Press.

1939 *Business Cycles.* New York: McGraw-Hill, 2 Vols.

1951 *Imperialism and Social Classes.* New York: Kelley.

Selznick, Philip 1957 *Leadership in Administration.* Evanston, Il: Row, Peterson.

Sheridan, Richard B. c.1779 *School for Scandal.* New York: Norton.

Simmel, Georg 1950 'The stranger.' Pp. 402–8 in Kurt H. Wolff (ed.), *The Sociology of Georg Simmel.* Glencoe, Il: The Free Press.

Simon, Herbert 1957a 'The compensation of executives.' *Sociometry* 20 (March):32–5.

1957b 'A formal theory of employment relation.' Pp. 183–95 in Herbert Simon (ed.), *Models of Man.* New York: Wiley.

Smelser, Neil J. 1962 *Theory of Collective Behavior*. New York: Free Press.

Sørensen, Aage and Nancy Tuma 1978 'Labor market structures and job mobility.' Paper presented at the International Sociological Association meeting in Uppsala, 1978, University of Wisconsin Institute for Research on Poverty, Discussion Papers No. 505–78.

Sorokin, Pitrim A. 1957 *Social and Cultural Dynamics*. Rev. and abridged. Boston: Sargent.

Statistisk Sentralbyrå 1972 *Standard for Naeringsgruppering*. Oslo: Håndbøker, No. 9.

Stinchcombe, Arthur L. 1959 'Bureaucratic and craft administration of production.' *Administrative Science Quarterly* 4:168–87.

1963 'Some empirical consequences of the Davis-Moore theory of stratification.' *American Sociological Review* 28 (October):805:8.

1964 *Rebellion in a High School*. Chicago: Quadrangle Books.

1968 *Constructing Social Theories*. New York: Harcourt, Brace, and World.

1974 *Creating Efficient Industrial Administrations*. New York: Academic Press.

1978 *Theoretical Methods in Social History*. New York: Academic Press.

Stolzenberg, Ross 1975 'Occupations, labor markets and the process of wage attainment.' *American Sociological Review* 40:645–65.

Stonier, Alfred W. and Douglas C. Hague 1972 *A Textbook of Economic Theory*. London: Longman.

Tannenbaum, Frank 1929 *The Mexican Agrarian Revolution*. New York: Macmillan Co.

Thompson, Edgar T. 1958 'The plantation as a race-making situation.' Pp. 506-7 in Leonard Broom and Philip Selznick (eds.), *Sociology*. Evanston, Il: Row, Peterson & Co.

Thrasher, Frederic M. 1936 *The Gang; A Study of 1,313 Gangs in Chicago*. 2nd rev. ed. Chicago: University of Chicago Press

Tocqueville, Alexis de 1955 *The Old Regime and the French Revolution*. Garden City, NY: Doubleday & Co.

Tomasevich, Jozo 1955 *Peasants, Politics, and Economic Change in Yugoslavia*. Stanford, Ca: Stanford University Press.

U.S. Bureau of the Census 1950 'Characteristics of the population.' *Population Census 1950*, vol. 2. Washington, D.C.: U.S. Government Printing Office.

1952 *Population census 1950*, vol. 2, part I. Washington, D.C.: U.S. Government Printing Office.

U.S. Bureau of Labor Statistics 1953 *Construction during Five Decades*. Bulletin no. 1146 (July 1): U.S. Government Printing Office.

Veblen, Thorstein 1921 *A Theory of Business Enterprise*. New York: Scribner's.

1948a 'Salesmanship and the Churches.' Pp. 499–506 in Max Lerner (ed.), *The Portable Veblen*. New York: The Viking Press.

1948b *The Portable Veblen*. Max Lerner (ed.). New York: The Viking Press.

Veyne, Paul 1976 *Le Pain et le cirque: sociologie historique d'un pluralisme politique*. Paris: Éditions du Seuil.

Vinogradoff, Paul 1905 *The Growth of the Manor*. London: Swan Sonnenschein.

Voltaire c.1929 *Candide*. Voltaire (Jean Marie Francois Arouet). New York: Random House.

von Neumann, John, and Oskar Morgenstern 1944 *Theory of Games and Economic Behavior*. New York: Wiley.

Waller, Willard 1938 *The Family: A Dynamic Interpretation*. New York: The Cordon Company.

1940 'War and social institutions.' Pp. 478–532 in Willard Waller (ed.), *War in the Twentieth Century*. New York: Dryden.

Wallerstein, Immanuel 1974 *The Modern World-System*. New York: Academic Press.

Warriner, Doreen 1957 *Land Reform and Development in the Middle East*. London: Royal Institute of International Affairs.

Weber, M. 1923 *General Economic History*. London: Allen & Unwin.

1924 *Gesammelte Aufsätze zur Sozial- und Wirtschaftsgeschichte*. Tübingen: J. C. B. Mohr.

1946a 'Protestant sects and the spirit of capitalism.' Pp. 302–23 in H. H. Gerth and C. Wright Mills (eds.) *From Max Weber: Essays in Sociology*. New York: Oxford University Press.

1946b *From Max Weber: Essays in Sociology*. H. H. Gerth and C. Wright Mills (eds.). New York: Oxford University Press.

1958 *The Protestant Ethic and the Spirit of Capitalism*. Translated by Talcott Parsons. New York: Scribner's.

1968 *Economy and Society*. Edited by Guenther Roth. New York: Bedminster Press.

Wendt, James C. 1978 'Toward an organizational theory of socio-economic achievement.' Unpublished paper, Columbia University.

Whyte, William Foote 1961 *Street Corner Society*. Chicago: University of Chicago Press.

1948 *Human Relations in the Restaurant Industry*. New York: McGraw-Hill.

Wiener, Norbert 1953 *Ex-Prodigy: My Childhood and Youth*. New York: Simon & Schuster.

Williamson, Oliver E. 1975 *Markets and Hierarchies: Analysis and Antitrust Implications*. New York: Free Press.

Wilson, Edward O. 1970 *The Insect Societies*. Cambridge, Mass: Belknap Press of Harvard University Press.

Wilson, James Q. 1968 *Varieties of Police Behavior*. Cambridge, Mass: Harvard University Press.

Wolfgang, Marvin, E. Martin Figlio, and Thorsten Sellin 1972 *Delinquency in a Birth Cohort*. Chicago: University of Chicago Press.

Wright, Eric and Lucca Perrone 1977 'Marxist class categories and income inequality.' *American Sociological Review* 42:32–55.

Zajonc, R. B. 1980 'Feeling and thinking: preferences need no inferences.' *American Psychologist* 35, No.2:151–175.

Zuckerman, Harriet, and Robert K. Merton 1971 'Patterns of evaluation in science: institutionalization structure and function of the referee system.; *Minerva* 9, No. 1 (January):66–100.

Name and place-name index

Adorno, T. W. 140, 364
Afghanistan 360
Africa 258
Alps 164
Aquitaine 164
Aristotle 42, 364
Arizona 20
Arnold, Sam 186–7, 364
Atlanta 17, 76, 82
Austen, Jane 154
Australia 252–3
Austro-Hungarian Empire 38

Bali 8
Baake, E. Wight 367
Baltimore 93, 342
Barnard, Chester I. 364
Becker, Gary 82, 91, 364
Becker, Howard 336
Bendix, Reinhard 33, 214, 283, 353, 364
Berlin 260
Berkeley *see* California
Bernard, Chester 242, 251, 364
Bertran, Gordon W. 188, 364
Bettleheim, Bruno 126, 364
Birmingham, Alabama 82
Birmingham, England 252–3
Blau, Peter 4, 66, 364
Blauner, Robert 33, 72–85, 91, 196, 364
Blum, Jerome 38, 364
Blumer, Herbert 356
Boothe, Viva 186–7, 363
Boudon, Raymond 326
Breton, Raymond 126, 364
Britain 138, 139 (see also England)
Brittany 164
Broom, Leonard 370
Bulgaria 44
Burke, Kenneth 357, 364

California 37, 44, 47, 342
Caplow, Theodore 214, 365
Cambodia 360
Cambridge 325, 331
Canada 128, 326
Caribbean 47
Carr, E. H. 279
Carrol, Lewis 323
Central America 47
Chandler, Alfred 265, 322, 365
Chapin, F. Stuart 361, 365
Charleston 17
Chicago 93, 229, 342
Chile 37, 327
China 36, 40–1, 74, 258
Chomsky, Noam 356
Clausen, Sten-Erik 86
Cohen, G. 356
Cole, Jonathan R. 348, 357, 365
Cole, Stephen 348, 357, 365
Colean, Miles J. 187, 365
Coleman, James S. 4, 33, 311, 324–6, 351, 358, 365
Commons, John R. 242, 365
Conrad, A. H. 198, 365
Coser, Lewis A. vii, viii
Crozier, Michael 222, 365
Cuba 74

Dahl, Robert A. 212, 365
Dallas 76, 82
Davis, James A. 349
Davis, Kingsley 52–69, 365
Denmark 49
Dentler, Robert A. 368
Detroit 340–1
Deutsch, Karl 127, 279, 365
Dewey, John 354–5, 365
Dore, Ronald P. 41–2, 44, 365
Dostoyevsky, Fyodor 154

373

Subject index